Global Governance and Japan

Global Governance and Japan examines the institutional mechanisms of governance at the global level and provides concrete evidence of the role Japan plays in these institutions. The main theoretical contribution of the volume is the analysis of how global governance *actually works* through the global institutional mechanisms of governance. It provides an up-to-date and contemporary analysis of the six most important global institutions, namely:

- the Group of Seven/Eight
- the Organization for Economic Cooperation and Development
- the World Bank
- the International Monetary Fund
- the World Trade Organization
- the United Nations.

Leading specialists from Europe and Japan provide a thorough and accessible discussion on Japan's role within these institutions and use supporting case studies to ask whether Japan is reactively or proactively involved in trying to shape these institutions in order to promote its own interests. At a time when the question of how the world is governed is of critical concern to policymakers and specialists alike, this book illuminates concretely how the institutional mechanisms of global governance are actually governing the world in the early twenty-first century.

Written clearly and concisely, this book will be an invaluable resource for undergraduates and scholars with an interest in global governance, Japanese politics and political economy.

Glenn D. Hook is Professor of Japanese Politics and International Relations and Director of the Graduate School of East Asian Studies at the University of Sheffield, UK. He is also the Director of the National Institute of Japanese Studies, an international centre of excellence established by the Universities of Sheffield and Leeds with funding from the UK authorities.

Hugo Dobson is Senior Lecturer in Japan's International Relations in the School of East Asian Studies at the University of Sheffield and at the National Institute of Japanese Studies, UK.

Sheffield Centre for Japanese Studies/Routledge Series

Series Editor: Glenn D. Hook

Professor of Japanese Politics and International Relations

This series, published by Routledge in association with the Centre for Japanese Studies at the University of Sheffield, both makes available original research on a wide range of subjects dealing with Japan and provides introductory overviews of key topics in Japanese Studies.

The Internationalization of Japan
*Edited by Glenn D. Hook and
Michael Weiner*

Race and Migration in Imperial Japan
Michael Weiner

Japan and the Pacific Free Trade Area
Pekka Korhonen

Greater China and Japan
Prospects for an economic partnership?
Robert Taylor

The Steel Industry in Japan
A comparison with the UK
Hasegawa Harukiyo

Race, Resistance and the Ainu of Japan
Richard Siddle

Japan's Minorities
The illusion of homogeneity
Edited by Michael Weiner

Japanese Business Management
Restructuring for low growth
and globalization
*Edited by Hasegawa Harukiyo and
Glenn D. Hook*

Japan and Asia Pacific Integration
Pacific romances 1968–1996
Pekka Korhonen

Japan's Economic Power and Security
Japan and North Korea
Christopher W. Hughes

Japan's Contested Constitution
Documents and analysis
Glenn D. Hook and Gavan McCormack

Japan's International Relations
Politics, economics and security
*Glenn D. Hook, Julie Gilson, Christopher W.
Hughes and Hugo Dobson*

Japanese Education Reform
Nakasone's legacy
Christopher P. Hood

**The Political Economy of
Japanese Globalisation**
*Glenn D. Hook and
Hasegawa Harukiyo*

Japan and Okinawa
Structure and subjectivity
*Edited by Glenn D. Hook and
Richard Siddle*

Global Governance and Japan

The institutional architecture

**Edited by
Glenn D. Hook
and Hugo Dobson**

Routledge
Taylor & Francis Group

LONDON AND NEW YORK

First published 2007
by Routledge
2 Park Square, Milton Park, Abingdon, Oxon OX14 4RN

Simultaneously published in the USA and Canada
by Routledge
711 Third Ave, New York, NY 10017

*Routledge is an imprint of the Taylor & Francis Group,
an informa business*

© 2007 Selection and editoral matter Glenn D. Hook and Hugo Dobson;
individual contributors for their contributions

Typeset in Times New Roman by
Newgen Imaging Systems (P) Ltd, Chennai, India

British Library Cataloguing in Publication Data
A catalogue record for this book is available
from the British Library

Library of Congress Cataloging in Publication Data
A catalog record for this book has been requested

ISBN10: 0–415–42400–3 (hbk)
ISBN10: 0–415–42401–1 (pbk)
ISBN10: 0–203–96366–0 (ebk)

ISBN13: 978–0–415–42400–4 (hbk)
ISBN13: 978–0–415–42401–1 (pbk)
ISBN13: 978–0–203–96366–1 (ebk)

Contents

Illustrations

Figures

Tables

Contributors

Amiya-Nakada Ryōsuke is Associate Professor of International Politics in the Department of International Studies, Meiji Gakuin University, Tokyo. His main research interests are in German political economy and the politics of European Integration. Publications in English include 'Functional Differentiation and Democracy', in *Anglo-Japanese Academy Proceedings* (University of Tokyo, 2002) and 'Constructing "Corporatist" State–Society Relations?: current discourses on the European NGOs and its democratic weakness', in *Kobe University Law Review*, 38 (2004).

Araki Ichirō is Professor of International Economic Law at the International Graduate School of Social Sciences, Yokohama National University. His main research interests include theory of public international law as it relates to cross-border economic activities, trade and development, dispute settlement in the WTO, and the political process of trade policy formulation. Publications include 'China and the Agreement on Technical Barriers to Trade', in *China and the World Trading System* (Cambridge University Press, 2003); 'Beyond Aggressive Legalism: Japan and the GATT/WTO Dispute', in *WTO and East Asia* (Cameron May, 2004); 'Industrial Policy in Japan', in *Developmental States: Relevancy, Redundancy or Reconfiguration* (Nova Science Publishers, 2004); and 'The Evolution of Japan's Aggressive Legalism', in *The World Economy* 29, 6 (2006).

Shaun Breslin is Professor of Politics at the University of Warwick and a co-editor of *Pacific Review*. His main research interests are in the political economy of globalization and regionalization and the Chinese political economy in the national, regional and international context. Recent publications include *Microregionalism and World Order* (co-editor, Palgrave, 2002); *New Regionalisms in the Global Political Economy: Theories and Cases* (co-editor, Routledge, 2002); and *China and the Global Political Economy* (Palgrave Macmillan, 2006).

Hugo Dobson is Senior Lecturer in Japan's International Relations in the School of East Asian Studies at the University of Sheffield and at the National Institute of Japanese Studies, UK. His main research interests are the G8, the international relations of Japan and the role of images in international relations.

Publications include *Japan and the G7/8, 1975–2002* (RoutledgeCurzon, 2004); *Japan's International Relations: Politics, Economics, and Security* (co-author, Routledge, 2005); and *The Group of 7/8* (Routledge, 2007).

Endō Seiji is Professor of International Politics at the Faculty of Law, Seikei University, Tokyo. His main research interests include theory of international politics, political theory of global order, globalization and the changing role of the state and transformation of war and conflict. Publications include *Gurōbaru Poritikusu: sekai no saikōzōka to atarashii seijigaku* (co-editor, Yūshindō, 2000); 'The Japanese state: surviving neoliberal political economy', in *The Political and Economic Transition in East Asia: Strong Market, Weakening State* (Curzon, 2001); 'Norms and structural change in international politics', in *Studies in International Politics 4: International Order in Transition* (University of Tokyo Press, 2004, in Japanese).

Andrew Gamble is Professor of Politics at the University of Cambridge and currently holds a Major Research Fellowship from the Leverhulme Trust. He has published widely on British politics, comparative and international political economy, and political ideologies including *Hayek: The Iron Cage of Liberty* (Polity, 1996); *Politics and Fate* (Polity, 2000); *Between Europe and America: The Future of British Politics* (Palgrave, 2003). In 2005 he was awarded the Sir Isaiah Berlin Prize for Lifetime Contribution to Political Studies.

Glenn D. Hook is Professor of Japanese Politics and International Relations and Director of the Graduate School of East Asian Studies at the University of Sheffield. He is also the Director of the National Institute of Japanese Studies, UK. His research interests are in Japan's international relations and the Japanese role in the regional political economy and security. His recent publications include the *Political Economy of Japanese Globalization* (co-editor, Routledge, 2001); *Contested Governance in Japan: Sites and Issues* (editor, Routledge, 2005); and *Japan's International Relations: Politics, Economics and Security* (co-author, Routedge, 2005).

Hoshino Toshiya is Professor of International Relations and United Nations Studies at the Osaka School of International Public Policy, Osaka University. His main research interests include the theory and practice of international security and multilateral diplomacy at the United Nations. Publications include 'Security communities, power sharing and preventive diplomacy', in *Containing Conflict: Cases in Preventive Diplomacy* (JCIE, 2003); 'Ningen no anzenhoshō to Nihon no kokusai seisaku', *Kokusai Anzenhoshō* 30, 3 (2002); *Global Governance:* 'Kokusai-heiwa kaifuku seisaku no kōsō to jissai: "takokukanshugi no kiki" o koete', in *Kokusai Seiji* 137, June (2004); and *'Aratana kyōi' to Kokuren, Amerika* (co-author, Nihon Keizai Shinpōsha, 2006).

Simon Lee is Senior Lecturer in Politics and Co-Director of the Centre for Democratic Governance in the Department of Politics and International Studies, Hull University, UK. His research interests are in comparative political economy, the political economy of the third way, and the politics and political economy of England. He has published work on the political economy of England, Britain, Canada and Japan. His publications include *Blair's Third Way* (Palgrave Macmillan, 2005) and *Neo-Liberalism, State Power and Global Governance* (co-editor, Kluwer, 2006). He was also a major contributor to the *Routledge Encyclopedia of International Political Economy*.

Anthony Payne is Professor of Politics at the University of Sheffield and was first Director and then Co-Director of the Political Economy Research Centre (PERC) at the same institution. His main research interests are in North–South relations in the context of globalization and theorizing new governance from an international political economy perspective. Recent publications include *Charting Caribbean Development* (co-author, Macmillan, 2001); *The New Regional Politics of Development* (editor, Palgrave, 2004); and *The Global Politics of Unequal Development* (Palgrave, 2005).

Nicola Phillips is Professor of Political Economy at the University of Manchester, UK. Her research interests are in comparative and international political economy, development and development theory, the political economy of the Americas, and the political economy of US power. Her recent publications include *New Regionalisms in the Global Political Economy: Theories and Cases* (co-editor, Routledge, 2002); *The Southern Cone Model: The Political Economy of Regional Capitalist Development in Latin America* (Routledge, 2004); and *Globalizing International Political Economy* (editor, Palgrave, 2005). She is the Managing Editor of the journal *New Political Economy* and co-editor of the Lynne Rienner International Political Economy Yearbook series. She holds or has held a number of visiting positions in various institutions in the UK, Europe and Latin America.

Sasuga Katsuhiro is Associate Professor in the Department of International Studies at Tōkai University, Tokyo. His research interests are in international political economy, globalization/regionalism, and East Asian political economy. Publications include 'Microregionalization across Southern China, Hong Kong and Taiwan', in *Microregionalism and World Order* (Palgrave Macmillan, 2002) and *Microregionalism and Governance in East Asia* (Routledge, 2004). His current teaching interests are in international business, international economics and international relations in East Asia.

Shirai Sayuri is Professor of Economics in the Faculty of Policy Management at Keio University, Tokyo. Her research interests are in international finance, finance and capital market development, fiscal decentralization in Japan, foreign aid policy, and the Asian economy. Book publications include *Currency Board no Keizaigaku* (Nihon Hyōronsha, 2000); *Megabank Kiki to IMF Keizaiseisaku* (Kadokawa Shoten, 2002); and *Jinmingen to Chūgoku Keizai* (Nihon Keizai Shinbunsha, 2004). She has also published numerous papers in *Asian Exchange*, *Asia-Pacific Development Journal*, *South Asia Economic Journal*, and *World Development*, as well as in a number of Japanese journals.

Rorden Wilkinson is Professor in International Relations and International Political Economy at the University of Manchester, UK. His research interests are in global governance, the regulation of international trade and international labour standards. His recent publications include *Multilateralism and the World Trade Organisation* (Routledge, 2000); *Global Governance: Critical Perspectives* (co-editor, Routledge, 2002); and *The Global Governance Reader* (editor, Routledge, 2005). His work has been published in, among others, *Global Governance*, the *Journal of World Trade*, *New Political Economy*, *Third World Quarterly*, the *British Journal of Politics and International Relations*, *Environment and Planning*, *International Studies Perspectives*, and *Environmental Politics*. He co-edits the *RIPE series in Global Political Economy* and the *Global Institutions Series*, both for Routledge.

Richard Woodward is Lecturer at the University of Hull, UK. His principal research interests are in the theory and practice of global governance, the OECD's role in global governance, offshore finance and small states. His publications include *Governing Financial Globalization: The Political Economy of Multi-level Governance* (co-editor, Routledge, 2005) and *The Organisation for Economic Cooperation and Development* (Routledge, 2007). His work has been published in *New Political Economy*, *World Today*, and *Cambridge Review of International Affairs*.

Preface

The genesis of this book is in discussions between Anthony Payne and Glenn Hook on the need to move the debate on global governance forward, but to do so taking into account the role of Japan. The contributors were selected and then invited to present drafts of their chapters at two workshops, the first held on 13–14 September 2004 at Dōshisha University, Kyoto and the second held on 29–31 January 2005 at Shrigley Hall, Pott Shrigley, near Manchester. The final versions included here were later revised based on comments by the participants, editors and anonymous referees. Thanks to all of the contributors for their chapters and to all those who commented on the drafts.

Acknowledgements

For financial assistance, we would like to thank the Daiwa Anglo-Japanese Foundation for support of the workshop at Dōshisha University, and the Toshiba International Foundation for support of the workshop at Shrigley Hall. We are also grateful to the Chūbu Electric Power Company for financial support.

Special thanks are due to President Hatta Eiji of Dōshisha University, for his generous hospitality, and to Hasegawa Harukiyo for making all of the local arrangements in Kyoto. I would also like to thank Hugo Dobson for agreeing to jointly edit this volume.

GDH

A note on the text

Following Japanese convention, the family name precedes the given name in the text. Long vowels are indicated by a macron, except in the case of common place and other names, such as Tokyo.

Abbreviations

ADB	Asian Development Bank
AMF	Asian Monetary Fund
ASEAN	Association of Southeast Asian Nations
ASEM	Asia–Europe Meeting
BIAC	Business and Industry Advisory Committee
BIS	Bank for International Settlements
BWP	Bretton Woods Project
CEA	Council of Economic Advisers
CSCE	Conference on Security and Cooperation in Europe
DAC	Development Assistance Committee
DDA	Doha Development Agenda
DfiD	Department for International Development
DSU	Dispute Settlement Understanding
EC	European Community
ESAF	Enhanced structural adjustment facility
EU	European Union
FDI	Foreign direct investment
G5	Group of Five
G7	Group of Seven
G8	Group of Eight
G24	Group of Twenty-four
G77	Group of Seventy-seven at the United Nations
GATS	General Agreement on Trade in Services
GATT	General Agreement on Tariffs and Trade
GDN	Global Development Network
GDP	Gross domestic product
GN	Guidance Note on Governance
GNP	Gross national product
HIPCs	Highly Indebted Poor Countries
HIV	Human Immunodeficiency Virus
HTC	Harmful tax competition
IBRD	International Bank for Reconstruction and Development
ICC	International Criminal Court

ICJ	International Court of Justice
ICSID	International Centre for the Settlement of Investor Disputes
IDA	International Development Association
IEO	Independent Evaluation Office (of the International Monetary Fund)
IFB	International Finance Bureau (of Ministry of Finance)
IFC	International Finance Corporation
IFIs	International financial institutions
IMF	International Monetary Fund
IMFC	International Monetary and Finance Committee
IPE	International political economy
ISO	International Organization for Standardization
IT	Information technology
ITO	International Trade Organization
ITU	International Telecommunications Union
JBIC	Japan Bank for International Cooperation
JFPR	Japan Fund for Poverty Reduction
JICA	Japan International Cooperation Agency
JSDF	Japan Social Development Fund
JSP	Japan Socialist Party
LDC	Less Developed Countries
LDP	Liberal Democratic Party
MAI	Multilateral Agreement on Investment
MDBs	Multilateral Development Banks
MDGs	Millennium development goals
MEIs	Multilateral economic institutions
METI	Ministry of Economy, Trade and Industry
MFA	Multi-fibre Agreement
MIGA	Multilateral Investment Guarantee Agency
MITI	Ministry of International Trade and Industry
MOF	Ministry of Finance
MOFA	Ministry of Foreign Affairs
NAMA	Non-agricultural market access
NATO	North Atlantic Treaty Organization
NEPAD	New Partnership for Africa's Development
NGO	Non-governmental organization
ODA	Official development assistance
OECD	Organization for Economic Cooperation and Development
OECF	Overseas Economic Cooperation Fund
OEEC	Organization for European Economic Cooperation
OMC	Open Methods of Competition
OOF	Other offical flows
OSCE	Organization for Security and Cooperation in Europe
P5	Permanent five (of the United Nations Security Council)
PHRD	Policy and Human Resources Development Fund
PIF	Pacific Islands Forum

PKO	Peacekeeping Operations
PRC	People's Republic of China
PRGF	Poverty Reduction Growth Facility
PRSP	Poverty Reduction Strategic Papers
PSIA	Poverty and social impact analysis
ROC	Republic of China
RTAA	Reciprocal Trade Agreements Act
SAF	Structured adjustment facility
SDF	Self-Defence Forces
SDRs	Special Drawing Rights
SPF	Spruce, Pine and Fir
TICAD	Tokyo International Conference on African Development
TRIMS	Agreement on Trade Related Investment Measures
TRIPs	Agreement on Trade-related Intellectual Property Rights
TUAC	Trade Union Advisory Committee
UNCTAD	United Nations Conference on Trade and Development
UNDP	United Nations Development Programme
UNHRC	United Nations Human Rights Commission
UNSC	United Nations Security Council
USSR	Union of Soviet Socialist Republics
VER	Voluntary export restraint
WBI	World Bank Institute
WEO	World Economic Organization
WHO	World Health Organization
WIPO	World Intellectual Property Organization
WTO	World Trade Organization

Introduction

Thinking about global governance and Japan

Glenn D. Hook and Anthony Payne

Introduction

The novelty and originality of this book is that it brings together in one volume consideration of two vitally important, yet still understudied, aspects of the contemporary world order, namely, the set of questions about power and global politics assembled of late under the rubric of 'global governance', and the collection of recurring themes which always seem to arise when Japan's role in international politics is subjected to analysis and reflection. Treated separately, neither is a straightforward matter on which easy agreement can quickly be reached. Few can as yet specify with precision what they mean by global governance; some deny its existence completely; and yet the phrase actually seems to have become ever more fashionable, as witnessed by the phalanx of commentators who use it as a way to try to capture something important about the current structure of the world order. Japan, too, has frequently been presented in the international relations literature as anomalous, if not aberrant or abnormal, due to the particular way in which Japanese policy makers have generally sought to configure and instrumentalize the country's power resources over the last twenty or thirty years. Yet Japan combines considerable economic weight, standing number two in the world in terms of gross national product (GNP), a strengthening civil society and a growing, if still constrained, security role. Treated together, none of the uncertainties of analysis pertaining to either global governance or the role of Japan necessarily disappear, but they can be interrogated in a new and potentially insightful way. This is the task that this book has set itself. The remainder of this introductory chapter seeks simply to set out the intellectual background on which such an enquiry must rest. It explores in turn the way that the debates about global governance and Japan have recently taken shape.

The global governance debate

As already indicated, global governance has become one of the mantras of our time. It is a turn of phrase increasingly widely used in both academic and political discourse, and yet its usage remains covered by ambiguity and indeed confusion. Nevertheless, it makes sense to think of global governance as being understood variously as an ideological project, as a theoretical orientation and as an emergent reality.

Global governance as ideological project

Much early discussion of global governance emerged as part of a conscious ideological project fashioned by clearly identifiable institutions and interests. Calls for more or better or renewed 'global governance' began to appear in the mid-1990s largely as a consequence of the ending of the cold war, the perceived trend towards the increasing pace of globalization and the apparent forging of a global civil society. What they generally sought under this rubric was reform and consequential strengthening of the various world organizations, principally the United Nations and/or the so-called Bretton Woods institutions by which was meant principally the World Bank and the International Monetary Fund (IMF). The forerunner within this movement was the self-named Commission on Global Governance, a group of senior politicians and public figures brought together in the early 1990s by the former Swedish prime minister Ingvar Carlsson and the former Commonwealth secretary general Shridath Ramphal with the explicit purpose of suggesting ways of consolidating the presumed revival of the United Nations (UN) in the aftermath of the 1991 Gulf War. Its preference for the notion of governance and its particular usage of the term was interesting and revealing. According to the Commission:

> Governance is the sum of the many ways individuals and institutions, public and private, manage their common affairs. It is a continuing process through which conflicting or diverse interests can be accommodated and cooperative action may be taken. It includes formal institutions and regimes empowered to enforce compliance, as well as informal arrangements that people and institutions either have agreed to or perceive to be in their interest.... At the global level, governance has been viewed primarily as intergovernmental relationships, but it must now be understood as also involving non-governmental organizations, citizens' movements, multinational corporations and the global market. Interacting with these are global mass media of dramatically enlarged influence.
>
> (Commission on Global Governance 1995: 2–3)

The Commission thus sought to shift attention away from the specificities of the particular powers of international organizations *per se* and reframe global governance as a process founded on accommodation and continual interaction between public and private actors. Unsurprisingly, the international system of states proved to be structurally unresponsive to this type of thinking and the many (broadly social democratic) reform proposals of the Commission generally fell by the wayside.

This did not, however, mean that other bodies and groups were not ready and willing to follow in its wake. A persistent theme in such discussions has been the need to reinstate the liberal international economic order initially put in place at Bretton Woods (Haq *et al.* 1995). This was pursued again with renewed urgency after the Asian financial crisis of 1997–8 (Michie and Smith 1999). Another such prospectus was offered up, with a considerable fanfare, by a group of economists linked to the United Nations Development Programme (UNDP). Their organizing insight was that 'today's turmoil reveals a serious under-provision of global public goods' (Kaul *et al.* 1999: xxi), understood in conventional terms as goods that are unlikely to be provided by unregulated markets. The way that the problem was posed inevitably gave away the means by which the UNDP believed it could be solved. Given that the intellectual origins of the theory of public goods go back, as is well known, to Samuelson (1954), Hardin (1968), Olson (1971) and Kindleberger (1986), the UNDP study was, as a consequence, irredeemably cast within the framework of liberal economics.

This highlighted a general lesson. Although, to be fair, much advocacy of this sort did lie more at the social democratic end of the spectrum, the truth is that global governance as an ideological project always fell within the broad embrace of liberal ideology. It also usually lacked a sharp grasp of politics – in particular, the political obstacles that might impede the realization of its vision – which tended to tar this early normative phase of the debate with a somewhat amorphous quality. This is perhaps what led Groom and Powell to suggest that global governance could be aptly described in this period as 'a theme in need of a focus' (1994: 81). What these projects really represented in their various ways were different strands of the politics of Western liberalism in the 1980s and 1990s, each revealing in its discourse the ongoing tension of that time between a neoliberalism that confidently asserted the limitations of state action and a social democracy that sought to defend and rethink the case for an active state. In sum, this part of the global governance debate does not provide the analytical tools needed for this study. Indeed, this literature needs to be unpicked and exposed as being explicitly ideological precisely as part of any serious attempt to come to grips with contemporary global governance as it has actually come to exist.

Global governance as theoretical orientation

International relations as a sub-field fell upon the concept of governance at about the same time as liberal ideology. The beginning of this part of the debate is usually traced to the publication in 1992 of *Governance Without Government: Order and Change in World Politics*, jointly edited by James Rosenau and Ernst-Otto Czempiel. Prior to this moment most attempts to understand 'government at the global level' had been made via rationalist studies of regime formation inspired by the work of Robert Keohane (1984). The central insight of this school was that, over time, states could learn to cooperate in non-zero-sum ways if they formed intergovernmental institutions, or regimes, in particular policy areas. Rosenau, who wrote the extended introductory chapter in *Governance without Government*, was clearly influenced by regime theorizing, although in this work with Czempiel he sought boldly and successfully to move the discussion forward. He set out the idea of governance as a set of 'regulatory mechanisms in a sphere of activity which function effectively even though they are not endowed with formal authority' (Rosenau 1992: 5). Governance thus differed from government in that 'it refers to activities backed by shared goals that may or may not derive from legal and formally prescribed responsibilities and that do not necessarily rely on police powers to overcome defiance and attain compliance' (Rosenau 1992: 4). It was, in other words, 'a more encompassing phenomenon' which 'embraces governmental institutions, but...also subsumes informal, non-governmental mechanisms' (Rosenau 1992: 4). Here lay the similarity to the conventional notion of regimes, except that regimes had generally been seen to exist in certain defined issue areas (Krasner 1983) and governance was used here by Rosenau in a manner which clearly tied the concept to the whole global order. In a later article in the first issue of the journal *Global Governance* Rosenau returned to these questions, defining global governance as 'systems of rule at all levels of human activity...in which the pursuit of goals through the exercise of control has transnational repercussions' (Rosenau 1995: 13). Finally, by the time this piece had been edited to reappear in his book, *Along the Domestic–Foreign Frontier*, the ultimate Rosenau definition of governance had been refined as 'spheres of authority...at all levels of human activity...that amount to systems of rule in which goals are pursued through the exercise of control' (Rosenau 1997: 145).

Many thought, and no doubt still think, that this was a very loose way of conceiving of the concept of governance. In a direct response to Rosenau, Lawrence Finkelstein suggested that it was hard to know what was excluded by such a formulation. He acknowledged, for example, that international crime syndicates, which Rosenau had included in his wide-ranging survey of existing agents of governance, were a factor to be dealt with in international relations, only then to ask caustically:

> Does it really clarify matters, however, or facilitate the research enterprise, to toss them in a hopper along with states, intergovernmental organizations, nongovernmental organizations, and Moody's Investor's Service?
>
> (Finkelstein 1995: 368)

Finkelstein's own approach was to insist that governance was 'an activity', not a system; it should be 'concerned with purposive acts, not tacit arrangements' (Finkelstein 1995: 4, 5). This was plausible, if no less vague than Rosenau, but only led in the end to the unoriginal claim that 'global governance is doing internationally what governments do at home' (Finkelstein 1995: 5). The main problem with this line of analysis, as Marie-Claude Smouts was quick to point out, was that it 'overlaps with multilateralism' (Smouts 1998: 82), which had served for a long while as a perfectly adequate way of coming to terms with what is done by international organizations (Ruggie 1983).

In fact, the appeal of Rosenau's working approach to governance was precisely its breadth. It was not at all, as alleged, a matter of bringing together different types of actors in some great 'spaghetti bowl' (another of Finkelstein's metaphors), but rather of sensitizing analysts to the changing patterns of international relations post-cold war to the extent of the mix of actors – governmental and non-governmental, public and private, legitimate and illegitimate – which had come to participate in the shaping of systems of global rule. Rosenau captured this very effectively. The problem with his analysis was rather different: it was, as Craig Murphy has noted, that he was 'less capable of explaining why so much of this creative movement in world politics seems to have added up to the supremacy of the neoliberal agenda both within and across states' (Murphy 2005: 796). To some extent this lacuna can be filled within international relations theory by incorporation of some of the insights from the constructivist school which has been so prominent of late, especially among American scholars (Finnemore 1996; Ruggie 1998; Wendt 1999). In the vision of constructivists all actors within international relations have the capacity in their exchanges to influence each other's understanding of their own interests, which means that the norms of those exchanges, the manner of the communication, matter. To follow Murphy again, in the contemporary era 'liberal norms ... exert power not due to their inherent validity or rightness, but because they are regularly enacted within certain realms, because some international actors have become convinced of their rightness and validity' (Murphy 2005: 797). Rosenau, plus a dash of constructivism, might therefore be said to be the best that the international relations sub-field has yet been able to offer to the study of global governance.

As an approach it is unquestionably useful. It has identified some of the ways in which international relations appear increasingly to be conducted outside the realist model, emphasizing in particular the growing significance of both new non-state actors and new processes such as intermediation, bargaining and networking. As such, it has pointed up some important shifts of behaviour in the international system. The problem is that, for all Rosenau's inventiveness, the mainstream international relations approach to governance remains grounded as a body of theory in the liberal institutionalist view of the world from which it originated. That means that it cannot but suffer from the flaws which have been associated over the years with that school of thought, namely, that it defines the essence of international relations too narrowly as process and that it ultimately lacks a convincing theory of power by which to explain why outcomes of a certain type keep on occurring.

Global governance as emergent reality

The third – and for present purposes the most important part – of the debate can be found in the sub-field of international political economy (IPE). As is well known, IPE is a notoriously diverse field of study, encompassing mainstream and critical traditions. According to Geoffrey Underhill, it is, however, held together by a core of shared conceptual assumptions, of which he highlighted three: '1) that the political and economic domains cannot be separated in any real sense, and even doing so for analytical purposes has its perils; 2) [that] political interaction is one of the principal means through which the economic structures of the market are established and in turn transformed; and 3) that there is an intimate connection between the domestic and international levels of analysis, and that the two cannot meaningfully be separated off from one another' (Underhill 2000: 806). To these should be added a fourth premise, namely, that in the best critical IPE there should also be an attempt to 'develop an integrated analysis, by combining parsimonious theories which analyse agency in terms of a conception of rationality with contextual theories which analyse structures institutionally and historically' (Gamble *et al.* 1996: 5–6). This is always a hard task, but it is not impossible.

As yet, the IPE literature on governance is best described as embryonic. The field's preoccupation of late has understandably been with the concept and process of globalization where the literature has genuinely been voluminous. But, from an agency-structure perspective, globalization is actually the right place from which to begin the analysis of global governance. Put more generally, the political economy (structure) must be understood before the politics (agency) can be grasped. To be specific, what is needed is a strong sense of the changed structural context brought out within the global political economy by the package of processes encapsulated by the term globalization before turning to ask: how is globalization governed? For the fact is that globalization is presently being governed. To borrow Rosenau's term, it has its own system of rule. It might not be ideal; it might be undemocratic; it might well be in need of reform in the direction of improved global governance; but it exists to some degree and in some fashion as emergent reality. It is incumbent on analysts, therefore, to try to make some sense of the complex facets of the way in which what may more accurately be described as the 'governance of globalization' actually occurs. Although it remains the case that this system is not understood very well as a totality, the good news is that there have emerged fragments of analysis which are relevant and illuminating and which can be assembled into an outline picture. This picture can be gradually built up by reference to five current areas of debate within IPE about the nature of contemporary global governance.

The ideological face of governance. Robert Cox, doyen of the critical school of IPE, has insisted for many years that ideational and material dimensions of power need to be understood as 'always bound together, mutually reinforcing one another, and not reducible one to the other' (Cox 1983: 168). Indeed, this insight is one of the distinguishing qualities of critical IPE. It needs therefore to be recognized that the world order, which is a notion conceptualized by Cox as 'the way things usually happen' (Cox 1981: 152), has an ideological, as well as a material, face. The latter, in relation to matters such as control over raw materials, markets, capital and the like, may be the more frequently analysed within IPE, and the easier to quantify, but the former is a vital part of the overall structure of power and, from a governance perspective, arguably even more important because it shapes the way that 'rulers' think about the possibilities of 'rule'. It raises the core Gramscian issue of who or what creates the 'common sense' of an era, the presumed, taken-for-granted norms and assumptions by which the wielding of power is classically masked.

As will be apparent, this is difficult terrain to research. Cox himself recognized this, at least implicitly, by deploying the French word *nébuleuse* in an attempt to catch the flavour of the way he saw this cloud of ideological forces exerting its impact (Cox 1996: 301). His elaboration of what this involved in the present era is worth quoting at length:

> There is a transnational process of consensus formation among the official caretakers of the global economy. This process generates consensual

guidelines, underpinned by an ideology of globalization, that are transmitted into the policy-making channels of national governments and big corporations. Part of this consensus-formation process takes place through unofficial forums like the Trilateral Commission, the Bilderberg conferences, or the more esoteric Mont Pélèrin Society. Part of it goes on through official bodies like the OECD, the Bank for International Settlements, the International Monetary Fund, and the G7. These shape the discourse within which policies are defined, the terms and concepts that circumscribe what can be thought and done.

(Cox 1996: 301)

It is no revelation to say that the leading discourse to have been shaped in this way over the past two decades has been neoliberalism. This unquestionably has been the dominant ideology of the globalization phase of world order and is still in broad terms the ruling orthodoxy of a majority of national governments throughout the world, no matter what varied rhetorical devices are employed to conceal this reality. It embraces within its orbit not only a whole series of practical stances towards markets, taxes, investments and the like, but also more intangible matters like attitudes, norms and styles, including those pertaining to modes of governing. As seen earlier, several explicit projects of governance have arisen out of the neoliberal well and have exerted their impact on the ways that people are actually governed. Neoliberal ideas have also unconsciously conditioned the thinking and behaviour of many actors involved in contemporary processes of governance. But it would be an exaggeration to imply that they have not been contested over the past twenty years. As indicated earlier, social democracy has fought a largely defensive battle on behalf of redistribution and continuing state intervention in the social sphere, regrouping lately under the banner of the 'Third Way' (Birnbaum 1999). Similarly, other competing 'models of capitalism' to the Anglo-American variant so revered in the neoliberal handbook have been discerned, and survive, albeit under steady pressure to liberalize. These too contribute to the ideological grounding of the theory and practice of gover- nance in the context of globalization. In short, the ideological (or normative) face of governance, as termed earlier, needs to be understood as constituting the very fabric of the picture of global governance that needs to be built up.

The global architecture of governance. At the institutional level there has also emerged what Paul Cammack has dubbed a 'global architecture of governance' (Cammack 2002). The reference here is not just or even predominantly to the United Nations system. The United Nations has been the embodiment of this aspiration since 1945, even if it largely failed to escape the constraints of superpower rivalry during the cold war era. Paul Taylor has shown, however, that during the 1990s it came to demonstrate a renewed activism in peace-keeping, in responding to emergencies and in promoting democracy and 'good governance'. He has argued that this reflected the force of a proactive cosmopolitanism which sought to ensure that all states are 'well-founded in the light of the standards of the international community' (Taylor 1999: 558). In his view this redefined sovereignty as, in effect, 'a licence from the international community to practice [*sic*] as an independent government in a particular territory' (Taylor 1999: 538). If he is right, then the

United Nations has won for itself a substantial role in policing the current terms of entry into the official state-based part of the contemporary system of rule.

Other global bodies have also acquired sufficient regulatory authority further to undermine the state's traditional monopoly of governance. They include, pre-eminently, the Group of 7/8 system, the World Bank, the IMF, the World Trade Organization and the Organization for Economic Cooperation and Development (OECD). Much is written, often in hyperbolic form, about the power of these institutions, and they have become the hate figures of the anti-globalization movement. However, good studies of how they actually operate politically are still thin on the ground. There is mainly Robert Wade's analysis of some of the internal mechanisms of governance of the World Bank in the early 1990s (Wade 1996), the study of relations between several of the multilateral economic institutions and global social movements by Robert O'Brien, Anne Marie Goetz, Jan Aart Scholte and Marc Williams (O'Brien *et al.* 2000), Cammack's exposition of the intended reach of the World Bank's new so-called Comprehensive Development Framework (Cammack 2002) and Rorden Wilkinson's critique of the workings of the World Trade Organization (Wilkinson 2000, 2002). These and other accounts do not generate a neat or simple picture of the way these bodies operate. As international organizations, each is different one from the other and they work in different ways at different times according to their own internal politics. There is thus a fluidity to their politics which is often under-played or even ignored completely. They are also still rooted in the politics of the states that constitute their membership. Yet it is also clear that these major global institutions do at the same time transcend their statist origins. They represent more than the sum of their parts and certainly command enough resources – of both a material and ideological nature – to qualify as significant agents of governance in their own right.

Multi-level governance. Regions (variously defined) have also been widely identified as new sites of governance. In a frequently quoted remark John Ruggie suggested several years ago that the European Union (EU) might be said to constitute 'the first "multi-perspectival polity" to emerge since the advent of the modern era' (Ruggie 1993: 172). This claim has been taken up and developed by Gary Marks, Liesbet Hooghe and Kermit Blank who have deployed the image of 'multi-level governance' to catch the essence of 'a polity creating process in which authority and policy-making influence are shared across multiple levels of government – subnational, national and supranational' (Marks *et al.* 1996: 342; see also Hooghe and Marks 2001). In effect, within the EU, perhaps more than in any other part of the world, states no longer monopolize governance: policy making is characterized instead by 'mutual dependence, complementary functions and overlapping competencies' (Marks *et al.* 1996: 372) among the supranational, national and subnational actors previously identified. The role played by the growth of sub-state regionalism within the EU model of multi-level governance has been explicitly treated by several authors, notably James Anderson and James Goodman. In a direct evocation of Ruggie, they have described how 'the related building of inter-regional linkages, formal associations of regional bodies, and collective institutional expressions of regional interests at the EU level, are all contributing to a multiple layering of power and to the process of selectively "unbundling" territoriality' (Anderson and Goodman 1995: 620; see Ruggie 1993: 171). What is more, this argument extends generally beyond the idea of a 'Europe of the regions' to provinces, federal states and municipalities in a variety of countries across the world and also, as Saskia Sassen has suggested, to the 'global city'. For her, cities are now vital parts of 'the global grid of places' (Sassen 1995: 46) and reflect globalization's continuing need for 'strategic sites with vast concentrations of resources and infrastructure' which may no longer be states *per se* but nevertheless still need to be 'situated in national territories' (Sassen 1995: 31).

The reorganization of the state. Notwithstanding some over-eager claims to the contrary, global governance, even within a global(izing) political economy, still derives fundamentally from what states do. In other words, states are only written out of the script at our peril. The point to stress is that states have always varied, and do still vary, inter alia in their degree of democracy, level of development, infrastructural power, national indebtedness and regional location. As Michael Mann has warned, even under conditions of globalization the patterns of change are simply too 'contradictory, and the future too murky, to permit us to argue simply that the nation and the nation-state system are either strengthening or weakening' (Mann 1997: 494, emphasis in original). A better, more nuanced thesis is that 'the processes of global restructuring are largely embedded within state structures and institutions, politically contingent on state policies and actions, and primarily about the reorganization of the state' (Amoore *et al.* 1997: 186).

This argument is now expressed in the literature in a range of forms. Cox, for example, initially referred to 'the internationalisation of the state' understood as a process that 'gives precedence to certain state agencies – notably ministries of finance and prime ministers' offices – which are key points in the adjustment of domestic to international economic policy' (Cox 1981: 146). Scholte has suggested that globalization has yielded 'a different kind of state . . . [which has]. . . . on the whole lost sovereignty, acquired supraterritorial constituents, retreated from interstate warfare (for the moment), frozen or reduced social security provisions, multiplied multilateral governance arrangements and lost considerable democratic potential' (Scholte 1997: 452). From further to the left Peter Burnham has drawn attention to what he sees as the widespread shift in the politics of economic management in advanced capitalist societies from 'politicised management (discretion-based)' to 'depoliticised management (rules-based)' (Burnham 1999: 43–4), the latter being characterized by attempts to reduce the former political character of economic decision making and re-position it as far as possible at one remove from government. Peter Evans, reflecting on 'stateness' in an era of globalization, has stressed the centrality of the hegemony of Anglo-American liberal thinking (again) in limiting belief in the efficacy of state action and charted accordingly the recent 'project of constructing a leaner, meaner kind of stateness' (Evans 1997: 85) lately associated with the 'Third Way' thinking of the Clinton, Blair and Schröder administrations in the United

States, the United Kingdom and Germany respectively. Linda Weiss similarly has insisted on the variety of 'state capacities' and has argued that 'adaptation is the very essence of the modern state by virtue of the fact that it is embedded in a dynamic economic and inter-state system' (Weiss 1997: 17). Although in some states certain policy instruments, particularly those associated with macroeconomic adjustment strategies, may be enfeebled by globalization, others, such as those related to industrial policy, may and do change in all manner of creative ways. It is therefore necessary always to look to a country's governing institutions and expect differences according to national orientation and capability. The lesson, in short, is that reorganized states still contribute in many important ways to reorganized global governance.

Privatized governance. The dispersal of contemporary global governance becomes still more apparent when the lens is extended beyond forms of public authority to the domain of the private. Drawing in good part on Susan Strange's last book on *The Retreat of the State* (Strange 1996), Murphy (2005: 794) has listed several 'global-level "private" authorities that regulate both states and much of transnational economic and social life', as follows:

- private bond-rating agencies that impose particular policies on governments at all levels;
- tight global oligopolies in reinsurance, accounting, high-level consulting that provide similar regulatory pressure;
- global and regional cartels in industries as diverse as mining and electrical products;
- the peculiar combination of oligopolistic regulation, *ad hoc* private regulation, and non-regulation that governs global telecommunications and the Internet;
- internationally integrated mafias; and
- a narrow group of economists who define the norms of that profession and thereby regulate the treasury ministries, the most powerful of the intergovernmental agencies, and the private institutions of financial regulation that want to adhere to economic orthodoxy.

His list is far from exhaustive and research into this aspect of governance within IPE is growing quite fast (Sinclair 1994; Cutler 1995; Weiss and Gordenker 1996; Cutler *et al.* 1999). It is too early at the moment to reach for generalized conclusions, for as yet there is nothing like a sufficiently full picture, either of the contemporary era or of the past. It is difficult, therefore, to establish how much is really new – for example, most of the 'authorities' identified by Murphy could be said to have had counterparts in the nineteenth century. Enough, however, has been said to have established that, within the study of contemporary global governance, the public/private interface has henceforth to be treated as notably fluid and uncertain. It is also worth pointing out here that the very notion of a clear separation between the public and the private is a feature of classical liberal thinking and does not therefore necessarily correspond with due expectation in many countries. Indeed, in many parts of the world it is not at all easy to distinguish effectively between 'public' and 'private' forms or agents of governance. At the very least there is a need to be extremely careful in the ways that these questions are approached if an appropriately inclusive, genuinely global understanding of privatized governance is to be reached.

Conclusion

The argument made in this final part of the first section of this chapter is that IPE has lately been responsible for quite a lot of work that can be gathered together to constitute a viable approach to the study of global governance. The central claim that has in effect been made is that in a period of globalization the number and type of sites of governance has multiplied to create a complex, multi-dimensional, multi-layered overall pattern. The explanatory link to the process of globalization is not always or necessarily made – that would be too crude a thesis – but it is rightly stressed within IPE that the package of trends encapsulated by the term globalization has significantly altered the structural contours within which global governance as an activity takes place. Certainly, in the best work a sense of the interlinking of structure and agency is provided and it can at least be said that globalization has acquired a distinctive, and increasingly well understood, apparatus of governance. Of course, it is the case that much more practical research needs to be done in all parts of the world in order to arrive at a genuinely global portrait of contemporary modes of governance. Unquestionably, one important missing dimension is a full understanding of the role played by Japan in these complex, emergent forms of global rule and so the discussion moves on to review by way of additional background the existing debate about Japan's role in the global political economy more generally.

The Japan debate

As already indicated, the international relations literature on Japan has frequently presented it as anomalous, if not aberrant or abnormal, due to the way in which the country instrumentalizes its power resources. Nevertheless, by the use of the appropriate tools, taking into account the three variables of structure, agency and norms, Japan can in fact be portrayed as a normal state, even if the debate on Japan in the world does not necessarily take all these variables into account.

Japan in the world

The debate on the role of Japan in the global political economy has been coloured by Japan's defeat in the Second World War and the double-digit economic growth the country achieved soon thereafter. The metaphor of the phoenix rising from the ashes has frequently been used to capture the general amazement at Japan's recovery soon after the dust from the war had settled. It is certainly true that, from the Meiji period (1868–1911) onwards, the Japanese state and its people have sought to catch up with the West, at times using war as an instrument of state policy as a means to try to achieve this goal. In the event, the sheer scale and rapidity of Japan's transformation quickly brought to centre stage the question of what kind of global role the country would play in the post-war era. Its rehabilitation following the defeat gave the United States a preponderance of power in reshaping the body politic during the Occupation (1945–52), which led, after a brief interlude of prioritizing the twin goals of demilitarization and democratization, to Japan being integrated into the cold war order as part of the Western camp. While one of the outcomes of the Occupation's policy of demilitarization was Article 9 of the 1947 Constitution (the famous 'peace clause'), the intensification of the cold war and the outbreak of the 'hot war' on the Korean peninsula in June 1950 meant that Japan was soon transformed into a bastion against communism in the Far East, not the unarmed, neutral state in the spirit of the Constitution and as proposed by the Japan Socialist Party (JSP) opposition (Hook and McCormack 2001). The conservative government of Prime Minister Yoshida Shigeru thus signed the US–Japan security treaty, along with the San Francisco peace treaty, to end the Occupation in 1952. It then put substantial energy into promoting development, with high economic growth following shortly thereafter, while relying on the United States for security guarantees.

At first, as a bastion against communism in the Far East, Japan's post-war role was very much constrained by the legacy of imperialism and the cold war division of the region and the globe, particularly in relation to the development of a regional policy with former colonies and other parts of East Asia that had suffered Japanese aggression. More generally, Japan was reliant on the sponsorship of the United States to re-enter international society. It was under US sponsorship in the 1950s, for instance, that it joined the key institutions of global governance, entering the IMF and the World Bank in 1952, and the predecessor to the WTO, the General Agreement on Tariffs and Trade, in 1955. It then joined the United Nations in 1956. In theory, Japan thereafter developed a 'UN-centred' foreign policy, but in reality its somewhat truncated global role was 'US-centred', with the country remaining overwhelmingly reliant on the United States in the political, economic and particularly the security dimensions of its international relations. These relations with the United States were sustained by the norm of bilateralism, which consistently underpinned the foreign policies pursued by the government, which from 1955, except for a brief period in the mid-1990s, has been formed by the conservative Liberal Democratic Party (LDP).

But the democratic reforms of the Occupation period and the existence of Article 9 of the Constitution created two alternative identities for Japan's role in the world: as an ally of the United States, on the one hand, or as a 'peace state', on the other. The JSP and other opponents of the ruling conservatives acted as a countervailing force against the LDP's attempts to strengthen especially the security relationship with the United States, preferring to try to realize the goal of becoming a 'peace state' through 'unarmed neutrality' rather than by means of the United States or indeed a potentially alternative Soviet alliance (for details, see Igarashi 1985). Although socialist and popular protest against the security treaty outside the Diet failed to halt its revision in 1960, the strength of the opposition was enough to lead to the downfall of the prime minister at the time, Kishi Nobusuke. In place of direct confrontation over the security policy to be pursued by Japan – the LDP's alliance with the United States or the JSP's policy of unarmed neutrality – the government focused on an 'income doubling' policy rather than foreign policy. This promoted a consumer culture as well as a boost in growth, with the appellation 'economic superpower' soon to follow. However, given the experience of the war, particularly the atomic bombings of Hiroshima and Nagasaki, issues of war and peace still continued to be of popular concern, bolstered by the gradual embedding of an anti-militarist norm at the popular level and, to a certain extent, also at the level of the policy-making elite. Indeed, Japanese policy-making agents at various times have taken advantage of this domestic resistance to the military to oppose US pressure to play a more active security role, whereas at others they have been prepared to challenge the norm as part of Japan playing more of a global role. Overall, the anti-militarist norm has acted as a constraint on the build-up of Japanese military forces and limited security cooperation with the United States, although over time Article 9 of the Constitution, the Self-defence Forces (SDF) and the US–Japan security treaty have gained popular acceptance. Certainly, the potential contradiction between the Constitution and the SDF and security treaty has never been resolved by the courts.

This combination of the US–Japan security treaty and the norm of bilateralism, on the one hand, and Article 9 of the Constitution and the norm of anti-militarism, on the other, gave shape to the debate on Japan's role in global politics during the cold war era, pitching 'realist' and 'idealist' scholars against one another (Nagai 1967; Sakamoto 1967). For the realists, communism was the greatest threat and, in order to protect the peace and security of Japan, the maintenance of the security treaty with the United States was seen to be essential. For the idealists, nuclear war was the greatest threat and, in order to protect the peace and security of Japan, not joining either of the two camps and thereby exacerbating international tensions was seen to be the preferred order of the day. With the demise of the cold war, however, the international stand-off between the two camps ended, thereby eroding the basis of the domestic cold war political order in Japan. For the realists, the end of the cold war undermined the basis for the security treaty: after all, if communism is for all intents and purpose dead, what is the purpose of the security treaty? For the idealists, if the cold war had ended, then what is the purpose of 'unarmed neutrality' as the means to prevent the exacerbation of international tensions and ensure that Japan is not dragged into a war of America's making? The final end was put to the cold war debate over Japan's role in global security with the formation of a coalition government between the LDP and its erstwhile enemy, the JSP, under the premiership of the leader of the socialist party, Murayama Tomiichi (1994–6). Shortly thereafter, the party dropped its opposition to the security treaty and the SDF, thereby removing an important brake on Japan's global security role. With the cold war points of contestation no longer valid in terms of the type of global role Japan should play, the question of how Japan should make an 'international contribution' now moved to centre stage.

Japan as a normal state

The question of how Japan should make an international contribution became particularly salient from the time of the 1990–1 Gulf crisis and war onwards. The debate pitted Article 9 of the Constitution, which placed restrictions on the international deployment of the Self-defence Forces, against Japan's obligation to fulfil its responsibilities as a member of the international community. For many, the economic superpower that had risen from 'the ashes' was not doing enough politically or militarily in support of the global order, not shouldering an appropriate burden as one of the major industrialized democracies. The demands of international society, especially the United States, were for Japan to 'do more'. Domestically, those in favour of Japan playing a greater global role joined the chorus. Taken together, these international and domestic pressures in effect constituted a call for Japan to deploy the SDF overseas. The end result, though, was not the despatch of the SDF to help in the Gulf War effort, but only the despatch of the Maritime SDF to help in mine-clearing operations after the end of the war. Japan's main contribution was financial: the provision of US$13 billion in support of the war. By sending money instead of troops the Japanese government was characterized as a 'cheque-book' diplomat, rather than as a responsible member of international society utilizing its economic power to make an international contribution. It seemed, to many, that Japan was somehow different from a 'normal' state in terms of its international behaviour.

The argument here, in essence, was that Japan did not seem 'normal' because it instrumentalized its power resources in ways that did not fit comfortably with the normative understanding of a 'normal' state – that is, one that uses the full complement of state power, including the military. One of the most influential politicians of the 1990s, Ozawa Ichirō, has been trying to make Japan a 'normal' state, but this is 'normal' in the sense of pursuing greater congruence with the established state norms of international society, which provide for the use of force (Ozawa 1994). As at the time of the Gulf crisis and war, Ozawa has sought to act as a conduit for American pressure on the Japanese government to despatch the SDF, leading to him being regarded by the Americans as a 'dependable Japanese leader' (Shinoda 2004a: 50). Thus his activities are in essence the manifestation of a political project aimed at transforming Japan into a state willing to utilize the full complement of its power capabilities, including the SDF. In pursuing this goal, Osawa has been making use of the Preface of the Constitution (not Article 9), which states that Japan desires to occupy an 'honoured place' in international society. His position was that, in order to occupy such a position, Japan needed to make a military contribution to global politics, and despatch the SDF, not be chained to the Constitution's 'peace clause'.

Certainly, Japan's role in the global political economy has often been presented as anomalous, if not aberrant or abnormal, depending on the variables used to account for its international behaviour. Three variables are crucial: structure, agency and norms. Some place greater weight on the structure of the international system, others on agency, and still others on norms in explaining how states behave. As is clear from American pressure on Japan to play a larger role in security, as called for at the time of the Gulf War, structural pressures have played an important role in moving Japan in the direction of the greater use of the SDF as an instrument of state policy. Indeed, in the early twenty-first century, Japan may well be emerging as a 'normal' military power (Hughes 2004). But this 'normal' Japan is not one likely to acquire nuclear weapons, in line with its capabilities as an economic superpower, as suggested from time to time by realist scholars (Waltz 1993: 55–61). So, while the dominant trend in the debate on Japan has been to pay attention to the structure of the international system in addressing Japan's role in global politics, or to pay attention to agency, by emphasizing the actors involved in the policy-making process, a number of scholars have come to see that it is not enough simply to examine structure and agency; there is also a need to place a much greater emphasis on how norms inform Japan's global role (Hook 1996; Katzenstein 1996; Berger 1998). By thus taking into account the normative orientation of domestic society towards support for non-military means as a way to carve out a global role, along with the anti-militarist Article 9 of the Constitution, Japan appears as a 'normal' state in a different way. For the global role pursued by Japan is 'normal' in the context of policy-making agents being sandwiched between the pressures from the international system and the pressures from anti-militarist norms.

Japan as a proactive state

As seen earlier, therefore, the role of Japan in the global political economy can be viewed as a product of the same variables, structure, agency and norms, as can be used to explain the behaviour of other states. However, following Calder's article on Japan as a 'reactive state' (1988), there has been a tendency in the debate on Japan to see the nation as anomalous not simply in terms of the way it instrumentalizes its power resources, but also in terms of the way it behaves: simply reacting to, rather than shaping, global politics. Some have deemed this to result from the 'immobilist' tendencies inherent in the policy-making process (Stockwin 1988); others, instead, see this to be linked to a lack of leadership, with there existing no centre of power capable of moving the policy-making process forwards (van Wolferen 1990). It is a characteristic that can be seen in economic as well as security policy, where Japan can sometimes simply appear to be reacting to international pressure. On the other hand, a number of commentators have instead pointed to Japanese proactivity, particularly in multilateral contexts (Yasutomo 1995). Indeed, whether in the case of Japan's normalization of relations with the Soviet Union in the mid-1950s, when the East–West cold war experienced a period of thaw, or the normalization of relations with the People's Republic of China at the beginning of the 1970s, which followed President Richard Nixon's decision to open up relations and the concomitant move of the international system towards multipolarity, Japanese policy makers have been proactive in responding to the opportunities provided by changes in the structure of the international system. Of course, creating a binary division between reactivity and proactivity is in some sense simply to highlight the two ends of a spectrum of international activity, as even 'proactive' states like the United States 'react' to international events like the 2001 terrorist attacks on New York and Washington. As has been pointed out, in certain areas of foreign policy, Japan is cautiously proactive, whereas in others it is reluctantly reactive (Hirata 2001).

Nevertheless, these two ways of characterizing Japan's international behaviour do serve a heuristic purpose in helping us to understand the way in which, by dubbing Japan 'reactive', the country is not being viewed as 'normal' in terms of the way it behaves; or, to put it another way, an advanced industrial democracy with the power resources of a country like Japan is expected to be more proactive.

This question of 'reactivity' and 'proactivity' is linked to the question of the nature of Japanese leadership: what kind of leadership role can and does Japan play in global politics? Given Japan's economic might, some have sought to find a similar potential for leadership as the United States: a pax Nipponica, as Vogel called it (1986). Others have seen the potential for joint cooperation between Japan and the United States: not so much the replacement of a pax Americana with a pax Nipponica, but the establishment of a 'bigemony' between the two powers (Inoguchi 1990). But these attempts to examine Japanese leadership by drawing on the material capabilities of the state as a way to speculate on the global role of Japan are in danger of missing the actual way Japanese policy-making agents practise leadership. How Japan behaves in terms of the style of leadership adopted has been variously characterized as 'leadership from behind' (Rix 1993) or, more provocatively, leadership by 'stealth' (Drifte 1998), or, as argued elsewhere, 'quiet diplomacy' (Hook *et al.* 2001). Certainly, in the early years of the twenty-first century, a greater recognition of the Japanese leadership role has become more salient, as these years have witnessed a much greater degree of proactivity on the part of Japan (Potter and Sueo 2003). It is possible to put such increased proactivity down to the ending of the cold war and the change in the structure of the international system this implies. The post-cold war environment has provided Japan with new opportunities to play a greater role in global politics, as in the increased tendency to utilize multilateral, rather than bilateral, channels to deal with trade conflicts with the United States. This can be seen, for instance, in the increased preference for taking conflicts to the World Trade Organization, as in the case of steel. In other cases, as with Japan's signing of an agreement in 2004 with Iran to develop the Azadegan oil fields, despite the George W. Bush administration's decision to declare Iran to be part of the 'axis of evil', proactivity is simply a reflection of the government pursuing its own national interests.

At the same time, however, given that a lot of this alleged proactivity has occurred during the period that Koizumi has been prime minister (2001–6), commentators paying attention to the role of agency as an explanatory variable have tended to see the hand of the prime minister in this more salient role. It is certainly true that, in terms of his attempts to normalize relations with North Korea as well as his support of Bush's 'war on terror', the prime minister has been much more prepared to deploy the SDF and offer strong political support to the United States than many of his predecessors would have been willing to do. Like Prime Minister Nakasone Yasuhiro (1982–7), Koizumi has tried to strengthen his political position in pushing forward controversial policies by appealing directly to his popular mandate (over 80 per cent of respondents supported his first cabinet), as well as by using expert advisory groups, as with the 2002 Advisory Group for International Cooperation on Peace. While agency cannot be totally ruled out, changes in the way the government is structured should nevertheless be noted, as these have provided a new policy-making infrastructure. In particular, the revision of the Cabinet Law in 1999 and a boost in the number of personnel working in the prime minister's office has created a policy-making process where the prime minister can more easily take on a proactive role (Shinoda 2004b). These changes suggest the greater potential for the government, whether headed by Koizumi or not, to avoid the sort of 'immobilist' tendencies pointed to earlier and to continue to play a more proactive role in global politics.

This more proactive role has been carved out in the context of the still remaining controversy over the legacy of the war, which makes it difficult for Japan to play a proactive leadership role in the region. While a number of apologies for the war have been made by Japanese political leaders, as at the time of the fifty-year anniversary of the war, when the socialist Murayama Tomiichi was prime minister (1994–6), there is still a call for a full apology, particularly from China and the two Koreas, at both the elite and mass levels. The issue of war-time responsibility has been made all the more difficult as a result of Koizumi's visit to Yasukuni Shrine, in which the spirits of Japanese war dead, including A-class war criminals, are interred. Although East Asian opposition to Japan playing a more proactive global role has weakened over time, especially in Southeast Asia, continuing concern still exists in Northeast Asia, suggesting that, even today, Japan still suffers from a 'legitimacy deficit' (Rapkin 1990: 195). For example, there currently exists strong Chinese and Korean opposition to Japan's ambition of becoming a permanent member of the United Nations Security Council, thereby demonstrating the extent to which the regional and global levels of governance are intricately intertwined.

Finally, with the end of the cold war and the demise of the JSP as an opposition party standing against the overseas deployment of the SDF and the existence of the US–Japan security treaty, the anti-militarist norm no longer has the same force in restricting the more proactive role Japan is playing in global politics. While there is still a strong preference on the popular level for Japan to play a global role through the use of political and economic, rather than military, means, a greater willingness now exists to support the overseas despatch of the SDF. However, as seen at the time of the decision to despatch troops as part of the US 'coalition of the willing' in the Iraq war, there remains strong opposition to Japan playing a full military role in the world (Curtin 2003). Japanese troops have been mainly involved in reconstruction and humanitarian work in Iraq, and have not joined the United States and other allies involved in the fighting. In short, there are still strong, albeit weakening, anti-militarist norms in domestic society that constrain the role Japan plays in global politics.

Conclusion

The argument made in this final part of the second section of this chapter is that Japan is clearly playing an important role in global politics, but that that role has not been clearly explicated due to a tendency for studies of Japan to be dominated by an approach paying undue attention to the structure of the international system and the material capabilities of the state. The central claim made here is that, by employing an approach based on an awareness of the need to take into account structure, agency and norms a much more nuanced explanation of Japan's role in the global political economy can be offered. Depending on the question asked, of course, one variable may be of greater utility in explaining Japanese behaviour than another. Certainly, there is no intention to deny the contribution of a wide range of scholars in deepening our understanding of Japan's role in the world by paying particular attention to say structure over norms or vice versa. However, as a result of Japan's instrumentalization of its power by mainly economic means, rather than by the full range of a state's capabilities, including the military, there perhaps has not been a full appreciation of the degree to which Japan has exercised leadership in order to pursue successfully its global interests. It is not, then, that Japan is an abnormal state, or solely a reactive state; rather that, just like any other state, Japan both reacts to and tries to shape international events and structures, using the most appropriate means, given the constraints and opportunities of the international system and the international and domestic norms informing the behaviour of policy-making agents. What does seem clear, however, is that, over time, Japan has become much more proactive in pursuing its global interests. This will become clear as the chapters investigate the role of Japan in the key international institutions at the heart of global governance.

Structure of the book

It is on the basis of this understanding of the debate about global governance and the debate about Japan that this project was conceived. Its purpose is to move the discussion forward on global governance by examining the role the six most important global institutions – the Group of 7/8 (G/8), the OECD, the World Bank, the IMF, the WTO and the UN – play in global governance. But this, on its own, is not enough, as simply dealing with the key global institutions would do nothing much more than give a nod in the direction of Japan. The second purpose is therefore to investigate what role Japan plays in these institutions, to find out, more specifically, whether Japan is simply reactively or proactively involved in trying to shape these institutions in order to promote its own interests. As seen earlier, global governance can be understood in a variety of ways, but here the explicit focus is on the *emergent reality* of global governance – that is, the chapters to follow investigate these institutions and Japan's role therein with a mandate to tell us how they function as mechanisms of global governance. This has been done by juxtaposing questions about how the global political economy is governed through the key global institutions with the power to establish the norms and rules for the management, regulation and ordering of international affairs, and then to ask, next, what role Japan is playing in these institutions. That is why the book is structured with a chapter on the institution followed by a chapter on Japan in the institution.

Of course, a focus on other actors, such as non-governmental organizations or private actors such as rating agencies, would also have helped to shed light on the governance of the global political economy and Japan's role therein. What a focus on these particular institutions most importantly does, though, is to provide an analysis of the backcloth against which many of the other apparatuses of global governance actually function: it is these institutions, it is argued, that establish the agendas, shape the values and norms, and exercise the power to put in place the rules and regulations for the actual governance of the globe. These institutions are, in essence, the actual architecture of global governance. Overall, what these chapters investigate is whether it is the case that, in an era of globalization, where both states and non-state actors are being forced to respond to a range of global pressures, a deeper institutionalisation of governance at the global level is being witnessed, with these six institutions at the very core of that process. Let us examine concretely, then, what role these institutions and Japan are playing in global governance, starting with the G8.

Note

It should be noted that the argument underpinning the first part of this chapter has been developed more fully in Anthony Payne, 'The study of governance in a global political economy', in Nicola Phillips (ed.) *Globalising International Political Economy*, London: Palgrave Macmillan, 2005, pp. 55–81; and that underpinning the second part in Glenn D. Hook, Julie Gilson, Christopher W. Hughes and Hugo Dobson, *Japan's International Relations: Politics, Economics and Security* (second edition), London: Routledge, 2005.

References

Amoore, Louise, Dodgson, Richard, Gills, Barry K., Langley, Paul, Marshall, Don and Watson, Iain (1997) 'Overturning "globalisation": resisting the teleological, reclaiming the "political" ', *New Political Economy* 2, 1: 179–95.

Anderson, James and Goodman, James (1995) 'Regions, states and the European Union: modernist reaction or postmodern adaptation?', *Review of International Political Economy* 2, 4: 600–31.

Berger, Thomas U. (1998) *Cultures of Antimilitarism: National Security in Germany and Japan*, Baltimore, MD: Johns Hopkins University Press.

Birnbaum, Norman (1999) 'Is the third way authentic?', *New Political Economy* 4, 3: 437–46.

Burnham, Peter (1999) 'The politics of economic management in the 1990s', *New Political Economy* 4, 1: 37–54.

Calder, Kent E. (1988) 'Japanese foreign economic policy formation: explaining the reactive state', *World Politics* 40, 4: 517–41.

Cammack, Paul (2002) 'The mother of all governments: the World Bank's matrix for global governance', in Rorden Wilkinson and Steve Hughes (eds) *Global Governance: Critical Perspectives*, London and New York: Routledge, pp. 36–53.

Commission on Global Governance, The (1995) *Our Global Neighbourhood: The Report of the Commission on Global Governance*, Oxford: Oxford University Press.

Cox, Robert W. (1981) 'Social forces, states and world orders: beyond international relations theory', *Millennium: Journal of International Studies* 10, 2: 126–55.

Cox, Robert W. (1983) 'Gramsci, hegemony and international relations: an essay in method', *Millennium: Journal of International Studies* 12, 2: 162–75.

—— (1996) 'Global *perestroika*', in Robert W. Cox with Timothy J. Sinclair (eds) *Approaches to World Order*, Cambridge: Cambridge University Press, pp. 296–313.

Curtin, J. Sean (2003) 'Japanese public opinion on the second Iraq war: part four – opinions about dispatching Japanese troops to postwar Iraq', available online at: http://www.glocom.org/special_topics/social_trends/20030724_trends_s49/, accessed on 5 April 2005.

Cutler, A. Claire (1995) 'Global capitalism and liberal myths: dispute settlement in private international trade relations', *Millennium: Journal of International Studies* 24, 3: 377–97.

Cutler, A. Claire, Haufler, Virginia and Porter, Tony (eds) (1999) *Private Authority and International Affairs*, Albany, NY: SUNY Press.

Drifte, Reinhard (1998) *Japan's Foreign Policy for the Twenty-first Century: From Economic Superpower to What Power?* (2nd edn of 1996 work), London: Macmillan.

Evans, Peter (1997) 'The eclipse of the state? Reflections on stateness in an era of globalization', *World Politics* 50, 1: 62–87.

Finkelstein, Lawrence S. (1995) 'What is global governance?', *Global Governance* 1, 4: 367–72.

Finnemore, Martha (1996) *National Interests in International Society*, Ithaca, NY: Cornell University Press.

Gamble, Andrew, Payne, Anthony, Hoogvelt, Ankie, Kenny, Michael and Dietrich, Michael (1996) 'Editorial: new political economy', *New Political Economy* 1, 1: 5–11.

Groom, A. J. R. and Powell, Dominic (1994) 'From world politics to global governance: a theme in need of a focus', in A. J. R. Groom and Margot Light (eds) *Contemporary International Relations: A Guide to Theory*, London and New York: Pinter, pp. 81–90.

Haq, Mahbubul, Jolly, Richard, Streeten, Paul and Haq, Khadija (eds) (1995) *The UN and the Bretton Woods Institutions*, London: Macmillan.

Hardin, Garrett (1968) 'The tragedy of the commons', *Science* 162 (December):1243–8.

Hirata, Keiko (2001) 'Cautious proactivism and reluctant reactivism: analysing Japan's foreign policy toward Indochina', in Akitoshi Miyashita and Yoichiro Sato (eds) *Japan's Foreign Policy in Asia and the Pacific: Domestic Interests, American Pressure and Regional Integration*, Basingstoke: Palgrave, pp. 75–100.

Hooghe, Liesbet and Marks, Gary (2001) *Multi-level Governance and European Integration*, Lanham, MD: Rowman & Littlefield.

Hook, Glenn D. (1996) *Militarization and Demilitarization in Contemporary Japan*, London: Routledge.

Hook, Glenn D. and McCormack, Gavan (2001) *Japan's Contested Constitution: Documents and Analysis*, London: Routledge.

Hook, Glenn D., Gilson, Julie, Hughes, Christopher W. and Dobson, Hugo (2001) *Japan's International Relations: Politics, Economics and Security*, London: Routledge.

Hughes, Christopher W. (2004) *Japan's Re-emergence as a 'Normal' Military Power*, Adelphi 368–9, Oxford: IISS/Oxford.

Igarashi, Takeshi (1985) 'Peace-making and party politics: the formation of the domestic foreign-policy system in postwar Japan', *Journal of Japanese Studies* 11, 2: 323–56.

Inoguchi, Takeshi (1990) 'Four Japanese scenarios for the future', in Kathleen Newland (ed.) *The International Relations of Japan*, Basingstoke: Macmillan, pp. 206–25.

Katzenstein, Peter (1996) *Cultural Norms and National Security: Police and Military in Postwar Japan*, Ithaca, NY: Cornell University Press.

Kaul, Inge, Grunberg, Isabelle and Stern, Marc A. (eds) (1999) *Global Public Goods: International Cooperation in the 21st Century*, New York and Oxford: Oxford University Press for the United Nations Development Programme.

Keohane, Robert O. (1984) *After Hegemony: Cooperation and Discord in the World Political Economy*, Princeton, NJ: Princeton University Press.

Kindleberger, Charles P. (1986) *The World in Depression 1929–39*, Berkeley, CA: University of California Press.

Krasner, Stephen D. (ed.) (1983) *International Regimes*, Ithaca, NY: Cornell University Press.

Mann, Michael (1997) 'Has globalization ended the rise and rise of the nation-state?', *Review of International Political Economy* 4, 3: 472–96.

Marks, Gary, Hooghe, Liesbet and Blank, Kermit (1996) 'European integration from the 1980s: state-centric v. multi-level governance', *Journal of Common Market Studies* 34, 3: 341–78.

Michie, Jonathan and Smith, John Grieve (eds) (1999) *Global Instability: The Political Economy of World Economic Governance*, London and New York: Routledge.

Murphy, Craig N. (1994) *International Organization and Industrial Change: Global Governance Since 1850*, Cambridge: Polity Press.

—— (2005) 'Global governance: poorly done and poorly understood', in Rorden Wilkinson (ed.) *The Global Governance Reader*, Routledge: London, pp. 90–104. (Originally published in *International Affairs* (2000) 76, 4: 789–803.)

Nagai, Yōnosuke (1967) *Heiwa no Daishō*, Tokyo: Chūō Kōronsha.

O'Brien, Robert, Goetz, Anne Marie, Scholte, Jan Aart and Williams, Marc (2000) *Contesting Global Governance: Multilateral Economic Institutions and Global Social Movements*, Cambridge: Cambridge University Press.

Olson, Mancur (1971) *The Logic of Collective Action*, Cambridge, MA: Harvard University Press.

Ozawa, Ichiro (1994) *Blueprint for a New Japan* (trans. Louisa Rubinfen, ed. Eric Gower), Tokyo: Kodansha.

Potter, D. and Sueo, S. (2003) 'Japanese foreign policy: no longer reactive?', *Political Studies Review* 1, 3: 317–32.

Rapkin, David P. (1990) 'Japan and world leadership', in David P. Rapkin (ed.) *World Leadership and Hegemony*, Boulder, CO: Lynne Rienner, pp. 191–212.

Rix, Alan (1993) 'Japan and the region', in Richard Higgott, Richard Leaver and John Ravenhill (eds) *Pacific Economic Relations in the 1990s: Cooperation or Conflict?*, St Leonards, Australia: Allen and Unwin, pp. 62–82.

Rosenau, James N. (1992) 'Governance, order, and change in world politics', in James N. Rosenau and Ernst-Otto Czempiel (eds) *Governance without Government: Order and Change in World Politics*, Cambridge: Cambridge University Press, pp. 1–29.

—— (1995) 'Governance in the twenty-first century', *Global Governance* 1, 1: 13–43.

—— (1997) *Along the Domestic–Foreign Frontier: Exploring Governance in a Turbulent World*, Cambridge: Cambridge University Press.

Ruggie, John G. (ed.) (1983) *Multilateralism Matters: The Theory and Praxis of an Institutional Form*, New York: Columbia University Press.

—— (1993) 'Territoriality and beyond: problematizing modernity in international relations', *International Organization* 47, 1: 139–74.

—— (1998) *Constructing the World Polity: Essays on International Institutionalism*, London: Routledge.

Sakamoto, Yoshikazu (1967) *Kakujidai no Seijigaku*, Tokyo: Iwanami Shoten.

Samuelson, Paul A. (1954) 'The pure theory of public expenditure', *Review of Economics and Statistics* 36 (November): 387–9.

Sassen, Saskia (1995) 'The state and the global city: notes towards a conception of place-centered governance', *Competition and Change* 1, 1: 31–50.

Scholte, Jan Aart (1997) 'Global capitalism and the state', *International Affairs* 73, 3: 427–52.

Shinoda, Tomohito (2004a) 'Ozawa Ichirō as an actor in foreign policy-making', *Japan Forum* 16, 1: 37–61.

—— (2004b) *Kantei gaikō seiji rīdāshippu no yukue*, Tokyo: Asahi Shimbunsha.

Sinclair, Timothy J. (1994) 'Passing judgement: credit rating processes as regulatory mechanisms of governance in the emerging world order', *Review of International Political Economy* 1, 1: 133–59.

Smouts, Marie-Claude (1998) 'The proper use of governance in international relations', *The International Social Science Journal* 155, 1: 81–9.

Stockwin, J. A. A. (1988) 'Dynamic and immobilist aspects of Japanese politics', in J. A. A. Stockwin, Alan Rix, Aurelia George, James Horne, Daiichi Ito and Martin Collick (eds) *Dynamic and Immobilist Politics in Japan*, London: Macmillan, pp. 1–21.

Strange, Susan (1996) *The Retreat of the State: The Diffusion of Power in the World Economy*, Cambridge: Cambridge University Press.

Taylor, Paul (1999) 'The United Nations in the 1990s: proactive cosmopolitanism and the issue of sovereignty', *Political Studies* 47, 3: 538–65.

Underhill, Geoffrey R. D. (2000) 'State, market, and global political economy: genealogy of an (inter-?) discipline', *International Affairs* 76, 4: 805–24.

van Wolferen, Karel G. (1990) *The Enigma of Japanese Power*, New York: Albert A. Knopf.

Vogel, Ezra (1986) 'Pax Nipponica?', *Foreign Affairs* 64, 4: 752–67.

Wade, Robert (1996) 'Japan, the World Bank, and the art of paradigm maintenance: *The East Asian Miracle* in political perspective', *New Left Review* 217: 3–36.

Waltz, Kenneth N. (1993) 'The emerging structure of international politics', *International Security* 18, 2: 44–79.

Weiss, Linda (1997) 'Globalization and the myth of the powerless state', *New Left Review* 225: 3–27.

Weiss, Thomas W. and Gordenker, Leon (eds) (1996) *NGOs, the UN, and Global Governance*, Boulder, CO: Lynne Rienner.

Wendt, Alexander (1999) *Social Theory of International Politics*, Cambridge: Cambridge University Press.

Wilkinson, Rorden (2000) *Multilateralism and the World Trade Organisation: The Architecture and Extension of International Trade Regulation*, London and New York: Routledge.

—— (2002) 'The world trade organisation', *New Political Economy* 7, 1: 129–41.

Yasutomo, Denis T. (1995) *The New Multilateralism in Japan's Foreign Policy*, New York: St Martin's Press.

1 Global governance and the Group of Seven/Eight

Hugo Dobson

Introduction

It has been estimated that almost one conference a week is held on the subject of governance and yet it remains a contested term, especially when the qualifying adjective 'global' is added (Valaskakis 2004: 3). In spite of this confusion, Rorden Wilkinson provides a road map for making sense of global governance:

> Global governance, then, is not defined simply by the emergence of new actors or nodes of authority; instead, it compromises a growing complexity in the way in which its actors interact and interrelate. Most certainly, some of the agents of global governance are newly emerged; others, however, are much longer established. Nevertheless, the key to understanding contemporary global governance is the capacity to identify the range of actors involved in the act of management, as well as to uncover the variety of ways in which they are connected to one another.
>
> (Wilkinson 2002: 2)

Although several studies of global governance have identified the range of actors involved in such a nexus and explored their interconnectivity, most of these studies more often than not omit the Group of Eight (G8). Instead, the UN, the International Monetary Fund (IMF), the World Bank and the World Trade Organization (WTO) are the 'usual suspects' when locating the relevant providers of global governance. The reason for this might lie in the openly declared and clearly articulated aims and evolution of these organizations, in contrast to the flexible goals and amorphous development of the G8. It is undeniable that a high degree of functional uncertainty surrounds the G8 to the degree that it is unclear what it is: international organization or institution, effective centre of global governance or meaningless junket? The objectives of this chapter are to establish what kind of entity the G8 is, adumbrate how it works and then explore how it is connected to other mechanisms involved in the provision of global governance. It does this by employing the metaphor of a concert and by fast-forwarding and rewinding between almost 200 years of international history to tease out a number of similarities between the G8 and its closest predecessor, the Concert of Europe.

The origins of the G8

The G8 represents a constantly evolving process that has redefined itself on a number of occasions. It first met as the Group of Six (France, Italy, Japan, UK, US and West Germany) from 15 to 17 November 1975 at the château of Rambouillet in France. This first meeting found its origins in an informal meeting of the Group of Four (G4) French, West German, UK and US finance ministers in the White House library in March 1973, later joined by Japan to form the Group of Five (G5), to discuss the state of the international monetary system. The perceived success of this style of meeting provided the impetus behind the Rambouillet meeting 'to recreate at the highest level the same sort of direct and informal exchange' (Hunt and Owen 1984: 658). Or, in the words of renowned summit-watcher, Sir Nicholas Bayne, the summit:

> was conceived as a personal encounter of the leaders of the world's most powerful economies. The founders believed that bringing the heads of government together would lead them to understand better both the domestic problems of their peers and the international responsibilities they all shared. This would enable them to solve, through personal interaction and original ideas, problems that had baffled their bureaucrats. The bureaucrats themselves ought to be kept out of the process entirely.
>
> (Bayne 2005: 174)

Unlike the more traditional international organizations explored in other chapters (even the Organization for Economic Cooperation and Development (OECD), the G8's closest relative), which are the result of an international agreement or formal treaty and display a high degree of institutionalization, the G8 has no legal basis and was originally intended as an impromptu, never-to-be-repeated, informal meeting in reaction to a series of 'tightly-spaced, partially-interrelated' crises of the early 1970s including conflict in the Middle East, the 1973 oil crisis and the collapse of the Bretton Woods system of fixed exchange rates (Kirton 1989). The utility of this forum as a unique meeting place for the world's leaders (in addition to President Gerald Ford's desire to use the summit as an electoral fillip at home) led to a second conference being held in San Juan, Puerto Rico in June 1976 at which Canada was added to form the Group of Seven (G7). Since then, other members with varying levels of status have joined the summit and their participation has contributed to the process of redefining the summit's nature and agenda. The European Community/European Union Commissioner participated from the 1977 London Summit. The meetings of the original G5 finance ministers, who had met irregularly in secret since the early 1970s, were brought into the open and expanded to include all seven members from the 1986 Tokyo Summit onwards. The 1990s witnessed the evolution of Russia's position from guest in 1991 through a range of statuses to a fully enfranchized member of the G8 by 2003. More recently, the G8 has engaged in a policy of 'outreach' to include non-G8 nations in individual summits and the further expansion of its membership – potential members currently include China and India – is regularly touted.

However, it was not long after the first summit that its original goals were abandoned. On the one hand, the remit of summit discussion expanded from chiefly economic issues to encompass political and security issues; while, on the other hand, the composition of summit delegations developed from the original idea of solely the leaders, accompanied by foreign and finance ministers, to embrace regular ministerial-level meetings on education, employment, energy, the environment, justice and trade. As a result, the administration and preparation for the annual summit, directed by the leaders' personal representatives, or sherpas, in turn supported by sous-sherpas, who meet regularly during the year preceding a summit, has led to an ever-increasing bureaucratic load that has become one of the main rods with which to beat the summit process over recent years.

Nevertheless, the G8 has 'hung together' and by 2004 the G8 was firmly entrenched into its fifth cycle of summitry, begun at the twenty-ninth summit in 2003 at Evian, and will meet again at the thirty-first summit to be held at the Gleneagles Hotel in Scotland from 6 to 8 July 2005. However, despite this degree of longevity, the G8 and its position within the global governance nexus is a mystery that has only recently begun to be explored as a result of the work of the G8 Research Group at Toronto University and the associated G8 and Global Governance series of books published by Ashgate. These summit-watchers believe the G8 to be 'emerging as an effective center, and is prospectively the effective center, of global governance' (Kirton 1999: 46). Although this claim may be more demonstrative of the enthusiasm of an academic defending his chosen subject of study, it would be difficult to deny that their work represents an overdue and welcome attempt to understand what kind of entity the G8 is and how it seeks to provide global governance. With the goal of shedding more light on these specific questions, the following sections highlight the way in which the G8 functions as an effective centre of global governance by comparing and contrasting it with a 200-year-old predecessor, the Concert of Europe. This exercise is all the more relevant as the embryonic summit process was originally credited as being the idea of US Secretary of State Henry Kissinger, author of one of the main studies of nineteenth-century diplomacy, *A World Restored*, who 'consciously sought to construct the modern equivalent of the nineteenth-century Concert of Europe' (Kirton 2001–2).

The Concert of Europe

Although its roots lie in the eighteenth century, the Concert of Europe existed in one form or another from its creation in the last years and immediate aftermath of the Napoleonic Wars until its final demise during the outbreak of the First World War. It was Napoleon's attempted domination of the European continent that

> finally convinced the statesmen of Europe, hard persons to teach, that what was at risk was not merely certain goods in international politics (peace,

security, territorial integrity) but the very life principle of European politics which made hese goods and others possible... [and thus, they] finally and suddenly succeeded in learning how to conduct international politics differently and better.

(Schroeder 1994: 395, vii)

The Concert of Europe was the manifestation of this learning process.

From 1815 to 1914, a 'system of governance was created by a five-power coalition, defined by it, and operated in terms of its members' interests' (Holsti 1993: 34). To this end, the European great powers of the day, namely Austria (Austro-Hungary from 1867), Britain, France, Prussia and Russia, held over thirty congresses and conferences and numerous smaller conferences attended by fewer of their number. Not only did it create a blueprint of how to organize (or not, as the case may be) future international organizations, such as the League of Nations and the UN (Mowat 1930: 362–4; Medlicott 1956: 315), it has been touted as the closest thing to a 'world government world federation, or even a worldwide pluralistic security community' (Jervis 1985: 58). However, perhaps a more accurate description of the Concert is of 'the great powers meeting together at times of international crisis to maintain peace and to develop European solutions to European problems' (Elrod 1976: 162).

The novelty of the Concert, and its chief similarity with the G8 summit, was its exclusive nature:

> Throughout the nineteenth century the European great powers claimed for themselves special rights and responsibilities which they were unwilling to accord to other states. They usually consulted each other, although not the small states, on major issues. They regarded themselves as the guardians of the peace of Europe, and they assumed responsibility for the maintenance of order within their neighbouring states. It was the strongest second-class states which resented the existence of this 'exclusive club' of great powers.
>
> (Bridge and Bullen 1980: 2)

This self-elected directorate shouldered exclusive responsibility for the security of Europe and the maintenance of the status quo in a spirit of cooperation. Or, in other words,

> the Concert would function as an informal consultative body of all the powers, handling each European question as it arose by *ad hoc* discussion, and finding a solution of differences between the great powers themselves in (presumably) the good fellowship and spirit of mutual concession which this friendly collaboration would foster.
>
> (Medlicott 1956: 34)

It sought to govern and negotiate any peaceful revisions to the post-war status quo on the basis of agreement *within* the concert system.

The Concert of Europe never constituted anything as formal as an institution or a regime. 'Regimes convert broad norms and principles into concrete rules and procedures.... While the Concert of Europe embodied principles and norms, however, it lacked rules and procedures for putting them into effect' (Rendall 2000: 87). Rather, the Concert was a forum based on the ideological convergence of the leading statesmen of the day as regards anti-revolutionism and general contentment with the status quo. Thus, 'concert' means something very different from institution or organization:

> In the language of diplomacy 'concert' originally meant either an *ad hoc* diplomatic arrangement involving some measure of cooperation between two or more powers or a temporary political situation implying some degree of agreement between the parties.
>
> (Holbraad 1970: 3)

Another important characteristic of the Concert of Europe is that it brought about a change in the behaviour of states in response to a crisis. The Concert was a reaction to the widespread destruction and anti-establishment ambitions unleashed by Revolutionary and Napoleonic France (Gulick 1955: 134–5; Bridge and Bullen 1980: 20–47). Both suppressing this revolutionary zeal and ensuring France would not become the destructive force it had been during the late eighteenth and early nineteenth centuries constituted a driving force and core principle of the Concert:

> The quarter of a century of turmoil to which Europe had been subjected created a strong and authentic desire for peace and order. At Vienna the clock was ostensibly set back and the Europe of 1815 may have seemed to the restorers little different from that of pre-1789. Yet it was also felt more than ever desirable that the competition of interests should proceed in orderly fashion: order could best be maintained by the clear assertion of the right and the responsibility of those possessed of power, the Great Powers. The conception was hardly new or original, and it was not formally institutionalized beyond the loose provision for the holding of future meetings of the Powers. Here lies the essence of the Concert of Europe.
>
> (Albrecht-Carrié 1968: 5)

So, '[t]he Concert of Europe was a loose concept rather than a formalized institution' (Albrecht-Carrié 1968: 59) and stressed multilateral, as opposed to unilateral or bilateral, solutions to issues of international diplomacy based on the 'conviction that the only satisfactory basis for intervention in the affairs of other states was in collaboration with other powers in the maintenance of the public life of Europe' (Medlicott 1956: 21). This was seen to be the only way 'which would permanently "neutralize and fetter and bind up" the selfish aims of each individual state' (Medlicott 1956: 305). This norm applied to containing smaller states, middle power and the dominant superpowers of the system, Russia and Great

Britain, and '[d]espite significant conflicts of interest among them, all the states shared the important interest of avoiding large wars and the need to maintain the new, more cooperative arrangements' (Jervis 1992: 719).

Thus, the Concert was an informal grouping of wartime allies who agreed to continue their frequent meetings and extend their spirit of unity into peacetime: '[t]he Concert of Europe, which brought a peace that although often disturbed did not shatter for a century, was due not only to the rough equilibrium of power after the Napoleonic wars but to the ability of statesmen to sense, appreciate, and solidify it' (Helprin 1996: 33). So, in order to realize the willingness to forego self-interest for the good of the group, the Concert worked for most of the time on the basis of individuals and personalities, and herein lies another important characteristic. In the case of the Concert, the inter-personal relationship between the British Foreign Minister from 1812 to 1822, Viscount Robert Castlereagh, the Austrian Foreign Minister from 1809 to 1848, Prince Klemens von Metternich, and the Russian Tsar from 1801 to 1825, Alexander I, has been credited as being integral to its successful functioning (Albrecht-Carrié 1968: 4). The fact that the statesmen of Europe, especially these three individuals, knew each other well having dealt with each other previously and respected each other's abilities and status drove the Concert during its early years while memories of the Napoleonic Wars were fresh. Moreover, stability in the relationships was encouraged by the fact that several of these statesmen were in power for extended periods of time, often more easily measured in decades than years, and their foreign ministries were often very small in size and number (Bridge and Bullen 1980: 17–18).

In addition to maintaining its own coherence through the ability of the individuals involved, the Concert demonstrated an ability to negotiate with third parties (Jervis 1985: 72). For example, France as the chief security concern in the immediate post-war period was admitted to the Concert in 1818 despite having been initially excluded. The Ottoman Empire, the management of whose decline proved to be the major issue of nineteenth-century international relations, was admitted to the Concert in 1856.

The 'intense diplomatic preparations' for each meeting of the Concert represent another characteristic worth mentioning. It has been noted that in preparation for Concert meetings:

> [s]ome delay was necessary...to give diplomats time to consult their colleagues and to work out their positions, and above all, to discover what would and what would not be palatable to the other powers in the conference. The requisite order included extensive *pourparlers*, perhaps a conference, and then a congress. This procedure insured that only those issues that were amenable to diplomatic treatment were introduced, and constituted a necessary precondition for successful summit diplomacy.
>
> (Elrod 1976: 168)

Thus, although intended as an *ad hoc* diplomatic instrument, the Concert, by necessity, developed formalized mechanisms to the degree that '[c]onsultation *prior* to taking major foreign policy actions had become the norm by the 1830s' (Holsti 1993: 39).

However, the Concert also displayed a number of weaknesses. The chief one being that it 'had no permanent organization, no standing council or committee. Thus its normal state was one of suspended animation; and it required to be called into being by the initiative of some Power or Powers at every fresh crisis.... What the Concert really needed in order that it might be effective was some permanent organization which could note the earliest signs of a European crisis and could at once offer its services for joint European action' (Mowat 1930: 363). As a result, towards the end of its lifetime, the Concert was no longer regarded as 'the moral consensus of a conservative coalition' (Bridge and Bullen 1980: 8), but rather in some quarters as a 'standing joke' and the 'crudest of all shams' (Medlicott 1956: 317–18), or as 'an unwieldy and often an ineffectual instrument' (Elrod 1976: 169).

Thus, the question is whether there was any great substance to the Concert, which

> seemed to many continental statesmen a mere phrase, a high-sounding nothing... In the ordinary language of continental diplomacy the Concert was something which existed when the great powers sat round a conference table, or found it expedient or convenient to join in collective action; there was a Concert of Europe when the action of the great powers was concerted, and when it was not there was not.
>
> (Medlicott 1956: 18)

Ultimately, the Concert could only work when the core national interests of the great powers were neither implicated nor threatened. And in this light, the record of the Concert can accurately be summarized in the following terms:

> At its worst, the Concert was an impotent assembly, merely adhering to the formalities, unable to resolve important and pressing issues. At its best, it represented a reasonably satisfactory solution to the most difficult problem of international systems: how to accommodate the forces of change and yet preserve peace and stability.
>
> (Elrod 1976: 169)

The G8 as a Concert

Thus, the key characteristics of the Concert of Europe as one of the first mechanisms of global governance are: (1) its origins in a crisis that demonstrated its utility and provided it with a subsequent *raison d'être*; (2) cooperation among the great powers of the day to maintain the status quo; (3) the informality of the process and resistance to any degree of institutionalization; (4) the emphasis placed upon the individual participants and the relationships between them; and (5) flexibility in agenda-setting and the ability to respond to situations as they arose and provide leadership when needed. These characteristics are also demonstrated by the G8 and the way in which it seeks to provide global governance.

Crisis-management

In the same way that the Concert of Europe was envisaged as an extemporaneous, *ad hoc* grouping borne of the Napoleonic Wars that was given a longer-lasting life and manifested a watershed in the way in which the great powers of the day conducted their relations, the first summit meeting of the G6 in France was an attempt to conduct international politics at a time of crisis in a different manner. The crisis in this case was the economic confusion caused by the oil crisis and collapse of the Bretton Woods system and

> the severity of these shocks was sufficient to destroy the prevailing international order and the economic, social and political stability of the western great powers. It was precisely to respond to this destroyed monetary and threatened trade system, and the much larger crisis of governability, that the seven-power summit was formed.
>
> (Kirton 1989)

However, once this initial crisis was forgotten, the summit entered into an evolutionary process and had to reinvent itself on a number of occasions throughout the subsequent decades by expanding the remit of its agenda and embracing other actors.

Maintenance of the status quo

Like the Concert of Europe, the G8 essentially preserves the right of the powerful – summit members account for roughly two-thirds of the world's gross domestic product – to take decisions on behalf of and without consulting the rest of the world. To this end, they are founded on agreed, although very different, norms and principles. On the one hand, the Concert emphasized the maintenance of the status quo through the right of the great European powers of the day to intervene in the affairs of smaller states to crush rebellion and maintain the larger status quo. On the other hand, the G8 has reiterated in its annual communiqués, declarations and chairman's statements (the chief mechanisms for disseminating its ideas) its own norms and principles, chiefly the promotion of democracy and free-market economic principles emphasizing non-inflationary growth, sound monetary policies and free trade. To this end, the summit process represents, in the broadest definition of the Coxian term, one element of a *nébuleuse* – the vaguely defined 'transnational process of consensus formation among the official caretakers of the global economy' that orients state behaviour towards the needs of the global economy (Cox 1996: 301; for a detailed discussion of how the G7 finance ministers in particular have promoted their own belief system, see Baker 2000).

Resistance to institutionalization

Similar to the Concert, the G8 has resisted any degree of institutionalization and, when it has emerged, has sought ways to return to the simplicity of its earlier meetings owing to a shared belief in the effectiveness and uniqueness of an informal gathering. As a result, both also lack their own ability to enforce its decisions. For some, this is a fatal weakness in the G8's credentials as an effective source of global governance (Gilpin 2002: 246). Nevertheless, the G8 does not seek to enforce policy or punish offenders. Its role is limited to that of a talking shop and thus it seeks to set the agenda, tone or mood for global governance while conscious of its position in relation to other, more formalized, mechanisms. If anything, it is the mouthpiece of the most powerful members of the international community closely interconnected with, while both relying upon and supported by, other mechanisms of global governance. In other words:

> The G7/8 is a forum, rather than an institution. It is useful as a closed international club of capitalist governments trying to raise consciousness, set an agenda, create networks, prod other institutions to do things that they should be doing, and, in some cases, to help create institutions that are suited to a particular task.
>
> (Hodges 1999: 69)

As regards the provision of global governance, the G8 depends especially on the moral weight of its communiqués and statements, and/or the delegation of an issue to a member state, fellow intergovernmental organization or appropriate non-governmental organization (NGO). Ultimately, the summit works as an annual forum for the informal and reiterative discussion of the main political and economic issues of the day and the incremental implementation of policy there-after. This approach was encapsulated by an editorial in *The Japan Times* prior to the San Juan Summit of June 1976, as relevant today as it was then:

> Rambouillet as well as the upcoming summit in Puerto Rico are unlikely to be remembered for having taken any historic, once-for-all decision to change the world's structure and the flow of history. But the free societies have a patent need for such consultative summits in a world as fluid and uncertain as it is today where old institutions have been discredited in the absence of a firm, new order.
>
> (*The Japan Times*, 5 June 1976: 12)

The role of the individual

The G8, like the Concert, emphasizes the role of the individual. His/her influence can be seen most starkly as impacting upon agenda-setting. The host is placed in a position whereby she/he is able to set the tone for the meeting as seen in Tony Blair's response to NGOs by placing debt relief on the agenda at the 1998 Birmingham Summit; Gerhard Schröder's conversion to the same issue at the 1999 Cologne Summit (contrasting with his predecessor's intransigence); Obuchi Keizō's desire to discuss information technology at the 2000 Okinawa Summit, an agenda item that survived despite his death before the summit; and Jean

Chrétien's insistence on limiting the size of summit delegations and length of statements at the 2002 Kananaskis Summit.

Moreover, the effective operation of both groupings is seen to be enhanced by the ability of the individuals involved and the atmosphere of cooperation they create. British Foreign Minister Lord Castlereagh referred to the meetings of the great powers as 'reunions' (Elrod 1976: 163); similarly, the original G7 was the creation and personal ambition of French President Valéry Giscard d'Estaing and West German Chancellor Helmut Schmidt, who had been finance ministers at the original meeting of the Library Group in 1973 and by 1975 had become leaders of their respective countries (Armstrong 1996: 42). The summit demonstrates the utility of a limited number of powerful states acting in cooperation. James Callaghan supported this claim by stating in 1976 that:

> [t]he numbers attending are small and compact. Discussions are businesslike and to the point. We do not make speeches at one another. We talk frankly but also as briefly as we can, and a lot of ground is covered.
>
> (quoted in Putnam and Bayne 1987: 44)

Thus, one of the main functions of the summit process has been as a mechanism to foster trust and hopefully coordination among the most powerful world leaders. This level of trust and intimacy is fostered by the use of first names between leaders. Equally, Blair and Bush met in the unlikely venue of the gym at 6:30 am during the 2002 Kananaskis Summit (Bayne 2005: 115). The maintenance of this intimacy has been a central concern of recent times as seen in Blair's initiative at the 1998 Birmingham Summit of separating the ministerial meetings from the leaders' meeting to create a 'heads-only' summit that continues today, and the post-9/11 tendency to select remote summit venues and place limits on the size of each delegation.

Flexibility

Both the Concert and the G8 are groupings flexible and amorphous enough to respond to changes in the international system. In this light, historical parallels can be drawn between the management of both post-Napoleonic France and post-Communist Russia: '[t]hough chastened, humiliated, and stripped of its empire, France was still a major power that, like Russia now, could not be ignored' (Helprin 1996: 32). Thus, throughout the 1990s, the G7 embraced Russia in a steadily increasing gradation of statuses as well as inviting other participants in order to address specific issues in the same way as France and the Ottoman Empire were included in the Concert. It is difficult to read the following sentence and not think of the Soviet Union/Russia: the 'formal admission of the Ottoman state to the Concert of Europe in 1856 ... could be read as a protectorate of sorts rather than as an admission to genuine parity of status' (Albrecht-Carrié 1968: 12).

Flexibility is evident not only in the membership but also the agenda of both groupings. The G8 and the Concert of Europe were created to deal with the problems of specific crises but thereafter were able to address broader issues in an iterative fashion and add pressing issues of the day to the agenda, such as, in the case of the G8, various terrorist attacks, the 1986 Chernobyl nuclear accident, Indian and Pakistani nuclear tests, social unrest in Indonesia and conflict in Kosovo (Hajnal and Kirton 2000: 8).

Beyond a Concert

However, the historical analogy with the Concert of Europe does not provide a complete picture of the way the G8 functions and two contemporary aspects in particular are not captured: (1) the G8's interconnectivity with the network of organizations, institutions and regimes that seek to provide global governance; and (2) its relationship with the NGOs that constitute civil society.

The G8 and other institutions

Echoing Wilkinson's plea, mentioned earlier, for students of global governance to discover the ways in which the various mechanisms of global governance are interconnected, the G8's position in the nexus of global governance can only be truly understood in relation to the other organizations discussed in this book.

The summit's communiqué and related documents have been used as a clarion call to coordinate and reform these organizations (for a detailed review of the summit's promotion of international organizations through communiqués and declarations, see Hajnal 1999: 45–55). For example, the final summit communiqués have repeatedly highlighted and endorsed various aspects of the work of the UN, in addition to calling for reforms in its structure. In particular, the 1996 Lyon Summit's communiqué focused upon institutional reform of the UN and made a number of suggestions (G7 1996). On occasion, the G8 has even replaced the UN. It was the G7, not the UN, which played a central role in coordinating Germany and Japan's financial support of the Gulf War of 1990–1, in addition to ending the Kosovo conflict of 1999 and proposing an African peacekeeping force to address the genocide in Sudan in 2004. Especially during the US-led war on Iraq of March 2003, which was instigated with little regard for the UN, it was suggested by some that real influence and authority was, or in the future will be, transferred to the G8 (Penttilä 2003: 46–50, 91–5; Sisci 2003). However, with their differing degrees of institutionalization and agenda, it is more accurate to claim that the G8 and the UN complement each other.

The G8's communiqués have also made reference to the World Bank and IMF. At the 1994 Naples Summit, the final communiqué stated that 'we agree to explore ways to mobilize more effectively the existing resources of the International Financial Institutions to respond to the special needs of countries emerging from economic and political disruption and the poorest most indebted countries' (G7 1994). At the Halifax Summit the following year a separate document was released on the review of the IMF and World Bank recommending a number of reforms in early-warning and surveillance, financial market supervision and the most effective use of resources (G7 1995a). However, the objective of the G8 member states has not been to pursue radical reform of these mechanisms of global governance, but rather 'to protect the existing system and make it work better', although for whose benefit is not immediately clear (Putnam and Bayne 1984: 141).

In addition, the G8 has supported the work of the General Agreement on Tariffs and Trade and the WTO by regularly encouraging the rapid conclusion of trade negotiations in its communiqués. In addition, the 1981 Ottawa Summit created the Trade Ministers' Quadrilateral attended by the trade ministers of the US, Canada, Japan and the EU, which was credited for galvanizing the previously stalled Uruguay Round of trade negotiations (Hajnal 1999: 35). In addition, the G8 has been linked to the OECD through certain customs such as regular meetings between sherpas and OECD officials and the practice from 1976 of holding the annual OECD Council meeting 4–6 weeks prior to the annual summit meeting (Bayne 2000: 53–4).

Within the framework of the G8 other groupings have been created when deemed necessary to address pressing global issues. For example, the Group of 20 finance ministers and central bank governors was created in September 1999 as a permanent grouping including several important developing countries in order to address financial and monetary reform in cooperation with the IMF and World Bank. Again, this suggests that the G8 has not eclipsed other international institutions, but rather has created a mutually reinforcing division of labour.

Thus, in short, what the G8 does best is offer a blueprint for global governance through its communiqués and declarations in order 'to provide political will and direction' (Hunt and Owen 1984: 659), and thereafter delegates to more appropriate or traditional international institutions to provide the specialization and implementation. If the origins of specific initiatives are traced, the trail will often lead back to the G8. For example, the Brady Plan, which was proposed by US Treasure Secretary Nicholas Brady in March 1989 to provide debt relief for developing countries in Latin America based on the resources of the World Bank and IMF, was originally based upon the Miyazawa Plan proposed at the 1988 Toronto Summit. Japan's Human Frontier Science Programme to develop cutting edge research in the pure sciences was adopted at the 1987 Venice Summit and continues to this day as an international organization in its own right. Ultimately, Bayne is correct in his assertion that 'the best future approach for the summits is that of catalyst, providing impulses to wider international institutions but not trying to do their work for them, either from inside or outside' (Bayne 1994: 20).

The G8 and civil society

Unlike the G8, meetings of the Concert of Europe did not take place while protestors in the streets outside demanded justice, transparency and accountability. Although Peter Hajnal has described the period from 1975 to 1983 as one of mutual ignorance between the summit process and civil society, in the mid-1980s civil society began to recognize the G8 and the G8 has returned the favour over the last decade (Hajnal 2002). For the G8, this is an attempt to address the problem that has haunted it since its inception: legitimacy. Accusations of being a closed rich man's club may deflect from an accurate understanding of the true nature, intent and functioning of the summit as a mechanism of global governance for fostering trust, coordination and concerted leadership among the leaders of the world's most powerful economies. However, this is a resonant accusation that was levelled specifically at the 1998 Birmingham Summit by the alternative forum of the People's Summit, and has been a constant criticism throughout the G8's history: '[m]any people question the right of eight countries...to take decisions affecting the rest of the world' (quoted in Patomäki 1999: 132). Thus, the G8 has responded to this by attempting to embrace the NGOs that constitute civil society. Demonstrative of its flexibility in responding to the trends of international relations, civil society was first mentioned in the communiqué issued at the 1995 Halifax Summit. Paragraph 25 of the communiqué states that the G8 nations will work with the UN and Bretton Woods institutions to:

> encourage countries to follow participatory development strategies and support governmental reforms that assure transparency and public account-ability, a stable rule of law, and an active civil society.
>
> (G7 1995b)

Later in the same document, paragraph 37 called for 'improved co-ordination among international organizations, bilateral donors and NGOs' – the first ever mention of NGOs. This trend continued with the communiqué issued at the 1996 Lyon Summit, which in paragraph 34 highlighted the need for 'a strengthened civil society' (G7 1996). Thereafter, year after year, the G8 has made increasingly numerous and positive references to civil society in its documentation (Hajnal 2002: 212–13). More concretely, a policy of what has been termed 'outreach' has been adopted in recent years. This is targeted at both non-G8 members, especially debt-crippled developing nations, and NGOs. Illustrative of the former, discussions on the second day of the 2002 Kananaskis Summit were also attended by leaders of Algeria, Nigeria, Senegal and South Africa and UN Secretary General Kofi Annan, and focused on large-scale aid to Africa in return for anti-corruption and free-market reforms in the recipient nations. On the afternoon of the first day of the 2003 Evian Summit the G8 leaders met with the leaders of Algeria, Brazil, China, Egypt, India, Malaysia, Mexico, Nigeria, Saudi Arabia, Senegal and South Africa, joined by the heads of the IMF, UN, World Bank and WTO, to take part in the enlarged dialogue working session.

As regards the latter, for the first time in summit history and in preparation for the 2000 Okinawa Summit, the Japanese government created the post of director-general for civil society participation, and as part of summit preparations, the Japanese sherpa Nogami Yoshiji met with representatives of charities such as Save the Children, Christian Aid and Amnesty International. On the morning of 21 July 2000, the first day of the summit, Prime Minister Mori Yoshirō met with the representatives of five NGOs calling for the cancellation of African debt, action on infectious diseases and a reduction in the US military presence in Okinawa. However, the most innovative and tangible action taken by the Japanese government was the construction of an NGO centre. This gave the 44 NGOs and 300 activists that registered a physical work space, base of operations and offered computers, telephones and photocopiers. This was symbolic of the first time that the importance of NGOs had been recognized by the host nation with the creation of physical space for them to conduct their operations. This was greeted with enthusiasm by one activist of Médecins Sans Frontières: 'I think the Japanese government made an effort to make this space for the NGOs and the chance to meet Prime Minister Mori. The equipment is great and people here are very helpful' (*The Japan Times*, 22 July 2000).

Jubilee 2000 probably represents the closest attempt at meaningful engagement between civil society and the G8 and has been dubbed by a World Bank spokesman as 'one of the most effective global lobbying campaigns I have ever seen' (cited in Hajnal 2002: 215). At the 1998 Birmingham Summit, the highpoint was a 'human chain' of 50–70,000 people (estimates differ) organized by Jubilee 2000 around the Birmingham convention centre where some of the G8 summit meetings took place (although the leaders retired to Weston Park on the day of the demonstration) and led Prime Minister Tony Blair to issue a *Response by the Presidency on Behalf of the G8 to the Jubilee 2000 Petition*, which acknowledged the efforts of Jubilee 2000:

> Your presence here is a truly impressive testimony to the solidarity of people in our own countries with those in the world's poorest and most indebted. It is also a public acknowledgement of the crucial importance of the question of debt.
>
> (G8 1998)

However, the momentum towards providing debt relief waned thereafter and the vague statement made on the first day of the Okinawa Summit was greeted with disappointment by NGO representatives. Ann Pettifor of Jubilee 2000 was quoted as saying: 'We are totally dismayed by this statement. The world's leaders have retreated to this remote island of Okinawa and have turned their backs on the poor, ignoring a call that is morally right, economically right and supported by millions around the world' (*The Japan Times*, 22 July 2000). In addition, the superficial nature of G8 engagement with civil society can be seen in the expression of doubt and fears of government surveillance that plagued the NGO centre. It was under-used, removed from the international media centre (from which NGOs were barred), cost ¥10,000 (US$91) per NGO to use, and involved procedures such as submitting individual photographs and registering details such as address and height. Representatives of Jubilee 2000 and the Okinawa Environmental Network were highly critical of the poor facilities provided in the NGO centre and the overly strict supervision by the Japanese Ministry of Foreign Affairs. Although similar NGO facilities were provided by the Italian government a year later at the 2001 Genoa Summit, the relationship between the G8 and civil society reached a low-point with the death of Italian protestor Carlo Giuliani. The reaction of the G8 to this violence and the events of

9/11 was to retreat to the isolated mountains of Kananaskis in the Canadian Rockies for their next summit. More recently, at the 2004 Sea Island Summit, engagement with civil society was evident by its absence.

Conclusions

The G8 constitutes an example of both 'nested' and 'overlapping' arrangements of global governance and to a much lesser degree an example of 'competing' arrangements (see Koenig-Archibugi 2002). On the one hand, this can be seen in the increasing number of global governance arrangements to which it has acted as midwife, in similar fashion to the UN family of agencies and organizations. On the other hand, with the expansion of its agenda, the G8 has intruded into areas of global governance for which it was not designed and in which institutions already exist. The G8's goal has not been to usurp these pre-existing arrangements but rather to provide leadership and direction. Some have suggested a more competitive relationship with the UN as to which will provide the central focus of global governance, especially after the 2003 Iraq War (Penttilä 2003: Sisci 2003; 46–50, 91–5). However, this is little more than speculation that ignores the concessions the G8 makes to the legitimacy of the UN. Rather than providing a concrete locus of global governance, the G8 continues to provide a talking shop for global governance. In the words of Bayne:

> The value of the G8 summit lies in its personal quality. It brings together the leaders of eight of the world's most powerful nations and reminds them of their responsibility to cooperate internationally, rather than acting unilaterally or giving way to domestic pressures. The results are often oversold in advance and disappoint in practice. But without the discipline of this regular encounter, it would be very easy for tensions and disputes to spread and to poison the underlying relationships between the G8 members. A world which did not have the safety-valve of the G8 summit would be an increasingly fractious and dangerous place.
>
> (Bayne 2005: 209)

If, as this chapter asserts, the G8 can be fairly represented as a modern application of a centuries-old idea of concert diplomacy with a strong emphasis upon great powers of the day, informality and flexibility in addition to the role of the individual, their relationships, personal initiatives and exchanges, then what implications does this have for Japan's role therein, especially considering the relatively weak position of the prime minister in Japanese politics, the emphasis in Japanese decision-making upon carefully constructed consensus, and Japan's unique position as the only non-Western representative?

Note

The second half of this chapter draws heavily upon ideas and evidence presented in Hugo Dobson (2004) *Japan and the G7/8, 1975–2004* (London: RoutledgeCurzon) and Hugo Dobson (2007) *The Group of 7/8* (London: Routledge).

References

Albrecht-Carrié, René (ed.) (1968) *The Concert of Europe*, London: Macmillan.

Armstrong, J. D. (1996) 'The Group of Seven summits', in David H. Dunn (ed.) *Diplomacy at the Highest Level: The Evolution of International Summitry*, Basingstoke: Macmillan, pp. 41–52.

Baker, Andrew (2000) 'The G7 as a global "ginger group": plurilateralism and four-dimensional diplomacy', *Global Governance* 6, 2: 165–89.

Bayne, Nicholas (1994) 'International economic relations after the cold war', *Government and Opposition* 29, 1: 3–21.

—— (2000) *Hanging in There: The G7 and G8 Summit in Maturity and Renewal*, Aldershot: Ashgate.

—— (2005) *Staying Together: The G8 Summit Confronts the 21st Century*, Aldershot: Ashgate.

Bridge, F. R. and Bullen, Roger (1980) *The Great Powers and the European States System 1815–1914*, London: Longman.

Cox, Robert W. (1996) 'Global *perestroika*', in Robert W. Cox with Timothy J. Sinclair, *Approaches to World Order*, Cambridge: Cambridge University Press, pp. 296–313.

Elrod, Richard B. (1976) 'The concert of Europe: a fresh look at an international system', *World Politics* 28, 2: 159–74.

G7 (1994) *Naples Summit Communiqué*, 9 July 1994. Available on-line at: http://www.g8.utoronto.ca/summit/1994naples/communique/index.html, accessed on 25 March 2005.

—— (1995a) *Review of the International Financial Institutions*. Available on-line at: http://www.g8.utoronto.ca/summit/1995halifax/financial/index.html, accessed on 25 March 2005.

—— (1995b) *Halifax Summit Communiqué*, 16 June 1995. Available on-line at: http://www.g8.utoronto.ca/summit/1995halifax/communique/development.html, accessed on 19 August 2004.

—— (1996) *Lyon Summit Economic Communiqué*, 28 June 1996. Available on-line at: http://web.archive.org/web/20040607002810/www.g8.utoronto.ca/summit/1996lyon/communique/eco4.htm, accessed on 25 March 2005.

G8 (1998) *Response by the Presidency on Behalf of the G8 to the Jubilee 2000 Petition*, 16 May 1998. Available on-line at: http://www.g8.utoronto.ca/summit/1998birmingham/2000.htm, accessed on 19 August 2004.

Gilpin, Robert (2002) 'A realist perspective on international governance', in David Held and Anthony G. McGrew (eds) *Governing Globalization: Power Authority and Global Governance*, Cambridge: Polity Press, pp. 237–48.

Gulick, Edward Vose (1955) *Europe's Classical Balance of Power: A Case History of the Theory and Practice of One of the Great Concepts of European Statecraft*, Ithaca, NY: Cornell University Press.

Hajnal, Peter I. (1999) *The G7/G8 System: Evolution, Role and Documentation*, Aldershot: Ashgate.

—— (2002) 'Partners or adversaries? The G7/8 encounters civil society', in John J. Kirton and Junichi Takase (eds) *New Directions in Global Political Governance: The G8 and International Order in the Twenty-First Century*, Aldershot: Ashgate, pp. 209–22.

Hajnal, Peter I. and Kirton, John (2000) 'The evolving role and agenda of the G7/G8: a North American perspective', *NIRA Review* 7, 2: 5–10.

Helprin, Mark (1996) 'For a new Concert of Europe', *Commentary* 101, 1: 30–7.

Hodges, Michael R. (1999) 'The G8 and the new political economy', in Michael R. Hodges, John J. Kirton and Joseph P. Daniels (eds) *The G8's Role in the New Millennium*, Aldershot: Ashgate, pp. 69–73.

Holbraad, Carsten (1970) *The Concert of Europe: A Study in German and British International theory 1815–1914*, London: Longman.

Holsti, K. J. (1993) 'Governance without government: polyarchy in nineteenth-century European international politics', in James N. Rosenau and Ernst-Otto Czempiel (eds) *Governance without Government: Order and Change in World Politics*, Cambridge: Cambridge University Press, pp. 30–57.

Hunt, John and Owen, Henry (1984) 'Taking stock of the seven-power summits: two views', *International Affairs* 60, 4: 657–61.

Jervis, Robert (1985) 'From balance to concert: a study of international security cooperation', *World Politics* 38, 1: 58–79.

—— (1992) 'A political science perspective on the balance of power and the Concert', *The American Historical Review* 97, 3: 716–24.

Kirton, John J. (1989) 'Contemporary concert diplomacy: the seven-power summit and the management of international order'. Available on-line at: http://www.g7.utoronto.ca/scholar/kirton198901/index.html, accessed on 3 August 2004.

—— (1999) 'Explaining G8 effectiveness', in Michael R. Hodges, John J. Kirton and Joseph P. Daniels (eds) *The G8's Role in the New Millennium*, Aldershot: Ashgate, pp. 45–68.

—— (2001–2) 'Guess who is coming to Kananaskis? Civil society and the G8 in Canada's year as host', *International Journal* 57, 1. Available on-line at: http://www.g7.utoronto.ca/scholar/kirton2002/020507.pdf, accessed on 7 May 2003.

Koenig-Archibugi, Mathias (2002) 'Mapping global governance', in David Held and Anthony G. McGrew (eds) *Governing Globalization: Power Authority and Global Governance*, Cambridge: Polity Press, pp. 46–69.

Medlicott, W. N. (1956) *Bismarck, Gladstone and the Concert of Europe*, London: Athlone.

Mowat, R. B. (1930) *The Concert of Europe*, London: Macmillan.

Patomäki, Heikki (1999) 'Good governance of the world economy', *Alternatives* 24, 1: 119–42.

Penttilä, Risto E. J. (2003) *The Role of the G8 in International Peace and Security*, Oxford: Oxford University Press.

Putnam, Robert D. and Bayne, Nicholas (1984) *Hanging Together: The Seven-Power Summits*, Cambridge: Harvard University Press.

—— (1987) *Hanging Together: Cooperation and Conflict in the Seven-Power Summits*, London: Sage.

Rendall, Matthew (2000) 'Russia, the Concert of Europe, and Greece, 1821–29: a test of hypotheses about the Vienna system', *Security Studies* 9, 4: 52–90.

Schröder, Paul W. (1994) *The Transformation of European Politics, 1763–1848*, Oxford: Clarendon Press.

Sisci, Francesco (2003) 'China goes down with UN defeat', *On-line Asia Times* 21 March. Available on-line at: http://www.atimes.com/atimes/China/EC21Ad01.html, accessed on 22 March 2003.

Valaskakis, Kimon (2004) 'Global governance'. Available on-line at: http://www.g8.utoronto.ca/g8online/2004/english/lectures/lecture04.pdf, accessed on 19 August 2004.

Wilkinson, Rorden (2002) 'Global governance: a preliminary interrogation', in Rorden Wilkinson and Steve Hughes (eds) *Global Governance: Critical Perspectives*, London: Routledge, pp. 1–13.

2 Global governance, Japan and the Group of Seven/Eight

Endō Seiji

Introduction

The Group of Seven (G7) and Group of Eight (G8) summit meetings are a very special and important forum for Japan. It represents one of the most important multilateral fora where Japan is a founding member, and up until the creation of the Asia-Pacific Economic Cooperation (APEC) and Association of Southeast Asian Nations (ASEAN) +3, it was virtually the only multilateral forum of great diplomatic and international significance for Japan.

As a defeated country in the Second World War, Japan accepted the existing institutional arrangement of the international order and benefited greatly while it was successfully operating during the 1960s. First, as a defeated country, Japan naturally could not participate in the construction of the postwar international system. At the United Nations, one of the most important pillars of its foreign policy, Japan was and is just one of some two hundred countries and it still senses a considerable gap in influence between the five permanent members (P5) of the UN Security Council and itself. At other multilateral institutions like the Organization for Economic Cooperation and Development, the General Agreement on Tariffs and Trade and the International Bank for Reconstruction and Development, Japanese influence was substantially extended over several decades, but its participation/accession was either not very welcome or its influence was highly limited.

Second, Japan is a non-Western country. Even today, the Euro-centred or Western-centred nature of the postwar global political economy has not changed altogether though the relative weight of the overall Asian region has increased greatly and the rise of China is changing the global balance of power. The Atlantic circuit of capital is still the core nexus of the global political economy and most of the international economic and financial institutions are still being run by Western standards (Hirst and Thompson 2000, cf. Van Der Pijl 1984). Back in the mid-1970s, the Atlantic-centred nature of the world economic system was even more self-evident.

With the postwar international economic order facing a serous crisis in the mid-1970s, a new international forum among the top leaders of the advanced capitalist countries, namely the G7, was called into being to manage international economic turbulence. This time, however, Japan was invited as a founding member. This forum was meant to stimulate spontaneous and lively discussions about stabilizing the international economic system and coordinating macro-economic policies among the leading global economic powers. When the original idea of the summit meeting was mooted by France and West Germany, it was still thought of in reality as a G4 meeting among France, the US, the UK and West Germany, with some face-saving representation by Japan and Italy. Some bureaucrats in the Japanese Ministry of Foreign Affairs were well aware of this and it was only after the 1979 Tokyo Summit that they became secure in their status as one of the founding members (Matsuura 1994). Nevertheless, the fact that Japan was an original member meant that its presence in the international economic system was recognized as having global significance by the most important Western powers. In addition and more importantly, the forum was not about the technical routines of functional issues but about the redesigning and management – more broadly, governance – of the international economic system as a whole at a time when the system was facing a serious crisis. Japan was now in a responsible position as an economic power to input its own resources and policy ideas for the governance of the system. This was a source of pride for the Japanese government and its people. Since then, Japan has secured a safe and significant seat at the high table of global economic management. The G7/8 is, thus, a very important and special forum for Japan.

The G7/8's history now spans more than thirty years. Both it and Japan have changed greatly over this period. There is no doubt now that Japan is an economic power of significant gravity and it plays an active and important role in the global political economy. When the G7 was first convened many Japanese were still sceptical and cautious about the larger role of their country in the management of the global economy, although the big power consciousness of Japanese policymakers had been emerging since the early 1970s. The Japanese people were deeply ambivalent about the conflicting self-images of a rising economic power, on the one hand, and a small vulnerable country with few natural resources facing serious economic difficulties after the collapse of the fixed exchange rate regime and the oil crisis, on the other hand (cf. Sakamoto 2004). Japanese foreign policy had long been deeply reactive rather than proactive and the public debate was profoundly inward-looking (Hook *et al.* 2005). It could be argued that it is through the G7 process that Japan started actively and formally to participate in the management of the global political economy. However, in order to fit this role, Japan's state structure, identities and foreign policy outlook needed to be transformed. In this sense, Japan's participation in the G7/8 had a catalytic influence in changing Japan's polity. In contrast, it could be argued that with the participation of Japan in the governing process of the international political economy, the G7/8 extended its own remit of governance from the original Atlantic base to cover the Asia-Pacific region.

Nevertheless, Japan's tangible achievements and contributions to the betterment of the world through the G7/8 process are not so clear. One of the reasons lies in the enigmatic nature of the G7/8 itself. Although it occupies the central position in the governance of the global political economy, it is not a formal international institution with an established bureaucracy (see Chapter 2 in this volume). The real significance of the G7/8 as a mechanism of global governance remains unclear but it is necessary to look at the G7/8 in a political context in which to assess Japan's achievements and contributions to global governance. The first section of this chapter briefly deals with this question.

Over the three decades, both the G7/8 and Japan have shown continuity and change. The second section focuses upon Japan's continuing structural problems that render a more assertive and vigorous leadership role difficult. Japan's state machine and society were, at first, both unprepared for a global role during the 1970s. On the one hand, there were and still are several structural problems within Japanese domestic politics that make it less prone to take a leadership role in global governance. On the other hand, Japan has changed substantially; it now occupies a far more important position in the global political economy compared with the mid-1970s and it has played an occasional leadership role on several issues. Several unique and consistent features of Japan's behaviour at the G7/8 summits thus can be discerned. The third section will capture both of these aspects of Japanese diplomacy.

After thirty years, the G8 is now facing several new challenges including the rise of China and increasing instability in the global economic system. The terrorist attacks of 11 September 2001 and the following militant and unilateralist foreign policies of the Bush administration, in particular, are posing a grave challenge to the existing Atlantic base of multilateral global governance. It is difficult to discern if and when the cleavages between the G7/8 countries revealed by the 2003 Iraq War will be overcome. The concluding section of this chapter will highlight these problems and assess Japan's position in creating a better framework for global governance.

Japan and the G7/8 as a mechanism of global governance

Although the G7 was originally created as a forum to deal with the turbulences in the international economy and problems of deepening interdependence during the 1970s, it now functions within the management process of a globalized political economy covering a variety of agendas and policy issues. Although Japan is politically and militarily a regional power, it has been an active participant in this global process of transition. The G7/8 seems to provide certain terms and conditions for those in power to occupy a safe and commanding position to play an active role in the management of global affairs. For example, after the cold war, the former superpower Russia was 'allowed' into the G7/8 because it was 'democratized' and had installed a full-fledged market economy. As is mentioned later, however, despite a sounding from Japan to invite China into this forum, other member states have been rather reluctant, because it is not a liberal democracy. In this way, the G7/8 has the virtual power to decide who manages and who is managed by limiting its membership and thereby informally demonstrating the international standard of political legitimacy. Through these developments, in some respects, the G7/8 controls the agenda of global concern by acting as a gatekeeper, with Japanese policymakers increasingly viewed as playing an active role in this process and the Japanese political economy as a whole occupying a significant position in it.

Yet the G7/8 is not just a series of meetings among the world's top leaders; it involves varieties of political processes and policy networks. The political economies of those advanced capitalist countries are, thus, organized into fuzzy interlocking networks of connections and influences. First, the G7/8 process involves wider bureaucratic machines and interest groups in these countries. They are quite active in attempting to influence the G7/8 negotiating process and shape what promises and pledges can and should be made. It is a formalized process through which the bureaucrats of these countries work together to bring about agreement as regards what constitutes the public agenda and general policy orientation on many issues; basically, the differing domestic policies of these countries are evaluated through agreed norms of policy orientation. Sometimes the real battle of words and ideas is fought among the bureaucrats involved. Through this process, bureaucrats from the G7/8 countries come into regular and close contact with each other, especially those working as assistants to their leaders: the sherpas. Their efforts before and during the summit meeting may create mutual confidence, private friendship and an *esprit de corps*. It is certainly an exaggeration to say that national bureaucracies are merged into a unified bureaucracy but regular contact across the nations has created a transnational policy network (Funabashi 1991; Matsuura 1994). Thus the G7/8 can be understood as the centre of a nexus of wider institutional frameworks of domestic societies and international organizations.

Second, the G7/8 is trying to 'outreach' to other states and groups of states of importance in the global political economy. For example, although China is not expected to become a fully fledged member of the G7/8 in the near future, its weight in the global economy is rapidly growing and the management of the global economy cannot be achieved without consultation with China on financial and monetary policies. It is currently invited to participate in the extended dialogue meetings of the leaders' summit and the extra-forum discussion connected to the G7 meetings of finance ministers and heads of central banks. Japan is eagerly promoting China's involvement in this process (Kirton 2001a). In this way, a variety of different states are invited either to the main G7/8 summits and related meetings depending upon the issues and timing. In this sense, the G7/8 is now trying to strengthen its representative function through the process of outreach, although in no way can it be thought of as full democratic representation.

Third, the interests of globally mobile capital are also organized in order to influence the process of the G7/8. The World Economic Forum, the Trilateral Commission and other similar organizations are thought of as transnational networking activities to set the agenda and 'orthodox' policy orientations (cf. Gill 1989, 1990). It cannot be said that the private activities of these transnational interest groups are directly connected with the activities of the G7/8, but there are dense networks and channels between them and member governments. In Japan, politicians, the bureaucracy and the business interests are closely associated with each other, and it is an established practice that high-ranking government officials meet with representatives from the business world before the summit meetings to listen to their opinions, preferences and expectations.

Fourth, the G7/8 process involves the wider public. The peoples of some G7/8 countries are paying more attention to and are more actively involved in the process. Now, the summit meeting is a formalized opportunity for the world's social movements and non-governmental organizations (NGOs) to express their concerns and voices against the established practices among the powerful nations and the powerful actors like multinational corporations. Japanese social movements are not as influential and capable as their European or US counterparts but they are trying to get their voices heard by the Japanese government, and the Japanese government is now less hostile to these voices than in the past.

The G7/8, thus, has a large *political* function and it is in this sense that it *governs* the world, the Japanese state and civil society. It does not and cannot implement policies as international organizations do. Rather, it is a forum to decide the global agenda and demonstrate general guidelines for policymakers of the world and assess the activities of other international organizations and countries around the world. In this sense, it can be said that the G7/8 is a powerful machine. Japan's role is, then, to organize its own economy and economic policy in tune with liberal norms and principles of current global political economy. In order to fulfil these functions, the state machine of Japan has exhibited numerous structural problems, which in turn have led to its transformation.

Conservative polity and foreign policy: durable impediments to multilateral diplomacy

The G7/8 summit meeting was originally meant to stimulate spontaneous and lively discussions among the top leaders of the global economic powers. The Japanese polity, however, has some characteristics which do not fit well with this idea. It does not have a prompt decision-making mechanism; leaders rarely lead, rather they are deeply enmeshed in the domestic political context. In addition, despite its sheer economic size and population, Japan's leadership role in global affairs has been limited in scope and vision because of its narrow foreign policy outlook.

When Prime Minister Miki Takeo was invited to the first summit meeting in 1975, it is reported that he was very happy and rightly realized that Japanese participation in this forum would open up a new chapter in the history of postwar Japan (Miki 1977; Matsuura 1994). But he was also gravely worried as Japanese politicians mostly had experience of bilateral talks, not multilateral fora. In addition, on most occasions of negotiating with other governments, Japanese politicians had been and still are accompanied by bureaucrats and interpreters. They had virtually no experience in the multilateral context of free and frank discussions with other top politicians. G7/8 discussions are conducted mainly in English and politicians from other countries have little difficulty in articulating their thoughts and ideas in English. The Japanese prime minister, however, required an interpreter.

For example, the former German Chancellor Helmut Schmidt, who had ample experience of the summit meetings and other top level discussions among politicians, regarded only Fukuda Takeo as a memorable Japanese politician with some vision and perspective (Schmidt 1989).

This is, however, not just a problem of personality, experience or a command of English. Rather, there are deep-rooted problems in the Japanese political system that do not fit very well with multilateral diplomacy among the world's top leaders. First, the bilateral relationship with the US has been the strongest (even naturalized) frame of reference for most of Japan's foreign policy elites. It is no exaggeration to say that Japan's foreign relations have been virtually dominated by the bilateral relationship with the US. It means that Japanese politicians and the public do not have much room for multilateral diplomacy. In the early 1970s, several important issues arose that made it clear that the US and Japan had different interests in the international arena. Two examples include their respective policies towards the Middle East and China, especially when the 1971 'Nixon shock' dealt a heavy diplomatic blow to Japan. Even then, most Japanese never thought creatively about their foreign political and military policies in an international environment with diminished US influence. Although there seem to be slight changes, it has long been an established mind-set that military security was dominated by the US; Japan would only pursue a junior partner role under US auspices. It rarely occurred to Japanese politicians to challenge cold war bipolarity, although Japan needed to develop a better relationship with China. In addition, the management of US–Japan relations since the mid-1970s was a very difficult task; the huge Japanese trade surplus with the US could not be reduced easily, despite various Japanese efforts, particularly on the part of the prime minister.

Second, the polycentric nature of Japanese politics and the weak power of the prime ministers is a disadvantage in summit diplomacy. Despite the image of *Japan Inc.*, the Japanese political system has been plagued by polycentricity. There are a myriad of organized interest groups from agriculture, fishery to manufacturing and finance, which are deeply intermeshed with the bureaucratic machinery and politicians from the ruling Liberal Democratic Party (LDP). They have vital interests and influence in the existing system and act as veto groups. It is, therefore, difficult for most political leaders from the LDP to exert strong leadership in a top-down style. This is why Japanese politics was, and in large measure still is today, operated by consensus among many interested parties. Even when a Japanese prime minister could express his personal ideas and preferences regarding global affairs at a G7/8 summit meeting, it has been extremely difficult for him to make firm pledges as there is always a possibility that his personal commitments may be turned down as a result of the domestic political process. In fact, Japanese prime ministers have to cope with severe power struggles among their fellow LDP politicians and it is very difficult to remain in office for a long period of time, even when the party itself manages to keep a relative majority in the Diet. Throughout the G7/8's history between 1975 and 2005, Japan has been represented by 14 prime ministers and 1 foreign minister, which is only comparable with Italy (13 prime ministers and 17 administrations).

Third, the Japanese public and politicians were, and still are, unaccustomed to thinking strategically in a turbulent international environment. Since Japan flourished economically under US hegemony, Japan's foreign policy rarely aimed at manipulating the international political configuration to create a new international environment for its own, or the international community's, interests. Rather, it has accepted the prevailing international environment as a given and tried to find a niche in which it could reap some rewards. Related to this tendency is the fact that the 'leadership' style of the dominant LDP has been more reactive than proactive and this has trickled down to the Japanese public.

Fourth, the Japanese public was, and in some sense still is, profoundly inward-looking and there has not been a mature environment for rational debates on concrete foreign policy strategies and their coherent implementation. There have certainly been several public debates conducted earnestly on how Japan should contribute to the global political economy, but these discussions have been rather abstract and lacking in concrete policy measures backed by rational calculations of Japanese resources and power. Even when new international economic arrangements were the real issue after the breakdown of the Bretton Woods system, Japan was still not very assertive internationally. It was, therefore, neither ready for the discussion of the wider rearrangement of the global political and economic systems, nor able to prepare its top politicians for the discussion of concrete policy reforms. All in all, these aspects of Japanese politics have been the structural impediment to Japan's positive contribution to the global political economy through multilateral diplomacy at the G7/8 summit.

As regards Japan's relations with capitalist countries in East Asia, however, it could be argued that Japan has played a kind of conservative governing role. Under the overall aegis of the US security and military network, Japan was actively engaged in protecting the capitalist or anti-communist camp in East Asia during the cold war era by bolstering authoritarian leaders and their regimes in East Asia (Borden 1984; Lee 1993; Endō 1995). Its main policy tools have basically been economic, namely, official development assistance (ODA), and its goal was to bring about stability in the regional political economy, thereby contributing to the overall governance of the global political economy. But this 'economic' nature of Japan's foreign policy style had a negative impact on the way the Japanese think about 'politics' in their diplomacy. Although Japan was politically active in maintaining the capitalist world by supporting authoritarian regimes in Asia, this was thought of as neutral, apolitical economic activity, despite the clearly political role Japan was playing through its use of ODA. As a nation that upholds the so-called peace Constitution, military affairs were viewed as something that Japan should not handle; rather, they should be addressed within the framework of the US–Japan relationship and basically left to the US. This is another structural impediment to Japan's active leadership role in the G7/8 and the wider world.

As for foreign economic policy, the principle of free trade has been the mantra of Japan since the mid-1970s. Despite its image of a mercantilist nation, Japan has vocally advocated the principles of free trade. It has produced trade surplus by exporting manufactured goods but it has also been very cautious and reluctant to open its markets, especially those of agricultural products mainly because of the rural power base of the ruling LDP. During the 1970s the Japanese market was not really open for foreign products and investment and it was not ready to carry a larger burden of maintaining free trade and a stable monetary system. The Japanese public still thought of itself as a very tiny and vulnerable defeated Asian country with few natural resources and heavily dependent upon imported oil, and thought that it was unfair of the bigger powers to ask Japan to take on 'international responsibilities'.

Even today it is the case that Japanese markets are not as open as other industrialized countries. Despite the fact that Japanese tariff levels are one of the lowest among advanced industrialized countries and that many Japanese companies are actively engaged in foreign trade and investment and they have created complex networks of transnational research, development, production and marketing, Japan's economy could not be said to form an integrated part of the global political economy. For example, Japan is still operating a huge trade surplus although its size is growing relatively smaller, and Japan's trade dependence has been declining although its dependence on imported goods is insurmountably heavy, especially in the supply of foodstuffs and grains other than rice. In addition, a mentality averse to foreign investment in Japan is still strong. The advocated principles of free trade and protectionism in reality have, therefore, been some-what contradictory, although Japan has consistently and repeatedly voiced strong support for free trade.

These were the structural problems for Japan and many of them still remain. In short, Japan's presence as an economic entity has become prominent, but the nation as a whole was not ready to take an active role in the redesigning and main-tenance of the international economic system during the mid-1970s. Even today, compared with its economic size, Japan's scope for leadership is still very limited. It could even be said that during the last decade of consistent economic downturn, the Japanese public's attitude has become more inward-looking. However, there have been significant changes as a result of the accumulated experience and education through participation in the G7/8 process over the last thirty years.

International recognition and greater responsibilities

During the late 1970s, Japan resolved its economic difficulties earlier than other G7 countries, which resulted in the large ongoing accumulated trade surplus of the 1980s. There was no doubt that Japan came to occupy a position of an economic superpower in the international system, although political leadership and the public were lagging far behind this increasing importance in the global political economy. Although the US and Europe considered the large trade surplus a source of systemic disequilibrium, the Japanese public regarded it and the nation's economic power as the result of their hard work and diligence and they did not see any reason why they should be blamed for it. Over the course of nearly three decades, however, the Japanese political scene and Japan's frame of reference for its foreign economic policies have significantly matured. The foreign policy perspectives of Japanese politicians, bureaucrats and the general public have been widened and Japan has become accustomed to its global responsibilities. On the one hand, in a sense, Japan has been educated into taking on this responsibility, at least, partly because of its participation in the G7/8 summit process. On the other hand, the Japanese political economy has gone through a transformation from the developmentalist state to a more market-oriented neoliberal political economy. This reform process began with the Nakasone administration and continued to the current structural reforms of the Koizumi administration. The Japanese polity, thus, is being transformed in line with the Western or Anglo-Saxon style of economic governance.

The transformation of the Japanese state

The first point to consider is the role of the prime minister. It was under the premiership of Fukuda that the term 'international commitment' (*kokusai kōyaku*) was first used in the Japanese political discourse. At the 1978 Bonn Summit, Fukuda pledged that Japan would absorb more foreign products, become the 'engine' of economic growth and make a greater effort to expand its ODA budget under pressure from other countries. Japan had set a tight budgetary ceiling at this time of economic difficulty, and Fukuda was the target of severe personal criticisms from his fellow LDP politicians for agreeing to expanded responsibilities at the summit meeting (Sakurada 1988). But Fukuda managed to gain support for his pledge and since then, 'international commitment' has entered the political vocabulary of Japan.

The administration of Prime Minister Nakasone Yasuhiro (1982–7) was a turning point in the Japanese position among the G7 countries. Although he was a conservative politician and an anti-communist leading a relatively minor political faction in the LDP, Nakasone had the political instinct to understand the meaning of the rising position of Japan in world affairs. He was a rare kind of leader among Japanese politicians and his proactive leadership role was thought of as president-like compared to other Japanese prime ministers who had played more the role of a mediator or arbitrator. He was quick to appeal to and flatter the changing psyche of the Japanese public which wanted more international prestige, recognition and respect as Japan was more successful than most other G7 members in running its economy. He first established a close, first-name, personal friendship with US President Ronald Reagan, known as the *Ron-Yasu* relationship. He asserted Japan's position more vocally at the summit meetings and he was virtually the first Japanese prime minister to take part actively in the discussions on security issues. Before him, Japanese prime ministers had largely kept silent on these matters in response to the Japanese political atmosphere at that time that did not allow the prime minister to take a more active *political*, namely military and security, role among the G7 or even in the bilateral relationship with the US (Seki and Takayanagi 1985).

Nakasone emphasized Japan's position as a part of the Western alliance against the Soviet Union, although it was almost taboo to describe the US–Japan relationship as an 'alliance' before his predecessor Suzuki Zenkō did so. This was in response to the Japanese public's feelings that Japan should not play a military role, even in the US–Japan relationship (Inoue 2003). Nakasone used confrontational language against the Soviet Union intentionally in order to show his own policy stance and create favourable conditions in domestic politics to compensate for his weak position in the LDP; certainly, a range of Japanese intellectuals and politicians preferred more nuanced and less confrontational language towards the Soviet Union, but his hawkish, clear-cut position against communism was successful in gaining some popular support. He also utilized his personal ties with Reagan. At the photo call for the 1983 Williamsburg Summit, for instance, he took a central position standing beside Reagan. The Japanese mass media rather sarcastically reported his tactics of sneaking up to Reagan but the public responded positively to the photo of their prime minister in a central position, which was seen as symbolically reflecting the increasing weight of Japan's status in world affairs.

While Nakasone was in power, a heated public debate on Japanese responsibilities in global affairs was conducted. With cold war tensions rising again, the US twin deficit running ever higher and the Japanese trade surplus at an historic high, Japan was harshly criticized by the US and European public and media. As suggested earlier, the Japanese public had not thought that the Japanese trade surplus was such a big problem for the world economy and people tended to think that it was more of a problem of those who bought more than they could earn and as a result ran a huge deficit (Kyōgoku 1983). In a sense, Nakasone tried to educate the Japanese public by running campaigns that promoted 'Japan as a political great power' (*seiji taikoku*) and encouraged the Japanese to 'buy foreign goods'. Alongside his purchase of American aircraft for government use and his hawkish security policy against the Soviet Union, these initiatives mitigated the severity of American criticism against Japanese economic prowess (cf. Inoguchi and Okimoto 1988; Nakasone *et al.* 1992).

The public gradually came to understand that Japan was now in a position to shoulder some burden in the Western alliance, and accepted the idea and usage of the phrases 'international responsibility' and 'burden sharing'. The public pledges by prime ministers at the G7 meetings came to be recognized as binding and started to take precedence over messy politicking within the LDP. One of the resulting changes could be seen in the rather smooth acceptance of the Plaza agreement of 1985 and the so-called Maekawa report. The former agreement brought about the rapid evaluation of the Japanese yen against the US dollar, which was a heavy blow to Japan's export industries, and the latter report aimed at structural change in the Japanese economy to grow depending more on domestic consumption than on export earnings. The Maekawa report may have not been successful enough to transform the Japanese economic system but people realized that Japan would need a more balanced trade position considerate of the economic situations in other G7 countries.

Activism based on the unique character of the prime minister, however, did not last long. There were a series of relatively weak prime ministers from the late 1980s, and the politicians' policy expertise, international network and reputation at the G7 were not necessarily reflected in election results. Prime Minister Miyazawa Kiichi was famous for his policy expertise and internationalist outlook, but he failed to win the election thereby ceding power to a non-LDP coalition government. LDP Prime Minister Hashimoto Ryūtarō had acquired a good reputation and policy expertise, especially on economic issues, while he served as Minister of International Trade and Industry, but again he lost the election. Prime Minister, Koizumi Junichirō, was known as an eccentric politician quite distinct from his fellow politicians in the LDP. Like Nakasone, he established a firm friendship with the US president. Although he liked to describe himself as a structural reformer of the Japanese political and economic system, he did not have any strong policy expertise other than to advocate, for example, the simple mantra of privatizing the Japanese postal service, suggesting his focus on the domestic rather than the multilateral forum of the G8. He was not a good communicator either and his political style was notorious for short and grossly simplified comments on many difficult and subtle issues. Nevertheless, he was able to maintain his popularity among the electorate and survive general elections with his populistic mobilization of the public (Yamaguchi 2004, 2005).

Nevertheless, the Japanese political economy went through a huge transformation during these twenty-five years. Starting from Nakasone's policy of privatization of the rail system, the focus of economic policy moved from state management to private sector initiative, and many national corporations were privatized following the neoliberal doctrine (Iio 1993; Vogel 1996).

Second, the transformation of the Japanese bureaucracy is also evident. The Japanese bureaucracy has been known as a well-oiled machine having a great deal of influence in governance, with an ability to take part in meticulous deliberations about wide-ranging issues in domestic politics. As the G7/8 came to be institutionalized as an annual event, the Japanese bureaucracy became accustomed to the process and has been successful in making its activities meet global requirements. As Robert Cox has suggested, in some issue areas, the state is functioning as a transmission belt of the decisions made at the international level. In this light, the Japanese bureaucracy has connected with global economic and financial issues, is increasingly internationalized and now forms a part of the mechanisms of global governance (Cox 1986). For example, the G7 meeting of the finance ministers and central bankers was more institutionalized with the Bank for International Settlements process than the summit meeting itself, as banking and financial sectors are the first to be globalized. The Japanese Ministry of Finance is the key player in changing the architecture of financial policy, financial regulation and the mechanisms of surveillance in line with the changes in global financial regulation (Funabashi 1988).

In addition, a large variety of international conferences have been held and discussions conducted around the G7/8 framework as it continues to cover an even wider range of social issues in addition to the original agenda of trade, macro-economic policy, financial globalization, security and political affairs. Even the most domestically oriented ministries now have to face up to their global connectedness as most of the Japanese bureaucratic system shares the governing responsibilities with the bureaucracies of other countries. In a sense, it could be argued that they are a part of the emergent global polity. Although the Japanese bureaucracy is relatively more reactive than proactive as is usually the case in Japanese politics, it is firmly and deeply enmeshed with the mechanisms of global governance.

However, the polycentredness of the political system has not changed much. The team for summit meetings is organized so that a variety of bureaucratic voices from different branches of the government are represented. Each bureaucratic section is a stakeholder and information is not shared in an efficient way in the Japanese bureaucracy. These different sections of the government have developed their transnational links without developing networks across the governmental agencies in Japan. Thus, in terms of the strategic mobility of Japanese foreign policymaking and implementation, the situation has not improved much since the 1970s, but this is partly a reflection of the changing nature of governance under globalization.

The Japanese way of global governance

What constitutes the Japanese way of global governance? Although it is difficult to identify and trace the points that Japan emphasizes in the G7/8 as there are so many issues discussed, several characteristics of Japan's role as an organ of global governance can be detected. The first is its economism and technological orientation, which could also be described as averseness towards 'politics'. The second is Asia-centredness. Throughout the process of its participation in the summit meetings, Japan has described itself as a representative of Asia. The third is the pursuit of national interests of an essentially bilateral nature by using the multilateral forum of the G7/8. Over time, however, it seems that multilateral issues are winning over the national and/or bilateral concerns.

As regards Japan's economism, for its size, it has not been very successful in making a positive and tangible contribution through the proposal of new agendas and creating new visions for the world. It is not that Japan does not have any positive ideas and that it has not put any creative thinking into the process of the G7/8, but it seems that it is not very good at selling ideas and ideals to the world in universal terms. 'Politics' in Japanese foreign policy terms has long been understood as military and security matters and Japan cannot and should not play a larger political role. For the tangible contribution, then, what remains is Japan's economic contribution.

As was mentioned earlier, Japan has consistently emphasized the importance of free trade and an open economy since the inception of the summit meeting, but there were serious problems in terms of the openness of the Japanese market to foreign products and investments. That is partly the reason why successive administrations tried, albeit inconsistently, to open the economy to foreign products and investment in order to respond to the demands of global governance. The far more important and effective factor was, however, US pressure to open the Japanese market, rather than Japanese consideration of the consistency of its policies with the G7/8.

At any rate, ideas mattered in Japanese policymaking too. At the summit meetings, the Japanese government used a promise to expand its own economy by fiscal measures and its ODA budget as one of the most important bargaining chips to show its power and international responsibility. During the 1980s, Japan's huge trade surplus was a main source of irritation for other member states. It was, therefore, essential that Japan show a way to reduce the trade surplus and promote the growth of the global economy. Japan's political leaders and bureaucrats worked hard to avoid a situation where Japan was directly targeted and named as the source of instability or disequilibrium in the global economy. Like any other country, Japan does not like public criticism and the Japanese media and public were troubled by critical assessments by other countries of its policy during the preparation for G7 summit meetings. It may be a small achievement that they avoided overt and harsh criticism of Japan, but through these negotiating processes the bureaucracy learned the positions and attitudes of other G7 nations and, in some cases, it came to be reflected in later policy and priority changes. It was, thus, essentially based on domestic policy that Japan tried to expand its economy, but it was framed as a part of its international policy as a responsible member of the capitalist world.

Issues concerning ODA can be understood in similar terms. Japanese ODA has been severely criticized because it has, after all, brought benefit to Japanese construction companies and authoritarian politicians in East Asia by promoting development projects (Murai *et al*. 1989). In other words, Japan's ODA is closely connected with the promotion of Japan's national and corporate interests. It has also been notorious for its low grant element. However, it was through its participation in the G7 that Japan expanded rapidly its ODA budget, extended into other areas outside East Asia and increased the amount of untied aid. It may look like only self-interest to expend huge amounts of ODA money throughout the world, but it is true that Japan has been an active advocate of addressing the North–South problem. Like the emphasis on the importance of free trade, emphasis on the North–South problem as a global issue could be detected from the time of Miki (Miki 1977). Japan's recent emphasis on IT, education and the digital divide at the 2000 Kyūshū/Okinawa Summit can be understood in the same vein (MOFA 2000). In this sense, economic development in the South could be regarded as a Japanese agenda item. Promoting development and bringing the fruits of economic growth to many poor people in the world through ODA was popular among the Japanese public, and Japan tried to sell its own experience of rapid economic development as a kind of model to other countries (Wade 1996). Japan boasted that it was the world's top donor of ODA for several years during the 1990s and the yen based ODA budget reached its peak in 1996 at about 120 billion yen. But the ODA budget has rapidly been reduced by one-third thereafter because of fiscal difficulties caused by rapidly accumulated government debt that had unsuccessfully stimulated economic growth during the 1990s. By 2005 the budget was reduced to US$7 billion. However, at the 2005 Gleneagles Summit, Japan expressed its intention 'to increase its ODA volume by US$10 billion in aggregate over the next five years', and committed 'to double its ODA to Africa over the next three years and launched the $5 billion "Health and Development Initiative" over the next five years' (G8 2005).

In many policy areas where Japanese interests and the interests of other G7 nations are not very different, Japan has carried the financial burden of the governing mechanisms of the G7. Japan's financial contribution should not be taken lightly and its generally positive attitude towards the G7/8 agenda can be evaluated as playing a positive and stabilizing role.

The second characteristic is an Asia-centred orientation. Japanese leaders from Miki onwards have responded positively to the idea of Japan as the representative of Asia and Japan has sought to include greater input from Asia into the G7/8. Because Japan fought and lost its imperial war in China and Southeast Asia, there was good reason for Japan to keep a low profile when advocating an Asian identity. In addition, Japan faced severe criticism from some of the Southeast Asian countries during the early 1970s when its economic power started to expand into the region. But Japan's Asian orientation at the G7/8 is not just a self-stylized image. It has been an established practice that Japanese ministers and/or top career diplomats travel around leading East Asian countries from China, South Korea, Indonesia, Thailand and so forth before and after the G7/8 summit meeting (Matsuura 1994; Dobson 2004a). They collect the opinions of Asian leaders before the summit and thereafter report back the results and what was discussed. It is not clear how far Japan has really been able to promote Asian interests against Western interests, but its emphasis on development and North–South problems mentioned earlier is connected and, at the least, Japan has shown respect to these Asian countries.

For example, Miyazawa tried to invite Indonesian President Suharto as a representative of the Non-aligned Movement to the 1993 Tokyo Summit. Japan also tried to set up an informal seat for China at the 2000 Kyūshū/Okinawa Summit and aired a proposal to invite China to the G8 after Russia became a formal member, saying that Asia's voice is not properly represented at this important forum (Kirton 2001b). Japan was unable to persuade other G7/8 countries, but it characteristically shows that Japan is earnestly trying to promote an Asian voice in global governance. The G7/8 is now trying to strengthen its 'outreach' to non-G8 members and Japan has attempted to assist this process by representing a variety of non-Western voices (Dobson 2004b). It is difficult to quantify the significance of this activity but in a sense Japan has contributed to the improvement in the levels of representation at the G7/8 summit, and at the same time adopted the role of the representative of Asian interests on the global political scene.

The third characteristic is the multilateralization of bilateral issues. The multi-lateral process of the G7/8 involves many reciprocal concessions and compromises. This gives Japan the chance to push its concerns up the international agenda by including them in some of the declarations issued by the G7/8. Regional stability on the Korean Peninsula, the problems of North Korean nuclear development and the multiple kidnappings of Japanese citizens by North Korean agents are salient examples. Another example is Japan's successful insertion of the bilateral territorial dispute with Soviet Union/Russia into the political declaration of the 1992 Munich Summit. Japan and Russia have yet to conclude a peace treaty after the Second World War because of an unresolved territorial dispute over the

'Northern Territories'. In other words, Japan sometimes uses the framework of the G7/8 as a foreign policy tool to promote national self-interest.

In this respect, however, the territorial dispute with Russia is important and interesting since this problem showed that Japanese national interests and the G7's capacity to accommodate Russia into a new international environment and support its efforts to introduce democracy and the market economy were potentially in conflict. It became a prominent issue when Miyazawa hosted the 1993 Tokyo Summit and the possibility arose of inviting Russian President Boris Yeltsin. During the early 1990s, the expectation of the island's return to Japanese sovereignty was high since Russia's position in world politics was faltering and Japan had greater financial leverage to persuade the leaders of Russia to return them to Japan. Thus, the Japanese government wanted to delay as much as possible the issue of a formal invitation to Yeltsin and keep its options open. In other words, the cold war had not ended yet in the early 1990s for Japan.

However, for other G7 nations, the cold war ended rapidly in the late 1980s and the creation of a new international institutional framework which accommodated Russia was a new and pressing agenda item. Thus, they wanted an earlier formal invitation to Russia. Japan's territorial interest and the G7's global interests were at odds with each other over this issue and the negotiations among the sherpas lasted a long time (Matsuura 1994). Miyazawa understood the difference between Japan and other nations very well but Japanese right-wing forces may well have reacted violently if Yeltsin had been invited without any firm commitment to return the islands. Miyazawa acted cleverly by not sticking to Japan's original position and instead giving its fellow G7 members greater preference than the narrowly defined Japanese national interest. In addition to inviting Yeltsin to Tokyo, the Japanese government decided to become an active supporter and positive source of finance for the Russian transition process from a socialist political economy to capitalist to support Russia, giving some US$6.6 billion between 1990 and 2001. It could, then, be said that Japanese leaders decided to give priority to the multilateral framework and global governance of the G7/8 over its own territorial issues. It could even be argued that the decision itself was a result of the learning and education process taking place through participation in the G7/8 for nearly two decades.

Like the issue of Russia's accommodation into the post-cold war international system, there have been many new issues concerning the redesigning of the global system during the 1990s. For the Japanese government and its people, however, many of the issues tend to be rather remote: protracted civil/international wars in the dissolving Yugoslavia; heavy-handed violence and resistance in the Israeli–Palestine conflict; protracted civil war in Somalia; genocide in Rwanda and its aftermath, and so on. Given that Japanese political and economic activity has little real contact with these areas, the Japanese are again being educated into the process of global crisis management by participating in the G7/8. Japan's active interests in Africa and its development may be cited as a result of the transformation of Japan's foreign policy outlook.

All in all, it could be argued that Japan has been a good and less selfish student in this multilateral process. Ultimately, it has learned a great deal by playing a positive role in bringing about stability in the process. But reflecting its traditional political style, it has been less proactive and more reactive. Given its economic size and financial contribution, Japan could have played a more proactive and salient role. The reason for this rather reactive attitude lies not in Japan's G7/8 policy but rather in its general foreign policy framework.

Japan's merit in the G7 has been rooted basically in its economic size and ability to play the role of a financier in G7/8 politics. As the image of robustness in the Japanese economy disappeared in the 1990s, it was difficult for Japanese leaders to assert strongly their position at the G7/8. With the highest rate of government debt per capita, an economic recession of more than a decade and a rapidly ageing population, Japanese politicians have struggled to play the role of a leading nation. In this sense, it is no longer just the personal performance of the top leaders that matters most in the G7/8's provision of governance.

Conclusion

A number of intertwined issues have led Japan to an important crossroads in terms both of its foreign policy outlook and domestic political structure. First, it has been trapped in an economic slump for well over a decade and its recovery is only recently nascent. Since its main source of power lies in its economy, Japan has been unable to assert a strong voice in global governance through the G8. Second, the long economic slump and lack of real reform has resulted in a variety of disruptions and cleavages in Japanese society: the erosion of the social security system, lowering worker morale and loss of job security, and a widening structural gap between the rich and the poor. Given this background, some populist right-wing politicians have gained popularity and some ground in persuading the public to unlearn the lessons of history, saying that the Japanese should have more pride in their history and the nation. This peculiar mixture of right-wing forces in Japan may undo the liberal aspects of Japanese polity and society (Yakushiji 2004).

Third, during the five years of the Koizumi administration, Japan's policy towards East Asia has been virtually in paralysis. In East Asia, China is rising fast as an economic power with huge exporting power and an expanding domestic consumer market. Japan has supported China's accommodation in the global political economy, as illustrated by the government's attempt to involve it in the G8 process. But Koizumi's personal creed of visiting Yasukuni Shrine, where Japanese war criminals are enshrined as war heroes, without due consideration of the region's history and the foreign policy positions of China and South Korea, makes Japan's relationship with them very bitter.

It could be argued that Japan and China are competing to win the position of leader in the East Asian region. China has been very proactive; for example, in concluding a free trade agreement with the Association of Southeast Asian Nations. Yet, Japan is trying to catch up in this area and it has concluded several free trade agreements with Asian countries and others are just waiting to be concluded. It is not, however, that Japan is just competing with China. Japan's role in the provision of global governance can be seen, for example, in the area of financial stability in the region. Japan has been very active in creating a series of foreign currency swap agreements among East Asian countries, which aim to provide a safety net at the time of financial crisis to save a country under pressure and prevent contagion. Although there is still much to be done, Japan and East Asian countries learned the lessons of the financial and economic crisis of 1997 (Itō 2001; Katada 2001). This and similar functional cooperation at the day-to-day administrative level in East Asia is developing smoothly in a number of fields: drug control, police technique, tsunami warning, financial regulation, piracy control, and so forth. This functional cooperation in the region results in rising East Asian expectations for the creation of an East Asian Community (Hook 1996; Kang 2001; Wada 2003; Endō 2005).

The emergence of right-wing elements, however, may all erode the accumulated assets of postwar Japanese diplomacy as a responsible economic power carrying the burden of global governance. Japan is, thus, now facing an important crossroads and will have to find a right course among competing identities, although they are not necessarily mutually exclusive. First, Japan's foreign policy activity is centred on the US–Japan bilateral relationship. Second, Japan has the identity of a large industrialized nation forming an important pillar in trilateral relations, which is exemplified in the membership of the G8. Third, Japan is obviously an Asian country and at the G8 Japan has adopted a self-nominated role as the voice of Asia. These roles have been compatible since the mid-1970s because forces supporting these identities have sustained each other.

However, these roles may not be compatible in the future. The most important pillar of Japanese foreign relations has been its bilateral ties with the US. But some high-ranking officials of the US are vocally against the idea of an East Asian Community if it is excluded. Given the frosty relations with China and South Korea, Japan under the Koizumi administration cannot legitimately call itself the representative voice of Asia. The G7/8 itself is not working effectively enough largely as a result of the US unilateralist position. In addition, isolationist and reactionary forces are gaining some ground in Japanese politics, which denies all of the three identities mentioned earlier.

Thus, it is important for Japan to strengthen its ties with all the members of the G7/8, not just the US, in addition to East Asian countries. It is not only for the sake of Japan's self-interest but for the sake of the globe. Japan can open up new opportunities for manoeuvre and possibly gain more leverage over the US and tame its destabilizing unilateralism towards cooperative multilateralism. By so doing, diverging identities of Japanese foreign policy outlook could again be made compatible and Japan could play a more positive and proactive role to govern global and regional affairs in a more creative way.

References

Borden, William S. (1984) *The Pacific Alliance: United States Foreign Economic Policy and Japanese Trade Recovery, 1947–1955*, Madison, WI: University of Wisconsin Press.

Cox, Robert W. (1986) 'Social forces, states and world orders: beyond international relations theory', in Robert O. Keohane (ed.) *Neorealism and Its Critics*, New York: Columbia University Press, pp. 204–54.

Dobson, Hugo (2004a) *Japan and the G7/8, 1975–2002*, London: RoutledgeCurzon.

—— (2004b) 'Japan and the G8 Evian Summit: bilateralism, East Asianism and multilateralization', *G8 Governance Working Papers* 9. Available on-line at: http://www.g8.utoronto.ca/governance/dobson_g8g.pdf, accessed on 9 May 2006.

Endō, Seiji (1995) 'East Asian security: issues in the post-cold war era', in Sekiguchi Sueo and Kawagoe Toshihiko (eds) *East Asian Economies: Transformation and Challenges*, Singapore: ISEAS, pp. 31–74.

—— (2005) 'Higashi Ajia kyōdōtai e no apurōchi: chiikiteki takokushugi no seidoka no kadai to genjitsu', *Seikatsu Keizai Seisaku* June, 101: 8–12.

Funabashi, Yōichi (1988) *Tsūka retsuretsu*, Tokyo: Asahi Shinbunsha.

—— (1991) *Samittokurashi*, Tokyo: Asahi Shinbunsha.

G8 (2005) *Gleneagles Communiqué on Africa*. Available on-line at: http://www.g8.utoronto.ca/summit/2005gleneagles/africa.html, accessed on 9 May 2006.

Gill, Stephen (ed.) (1989) *Atlantic Relations: Beyond the Reagan Era*, New York: Harvester Wheatsheaf.

—— (1990) *American Hegemony and the Trilateral Commission*, Cambridge: Cambridge University Press.

Hirst, Paul and Thompson, Grahame (2000) *Globalization in Question: The International Economy and the Possibilities of Governance*, Cambridge: Polity (second edition).

Hook, Glenn D. (1996) 'Japan and the construction of Asia-Pacific', in Andrew Gamble and Anthony Payne (eds) *Regionalism and World Order*, Basingstoke: Macmillan, pp. 169–206.

Hook, Glenn D, Gilson, Julie, Hughes, Christopher W. and Dobson, Hugo (2005) *Japan's International Relations: Politics, Economics and Security*, London and New York: Routledge (second edition).

Iio, Jun (1993) *Mineika no Seijikatei: Rinchōgata Seiji no Seika to Genkai*, Tokyo: University of Tokyo Press.

Inoguchi, Takashi and Daniel Okimoto (1988) *The Political Economy of Japan: The Changing International Context*, Stanford: Stanford University Press.

Inoue, Toshikazu (2003) *Nippon Gaikōshi Kōgi*, Tokyo: Iwanami Shoten.

Itō, Kunihiko (2001) 'Japan, the Asian economy, the international financial system and the G8: a critical perspective', in John J. Kirton and George M. von Furstenberg (eds) *New Directions in Global Economic Governance: Managing Globalization in the Twenty-first Century*, Aldershot: Ashgate, pp.127–42.

Kang, Sanjung (2001) *Tōhoku Ajia Kyōdō no Ie o Mezashite*, Tokyo: Heibonsha.

Katada, Saori N. (2001) 'Japan's approach to shaping a new international financial architecture', in John J. Kirton and George M. von Furstenberg (eds) *New Directions in Global Economic Governance: Managing Globalization in the Twenty-first Century*, Aldershot: Ashgate, pp. 113–26.

Kirton, John J. (2001a) 'The G20: representativeness, effectiveness, and leadership in global governance', in John J. Kirton, Joseph P. Daniels and Andreas Freytag (eds) *Guiding Global Order: G8 Governance in the Twenty-first Century*, Aldershot: Ashgate, pp. 143–72.

—— (2001b) 'The G7/8 and China: toward a closer association', in John J. Kirton, Joseph P. Daniels and Andreas Freytag (eds) *Guiding Global Order: G8 Governance in the Twenty-first Century*, Aldershot: Ashgate, pp. 189–222.

Kirton, John J., Daniels, Joseph P. and Freytag, Andreas (eds) (2001) *Guiding Global Order: G8 Governance in the Twenty-first Century*, Aldershot: Ashgate.

Kyōgoku, Junichi (1983) *Nippon no Seiji*, Tokyo: University of Tokyo Press.

Lee, Jong Won (1993) 'Higashiajia ni okeru reisen to chiikishugi: amerika no seisaku wo chūshin ni', in Kamo Takehiko (ed.) *Koza seikikan no sekai seiji vol.3 Ajia no kokusai chitsujo, datsu reisen no eikyo*, Tokyo: Nihon Hyōronsha, pp. 185–239.

Matsuura, Kōichirō (1994) *Senshinkoku Samitto: rekishi to tenbō*, Tokyo: Saimaru Shuppankai.

MOFA (2000) *Okinawa Charter on Global Information Society*. Available on-line at: http://www.mofa.go.jp/policy/economy/summit/2000/charter.html, accessed on 9 May 2006.

Murai, Yoshinori and ODA Chōsa Kenkyūkai (eds) (1989) *Musekinin ODA Taikoku Nippon: Firipin, Tai, Indonesia genchi kinkyū ripōto*, Tokyo: JICC Shuppankyoku.

Miki Naikaku Sōridaijin Enzetsushū in Naikaku Sōridaijin Kanbō Kanshū (ed.) (1977) Tokyo: Nippon Kōhō Kyōkai.

Nakasone, Yasuhiro, Murakami, Yasusuke, Satō, Seizaburō and Nishibe, Osamu, (1992) *Kyōdō Kenkyū 'Reisen igo'*, Tokyo: Bungeishunju.

Sakamoto, Yoshikazu (2004) *Nippon no Ikikata, Sakamoto Yoshikazu Shū vol. 4*, Tokyo: Iwanami Shoten.

Sakurada, Daizō (1988) 'Japan and the management of the international political economy: Japan's seven power summit diplomacy'. Available on-line at: http://www.g8.utoronto.ca/scholar/sakurada1988, accessed on 9 May 2006.

Schmidt, Helmut (1989) *Shumitto Gaikō Kaisōroku*, Tokyo: Iwanami Shoten.

Seki, Hiroharu and Takayanagi, Sakio, (1985) *Dōjidai e no Shiza: gunkaku, detanto, daisan sekai*, Kyoto: Sanrei Shobō.

Van Der Pijl, Kees (1984) *The Making of an Atlantic Ruling Class*, London: Verso.

Vogel, Stephen (1996) *Freer Markets, More Rules: Regulatory Reform in Advanced Industrial Countries*, Ithaca, NY: Cornell University Press.

Wada, Haruki (2003) *Tōhoku Ajia Kyōdō no Ie: shinchiikishugi sengen,* Tokyo: Heibonsha.

Wade, Robert (1996) 'Japan, the World Bank, and the art of paradigm maintenance: the East Asian miracle in political perspective', *New Left Review* 217, May/June: 3–36.

Yakushiji, Katsuyuki (2004) 'Jimintō wa "Kyokū Seitō" ni naru no desu ka', *Sekai* October: 170–7.

Yamaguchi, Jirō (2004) *Sengo seiji no hōkai: demokurashi wa doko e yuku ka*, Tokyo: Iwanami Shoten.

—— (2005) 'Minshutō wa ima nani o subeki ka', *Sekai* December: 75–81.

3 Global governance and the Organization for Economic Cooperation and Development

Richard Woodward

Introduction

The Organization for Economic Cooperation and Development (OECD) is the least written about and least well understood of the global multilateral economic institutions. Paradoxically, leading commentators ceaselessly refer to the centrality of the OECD to contemporary global governance, yet rarely has the organization been the subject of sustained academic scrutiny. For instance, Joseph Nye (2002: 144) argued that the OECD, in collaboration with the International Monetary Fund (IMF) and the World Trade Organization (WTO), provides 'a framework of rules for the global economy'. Similarly, Held *et al.* (1999: 84) cite the OECD among the 'key multilateral economic fora' common to all 'states in advanced capitalist societies'. Nevertheless, having identified the importance of the OECD, these and many other observers proceed to marginalize the role of the organization preferring instead to focus on the IMF, the World Bank and the WTO. Equally, as the other contributions to this volume testify, book-length accounts of the activities of the WTO, the IMF, the World Bank and other leading institutions such as the Group of 7/8 (G7/8), which now has an entire book series devoted to it, are commonplace. In contrast, apart from a smattering of texts authored by the OECD's own staff (OECD 1971; Sullivan 1997) and a small literature examining the organization's role in the global trading system (Blair 1993; Cohn 2002), the last single-authored book written in English by an outsider and focussing exclusively on the OECD's role in global affairs was published nearly forty years ago (Aubrey 1967; Woodward 2007a). More specialized work detailing the history and evolution of transatlantic governance is largely devoid of references to the OECD. One contributor to Gardner and Stefanova's collection *The New Transatlantic Agenda* (2001) asserts that 'the "OECD world" is, first of all, a transatlantic world' (May 2001: 185) but there is only one further reference to the organization in the volume. Pollack and Shaffer's (2001) *Transatlantic Governance in the Global Economy* and Richard Cooper's (1968) classic study of economic management among the Atlantic community, *The Economics of Interdependence*, provide greater coverage of the OECD and its predecessor the Organization for European Economic Cooperation (OEEC) but again these references are sporadic and fragmented. A cursory survey of articles published in the last decade by what, according to the ISI Social Sciences Citation Index, are the

Table 3.1 Articles about key global multilateral institutions in leading international relations journals, 1995–2004

Journals	WTO	IMF	World Bank	G7/G8	OECD
International Organization	2	3	1	0	6
International Security	0	0	0	0	0
World Politics	0	1	0	0	1
International Studies Quarterly	0	3	1	0	3
American Journal of International Law	14	1	1	1	0
Journal of Conflict Resolution	0	0	1	1	0
Foreign Affairs	3	9	4	0	0
Journal of Peace Research	0	0	2	0	2
European Journal of International Relations	0	0	1	0	0
Journal of Common Market Studies	3	0	0	0	2
Columbia Journal of Transnational Law	2	4	2	0	0
Survival	0	1	0	0	0
Security Studies	0	0	0	0	0
Journal of World Trade	131	3	3	0	9
World Economy	48	16	7	0	7
Foreign Policy	2	5	1	0	1
Common Market Law Review	2	0	0	0	0
Post Soviet Affairs	0	0	0	0	1
Stanford Journal of International Law	0	0	0	0	0
International Affairs	4	2	2	3	2
Totals	**211**	**48**	**26**	**5**	**34**

Source: ISI/BIDS.

Note
Census date: 7 June 2004. Search criteria: for all available alternatives in the full abstract (e.g. IMF, International Monetary Fund and so on), for articles 1995–2004.

twenty highest impact international relations journals reveals a comparable pattern (see Table 3.1). In purely quantitative terms the OECD does not fair too badly. The WTO is clearly the frontrunner, being the subject of 211 articles during the period, but the OECD with thirty-four articles is only slightly behind the IMF (48) and is ahead of the World Bank (26) and the G7/8 (5). However, only 15 of these 34 articles contain substantive material about the organization, its work or its broader contribution to global governance. The remaining articles were using OECD countries as a basis for comparison. Finally, the OECD lacks the public profile associated with other international organizations. Anti-globalization protests have marred OECD gatherings in Paris (February 1998), Bologna (June 2000) and Naples (March 2001) but typically OECD meetings are low-key affairs passing off without the media comment, sabre rattling and general razzmatazz that accompany the IMF, WTO and the G8.

In short, the OECD is the forgotten institution of global governance. Given this minimal literature the next section sketches a framework for understanding the OECD's contribution to global governance before going on to suggest that despite its achievements and longevity changing circumstances are raising formidable obstacles to the OECD's operations. The chapter goes on to outline the OECD's response to these changes and assesses whether revamping relations with civil society and enlarging the membership are likely to prove the organization's salvation. The chapter concludes that the organization's reaction, though intuitively sensible, could be self-defeating and that a more radical overhaul may be needed to convince member governments that the OECD is worth retaining.

Global governance and the OECD

In theory, the role and purpose of the OECD is straightforward. Article 1 of the OECD Convention states:

the aims of the Organization ... shall be to promote policies designed:

- to achieve the highest sustainable economic growth and employment and a rising standard of living in Member countries, while maintaining financial stability, and thus to contribute to the development of the world economy;
- to contribute to sound economic expansion in Member as well as non-member countries in the process of economic development; and
- to contribute to the expansion of world trade on a multilateral, non-discriminatory basis in accordance with international obligations.

In support of these aims Members agree under Article 3 to:

- keep each other informed and furnish the Organization with the information necessary for the accomplishment of its tasks;
- consult together on a continuing basis, carry out studies and participate in agreed projects; and
- cooperate closely and where appropriate take co-ordinated action.

Thus, in theory, the OECD possesses a clear set of ends (promoting sustainable economic growth and development, raising standards of living and supporting the multilateral trading order) and a clear set of means (cooperative ventures between and among member countries). However, in practice things are much more complicated. First, the significance of the founding Convention lies not just in what it says but what it does not. Unlike other international organizations covered by this volume, the OECD is not accorded an exclusive or leading role in any policy domain. The OECD is normally one of many institutions active in a given area but it is unusual for the OECD to take the leading role. To borrow a musical analogy, the OECD is often a valuable member of the orchestra but rarely will it act as conductor. Second, the OECD has no formal powers or regulatory function. The question therefore arises as to how the OECD governs. There is an assumption that cooperation is a necessary and sufficient condition for achieving desired outcomes, but cooperation in international affairs is a variable and no clues are offered as to how the OECD promotes cooperative behaviour. The answer, in the majority of cases, is that cooperative activity is pursued through a labyrinth of committees composed of members of the OECD Secretariat and officials from national capitals. These committees perform many functions but arguably their most important is to afford senior bureaucrats an opportunity to network, exchange ideas and experiences and to better understand the policy challenges confronting states both individually and collectively.

The absence of formally transcribed powers and a precise functional domain combined with opaque internal processes have contributed to the OECD's reputation as a vague and disparate body with 'no widely agreed raison d'être, no clear purpose, few very precise commitments which governments were pledged to carry out, and no simple goals which commanded public understanding' (Camps 1975: 10, quoted in Woodward 2004: 114). Instead, the majority of authors satisfy themselves by applying imprecise soubriquets to the OECD describing it as a 'consultative forum' (Aubrey 1967: 102), a 'think tank' (*Financial Times* 2002), a 'rich man's' or 'rich country club' (Camps 1975: 10; Gilpin 2000: 184), 'a pool of statistical and economic expertise' (Sullivan 1997: 6), and a 'club of government economic analysts and forecasters' (Hutton 2002: 218). Each of these appellations touches upon aspects of the OECD's work but none of them provides a synoptic or comprehensive account of the organization's activities, particularly in respect of its role in global governance.

Exceptionally, Marcussen (2004) has suggested that the OECD's roles and responsibilities boil down to three interrelated modes of governance: the cognitive, legal and normative. This chapter suggests that, in addition, the OECD's has a fourth mode, 'palliative governance'. According to Marcussen (2004) the cognitive dimension of OECD governance refers to its ability to construct, sustain and propagate a common set of principles, viewpoints and discourses about global governance. Any state which is committed to maintaining a market economy and a pluralistic democracy is eligible to join the OECD. From the beginning the OECD 'symbolized a consensus about the superiority of capitalism and democracy as the organizing principles for global governance' (Woodward 2007b). At the time of the OECD's creation central planning and authoritarian rule loomed large as competing and seemingly viable alternatives to capitalist and democratic modes of governance. The intensification of the cold war made it imperative that there was a strong Atlantic economic community to underscore political and military alliances. Indeed the OECD is sometimes viewed as the 'economic counterpart to NATO' (OECD 2004a), a beacon of free markets and democracy to counteract the communist bloc. Moreover, whereas the OEEC had primarily been an inward looking organization concerned with the reconstruction of Europe, the OECD explicitly recognized the obligations of the industrialized countries of the North to the developing countries of the South. This sudden concern for developing nations may have been prompted by altruistic motives but it also reflected the realization that decolonization was creating new suitors for the rival superpowers. Though some European nations were initially ambivalent, or even hostile, to the decolonization process, the US in particular recognized that if development assistance was not forthcoming from the industrialized democracies of North America and Western Europe the void would be filled by the Soviet Union. Though the OECD does not disburse development assistance it does provide the Development Assistance Committee (DAC), a forum where the world's major bilateral aid donors could meet to review and coordinate aid policy with the objective of expanding the volume and effectiveness of official resource transfers to developing nations.

OECD members shared a vision about the fundamental principles which should underpin the architecture of global governance but they also recognized that the survival of the liberal democratic order demanded a robust framework of rules. '*Legal* governance', devising and disseminating international rules and standards, is the task for which the OECD is most renowned. Rules formulated at the OECD pervade almost every facet of global economic activity. The majority of OECD rules are concerned with esoteric matters. Most citizens in industrialized countries are unaware that the symbols on the sides of tankers carrying volatile chemical substances will be conforming to the OECD's Globally Harmonized System for the Classification and Labelling of Hazardous Chemicals, that the trade in agricultural seeds is governed by the OECD Scheme for Seed Certification, or that the companies in which they hold shares should conform to the Principles of Corporate Governance. Though they do not command broad public understanding, OECD standards penetrate everyday life and are highly regarded by specialists working in these areas (OECD 2004a: 18–19).

However, there are a number of caveats to the OECD's function as a legal governor. First, the OECD is hardly a prolific legislator. By April 2006 it had only passed 189 Acts, fewer than five per annum. Moreover, though the OECD has legislated in a vast number of areas most are concentrated into environmental standards (accounting for one-third of OECD Acts), fiscal affairs and international investment (see Woodward 2004: 116). Second, *only* those OECD Acts described as Decisions and Conventions are legally binding and then *only* on OECD members. Only thirty-six of the Acts passed by the OECD fall into these categories. In addition, the OECD also has no sanctions to punish disobedient members and therefore compliance depends predominantly on 'soft' mechanisms including moral suasion exerted through ongoing surveillance and periodic peer review. Third, that OECD rules apply only to members places restrictions on the geographical scope of the OECD's authority. Non-member states can voluntarily submit to OECD regulations and are expected to abide by them as if they were full members. The OECD Guidelines on Multinational Enterprises have been ratified by Argentina, Brazil, Chile, Estonia, Latvia, Lithuania and Slovenia while Argentina, Brazil, Bulgaria, Chile and Slovenia are signatories to the OECD Convention on Combating Bribery of Foreign Public Officials in International Business Transactions. However, as the ill-fated Harmful Tax Competition initiative vividly demonstrated, the OECD 'lacks the legitimacy and legal authority to forcibly make non-members party to its rules' (Woodward 2007b).

The ability of the OECD to secure compliance through 'soft' and informal mechanisms underscores the notion of *normative* governance. Normative governance 'refers to the formation and dissemination of key ideas and expected standards of behaviour resulting from repeated social interactions in OECD committees and working groups' (Woodward 2007b following Marcussen 2004). Countries adhere to the demands of the OECD because they feel it is a policy they *ought* to pursue if for no other reason than to avoid the damage to their reputation among their peers.

Finally, *palliative* governance refers to the organization's capacity to lubricate the processes of global governance by acting as a caucusing group for industrialized states, nudging the global policy agenda, providing analytical expertise to other international institutions and generating rules and norms for emergent or neglected areas of concern. The OECD 'has proved especially adept at concocting benchmarks for emerging issues and problems and has often been the progenitor of what later came to be seen as conventional wisdom' (Woodward 2007b). For example, in 1972 the Report of the OECD's High Level Group on Trade and Related Problems (the 'Rey Group') was the first public document to deploy the term 'trade in services' (Cohn 2002: 159). The Group's pioneering work in this field later became the basis for progress during the Tokyo and Uruguay trade rounds. The OECD is still engaged in trailblazing research and rule-making to solve emergent problems. Recent developments include guidelines to promote online security, deterring unsolicited e-mail, plus the development of codes of practice to govern the handling and licensing of human genetic data.

The OECD's other palliative function is to reinforce and further the work being undertaken in other international fora, chiefly the WTO (Cohn 2002) and the Group of 7/8 family (Ougaard 2004). As Marcussen (2001) has observed, 'an international organization may be important, not for what it "does" in legalistic terms, but for what it helps other organizations do and for what it helps its own members accomplish outside', so it is for the OECD. The OECD undertakes the discreet, behind the scenes tasks that sustain the impetus between the meetings of other institutions of global governance. Fittingly, Nicholas Bayne (1987: 30), a former UK Permanent Representative to the OECD, has characterized the organization as 'something of a Cinderella... it does not always go to the balls like its grander sister organizations, though it often runs up their dresses and sometimes clears up the mess after the party'. Every year the OECD publishes more than 250 books and 40 databases, and is widely seen as an 'authoritative source of independent data' (Salzman 2000). Thus, the OECD is responsible for 'much of the statistical information and analytical muscle essential to the work of other international bodies' (Woodward 2007b). For instance, the WTO Secretariat employs only 630 bureaucrats and can hardly be expected to resolve the multifarious and intricate conundrums of global trade governance. Consequently, in areas such as agricultural trade, export credits and competition policy the WTO's work relies heavily on the analysis and expertise provided by the OECD. For example, Cohn (2002: 182–5) outlines how analytical and conceptual work undertaken in the OECD regarding the measurement of agricultural subsidies helped to diffuse tensions between the US and the European Union (EU) paving the way for the successful completion of the Uruguay Round of trade negotiations. Though it is beyond the scope of this chapter, an interesting question to be addressed by future research is *why* OECD data is viewed credibly by so many actors (see Woodward 2007a). Despite the mushrooming of G7 institutions and the topics they cover, there has been a general reticence to introduce anything approximating a G7 Secretariat. The result is a qualitative and quantitative expansion in the G7's reliance on the OECD. Between 1975 and 1999 the G7 Communiqués contained some sixty-four references to the work of the OECD. The majority of these (forty-one) occurred between 1990 and 1999. Moreover, in the 1990s the G7 increasingly looked towards the OECD to pursue initiatives on its behalf. On fifteen separate occasions the G7 pledged to commence cooperative activity within the OECD or encouraged the OECD to investigate a specific problem (Ougaard 2004: 78–80). The increasingly institutionalised relationship between the G7 and the OECD, culminating in 2000 with the appointment of Japanese Ambassador Kondō Seiichi as an official go-between for the two bodies, has contributed to a growing perception that the OECD is the *de facto* G7 Secretariat.

The OECD also supports the work of other bodies by acting as a 'pre-negotiating forum' (Cohn 2002) and 'caucusing group' (Murphy 2001) for advanced industrialized countries. Discussions at the OECD have allowed advanced industrialized countries to thrash out agreements on some of the more intractable problems of global governance. The example of agricultural subsidies referred to earlier is a good case in point. The analytical evidence would have been redundant without political momentum to ensure that agriculture would become subject to world trade law. It was in discussions at the OECD that countries finally acknowledged the distortions introduced into global agricultural markets by national agricultural policies and that as such these policies should be covered under the auspices of the General Agreement on Tariffs and Trade (GATT) (Cohn 2002: 183). For the purposes of debate and seeking consensus the OECD carries a number of advantages over other international organizations. As the chapter has already argued, OECD membership encompasses a shared vision about what the world ought to look like and so it is not hampered by the need to reconcile incompatible visions of global governance. States also tend to be more flexible in the OECD context because the discussions are in private and their outcomes are non-binding. Publicly states may be deterred from compromising for fear that it may be interpreted as a sign of weakness but in private may be more willing to concede ground. In terms of the second element, the non-binding nature of the agreements reached, the OECD is primarily a deliberative rather than distributional body. That is to say, talks at the OECD are aimed primarily at exploring the issue, consulting with like-minded countries and seeking a consensus on a suitable way forward rather than seeking to reach a decision that will apportion costs and benefits to the participants (Aubrey 1967). As soon as bargaining and final negotiation about the distribution of costs and benefits assume a greater prominence national positions tend to become more entrenched and agreement more difficult to reach. Unless the discussions yield an OECD decision, the agreements reached have the status of a 'gentlemen's agreement' and are subject only to the soft law procedures available to the institution's members. As a consequence, countries will sometimes be more willing to discuss matters in the less formal deliberative setting of the OECD than in more formalized settings. Countries that resisted the inclusion of the 'Singapore issues' (investment, competition policy and government procurement) at the WTO Ministerial Meeting in Cancun, for instance, have quite happily participated in discussions on these matters at the OECD.

Challenges for the OECD

The OECD (1997, 2003) acknowledges that it faces growing challenges resulting from intensified institutional competition, geo-political and economic upheaval and high profile policy failures.

The elasticity of the OECD's mission has unquestionably contributed to its durability as a mechanism of global governance. The organization perpetually refurbishes its portfolio of responsibilities to meet the exigencies both of its members and its fellow institutions of global governance. Equally, the absence of a specific purpose is a major source of vulnerability for the OECD because its functions can be appropriated or replicated by other institutions. A 'gaggle of Gs' (G8, G20 and so on) (Culpeper 2000), a rejuvenated EU (to which 19 of the OECD's 30 members will shortly belong), a proliferation of think tanks and international meetings such as the World Economic Forum, and private sector structures of authority (Julin 2003) have all emerged as competitors to the OECD. In one sense this matters little. Many of these institutions are proponents, at least at a rhetorical level, of the market friendly and pro-democracy stance championed at and by the organization and as such do not directly challenge the cognitive dimension of OECD governance. However, the legal and normative elements of OECD governance are more seriously impaired. The OECD's standards and codes must clamour for recognition alongside those developed by other bodies. More seriously, from the OECD's perspective, many bodies have identified the promise of 'soft' approaches to enforcement and are now impersonating them. The OECD can coexist with these new institutions; indeed they can open up new avenues of activity, as has been the case with the G7. Nevertheless, together these developments have eroded the distinctiveness of the OECD and have begun to constrict the arenas in which it is the accepted governor.

Changing geo-political circumstances pose a second clutch of challenges to the OECD. The end of the cold war and the collapse of European communism signalled the triumph of capitalist and democratic values being upheld by the OECD, but paradoxically led to something of an identity crisis within the organization. With the removal of the 'other' against which the OECD had aligned itself, some began to question what the organization was for. In addition, less spectacular changes to the global political and economic map were also taking place. In the 1960s the OECD could rightfully claim that:

> as the most inclusive grouping of industrialized countries...the OECD marshals some formidable and unique capabilities. Here, among its members, is the most massive accumulation of savings available for investment not

only at home but potentially in the rest of the world. Its members control all the key currencies, too. Thus, by way of capital supply, exchange availabilities, financial expertise, the group represents an unmatched capacity for capital exports. Since goods and funds go together in many guises, the OECD membership weighs heavily in the three spheres of world production, trade and finance.

(Aubrey 1967: 97)

At the turn of the twenty-first century OECD countries still collectively account for 59 per cent of the world's Gross National Income, 75 per cent of global trade, 95 per cent of official development assistance, 51 per cent of carbon dioxide emissions and consume 52 per cent of the world's energy (OECD 2005: 6). However, the global significance of OECD economies has waned and with the rapid growth of economies such as China and India this trend seems set to accelerate. This will undermine the legal and palliative domains of OECD governance. As the chapter has already stated, the OECD has previously been a forum for industrialized countries to seek consensus on the more insoluble problems of global governance. The organization was an eminently sensible choice at a time when the majority of globally significant economies belonged to the institution. There are still many areas, such as the steel and shipbuilding industries, where OECD countries continue to dominate and where it is a reasonable forum for discussion. Elsewhere the continuing absence of China, Russia, the majority of the newly industrialized countries of East Asia and large industrial economies of Latin America, such as Brazil and Argentina, has devalued the OECD's role as a preparatory venue for industrialized states. A second problem for the OECD is a lack of legitimacy. OECD countries still dominate the economic landscape but they are home to only 18 per cent of the world's population (OECD 2005: 6). The OECD likes to think of itself as a setter of *global* standards. However, many nonmember states are suspicious of the organization and its motives and have, most conspicuously with the harmful tax competition (HTC) initiative, vehemently opposed moves by the OECD to unilaterally impose its rules upon them.

Finally, the image of the OECD has been dented by the failure of flagship policies, most notably the Multilateral Agreement on Investment (MAI) in 1998. The MAI was intended as a blueprint for the governance of foreign investment. From the outset the MAI was bedevilled by controversy. OECD countries including France and the US opposed the agreement because they wanted greater latitude to protect certain industry sectors. Non-OECD members felt no compunction to become signatories to an agreement over whose design they had had no control. Finally, civil society groups maintained that the MAI prioritized the rights of investors paying insufficient attention to impact of foreign investment on labour and the environment (Rugman 1998). While the embers of the MAI fiasco were still being raked over the OECD quietly launched its HTC initiative designed to diminish tax avoidance by forcing member and non-member states to eradicate the opacity of their financial systems and exchange information about nonresidents investors. Non-member states (but not member states) which failed to make the necessary adjustments would be placed on a list of uncooperative tax havens and would be liable to countermeasures from OECD members. As with the MAI, the OECD encountered virulent resistance both from its own members and from outside. OECD members Luxembourg and Switzerland abstained from the HTC citing their refusal to accede to any agreement aimed at diluting banking secrecy. In 2000, the HTC fell victim of the 'tax and regulatory bonfire' (Hutton 2002) in the aftermath of George W. Bush's election to the White House. Opposition from outside the OECD originated from the many small jurisdictions being targeted by the HTC whose economies were heavily dependent on revenue generated by off-shore financial activities and an 'unholy alliance of libertarian think tanks, big business and those campaigning on developmental issues' (Woodward 2005: 208). The MAI and HTC initiatives laid bare the limitations of the OECD and its future contribution to global governance. Not only had it failed to apply its standards beyond its own restricted membership but it has been debilitated by the inability of its own members to reach a consensus. The result is 'diminished interest in capitals to make use of the OECD as a practical means to bring about institutional and policy change' (OECD 2004b: 7).

OECD reform

In 1996 Donald Johnston became Secretary General of the OECD. Johnston, a Canadian who occupied a number of senior ministerial positions in Pierre Trudeau's government in the early 1980s and a lawyer by profession, instantly recognized that reasserting the OECD's authority and legitimacy and securing its position in the architecture of global governance would necessitate serious reform. In the same year the OECD's Annual Ministerial Meeting called on the organization to 'accelerate the process of structural change ... with a view to further enhancing the relevance, efficiency and effectiveness of the Organization' (OECD 1996). Much of the initial reform programme consisted of minor tinker-ing with the committee system, reforms to the financial and budgetary systems, and instituting more scientific, output-oriented management techniques (OECD 2003). These reforms did not address the problems of legitimacy, intensified com-petition and the organization's tarnished image that had led to the initial calls for reform. Johnston thus endorsed a bolder set of more substantive reforms which would involve the expansion of OECD membership and the fortifying of relations with non-members and civil society.

Since 1961 membership of the OECD has expanded numerically (from 19 to 30) and geographically (now encompassing members from all but the African continent) (see Table 3.2). However, the process of OECD enlargement has been largely driven by the exigencies of US foreign policy resulting in an organization whose composition 'owes more to history than logic' (Bayne 1987: 27). In November 2002 the OECD assembled a 'Working Group on the Enlargement Strategy and Outreach' under the chairmanship of the Japanese Ambassador to the OECD, Noboru Seiichirō. This body was mandated to evaluate the effects of enlargement on the personality of the OECD and its working methods. The Working Group's

Table 3.2 Membership of the OECD (progressive)

Country	Date of ratification of OECD Convention
Canada	10 April 1961
United States	12 April 1961
United Kingdom	2 May 1961
Denmark	30 May 1961
Iceland	5 June 1961
Norway	4 July 1961
Turkey	2 August 1961
Spain	3 August 1961
Portugal	4 August 1961
France	7 August 1961
Ireland	17 August 1961
Belgium	13 September 1961
Greece	27 September 1961
Germany	27 September 1961
Switzerland	28 September 1961
Sweden	28 September 1961
Austria	29 September 1961
Netherlands	13 November 1961
Luxembourg	7 December 1961
Italy	29 March 1962
Japan	28 April 1964
Finland	28 January 1969
Australia	7 June 1971
New Zealand	29 May 1973
Mexico	18 May 1994
Czech Republic	21 December 1995
Hungary	7 May 1996
Poland	22 November 1996
South Korea	12 December 1996
Slovak Republic	14 December 2000

Source: OECD (2004c).

findings were published in a report entitled *A Strategy for Enlargement and Outreach* (OECD 2004b) which was endorsed by Annual Ministerial Meeting in May 2004. The Working Group concluded that there was a robust case for the enlargement of the OECD and discovered that there was a baseline agreement among member states about suitable benchmarks to gauge prospective members and how the accession process ought to be managed. Enlargement must be 'innovative and strategically selective' (OECD 2004b: 14) and prospective members must be 'like-minded' and 'significant players' (OECD 2004b: 16) in order that they would supplement both the quality of the OECD's work and promote its world-wide influence. The report also specified that many delegations wish to see an upper limit of somewhere between 40 and 45 members so as not to impair the efficiency of the OECD. Nonetheless, the report also revealed considerable divergence in the positions of different national delegations on issues surrounding modifications to decision-making procedures in the light of expanded membership and how an enlarged OECD would be funded.

The case for increased membership can be interpreted through the four modes of governance previously specified. The OECD would retain 'fundamental concepts like market-based economy and democratic principles' (OECD 2004b: 16) as key yardsticks for gauging any fresh member. In addition, legal governance would be enhanced by incorporating a greater proportion of economic production and the global population, broadening the legitimate applicability of OECD rules and standards. The prospects for normative governance look promising with new members bringing different perspectives hopefully sparking vigorous debates in OECD committees leading to novel solutions to existing and future problems. Finally, all of these things would underpin the OECD's palliative function. An expanded and revitalized OECD might once again emerge as the forum of choice for debate, analysis and expertise by industrialized countries and leading international organizations.

Undoubtedly, OECD enlargement will bestow some of the advantages forecast by the Working Group. That said, there are reasons to believe that the Working Group is overly optimistic and there are considerable risks associated with the enlargement strategy. Hitherto the efficacy of the OECD has hinged on it being a small, tightly knit alliance operating on a consensual basis. The architects of the enlargement strategy believe that the cognitive dimension of governance can be protected by their insistence that new members will be expected to extol the virtues of free markets and democracy. Nevertheless, the 'importation of significant numbers of new members still threatens to dilute this consensus resulting in the ossification and paralysis which plague more universally based international organizations' (Woodward 2007b). Moreover, the OECD's palliative, normative and legal function requires an efficient committee structure. New members seem almost certain to result in a prolonged and ungainly decision-making system negating the improvements resulting from the restructuring of the committee system. Thus far the Working Group has acknowledged these concerns but has offered little in the way of a solution to them. The price of inclusivity may prove to be inflexibility.

There are also more practical issues to be overcome. The OECD maintains that sixteen states have articulated an interest in joining the organization (OECD 2004b: 7) which would bring membership to the sort of figure being proposed by most national delegations. However, the danger is that this is the first step on the route to becoming a universal institution. The likelihood is that in 5, 10 or 15 years time the shifting sands of the global economy may well unearth a new group of economies deserving of membership. Unless the OECD is willing to jettison some of its declining members it will quickly become a more universalist institution undermining the uniqueness which the OECD claims lies at the heart of its comparative advantage, saddling it with the difficulties that have paralysed bodies such as the UN but without the coercive powers to resolve the tensions. With the exception of Russia, the OECD has never openly stated which states have expressed an interest in membership. However, it seems reasonable to speculate that to meet the objectives of its reforms the OECD would wish to incorporate what it calls the 'Big Six' (*Financial Times* 2003) systemically significant economies (Russia, India, China, Brazil, South Africa and Indonesia) currently lying outside the OECD alliance. At present the accession of any of these countries is problematic. China, and to a lesser degree Russia and Indonesia, would fall foul of the democratic requirements of OECD membership. India, the world's largest democracy with a growing reputation for its pro-market stance, would need to dismantle capital controls to comply with the OECD Codes on Liberalization, something it is reluctant to do. Finally, South Africa's atrocious human rights record and the ongoing tribulations of the Brazilian economy seem set to preclude their accession for the foreseeable future. As before there is a trade-off for the OECD. If the OECD wishes to re-establish its position in global governance it must admit these economies, but in so doing the like-mindedness that has been one of the organization's greatest strengths will inevitably be undermined.

Finally, there are the financial repercussions of expansion. Currently, 80 per cent of the OECD's official budget is contributed by G7 countries while just two countries, Japan and the US, provide half of the OECD's funds (see Chapter 4; Woodward 2004: 123). It might be argued that extending the membership could be an opportunity to reduce the burden on G7 countries but the probability is that the burden will increase. Already the OECD budget is stretched to bursting point and it 'has come to rely heavily on voluntary contributions to accomplish its work programme' (OECD 2003: 7). Indeed of the OECD's 227.7 million euro budget in 2002, 17.7 per cent came from voluntary contributions compared with 6.3 per cent in 1995 (figures derived from OECD 2004a: 29). The costs of surveys, surveillance and peer review means that every new member adds around one per cent to the OECD's expenditure (*Financial Times* 2003) putting further stress on an already tight budgetary situation.

The second major strand of the OECD's strategy is to extend its ties with civil society. Unlike some of the institutions covered by this volume the OECD has a long-standing commitment to consulting key stakeholders. This has been achieved primarily through the Business and Industry Advisory Committee (BIAC) and the Trade Union Advisory Committee (TUAC), both formally designated by the OECD Council in 1962, as mechanisms whereby business and trades unions could have a direct input into OECD work. The widespread opposition to the MAI orchestrated by civil society groups convinced the OECD that these arteries of communication should be widened. The 1999 Annual Ministerial Communiqué noted that the 'political, economic and social challenges of the next century require informed and actively participating citizens' and 'looked to the Organization to assist governments in the important task of improving communication and consultation with civil society' (OECD 1999).

Since this clarion call the OECD has worked feverishly to increase levels of informal communication, promote collaborative analytical work, regularize consultation and occasionally employing the expertise of groups to assist in the monitoring of OECD rules (OECD Policy Brief 2002). The modernization of

OECD procedures has also been accompanied by substantive innovations, most notably the instigation in 2000 of the OECD Annual Forum. The Annual Forum allows ministers, heads of government, international organizations, civil servants and representatives of business and NGOs 'to impart and share information, improve communication, and foster a climate of enlightened policy making' (OECD Observer 1999). The Forum is organized around a central theme and is timed to coincide with the Annual Ministerial Meeting. The Forum is proving increasingly popular. Since the inaugural meeting event in 2000 on the topic of 'Partnerships in the New Economy' the Annual Forums have attracted more than 6000 delegates from nearly ninety countries.

The OECD has made a number of bullish assessments about the Forum with Donald Johnston referring to it as a 'landmark in the life of the organization' (quoted in Woodward 2004: 120). Again there is a belief that connecting with a broader audience will confer legitimacy on OECD decisions and that it will introduce new perspectives enhancing the normative aspects of OECD governance. So far, however, these reforms have not lived up to expectations. The Forum has succeeded in attracting participants from all over the world but the majority of delegates are drawn from among OECD countries. Figures for the 2002 Forum show that almost three-quarters of delegates were deputed from ten OECD countries (Woodward 2004: 120). This bias is even more pronounced among those who get to make presentations at the Forum. Since 2000, 716 presentations have been made at the Annual Forum of which just under 90 per cent were made by speakers hailing from OECD countries (see Table 3.3) while there have been only thirteen speeches made by representatives of African nations. Furthermore, it is noticeable that the pressure groups who attend are worthy, but nevertheless mainstream, organizations such as ATTAC, Oxfam and Médecins Sans Frontières. While the OECD cannot be held responsible for the non-attendance of more radical groups it does undermine the contention that they are listening to a greater diversity of voices. The opinion of these groups is also likely to be drowned out by the large commercial interests whose delegates outnumber them and who sponsor the event. Theoretically, the Forum provides a conduit for alternative opinions to reach the ears of OECD ministers and bureaucrats but in practice it has become a pedestal from which to rehearse tired arguments about the promise of market forces as a panacea for global governance.

Table 3.3 Breakdown of speakers by country of origin at the OECD Forum 2000–5

Speakers	2000	2001	2002	2003	2004	2005	Total	%
From OECD members	92	112	137	107	95	96	639	89.2
From non-OECD high/middle income countries	12	9	14	3	7	13	58	8.1
From non-OECD low income countries	4	6	3	1	0	5	19	2.7
Total	108	127	154	111	102	114	716	100

Conclusion

The world at the turn of the twenty-first century is almost unrecognizable from that into which the OECD was born in 1961. The roles played by the OECD in global governance are indispensable but there is a gathering feeling that it might not be the right agency to undertake them. Changing geo-political realities, intensified institutional competition and high profile policy failures have combined to undermine both the ability and suitability of the OECD to execute the functions of governance for which it was conceived. Faced with the prospect of becoming a marginal player in the architecture of global governance the OECD sought to enhance its appeal by streamlining its internal organization, proposals to expand the membership and reaching out to civil society. This chapter has argued that these are sensible, admirable and crucial responses to the criticisms made of the OECD but that the strategy appears beset with contradictions which may ultimately prove self-defeating. In particular, the OECD seems to have placed excessive emphasis on dealing with the issue of the legitimacy of its legal governance but the fallout from these changes could undermine the normative and cognitive dimensions on which its legal governance depends. The strategy of inclusiveness is commendable but it raises the spectre of inflexibility.

This said, it is difficult to envisage a world without the OECD and most leading states accept that an OECD-type body is worth retaining. In this regard there are a number of aspects of the OECD which need to be addressed by future research. First, there are the more practical, policy-oriented debates that have formed the basis of this chapter surrounding the future of the OECD as an organ of global governance. Though this chapter is somewhat downbeat about the OECD's prospects it is possible to be more positive. For example, a number of commentators have championed the cause of the Group of 20 (G20) as a long-term replacement for the G8 because its greater inclusivity will accord it greater legitimacy than the G8 and enable it to tackle the growing number of problems emanating from outside the G8 polities (Bradford and Linn 2004; Slaughter 2004). These analyses are presented as though the OECD does not exist. The purported advantages of the G20 apply equally if not more so to the OECD, particularly a reformed OECD, which has a track record of managing interdependence and has an effective committee system, expert bureaucracy and decision-making system already in place (Woodward 2007b). Second, this chapter is exclusively concerned with *how* the OECD governs. It has assumed the OECD is imbued with power and/or authority and the primary task is to identify and understand the dimensions through which it is exercised. However, there is need to go back one stage further and to identify the *sources* of the OECD's power and authority; to ask *why* the OECD is able to govern and *why* it is this enigmatic institution that is allowed to govern behaviour and determine outcomes in the nascent global economy.

References

Aubrey, Henry G. (1967) *Atlantic Economic Cooperation: The Case of the OECD*, New York: Frederick A. Praeger.

Bayne, Nicholas (1987) 'Making sense of western economic policies: the role of the OECD', *World Today* 43, 2: 27–30.

Blair, David J. (1993) *Trade Negotiations in the OECD: Structures, Institutions and States*, London: Kegan Paul International.

Bradford, Colin I. and Linn, Johannes F. (2004) 'Global economic governance at a crossroads: replacing the G7 with the G20', *The Brookings Institution Policy Brief* 131.

Camps, Miriam (1975) *'First World' Relationships: the role of the OECD*, Council Papers on International Affairs: 5, Paris: The Atlantic Institute for International Affairs.

Cohn, Theodore H. (2002) *Governing Global Trade: International Institutions in Conflict and Convergence*, Aldershot: Ashgate.

Cooper, Richard N. (1968) *The Economics of Interdependence: Economic Policy in the Atlantic Community*, New York: McGraw Hill.

Culpeper, Roy (2000) 'Systemic reform at a standstill: a flock of "Gs" in search of global financial stability'. Available online at: http://www.g8.utoronto.ca/scholar/culpeper 2000/index.html, accessed on 20 May 2005.

Financial Times (2002) 'OECD fails to put its own house in order', 28 May: 9.

—— (2003) 'Navigating the OECD "supertanker" ', 3 March: 13.

Gardner, Hall and Stefanova, Radoslava (eds) (2001) *The New Transatlantic Agenda: Facing the Challenges of Global Governance*, Ashgate: Aldershot.

Gilpin, Robert (2000) *The Challenge of Global Capitalism: The World Economy in the 21st Century*, Princeton, NJ: Princeton University Press.

Held, David, McGrew, Anthony, Goldblatt, David and Perraton, Jonathan (1999) *Global Transformations: Politics, Economics and Culture*, Cambridge: Polity.

Hutton, Will (2002) *The World We're In*, London: Little Brown.

Marcussen, Martin (2001) 'The OECD in search of a role: playing the idea game', *Paper presented at the European Consortium for Political Research (ECPR), 29th Joint Sessions*, Grenoble, France, 6–11 April.

—— (2004) 'OECD governance through soft law', in Ulrika Mörth (ed.) *Soft Law in Governance and Regulation: An Interdisciplinary Analysis*, Cheltenham: Edward Elgar.

May, Bernhard (2001) 'New challenges for transatlantic economic relations', in Hall Gardner and Radoslava Stefanova (eds) *The New Transatlantic Governance: Facing the Challenges of Global Governance*, Ashgate: Aldershot, pp. 173–90.

Murphy, Craig N. (2001) 'Organization for economic cooperation and development', in Joel Kreiger (ed.) *The Oxford Companion to the Politics of the World*, Oxford: Oxford University Press, pp. 618–19.

Nye, Joseph S. (2002) *The Paradox of American Power: Why the World's only Superpower Can't go it Alone*, Oxford: Oxford University Press.

OECD (1971) *OECD: History, Aims, Structure*, Paris: OECD.

—— (1996) *Meeting of the Council at Ministerial Level Paris, 21–22 May 1996*. Available online at: http://www.g7.utoronto.ca/oecd/oecd96.htm accessed on 20 May 2005.

—— (1997) *The OECD: Challenges and Strategic Objectives: 1997: Note by the Secretary General*, C(97)180, Pairs: OECD.

—— (1999) *Meeting of the Council at Ministerial Level Paris, 26–27 May 1999*. Available online at: http://www.g7.utoronto.ca/oecd/oecd99.htm accessed on 20 May 2005.

—— (2003) *Reform and Modernization of the OECD*, C/MIN (2003) 6, Paris: OECD.

—— (2004a) *Getting to Grips with Globalization: The OECD in a Changing World*, Paris: OECD.

—— (2004b) *A Strategy for Enlargement and Outreach: Report by the Chair of the Heads of Delegation Working Group on the Enlargement Strategy and Outreach, Ambassador Seiichirō Noboru*, Paris: OECD.

—— (2005) *OECD Annual Report 2005*, Paris: OECD.

OECD Observer (1999) 'Announcing OECD Forum 2000'. Available online at: http://www.oecdobserver.org/news/archivestory.php/aid/167/Announcing_OECD_Forum_2000.html, accessed on 23 August 2003.

OECD Policy Brief (2002) *Civil Society and the OECD – November 2002 Update*, Paris: OECD.

Ougaard, Morten (2004) *Political Globalization: State, Power and Social Forces*, Basingstoke: Palgrave.

Pollack, Mark A. and Shaffer, Gregory C. (eds) (2001) *Transatlantic Governance in the Global Economy*, Lanham, MD: Rowman & Littlefield.

Rugman, Alan (1998) 'The political economy of the multilateral agreement on investment'. Available online at: http://www.g7.utoronto.ca/annual/rugman1998/index.html, accessed on 20 May 2005.

Salzman, James (2000) 'Labour rights, globalization and institutions: the role and influence of the Organization for Economic Cooperation and Development', *Michigan Journal of International Law*, 21: 769–848.

Slaughter, Anne-Marie (2004) 'Disaggregated sovereignty: towards the public account-ability of global government networks', *Government and Opposition* 39, 2: 159–90.

Sullivan, Scott (1997) *From War to Wealth: Fifty Years of Innovation*, Paris: OECD.

Woodward, Richard (2004) 'The organization for economic cooperation and development', *New Political Economy* 9, 1: 113–27.

—— (2005) 'Offshore or "shorn off"? The OECD's harmful tax competition initiative and development in small island economies', in Graham Harrison (ed.) *Global Encounters: International Political Economy, Development and Globalization*, Basingstoke: Palgrave, pp. 195–212.

—— (2007a) *The Organization for Economic Cooperation and Development*, London: Routledge.

—— (2007b) 'The OECD: meeting the challenges of the 21st century', in Simon Lee and Stephen McBride (eds) *Neo-liberalism, State Power and Global Governance*, New York: Kluwer.

—— (2007c) 'Right idea, wrong institution: why the OECD and not the G20 should replace the G8', *Centre for Democratic Governance Working Paper*, Department of Politics and International Relations, University of Hull.

4 Global governance, Japan and the Organization for Economic Cooperation and Development

Amiya-Nakada Ryōsuke

Introduction

Among the various international organizations dealt with in this book, the Organization for Economic Cooperation and Development (OECD) occupies a unique position. It has neither the decision-making competences nor economic capacity to achieve specific policy objectives. Rather, it is often described as a 'club', a 'forum' or a 'think-tank'. Moreover, its true singularity lies in the fact that the OECD itself does not strive to acquire 'decision-making' capacity and finds its identity in being 'soft'. Therefore, in contrast to its presence, the OECD is one of the least frequently studied international organizations. On the one hand, Realists find no reason to pay attention to such a 'powerless' organization, while on the other hand, its club-like character (exclusiveness, informality and even secrecy) and intergovernmental nature discourage the Constructivists who are generally more interested in such fields as human rights where the topic is universal and non-governmental organizations (NGOs) or 'civil society' have some say.[1]

Given its softness and invisibility, and faced with a lacuna in its study, this chapter limits itself to providing an overview on the relationship between Japan and the OECD. The aim of the chapter is to illuminate some aspects of Japan–OECD relations and changes over time. These aspects include:

- Japan's contribution to the OECD in terms of personnel and budget;
- Japan's perception of the OECD and change in the organization; and
- the impact of the OECD recommendations on Japan's domestic politics.

The chapter contends that a section of the Japanese bureaucracy gives due attention to the organization and has despatched competent officials to its offices. In fact, Japan has occupied the structurally unique position of a non-Western member and generous donor of development aid. But, at the same time, the chapter also stresses the inherent limit to Japanese proactivism in the OECD.

The argument proceeds in the following manner. In the following section, the Japanese accession process to the OECD is briefly reviewed. Then, in the third section, the role played by the Japanese delegation in the OECD is analysed. Here, the basic contention is that the OECD is regarded as an important forum by the multilateralists in the Japanese Ministry of Foreign Affairs (MOFA). In the fourth section, the changing perception of the OECD among the Japanese public, especially that of politicians and the media, is analysed. Although it may be expected that the increasing importance of multilateral organizations would be reflected in more frequent references to the OECD, and despite the recognition of its importance by some bureaucrats, public recourse to the OECD reports has been in decline. In the conclusion, the chapter relates this paradoxical finding to a broader issue, namely, Japanese perception and understanding of international relations in general.

Japanese accession to the OECD

Japan joined the OECD in April 1964. Prior to its admission, Japan had already been invited to the first meeting of the Development Aid Group in March 1960, which was set up in the reorganization process of the Organization for European Economic Cooperation, the forerunner of the OECD. In fact, the US government was said to have intended to involve Japan during the reorganization, but there was disagreement between the US-led group and some European states like Switzerland over the characteristics of the new organization, its scope of activities and its regional character. The former, including the US, the UK and France, saw the prime objective of the new organization in the provision of development aid, while the latter insisted on the continued importance of trade affairs in the new organization and its regional character as being transatlantic. As a result of compromise between the two groups, Japanese participation was not on the agenda at that time.

Nevertheless, the Japanese government dispatched its Foreign Minister to the first Ministerial Council of the OECD in November 1961 to participate in the discussion of developmental aid, demonstrating the Japanese government's interest in the OECD. In the summer of 1961, the Japanese government consulted the OECD-bureau and the British, West German and French governments on Japanese participation. However, there was the concern that Japanese accession might induce a wave of applications from other non-member countries like Australia and New Zealand, which might lead to the paralysis of the new organization. Therefore, Japan's first consultation bore little fruit.

In the autumn of 1962, Prime Minister Ikeda Hayato visited several European states. This time, backed by the US, Japan's planned accession was generally welcomed as it was already clear that other potential candidates had no intention of applying for membership. In November 1962, the US and the UK proposed Japanese accession in the Council meeting of the OECD, which led to negotiations between the OECD and the Japanese government.

On the Japanese side, MOFA was positive from the beginning. But the Ministry of Trade and Industry was deeply, concerned about the effect of liberalization measures on Japanese industry, especially on small- and medium-sized enterprises. In actual fact, the negotiations conducted in the first half of 1963 were intense. Among the main problems were liberalization of capital mobility and shipping;

as a result, the postponement of accession was even suggested. Nevertheless, in 1963 negotiations proceeded and the memorandum was signed on 26 July of that year.

The Japanese government and the OECD: roles and perceptions

Japanese influence in the OECD in figures

The Japanese have been a silent participant in the OECD since accession in 1964 and were said to 'spen[d] their years baffling their colleagues with their apparent reserve, even with passivity. According to the old-timers, delegations from Tokyo sat through day-long meetings in utter silence, busily taking notes' (Sullivan 1997: 60).

However, recently the Japanese have been assuming more active roles. At the time of accession, Japan paid only 7 per cent of the OECD budget, while the US paid 25 per cent and Germany 14 per cent. Now Japan is the second largest contributor to the OECD with a contribution that amounts to 23.128 per cent of the budget (2003), following the US (24.975 per cent) and far exceeding major European countries (Germany: 9.467 per cent; UK: 6.885 per cent; and France: 6.382 per cent). This figure, which exceeds the 19.5 per cent to the UN and 10.1 per cent to the International Monetary Fund (IMF), is the highest among Japanese contributions to the major international organizations.

In contrast to its contribution to the budget, the number of Japanese staff working in the OECD is still low. The number of Japanese staff in the late 1970s was more than twenty (Fujiwara 1978), a figure that has since increased to sixty-nine by 2003 but which still amounts to just 3 per cent of the whole staff (MOFA 2003). Yet, it must be added that 1 of the 4 Deputy Secretaries-General has been Japanese since 1990, which may reflect the consolidation of Japan's presence in the OECD.

In the intergovernmental arena, the presence of the Japanese delegation is more prominent. According to the On-Line Guide to OECD Intergovernmental Activity, the OECD bodies chaired by Japanese nationals comprise only 3.3 per cent (6 out of 184), but when we add the number of vice-chairs, Japanese share amounts to 8.6 per cent (52 out of 603), which ranks third following the US (10.9 per cent) and Canada (10.6 per cent), but exceeding France (7.0 per cent), the UK (6.0 per cent) and Germany (4.6 per cent).

The OECD as an important forum for MOFA's multilateralists

One way of gauging the importance attached to the OECD by the Japanese government is to analyse who has been sent to the OECD (see Tables 4.1, 4.2 and 4.3). Judging from the career path, the post of the permanent representative to the OECD seems to be highly regarded in the MOFA. OECD affairs have been a matter of the Economic Affairs Bureau in the MOFA (OECD Division). The post is located nearly at the end of the career path for those working around the

Table 4.1 Chairs of the bodies in the OECD held by respective countries

Chair		Vice-chair		Total chairs	
Canada	25	Japan	46	US	66
US	24	US	42	Canada	64
UK	17	Canada	39	Japan	52
Australia	14	France	32	France	42
Netherlands	13	Italy	25	UK	37
Sweden	11	Sweden	23	Italy	34
France	10	Germany	21	Sweden	34
Italy	9	UK	20	Australia	32
Switzerland	8	Australia	18	Germany	28
Germany	7	Finland	15	Switzerland	22
Japan	6	Switzerland	14		
Denmark	6	Netherlands	12		
Norway	5	Spain	11		
OECD	5	Norway	11		
Austria	5	Korea	11		
Belgium	5				
Total	184		419		603

Source: Compiled by the author from the data on On-Line Guide to OECD Intergovernmental Activity (http://webnet3.oecd.org/OECDgroups/).

Table 4.2 Important positions held by Japanese nationals (period, name and previous affiliation)

Deputy Secretary-General		
1990–96	Taniguchi Makoto	MOFA (Ambassador to the UN)
1997–99	Shigehara Kumiharu	Bank of Japan
1999–2003	Kondō Seiichi	MOFA (Economic Affairs Bureau)
2003–	Akasaka Kiyotaka	MOFA (Ambassador to the UN)
Chairs of the Economic Policy Committee		
1994, 95	Tanaka Tsutomu	Economic Planning Agency
1997, 98	Ōkita Yōichi	Economic Planning Agency
2004	Ushijima Shunichirō	Economic Planning Agency
Chairs of the Working Party No. 3		
1977–79	Miyakawa Michiya	Ministry of Finance
1988–89	Gyōten Toyō	Ministry of Finance

Economic Affairs Bureau. Among the fifteen representatives to date, many have acted as head of the Economic Affairs Bureau before going to the OECD. After working at the OECD, two were promoted to the position of Secretary of Foreign Affairs (Owada Hisashi and Nogami Yoshiji) and seven became ambassador to

Table 4.3 Japan's Permanent Representative to the OECD and main previous positions (at the Director-General of Bureau level)

1964–67	Mori Harukiyo	American Affairs Bureau
1967–70	Katō Tadao	Economic Affairs Bureau
1970–72	Tsurumi Kiyohiko	Economic Affairs Bureau
1972–75	Yoshino Bunroku	North American Affairs Bureau
1975–80	Hirahara Tsuyoshi	Economic Affairs Bureau
1980–82	Miyazaki Hiromichi	Economic Affairs Bureau
1982–84	Teshima Reishi	Economic Affairs Bureau
1984–88	Fukuda Hiromu	Economic Affairs Bureau
1988–89	Owada Hisashi	International Legal Affairs Bureau
1989–92	Fujii Hiroaki	North American Affairs Bureau
1992–95	Satō Yoshiyasu	Economic Affairs Bureau
1995–97	Takahashi Masaji	Immigration and Control Bureau of the Ministry of Justice
1997–99	Nogami Yoshiji	Economic Affairs Bureau
1999–2002	Nishimura Mutsuyoshi	European and Asian Affairs Bureau
2002–	Noboru Seiichirō	Middle Eastern and African Affairs Bureau

major countries like the UK, Germany or China. Hirahara Tsuyoshi contends that the MOFA and other ministries have regularly sent competent personnel to the Japanese delegation to the OECD (Hirahara 1995: 206).

Moreover, those sent to the OECD seem to have a specific policy orientation, somewhat different from others in the MOFA. According to Fujiwara Kiichi, the Economic Affairs Bureau and bureaucrats like Kondō Seiichi, a former Deputy Secretary-General of the OECD, tend to see multilateral frameworks including the US as more important than the bilateral alliance, as is common to specialists in the economic affairs of the other OECD countries. They want to tie the US to multilateral frameworks of coordination, through which policy options for the US are reduced and it is forced to choose between policy coordination and potential conflict. These MOFA officials are not anti-American in the sense that they do not regard the relationship with the US as unimportant, but they strive to enclose it in institutionalized coordination (Fujiwara 2002a). We may call them MOFA's multilateralists.

One of these multilateralists, Taniguchi Makoto, the first Japanese Deputy Secretary-General, is among the most unequivocal advocate of the East Asian Community. In his recent book on the topic, he often draws on his experiences in the OECD and criticizes MOFA's recent policy as unbalanced. He writes that the Japanese 'no' to the East Asian Economic Caucus initiative by the Malaysian Prime Minister Mahathir at the 1991 meeting of the Pacific Economic Cooperation Council, in which he participated as representative of the OECD-bureau, was a great disappointment to East Asian countries. In the meeting, the Japanese representative spoke frankly of the consideration given to relations with the US as a reason behind this. According to Taniguchi, MOFA is putting too heavy a weight on the relationship with the US, which results in unprincipled policies towards East Asia and a lack of initiatives vis-à-vis China (Taniguchi 2004: 64–8).

In reality, the existence of the multilateralist current in MOFA, as shown earlier, is always overshadowed by the mainstream which place the emphasis on the relationship with the US and tend to disregard multilateralism. Taniguchi refers to an interesting, related episode. The OECD's report entitled *The World in 2020*, written under Taniguchi's initiative, offended the mainstream in MOFA because the report predicted China's possible overtaking of the US and Japan in GDP measured by purchase power parity. Some even suggested that Japan should withdraw from the OECD for having conducted such an absurd research project. In fact, Japan broke away from the Development Centre of the OECD after the US had already left the body (Taniguchi 2004: 71–2).

Japanese contribution in specific policy proposals

Japan has played a role in a number of contentious issues concerning the OECD such as harmful tax competition and the Multilateral Agreement on Investment (MAI). On harmful tax competition, Japan chaired, together with France, the Harmful Tax Competition Project in the OECD Fiscal Committee, which drafted the 1998 report. Based on the report, the Tax Competition Forum was set up in October 1998 with Japan acting as vice-chair and which published the 2000 Report on the matter. In connection to this, Japan has also co-chaired the Board for Cooperation with Non-OECD Economies established in 2001 (Sugie 2000). Thereafter, Japan hosted a workshop on tax issues in the global environment in Tokyo from 15 to 16 February 2001. This workshop was said to be designed

> to facilitate further the partnership between Japan and the Pacific Islands Forum (PIF). It was also designed to provide an international forum where the PIF and OECD countries could discuss and enhance their mutual understanding on international tax issues, including the issue of harmful tax practices.
>
> (OECD 2001)

On the subject of MAI, Foreign Minister Ikeda Yukihiko referred to Japan's contribution to the issue in his annual addresses in 1996 and 1997, saying that Japan had been making efforts to conclude negotiations on the MAI (MOFA 1997). Japan's efforts were made in coordination with European countries in order to induce the US to act in a multilateral framework (Sakurai 2000).

Japan has also played an active role in formulating the New Development Strategy by the OECD's Development Assistance Committee (DAC). According to MOFA, Japan had been one of the first countries to take a number of initiatives to promote the New Development Strategy. In 1993, Japan stressed at the Tokyo Summit the need for a new approach towards development and convened the first Tokyo International Conference on African Development (TICAD I) under the joint auspices of the UN and the Global Coalition for Africa as a practical step towards the implementation of the new strategy. As a result, a report entitled *Shaping the 21st Century: the Contribution of Development Cooperation* was adopted by DAC in May 1996. Japan played a key role in the preparation process of this document by, for example, proposing specific development goals. As part of the process of implementing this strategy, Japan hosted the second Tokyo International Conference on African Development (TICAD II) in October 1998 with the participation of a number of high-level leaders from African and Asian donor countries and international organizations including the UN. The Conference adopted the *Tokyo Agenda for Action for 21st Century African Development*, which contained concrete objectives and priority policy tools in three fields: social development; economic development and premises for development such as good governance; and conflict prevention (MOFA 1996; Owada 1998; MOFA 2000).

The Japanese public's changing perceptions of the OECD and its decreasing salience

The previous section has analysed Japan's relationship with the OECD by focussing on the governmental level, especially MOFA. This section deals with the broader context of the relationship, namely, changing perceptions of the OECD as expressed in the formation of public opinion by analysing debates in the Japanese parliament (Diet) and journal articles.

The OECD as a 'club' of advanced industrial nations and a 'liberalizer'

In May 1961, the OECD became a topic in Diet debates for the first time (*Gaimu Iinkai, Shūgiin*, 11 May 1961). This was initiated by Sugihara Arata, a Diet member from the governing Liberal Democratic Party (LDP), who was an official in MOFA until the end of the Second World War and served as chairperson of the Foreign Policy Committee of the Upper House (*Sangiin*) and the Director General of the nascent Defence Agency. Against this background, he posed a question on accession to the OECD that had no relation to the tabled agenda. In reply, Foreign Minister Kosaka Zentarō stated that the OECD was the most important international economic organization of the free world and regarded the fact that Japan was the only large industrialized country that did not participate as a serious problem. He even wondered why there was no surge of opinion in favour of accession. It appears that the debate was arranged to promote the government's effort towards accession.

Thus, on the one hand, accession to the OECD was discussed first and foremost as a status problem and it was regarded as a milestone in Japan's post-war development as an advanced industrialized country. It was argued that greater interaction in the economic arena would facilitate understanding and lead to better political cooperation, which would ultimately strengthen Japan's position in the international arena.

On the other hand, membership of the OECD represented a challenge for Japanese policymakers and industrialists, who regarded Japan as *chūshinkoku* (middle-level developed country). According to a Ministry of Finance official, the Japanese delegation to the negotiations insisted that Japan was a first-class nation in terms of GNP but not in national income per capita, which amounted to only US$500, and pointed out the problems of medium- and small-sized enterprises. It was even reported that some parts of the bureaucracy and industrial sectors, such as ship-building and steel, embraced 'OECD-phobia', which saw the OECD as a 'gathering of the advanced countries trying to regulate Japan in any way possible' (Masuyama 1964). It was also argued that Japan would be stripped of its freedom of action by being subject to the same criteria as other advanced countries.

For industrialists, the OECD was in particular a powerful 'liberalizer' of capital markets and transactions. Pointing to the complicated dual structure of Japanese industry, Kanazawa (1963: 3) argued that 'the OECD will pose excessive demands upon Japan, but there is no reason for Japanese industry to be forced to fall prey'. As a result, Japanese industrialists paid considerable attention to Japan's accession. In its monthly journal *Keidanren Geppō*, the *Keidanren*, an influential organization of industrialists, has continuously reported on the OECD from its inception.

In actual fact, with a similar transition of status in the IMF, first to a Clause 11 state (no trade restrictions permissible on the grounds of balance of payment) in 1963, then to a Clause 8 state (no exchange restrictions permissible on the grounds of balance of payment) in 1964, the brief period from 1963 to 1964 was often regarded as a milestone in post-war Japanese economic history, especially in terms of the beginning of economic liberalization. The 1964 *Unyū Hakusho* (White Paper on Transportation) included a section entitled 'a harsher international environment' in relation to the transition to a Clause 8 state and accession to the OECD. In addition, a leading Japanese legal journal entitled *Jurisuto* (Jurist) published a special issue on liberalization in January 1964.

In an attempt to counter sceptics, more concrete arguments for accession were deployed. First, it was expected that Japan would have a better knowledge of international economic affairs. There was a general feeling among politicians, bureaucrats and business people that Japan was excluded from international agenda-setting and the flow of information. According to a contemporary commentator, it was expected that 'through accession to this organization, Japan's standpoints will be better emphasized and its interests better defended. Because the agenda of international discussions at various international meetings, such as the UN, General Agreement on Tariffs and Trade (GATT) or IMF, is scrutinized by this organization beforehand, it is possible to exchange views and acquire important information earlier' (Kanazawa 1963: 3). Gaining access to new information and ideas, concretely in the form of documents, was an important benefit of the accession.

Second, especially in relation to the European countries, the OECD was needed as a talking shop. It was recognized that discriminatory treatment by some European countries under Article 35 of GATT has impeded Japan's export to Europe. It was thought that this discrimination was based upon unnecessary concern and misunderstanding, which would be resolved through confidence-building in the OECD. In this way, the OECD was paid considerable attention and reported widely upon during the 1960s.

The OECD as a 'macroeconomic forum'

After this initial attention faded in subsequent years, the OECD came to the fore again at the end of the 1970s and during the 1980s. In this second phase, the role of the OECD was discussed in the context of macroeconomic policy coordination and trade friction with the US and European countries, which reflected Japan's growing economic power. At that time, 'multi-polarization' or the 'Japan–US–Europe trilateral structure' were often spoken of, reflecting the relative decline of the US economy. The OECD was seen in this context as a mechanism for sustaining trilateral relations.

In this period, the OECD was also seen as a vehicle to keep regular contact with West European countries. When trade friction occurred between Japan and the European countries, it was a grave concern of the Japanese business community that European countries took protectionist measures through the EC, thereby bypassing the OECD. For example, Miyazaki Hiromichi, a former permanent representative to the OECD, wrote in 1980, 'if the EC places greater weight on internal coordination and disregards deliberation in the OECD, then this is a big problem' (Miyazaki 1980).

As for macroeconomic policy, the OECD was used to sustain the argument in favour of fiscal stimulation and expansion of the domestic economy, as opposed to export-led growth. In November 1977, the Brookings Institute published a report by economists from the US, Europe and Japan, which propagated common macroeconomic stimulation by the three poles. This was the beginning of the so-called locomotive theory. The OECD followed suit and recommended fiscal expansion for Japan (Tadokoro 2003). For example, in Diet debates in 1983, an opposition member Osada Takeshi referred to the OECD's *Economic Survey of Japan* when urging the government to under-take fiscal expansion. He argued that 'according to the OECD's *Economic Survey of Japan, 1983*, it is said that the recent Japanese recovery is export-led . . . and that the expansion of domestic demand should be aimed at'. Such political use of the OECD surveys continued for several years. It is also note-worthy that OECD reports were seen not as that of an international organiza-tion but as reflecting the opinion of the US and European governments. Osada continued: 'I think such an OECD report proves the existence of criticism within the US and European governments towards Japanese macroeconomic management' (*Shōkō Iinkai, Shūgiin*, 4 October 1983; see also *Bukka Mondai ni kansuru Tokubetsu Iinkai, Shūgiin*, 10 August 1982 and *Shōkō Iinkai, Shūgiin*, 13 April 1984).

Accordingly, the Japanese government displayed an interest in the reports and debate occurred concerning policy recommendations. Shigehara Kumiharu, a former Deputy Secretary-General of the OECD, recalls that tough discussions took place in preparation for the OECD Ministerial Council in the spring of 1982 concerning Japanese monetary and fiscal policies in reaction to the rise of the dollar (Shigehara 1984).

Another issue, which was not publicly debated in terms of fiscal expansion, was industrial policy. On the one hand, the Japanese government had to take measures to help small- and medium-sized enterprises in industrial restructuring resulting from the appreciation of the yen. On the other hand, growing exports to the US and Europe caused 'trade friction' and the possibility of protectionism. Therefore, the Japanese government referred to the OECD's 'Positive Adjustment Policy' guideline, which aimed at promoting the expansion of growing industries against protectionism, almost every year in its White Papers from 1980 to 1986 as a way of attaining both objects simultaneously.

The OECD in the shade

Since the latter half of the 1990s, the OECD's economic policy recommendations have commanded less attention. Because structural reform of the Japanese economy has been on the agenda, one might expect the OECD to act as a trigger or accelerator of reform, as was observed in some European countries. However, this has not been the case.

One of the main issues in the OECD's Economic Surveys is the use of monetary policy to counter deflationary tendencies. The Economic Survey for 2000 pointed out that:

> [w]ith respect to the need to control expectations of further rate increases, it is imperative for the Bank of Japan (BOJ) to move quickly to establish an explicit policy framework to guide expectations in what amounts to a new regime. [I]t would be important for the bank to give more concise form to its inflation objectives in terms of specifying what inflation rate or range is considered appropriate.

In the 2005 Survey, this recommendation is reiterated:

> [t]he priority should be to end six years of deflation by maintaining the quantitative easing policy until inflation is sufficiently high so as to make the risk of falling back into deflation negligible. Setting a higher inflation threshold as a condition for changing monetary policy would also help guide private-sector expectations and help limit the reaction in markets.
>
> (OECD 2005)

Yet, it is remarkable that there was no political support for the deflationary measure of 'inflation targeting'. Only once has an opposition member of the Diet, Furukawa Motohisa of the Democratic Party of Japan (DPJ), posed questions to the government and the BOJ in the Budgetary Committee debate (*Yosan Iinkai, Shūgiin*, 17 December 2001). There is no systematic questioning by the DPJ thereafter.

Ronald Dore (2003) has pointed out that the discussion on measures to combat deflation has faded away and that deflation came to be regarded as unavoidable. Dore has even advocated a coordinated wage push by the trade unions, but this proposal has elicited no response from journalists and labour unions.

Such neglect of OECD recommendations is not restricted to general economic policy, where the recommendations partly contradict the declared stance of the Koizumi government. As regards regulatory reform, an issue upon which the government placed the highest priority and congruence between the recommendations and governmental policy is higher, one might expect the political use of OECD recommendations by the government.

Prime Minister Koizumi Junichirō took office on 26 April 2001, claiming 'structural reform without haven' as the prime task for the new government. The formation of the Koizumi government was welcomed by the OECD Survey. The 2001 Survey states, 'The new government of Prime Minister Koizumi has quite correctly put a top priority on structural reforms and budgetary discipline to revitalize the Japanese Economy'. But the Koizumi government seldom refers to the OECD report. In fact, the Economic Surveys and 'Regulatory Reform in Japan' are never reflected in the White Paper on the Economy. In July 2004 the OECD released a follow-up report on regulatory reform entitled *Japan: progress in implementing regulatory reform*. In March earlier that year, the three-year plan for regulatory reform was adopted by the cabinet and the privatization of the Japan Post was placed high on the agenda. However, the report was almost completely disregarded by the government. It is only natural that opposition parties do not refer to such reports that are generally favourable to the government. But the government only once referred to the OECD's reports simply to cite the positive overall economic prospects identified by the Survey (*Yosan Iinkai, Shūgiin*, 31 January 2005).

This disregard is in stark contrast to Germany, where the policy evaluations and recommendations of the OECD have been reported on television news and the government often releases press statements concerning the OECD reports. For example, the Schröder government was said to have put pressure on the OECD in 2002 to water down its recommendations on labour market flexibility and pension reforms (EIROnline 2003). On the occasion of the recent report *Economic Survey – Germany 2004*, the German Government and the Ministry of Economic Affairs released press releases respectively entitled *The OECD appreciates structural reform in Germany* and *The OECD praises reform policy*. Following the report, the weekly newspaper *Die Zeit* published an interview with an OECD researcher on the prospect of labour market reform (*Die Zeit*, 15 July 2004).

It was not the case that the Japanese government had completely lost interest in the work of the OECD. As regards the drafting of the regulatory reform survey of 1999, a labour union representative of the Trade Union Advisory Committee to the OECD expressed his concern about the political use of the report. He pointed out that the Japanese government had demonstrated its intention to treat the OECD report as *gaiatsu* (external pressure), in spite of the assertion in the OECD survey itself, which assigns respective governments the right to decide on the appropriate measures to be taken (Kimura 1997).

Such disregard can be also explained by the current political constellation. Both the Koizumi government and the opposition DPJ are competing in claiming credit as the 'true' promoter of 'structural reform'. Major newspapers are by and large singing from the same hymnbook. In this sense, there is a consensus on the direction of policy and the recommendations of the OECD cannot find supporters and promoters in the political arena.

Part of the reason also lies in the international environment. In the 1960s and 1970s, Japan's problems were not only with the US but also with European countries. Thus, the OECD was an appropriate problem-solving framework. When the US became the main claimant of unfair trade and economic practices, it was only natural that bilateral negotiations came to the fore.

It is also notable that such a contentious issue for the OECD as the MAI was paid little attention, although Japan had played some role in its formulation. The topic was referred to in Diet debates only eight times, half of which were initiated by a Social Democratic member of the Diet. Besides explanation from the government, no serious discussion on the agreement itself was conducted. On harmful tax competition, Diet discussions were initiated by various members on ten occasions and the debate was more substantial. However, such debate was not concerned with how to establish new norms of behaviour but rather how to adapt to the established norm. In other words, the whole discussion concerning the OECD was based on the stance not of a policymaker but a 'policy-taker'.

The former Deputy Secretary-General Kondō was said to have commented that it was wrong to regard the US's consideration of domestic opinion as a constraint and that it was rather a strength of US foreign policy (Fujiwara 2002b). If we apply the same logic to Japan–OECD relations, Japan's possible role in the OECD is limited because the problem of what stance Japan should take towards multilateral international organizations in general lacks political salience.

Conclusion and prospects

Japan has recognized the importance of the OECD as a forum of the advanced industrialized countries. This importance has been reflected in the career path of the Japanese delegates and some specific policy proposals. Is it possible to say that Japan will play a greater role in the OECD as a part of the arrangements for the provision of global governance? It is true that in relation to the new challenges of enlargement (see Chapter 3) and the non-member states in Asia-Pacific, Japan has a unique role to play, as is exemplified in the workshop on tax competition held in Tokyo mentioned earlier. This geopolitical importance is reflected in an interview with the previous OECD Secretary-General David Johnston, which suggested the first candidate to his successor be Japanese (*Asahi Shimbun*, 26 February 2005).

Speculating from the earlier insights, however, it is unlikely that Japan will make more use of the OECD as a mechanism of global governance. First, Japanese perception of the OECD is narrow in two senses. In scope, the presence of the OECD in public debates is declining compared with the 1960s or 1980s and this diminishes the effect of soft policy-coordination mechanisms. In depth, Japanese perceptions are limited to one aspect, the OECD as a 'club'. True, those who have experience of working in or with the OECD have stressed such aspects as norm-finding and settling, or policy learning through a peer review system. For example, Inoue Minoru, Vice-President of the Business and Industry Advisory Committee (BIAC) to the OECD, wrote that the OECD was not a place for negotiation but a think-tank of the twenty-five participating countries, which has conducted various analyses and made guidelines and rules. But this understanding is not widely accepted. In the recent Blue Paper on Foreign Relations 2004 (MOFA 2004), the position of the current Deputy Secretary-General Akasaka Kiyotaka is referred to in the section dedicated to the reform of the UN and the upgrading of Japan's position in the international arena. This gives the impression that the OECD is treated as an issue of status or power rather than policy – not dissimilar to arguments made at the time of Japan's accession to the OECD.

This lack of understanding has several reasons. First, former Deputy Secretary-General Shigehara wrote that peer-pressure was sometimes more effective in a regional organization like the EU, to which Japan has no equivalence. He also pointed out the importance of the publication of the Economic Survey as a result of multilateral peer review, which would stimulate public discussion. As was demonstrated earlier, this is not the case in Japan–OECD relations because media attention towards and political use of the Survey are in decline.

Second, the OECD historically came to the fore when economic relations with Europe caused policy problems for government and business. In recent years, however, this is not the case. There is neither major trade friction comparable to that of the 1960s and 1980s, nor concern for the export of Japanese production styles to the European branches of Japanese companies, as was the case in the 1980s. Rather, in cases such as the reduction of greenhouse gas emissions in line with the Kyoto Protocol and the World Trade Organization's agricultural negotiations, Japan has some common interests with Europe against the US. In short, if the relationship with the US were the only major problem, the established bilateral channel would be preferred.

Third, there is a more immediate reason. While the bilateralists have remained central within MOFA, the multilateralists with experience of the OECD were severely discredited by several scandals in MOFA over recent years. Under the first Koizumi administration, there was a clash between Foreign Minister Tanaka Makiko and the bureaucrats, headed by Secretary of State Nogami Yoshiji, who was previously permanent representative to the OECD. It was revealed that Nogami and others in MOFA had close connections with LDP politician Suzuki Muneo and that they had made decisions beneficial to Suzuki. Moreover, Nogami was said to have excluded a number of NGO representatives from the International Conference on Reconstruction Assistance to Afghanistan held in Tokyo in January 2002, following Suzuki's suggestion. Nogami was forced to resign and Nishimura Mutsuyoshi, Nogami's successor as permanent representative to OECD, was also passed over.

It should also be noted here that even the multilateralists have their own limits in regard to new strategies originating with the OECD (see Chapter 3). As is clear in the episode mentioned earlier, the multilateralists do not necessarily value the inclusion of civil society. In this regard, it is unlikely that Japan would take the lead in cultivating links between the OECD and civil society.

Finally, it might be conceivable that the Japanese stance regarding the OECD is a reflection of a deeper Japanese perspective on international relations. It is interesting here to make comparison with the case of Germany. Although in a different context, Peter J. Katzenstein wrote:

> Germany's active involvement in the evolution of international norms conveyed a conception of belonging to and participating in an international Grotian community. Japan's lack of concern for the consequences of pushing Japanese terrorists abroad and its generally passive stance was based on a Hobbesian view of the international system.
>
> (Katzenstein 1993: 266)

What makes such a difference? It may be related to the internationalization of national identity after the Second World War. In the case of Germany, Katzenstein contends that German power was institutionalized in regional frameworks such as the EU and the North Atlantic Treaty Organization, which transformed and internationalized German identity (Katzenstein 1997). In contrast, no multilateral framework existed in East Asia even among the members of the 'Western camp', like Japan, South Korea and the Philippines. Generally speaking, US foreign policy had aimed at the construction of a regional framework in East Asia analogous to NATO, through which the US's own burden would be lessened. However, because of Japan–Korea rivalry and differences in economic development, such visions were never realized (Lee 1996. See also Hemmer and Katzenstein 2002). It is also noteworthy that leading left-leaning, liberal intellectuals in Japan like Maruyama Masao were sympathetic to East Asian nationalism, partly because the regional vision of the pre-war generation, namely the Greater East Asian Co-prosperity Sphere (*Daitōa kyōeiken*), had in the end degenerated into a *façade* for the expansionist project of the government (Sakai 1996). Thinking in regional terms had been suspect in the post-war Japanese liberal *milieu*.

In the 1980 special issue of the Japanese journal *Keizai to Gaikō* (Economy and Diplomacy) on the twentieth anniversary of the establishment of the OECD, many contributors with varying degrees of experience of work in the OECD pointed out the lack of Japanese interest in and experience of multilateral fora and stressed their importance. For example, Ariyoshi Yoshiya, a past president of shipping company *Nippon Yusen*, who was once a Japanese representative to BIAC and served as its chair for two years, said:

> Japanese businessmen were doing their best in international activities, but only in a bilateral manner. For example, as regards US–Japanese, Anglo–Japanese, or German–Japanese relations, there are concrete merits and demerits and therefore many go to the countries and devote their energies. As for multilateral organizations such as BIAC or the OECD, however, few feel like going there to have their say and to represent Japanese opinion.
>
> (Ōkita *et al.* 1980: 18)

This testimony, made a quarter century ago, still holds explanatory power for the Japanese stance towards the OECD today, and perhaps multilateral international organizations in general.

Note

1 Recently, however, light has been thrown on the OECD from an unexpected direction. In the policy development of the European Union (EU), new methods of governance were introduced during the latter half of the 1990s, among which the 'Open Methods of Co-ordination' (OMC) is the most prominent. The core of the OMC lies in collective policy learning among member states through policy monitoring and peer review. In this regard, the OECD was 'discovered' as a predecessor to the OMC in EU studies. Scholars of international relations have also shown a growing interest in international 'soft law'. From these two perspectives, the OECD can be investigated in more detail. These new currents of research include Dostal (2004), Martens and Balzer (2004), Schaefer (2004) and Webb (2004).

References

Dore, Ronald (2003) 'Koe naki koe ni natta defure taiji ron', *RIETI Policy Discussion* 10. Available on-line at: http://www.rieti.go.jp/jp/special/policy_discussion/10.html, accessed on 14 February 2005.

Dostal, Jörg Michael (2004) 'Campaigning on expertise: how the OECD framed EU welfare and labour market policies – and why success could trigger failure', *Journal of European Public Policy* 11, 3: 440–60.

EIROnline (European Industrial Relations Observatory On-line) (2003) 'Newspaper claims OECD was urged to rewrite policy recommendations on Germany'. Available on-line at: http://www.eiro.eurofound.eu.int/2003/06/inbrief/de0306106n.html, accessed on 21 July 2005.

Fujiwara, Buheita (1978) 'OECD jimukyoku kinmu are kore', *Tsūsan Jyānaru* 11: 44–9.

Fujiwara, Kiichi (2002a) 'Shokuminchi naki teikoku: Amerika taigai seisaku to chiiki', Presentation at the 38th Project Seminar of the Institute of Social Science at the University of Tokyo, 27 June. Available on-line at: http://project.iss.u-tokyo.ac.jp/seminar/fujiwara_main.pdf, accessed on 14 February 2005.

—— (2002b) 'Higashi Ajia no heiwa kōsō', *Human Security* 6. Available on-line at: http://www.tokai.ac.jp/spirit/archives/human/pdf/hs06/02_01.pdf, accessed on 14 February 2005.

Hemmer, Christopher and Katzenstein, Peter J. (2002) 'Why is there no NATO in Asia? Collective identity, regionalism, and the origins of multilateralism', *International Organization* 56: 575–607.

Hirahara, Tsuyoshi (1995) *Eikoku Taishi no Gaikō Jinsei*, Tokyo: Kawaide Shobō Shinsha.

Kanazawa, Shigeru (1963) 'OECD o meguru shomondai', *Sekai no Rōdō* 13: 2–6.

Katzenstein, Peter J. (1993) 'Coping with terrorism: norms and internal security in Germany and Japan', in Judith Goldstein and Robert E. Keohane (eds) *Ideas and Foreign Policy*, Ithaca, NY: Cornell University Press, pp. 265–95.

—— (1997) 'United Germany in an integrating Europe', in Peter J. Katzenstein (ed.) *Tamed Power: Germany in Europe*, Ithaca, NY: Cornell University Press, pp. 1–48.

Kimura, Hiroshi (1997) 'Hōdō de wa tsutawara nai OECD ni okeru kisei kanwa no rongi', *Sekai no Rōdō* 47: 20–3.

Lee, Jong Won (1996) *Higashi Ajia Reisen to Kan-Nichi-Bei Kankei*, Tokyo: Tokyo Daigaku Shuppankai.

Martens, Kerstin and Balzer, Carolin (2004) 'Comparing governance of international organisations – the EU, the OECD and educational policy'. Paper presented to the ECPR Joint Sessions, Uppsala, 13–18 April.

Masuyama, Eitarō (1964) 'OECD "kyōfushō" kieru', *Sekai Shūhō* 45: 20–5.

Miyazaki, Hiromichi (1980) 'OECD to sono kadai', *Keizai to Gaikō* 703: 23–6.

MOFA (1996) Japan's ODA Annual Report (Summary) 1996. Available on-line at: http://www.mofa.go.jp/policy/oda/summary/1996/index.html, accessed on 21 July 2006.

—— (1997) *Gaikō Seisho 1997*. Available on-line at: http://www.mofa.go.jp/mofaj/gaiko/bluebook/97/index.html, accessed on 21 July 2006.

—— (2000) *Nihon to Kokuren*. Available on-line at: http://www.mofa.go.jp/mofaj/press/pr/pub/pamph/un_jp.html, accessed on 21 July 2006.

—— (2003) *Kokusai Kikan tou e no kyōshutsukin, shussikin ni kansuru hōkokusho*. Available on-line at: http://www.mofa.go.jp/mofaj/gaiko/oda/shiryo/sonota/k_kikan_15/index.html, accessed on 21 July 2006.

—— (2004) *Gaikō Seisho 2004*. Available on-line at: http://www.mofa.go.jp/mofaj/gaiko/bluebook/2004/index.html, accessed on 21 July 2006.

OECD (2001) 'Ministers and senior policymakers from Pacific Island Forum and OECD countries met for the workshop on tax issues', 15–16 February. Available on-line at: http://www.oecd.org/document/7/0,2340,en_2649_37427_2351495_1_1_1_37427,00.html, accessed on 13 June 2006.

—— (2005) 'Economic Survey of Japan, 2005'. Available on-line at: http://www.oecd.org/dataoecd/50/37/34286799.pdf, accessed on 21 July 2006.

Ōkita, Saburō, Inose, Hiroshi, Ariyoshi, Yoshiya and Fukada, Hiroshi (1980) 'OECD to Nihon: 20-nenkan no ayumi to sono shōrai', *Keizai to Gaikō* 703: 4–22.

Owada, Hisashi (1998) 'Global partnership towards the 21st century: new development strategy and the role of international organizations', Speech to the High-level Open Symposium on Development Cooperation 'Donor Coordination and the Effectiveness of Development Assistance', Tokyo, 22 June. Available on-line at: http://www.unu.edu/hq/public-lectures/owada.html, accessed on 19 March 2005.

Sakai, Tetsuya (1996) 'Sengo gaikōron ni okeru risōshugi to genjitsushugi', *Kokusai Mondai* 432: 24–38.

Sakurai, Masao (2000) 'Takokukan tōshi kyōtei', *Kokusai Zeimu* 20: 8–9.

Schaefer, Armin (2004) 'A new and effective form of governance? Comparing the OMC to multilateral surveillance by the IMF and the OECD', Paper for the 2004 Conference of Europeanists, Chicago, 11–13 March 2004.

Shigehara, Kumiharu (1984) 'OECD no omoide', *Chochiku to Keizai* 139. Available on-line at: http://office.shigehara.online.fr/jp/chatting/omoide.html, accessed on 21 July 2006.

Sugie, Jun (2000) 'OECD ni okeru yūgai na zei no kyōsō purojekuto ni tsuite', *Sozei Kenkyū* 612: 76–81.

Sullivan, Scott (1997) *From War to Wealth: 50 Years of Innovation*, Paris: OECD.

Tadokoro, Masayuki (2003) 'Makuro keizai seisaku no kokusai kyōchō to Nihon: 1967-nen – 79-nen', *Hōgaku Kenkyū* 76: 1–29.

Taniguchi, Makoto (2004) *Higashi Ajia Kyōdōtai*, Tokyo: Iwanami Shoten.

Webb, Michael C. (2004) 'Defining the boundaries of legitimate state practice: norms, transnational actors and the OECD's Project on Harmful Tax Competition', *Review of International Political Economy* 11, 4: 787–827.

5 Global governance and the World Bank

Nicola Phillips

Introduction

The aim of this chapter is to put forward a set of ideas about how best to understand the place and significance of the World Bank within the structures that are considered to constitute the architecture of global governance. It takes as its point of departure the contention that analyses of the World Bank are informed intrinsically, in a way not often made explicit, on the particular understandings of what 'global governance' means that are brought to bear on them. Indeed, the debate about the various institutions of global governance, including the Bank, has generally been conducted in an unsatisfactory manner, inasmuch as it features a pronounced bifurcation between two distinct and, ultimately, contradictory perspectives: either the focus falls on the institution itself, ignoring the structural context into which it is inserted and of which it is intrinsically representative, or it falls on the structural context and the significance of the institution within the contemporary world order, saying next to nothing about the nature of the institution, its operations or the impact of its activities. The former approach emphasizes the shortcomings of the Bank and the limitations of its influence; the latter observes the complex, extensive and unprecedented power and influence that the World Bank both realizes and exercises. We are thus left predominantly with a set of contradictory analyses and conclusions concerning institutions like the World Bank in global governance, which offer only very partial purchase on the nature of their power, influence and significance.

It is this tension in the debate surrounding the World Bank that this chapter sets out to address. It does so by posing the problem as a question, namely, why is it that the Bank should have been widely recognized to have achieved unprecedented levels of 'structural power' and penetration of national development processes, and to be situated at the very heart of a structure of global governance that is embedded in and serves to entrench the ideological hegemony of neoliberalism, while at the same time being characterized as of signally limited efficacy in achieving its objectives and widely criticized as moribund or in need of substantial reform? In other words, why has there developed such a marked disjuncture between the structural power possessed by the World Bank and its ability effectively and systematically to achieve its objectives in the outcomes of its lending strategies? It is argued that the difficulty arises in the first instance from the lack of conceptual clarity that characterizes the now truly enormous cottage industry that has grown up around the notion of global governance. What is consequently needed is a more fruitful approach to understanding the key institutions of global governance, which is capable of reconciling the disjointed conceptual and empirical understandings of global governance itself that prevail in the literature, and which offers a conducive platform from which to address the specific reasons for the disjuncture outlined here. These reasons, it is argued, cluster principally around the *absence* of ideological and ideational consensus in the global political economy, the existence of competing structures and modes of governance and associated tensions between the national and 'global' governance agendas, and the institutional and organizational character of the World Bank itself.

Conceptualizing global governance

There is a striking bifurcation in the study of global governance between those approaches which conceive of global governance as the study of agency and actors in world politics, and those which adopt a structuralist understanding of global governance. Perhaps the difference is well captured in the distinction suggested by James Rosenau (2002) between governance *in* and governance *of* world politics. His explicit acknowledgement that his own conceptualization of global governance (which, as argued in the introduction to this volume, has become widely accepted as 'the' IR definition) is premised on a notion of -- governance *in* world politics is useful in characterizing the bulk of the contemporary literature on global governance. Cognizant of the need to expand the terrain of global governance from the traditional, restrictive focus on multilateral institutions and encompass a much greater degree of complexity and a much wider array of actors, the primary concern of most students of global governance lies with what happens *within* the system, rather than with the overarching nature of the system itself and the sort of system of rule it represents. In other words, the bulk of the global governance literature has come on this basis to substitute the focus on institutions with a wider focus on agency. Rorden Wilkinson and Steve Hughes' (2002) authoritative volume, for instance, starts by drawing attention to the two-fold distinctiveness of global governance: the array of actors it comprises, and 'the way in which varieties of actors are increasingly combining to manage – and, in many case, micro-manage – a growing range of political, economic and social affairs' (Wilkinson 2002: 2). Miles Kahler and David Lake (2003) have focused on the slightly different notion of 'political authority' as the core concept pulling together the essays in their volume. But the general thrust is that the study of governance is essentially the study of actors and what actors do. Governance is understood as an activity, usually as the 'management' of world affairs, and therefore corresponds with what Finkelstein (1995: 4–5) advocated as a focus on 'purposive acts' rather than 'tacit arrangements' as the core of the study of global governance.

This approach is problematic for a number of reasons, which cluster around its neglect of the crucial question of structure within which what is understood to be the 'activity' of global governance takes place. Scholars approaching global governance from a broadly critical international political economy (IPE) perspective would locate this problem within their longstanding observation of the shortcomings of mainstream, 'problem-solving' theory. That is, these approaches fail to offer an understanding of the particular nature of the contemporary world order, how it came into being and its structural significance; consequently, they have few understandings of any substance to offer on the nature of the system that is being governed. Perhaps the most important dimension of this difficulty is the neglect of the ideological foundations of the system and the failure to shed light on the manner in which the exercise of agency and authority in world politics is intrinsically shaped by prevailing ideological structures. As noted in the introduction, Craig Murphy (2000: 796) has pinpointed the problem in his observation of the inability of many approaches to global governance to account for 'why so much of this creative movement in world politics seems to have added up to the supremacy of the neoliberal agenda both within and across states'. Yet the issue is not *only* that much of the global governance literature neglects the issue of ideology, but also – and perhaps moreover – that it is presented as ideologically *neutral*. It is this shroud of neutrality that, as Anthony Payne (2005a) has argued, obscures the key point that global governance is in essence an ideological *project* which aims to sustain a particular neoliberal world order.

These agency-centred approaches to global governance tend also to share certain conceptualizations of 'politics' that have frequently posed limitations to our ability to understand the nature of global governance itself. That is, the commonly accepted Laswellian definition of politics – as the struggle over who gets what, when and how – has tended, particularly in neoliberal scholarship, to give rise to understandings of politics essentially as processes of *bargaining*. While power is of course intrinsic to these processes and recognized as such, the emphasis in much of the global governance literature is effectively on the bargaining dynamics among different groups of actors for a variety of resources (including power itself). Global governance is thus often understood as the 'organization of collective action' (Prakash and Hart 1999), or alternatively as the provision of services and public goods within the global political economy (Kaul *et al.* 1999; McGinnis 1999). These conceptualizations of global governance fall short inasmuch as they fail, in the main, to give adequate account of the notion of coercion and control.

Lake (1999) has offered an interesting take on this in his idea of 'contracting'. Rather than focusing on the processes by which bargains are reached, Lake advocates an emphasis on the enforcement of already existing bargains, in an effort to counter the notion that everything is 'up for grabs' in global governance. Indeed, in this he coincides well with the emphases on global governance as control, and on its coercive expressions, that are found in a good deal of the IPE approaches that have emerged. We will turn to these approaches shortly. The problems with a focus on contracting along these lines, however, are two-fold: first, that it fails to account for the nature of the already existing overarching bargains and the processes of their formation – that is, the question of how and why these bargains came into being in the first place; and second, it precludes a serious normative discussion about the nature of world order and global governance. Lake's own approach relies on a rational choice-based theory of contracting which offers a useful insight into the dimensions of governance that are intrinsically about control, but nevertheless offers little historical or structural perspective on the nature of the 'grand' bargains that constitute the structure of the particular world order in which we currently live.

The counterpoints to this raft of 'agency-centred' approaches to the study of global governance are found in an alternative, 'structuralist' approach, which attempts to address precisely this neglect of the nature of the system. Rather than conceiving of governance 'in' world politics, these structuralist perspectives can be thought of as concerning themselves more with the notion of governance 'of' world politics. The works surveyed in the introduction of Robert Cox and Paul Cammack, among others, are emblematic of the approaches which see structure as the key to understanding global governance. Yet, despite their useful correctives to the problems of excessively agency-centred analysis, the difficulty with both of these structuralist perspectives is that we are left with rather confused conclusions about what, then, governance or global governance actually is. Cox's (1996) *nébuleuse* implicitly indicates an understanding of global governance as an ideological construct that is made concrete by its filtration through the multilateral institutions and other agents of the global economy. More to the point, for Cox and others of a similar persuasion (recalling Murphy's observations earlier), global governance is, in essence, neoliberalism. It is ideology itself which is the governance structure – in the formulation of Stephen Gill (1995) or Andrew Gamble (2000), the 'constitution' which itself 'governs' world politics and development.

This is quite different from seeing governance as essentially a management activity through the actor-centred lenses we highlighted earlier on, and is unquestionably a useful insight. The question that is immediately raised is how, then, is governance different from the term 'structure' that we are already so used to using. Indeed, it is entirely possible to see the concept of global governance as a whole as signifying nothing more, but equally nothing less, than 'the politics of globalization' – or, perhaps even more appositely, 'the globalization of politics'. But whether or not we agree that the term governance represents nothing newer than or different from the term 'politics', the point can simply be harnessed to put forward the central contention that governance is essentially *about* politics; consequently, we need to sort out what we mean by politics in order to understand what we might mean by governance. Politics is not just about bargaining and distribution but also about coercion and control and, moreover, as much about structure as about agency.

Understood in this way, we are drawn to the compelling argument advanced in the Introduction to this volume for locating the study of global governance within the frameworks offered by critical IPE. In this light, a fruitful theoretical and conceptual apparatus for understanding and analysing global governance and, more specifically, the key institutions of global governance can be put forward, which involves an appropriately integrated understanding and account of structure and agency, on the one hand, and the coercive (control) and the consensual dimensions of governance, on the other. In the context of the present volume, these then need to be combined with due attention to the institutions of global governance themselves, their organizational characteristics and operations, the politics surrounding their activities and, in particular, the nature of their impact 'on the ground'.

The need for integrating this institutional analysis becomes readily apparent in the context of the observation made at the start of the chapter: that there is a striking discrepancy between those (structuralist) accounts that see the World Bank and other organizations as having achieved unprecedented levels of power and influence and those (institutionalist) accounts that would draw attention to the failings and limitations of the Bank as an 'actor' in the global political economy. Structuralist analyses of the World Bank's documented strategies and action plans can, in this sense, be criticized for some inattention to how these strategies fare when put into practice and whether the Bank is effective in achieving its own stated objectives in its lending programmes. Moreover, they can be upbraided for their frequent failure to demonstrate exactly how much of any observed process of change can be attributed directly to the World Bank's activities, rather than to a broader and more diffuse constellation of ideological forces that underpin the contemporary world order. The causality tends, at least in part, to be imputed rather than demonstrated. It often seems that it is less the impact of the World Bank specifically that is being measured and assessed than the impact of the broader confluence of ideological, political and economic forces associated with globalization. Equally, however, those accounts of the World Bank which focus solely on the institution itself miss the key questions concerning the place of the Bank in the overarching system of global governance and the ideological force it represents. The Bank is both a product of that system and a key agent in its shaping, and its implications cannot be understood purely in terms of its efficacy in achieving specific policy reforms in particular countries.

In summary, then, the bifurcation in the global governance debate between agency-centred and structuralist approaches has been reflected in the analysis of key institutions of global governance, including the World Bank, and has hampered their full understanding and analysis. The conclusions thereby generated are contradictory and unhelpfully stark, dividing as they do between those that see the World Bank as an ineffective and limited agent of global governance, and those that observe its unprecedented reach into all areas of national political, economic and social systems. More to the point, it has thus obscured what, it is argued here, is the central question or 'puzzle' that needs to be addressed – namely, the reasons for the apparent co-existence of, and discrepancy between, the immense structural (ideological) power wielded by the Bank and its relative effectiveness in exercising that power effectively and systematically achieving its objectives. It is to the Bank specifically, then, that we now turn our attention.

The World Bank and global governance

The remit and scope of the World Bank since its inception as one of the Bretton Woods institutions created in 1945 has been strikingly wide-ranging. The

International Bank for Reconstruction and Development (IBRD) – the original 'World Bank' – was established to provide development loans for the economic reconstruction primarily of the war-torn European countries. It has since been joined by four other institutions with supplementary mandates: the International Development Association (IDA), providing concessional loans to small countries; the International Finance Corporation (IFC), lending to private sector enterprises investing in poorer countries; the Multilateral Investment Guarantee Agency (MIGA), insuring foreign direct investors against non-commercial risks; and the International Centre for the Settlement of Investor Disputes (ICSID), providing a mechanism for the arbitration of disputes between states and investors. The diverse and competing strands of its remit have generated consistent debate – often, confusion – for the last sixty years over what the role of the Bank is or should be, and in particular what is or should be its relationship with its twin financial institution, the International Monetary Fund (IMF). At the time of the establishment of these institutions, there was a clear division of labour between the two institutions: the IMF's functions were defined as relating to the provision of liquidity and 'lender of last resort' activities, while the Bank's were concentrated in the area of structural adjustment and reform. But, for much of the post-war period, the activities of the Bank and the IMF were closely integrated, with the salient exception of the late 1980s. The differences that emerged at that time were manifested most sharply in the case of the 1987 Trade Policy Loans to Argentina, in which, for the first time, the Bank acted unilaterally and without consultation with the IMF (Tussie and Botzman 1992).

During the 1990s a much closer relationship was re-established as the emphasis shifted away from structural adjustment towards a more self-consciously 'developmental' agenda for the international financial institutions (IFIs) premised on notions of 'governance'. This new agenda was associated primarily with the World Bank, and indeed formed the basis of a revitalization of its identity as a development organization and its new self-styling as a 'knowledge bank'. This strategy was driven primarily by the Bank's Chief Economist, Joseph Stiglitz, and its president, James Wolfensohn, and involved a shift away from structural adjustment lending to a so-called Comprehensive Development Framework that was laid out by Wolfensohn in 1999 (see Standing 2000; Cammack 2004; Charnock 2005). In essence, the Bank has sought to position itself as the primary agency involved in the generation and dissemination of ideas about development and the provision of the financial and technical assistance necessary to start to translate knowledge into policy practice. The good governance agenda is the most commonly cited example, along with the Washington Consensus, post-Washington Consensus and poverty reduction strategies, among many others. More lately, initiatives such as the Global Development Network (GDN) have formed part and parcel of this new-found 'knowledge bank' identity that the World Bank has sought to claim for itself. The GDN's description of its functions are, in many ways, equally descriptions of the World Bank's broader project: among other things, it aims to promote 'the generation of local knowledge in developing and transition countries', produce 'policy relevant knowledge on a global scale' and disseminate 'development knowledge to the public and policymakers' (Global Development Network 2005).

This rethinking of the Bank's agenda, and indeed the prioritization of governance as embodying the Bank's thinking on development, emerged from the manifest failures of the structural adjustment strategies of the 1980s. It was precipitated most immediately by the situation of the sub-Saharan African region by the end of that decade, which was diagnosed by the World Bank as a 'crisis of governance' rather than a crisis of primarily economic dimensions (World Bank 1989). The Bank contended that the relatively healthy growth figures for developing countries between 1965 and 1980 concealed 'deep-seated problems of governance' that only became exposed with the widespread economic crisis of the 1980s, and that the problems that subsequently became apparent with structural adjustment lending provided evidence of the importance of 'further improvements in the institutional framework for development management' (World Bank 1992).

The governance agenda, as is well-known, is founded on a contention that a neutral and effective state, of a sort consistent with the tenets of the neoliberal project, depends intrinsically on a 'corresponding liberal public sphere' characterized by an increasingly empowered civil society and enhanced technical and institutional effectiveness (Williams and Young 1994: 93–4). The Bank's much-touted initiative to reformulate the orthodox neoliberalism of the 1980s into a framework which gives due centrality to institutions, politics and governance is concerned fundamentally with ensuring the more effective functioning of the neoliberal market system and a process of market 'completion'. The thrust of the post-Washington Consensus and 'second-generation' reform agendas – involving reforms that go beyond the initial agendas of trade liberalization, privatization and financial deregulation to encompass such areas as judicial reform, tax and fiscal reforms, labour flexibilization and institutional reforms captured under the banner of 'the modernization of the state' – deems institutional reform to be necessary specifically for the purposes of achieving the optimal functioning of markets and economic efficiency through institutional reform (World Bank 1997). Greater participation by civil societies is in turn required for the purposes of enhancing the 'legitimacy' of the Bank's programmes and thereby circumventing political opposition to neoliberal reform. The self-consciously more 'progressive' agenda pushed by the Bank in its second-generation reform agenda is therefore one of promoting competition, reducing the political obstacles encountered by reforming national governments and advancing an agenda of 'completing' national reform programmes.

The governance agenda signified in some ways an important shift in the way in which the Bank conceived of its role and its concerns with the political aspects of development. Traditionally, as is well-known, the Bank adhered to the stipulations in its Articles of Agreement that its lending strategies were entirely of an apolitical nature in their design and execution. The Bank's ethos during the post-war period, and certainly during the 1980s, was one based on a notion of 'economic neutrality' (Swedberg 1986) – that is, the Bank was not permitted to be influenced in its decision-making processes by the political nature of a member country, to interfere in partisan politics, to act on behalf of an industrial member country to influence the political system or behaviour of a borrowing member, to be influenced by political factors that had no direct economic implications, or to be influenced by the possible reactions of member countries to its policies or decisions (see Shihata 1991: 79–84; World Bank 1992). In the new context of governance, however, this founding conception of apoliticism required some modification. In one sense, governance issues were deemed to be relevant when placed in the context of order and discipline in the management of national resources (World Bank 1992: 5), and information about the political situation was valid inasmuch as it influenced assessments of the prospects for successful implementation of reforms. In another sense, and more obviously, the governance agenda represented an unprecedented reach into the political and institutional systems of countries, on the basis of the new concerns with accountability and transparency, judicial systems, public adminis-tration, corruption, competition, the rule of law and so on. Even while a more explicitly political conception of governance has been embraced only haltingly and with some equivocation by the Bank (Harrison 2005: 240), nevertheless, the rhetoric of apoliticism has been largely abandoned and the governance agenda represents unquestionably a deeper political strategy that stretches widely across social, political and institutional arrangements in huge swathes of the world.

Nevertheless, despite the magnitude of the shift in the remit of the Bank's development agenda, the second-generation and post-Washington Consensus agendas represent little that is of *fundamental* novelty in the Bank's development orthodoxy. The new 'politicism' is of a distinctly economic sort; moreover, it is distinctly 'economistic' in its foundations. The Comprehensive Development Framework and good governance agenda focus, in essence, on putting in place the conditions in which the founding principles of the Washington Consensus itself might be made to work better after a decade in which the results of neoliberal reform have been, at best, patchy and, at worst, disastrous. The post-Washington Consensus agenda constitutes more an agenda of 'Washington Consensus-plus' than any meaningful new direction in the way development is conceived or development strategies are designed. It also continues to rely on a particular interpretation of widespread development failures in the 1990s (particularly in Latin America) as being of intrinsically endogenous provenance. Consistent with neoliberal understandings of development as an inherently national process, development failures are understood to arise from 'incorrect' government policies, incomplete implementation of market reform agendas, the shortcomings of political systems (particularly high levels of corruption), domestic political opposition and resistance and so on. The Bank's development orthodoxy thus represents an agenda of *internal* policy reform which has left entirely untouched the issues of the global environment within which these policies have been pursued (Phillips 2005a). In a nutshell, the governance agenda suffered from the same failings as its structural adjustment-oriented predecessors, namely, that it was 'too idealistic, insufficiently historically specific and over-confident in respect of what we do know and can know about the politics of development' (Philip 1999: 226).

What lies at the heart of the World Bank's place in global governance – both as a refractor of the world order and as a force constitutive of it – is thus that its role as a knowledge bank is deployed for the purposes of furthering a particular ideological project, and the knowledge that it generates represents a development orthodoxy of a particular kind. Aside from the magnitude of funds at its disposal (in the region of US$20 billion), in this sense, the *structural* power of the World Bank is in large part of an ideological variety. The Bank has positioned itself since the 1980s as *the* prime agency responsible for generating the ideational foundations of prevailing development orthodoxy within the architecture of global governance. Its lending strategies, along with those of the IMF and the conditions attaching to loans from private creditors, aim to embed at the national level a set of norms that privilege the institutional, macroeconomic and microeconomic conditions and the forms of social organization necessary for their realization.

Yet the ability of the Bank to translate its strategies into concrete, 'successful' policy initiatives has been strikingly patchy and complicated. The financial and economic crises that spread across East Asia, Russia, Brazil and Argentina between 1997 and 2002, and the generalized failures of development across the world over the 1990s – leading, for example, to another 'lost half-decade' for much of Latin America (ECLAC 2002) in which per capita GDP was 1.5 per cent lower than in 1997 and levels of poverty reached 44 per cent of the total population of the region – have led to stinging critiques of the IFIs for both their ideas and policy agendas and their failures adequately to manage the crises themselves. Critics have, inevitably, come from both the left and the right, variously attacking the IFIs' strategies as responsible for the crises or attributing the crises to the failures of national governments adequately to implement their prescriptions. They have also come from within the institutions themselves, famously from Joseph Stiglitz (2002) after his departure from the World Bank.

Stiglitz, perhaps not surprisingly, aimed the bulk of his ammunition at the IMF rather than at the Bank, and the Bank has endeavoured since the time of the crises to establish 'intellectual and institutional distance' from the IMF (Standing 2000). In an immediate sense, in any case, much more criticism attached to the IMF over its handling of the international financial crises that erupted in these various parts of the world. Nevertheless, the 'backlash' before and, particularly, since the late 1990s has been against the neoliberal development orthodoxy in the broadest sense and its failure to produce sustained growth, stability and developmental progress. Moreover, it has widely been deemed, particularly in Latin America, Asia and Africa, to have acted directly to increase inequality and poverty and to exacerbate the socioeconomic and development problems faced by the vast majority of the world's societies. The Bank has also found itself frustrated by a failure to achieve many of the reforms that it has sought to promote in recipient countries, as a result of patchy or incomplete implementation, an unwillingness on the part of national policy elites to undertake particular reforms, the emergence of disabling political and societal resistance, and the obstacles – or, indeed, the catastrophic disruptions – occasioned by the functioning of the global political economy, whether in the form of volatility in financial markets or the persistent barriers to trade associated with protectionism in the advanced industrialized economies.

Despite the enormous degree of structural power and leverage that the World Bank possesses within the architecture of global governance, then, it has been unable to translate it into power of a more 'agential' kind through which it is able consistently to achieve its objectives in its lending strategies. In other words, it has been more effective as a force shaping the prevailing political, economic and ideological foundations of the contemporary global structure, but much less effective as an agent within that structure. But how then to understand the specific reasons for this disjuncture? It was suggested at the outset that there are three key issues which need to be taken into account, which we will take in turn.

The absence of ideological and ideational consensus

What the politics of the World Bank's activities in developing countries has shown, above all else, is that its ideological agenda is by no means as monolithic in the contemporary world order as many observers would like to suggest. On the one hand, it must be conceded that the Bank's greater involvement than the IMF with *debates* about development has made it 'even less the monolithic or mono-logical body which it has often been charged with being by over-hasty critics on both the left and the right' (Payne 2005b: 113). That is to say, as a self-styled 'knowledge bank' or development organization, some onus has come to rest on the Bank to engage with broader debates about development and changing ortho-doxies in the wider academy and policy community. In this regard, at least, while we have argued that there is little novelty of any fundamental substance in the path the Bank's ideas have charted from the Washington Consensus to the governance and second-generation reform agendas, the extent of the evolution of its official 'thinking' has been considerably greater than in the IMF, an evolution that is perhaps most evident in the governance agenda.

On the other hand, depictions of the pervasive and penetrating hegemony of neoliberalism – such as that offered by Cammack and many critical IPE approaches – are frequently blind to the ways in which that ideological hegemony is deeply contested and inherently fragile. Structuralist accounts of global gover-nance are frequently marked by an over-statement of the extent to which any ideological consensus which underpins the contemporary world order, repre-sented by or refracted through the structures of global governance, is of genuinely 'global' reach. There is a tendency, in discussions about epistemic communities, global technocratic elites, transnational historic blocs and global development, to underplay the fact that the dissemination of the Washington Consensus and other such ideas has not led to a global convergence on these principles, whether we would celebrate or lament such an eventuality. The contestation of the dominant ideological framework is, if anything, growing rather than attenuating in world politics and across the developing world.

It is of course the case that there has been a movement in large parts of the world to adopt a neoliberal model of social, political and economic organization. It is also the case that many leftist governments in, for example, Latin America that seek to challenge the prevailing neoliberal orthodoxy stop a good way short of abandoning a market-led model of development. A good part of the reason for this does indeed lie in the pressures and structural constraints imposed by the World Bank and other institutions of global governance, to which most governments in Latin America, Africa, Asia and elsewhere remain tied as a result of existing debt and the continuing need for financing. Yet, there remains a tendency, particularly from the left, to underplay the degree to which even national governments of a broadly neoliberal persuasion are vehemently hostile to the sorts of policy agendas pushed by the IFIs and other agents of the international financial community and 'Western' creditor communities. The development ideas of the World Bank and the notion of global governance itself remain intrinsically 'Western', or more properly 'Anglo-American' in both their genesis and their ongoing realization. Just as the processes of 'globalization' are not truly global but rather concentrated in the 'core' countries of the Organization for Economic Cooperation and Development (OECD), and the idea of an 'international community' corresponds with exactly the same, small, group of countries, so the notion of 'global governance' is a concern of distinctly 'Western' provenance and a liberal project associated with the corresponding power structures (Phillips 2005b). It is at the intersection of the rejections of US hegemony and Anglo-American neoliberalism, as well as resentment generated by widespread development failures, that the fragility of the ideological 'consensus' pursued by the institutions of global governance arises.

However, what is particularly important about the resurgent ideological and ideational contestations in the world is that they have emerged at least as much *within* what we might call the transnational neoliberal elite as outside it. This is not, in other words, a contestation that emanates only from disaffected parts of national and global civil societies or within parts of the world where a rejection of the 'Western' world order is prevalent. Nor is it solely the politics of opposition from those parts of societies that represent the 'losers' from globalization, neoliberal reform processes and financial crisis. Rather, Payne (2005b: 90), for example, has demonstrated how the predominant challenge to the post-Washington Consensus has come not from leftist or radical quarters but from the 'ambitious reassertion of right-wing politics and political economy mounted... in Washington in the very heart of the new US administration formed by George W. Bush'. He demonstrates how the tenets of the post-Washington Consensus were assailed by the dominance within these circles of 'mainstream liberal Republican economic values, suspicion of aid and relative hostility to the management of the global political economy by the multilateral institutions' (Payne 2005b: 136; see also Soederberg 2004). At least during the Bush administration, then, the development orthodoxy espoused by the World Bank – and, indeed, the importance of World Bank itself – have been questioned and marginalized by the government of the country which has long dominated the institution's decision-making processes and ideational foundations. It remains to be seen whether these trends are continued after the change of government in 2008.

The Bank has also found itself embroiled in a wider challenge to the structures and institutions of international financial governance. This was given particular impetus by the financial crises that spread across the world from the late 1980s, but was spearheaded, in some ways, from within that financial community by Stiglitz. While, as noted earlier, Stiglitz vented most of his spleen on the IMF, the Bank was equally caught up in the wider debate about whether the IFIs themselves should be demolished or, alternatively, in what ways they should be substantially reformed. Aside from the radical and leftist sources of this debate, which were founded on a fundamental contestation of the ideological power embodied by these institutions, it was conducted also within the transnational neoliberal community itself in a questioning of the ideational principles on which the system rested and which it was designed to serve, given the sharp demonstration of the failure of the IFIs' reform agendas to prevent either explosive crisis or continued stagnation. As such, the extent of both global convergence on the tenets of the neoliberal development orthodoxy and cohesion within the 'bloc' or 'community' associated with this dominant ideological project have been considerably over-stated in analyses of the World Bank and global governance, from both the left and the right. What is needed, instead, is an appreciation of the intrinsic fragility of the neoliberal ideological project and an awareness of the ways in which this has diminished the capacity of organizations like the World Bank effectively to translate its structural power into the consistently effective realization of its objectives in its lending strategies.

Competing structures and modes of governance

Related to the earlier arguments about ideological challenges to the Bank's exercise of power is a second set of points about the ways in which 'global' governance clashes in important ways with regionally and nationally specific structures and modes of governance. Much of the global governance literature is based on two pervasive assumptions or arguments: first, that global governance is indeed, as Rosenau (1997: 145) has it, about governance at *all* levels and thus draws national, regional, subnational, supranational and all other 'levels' of governance into an overarching 'global' whole; and second, that the emerging global governance structure is in essence a *single* umbrella structure which presides over and shapes world politics. Global governance is only unhelpfully understood in this manner. If it is to be understood adequately, governance has to be conceptualized as a plethora of systems of rule which do *not* coalesce into a single architecture of 'global governance'. What the explosive tensions and the persistent failures surrounding the World Bank's operations and activities demonstrate clearly is that there is no one governance structure currently in evidence, but rather a raft of different, overlapping and *competing* structures and modes of governance. The customary response to these sorts of points is that global governance is only emerging, that it is in the process of crystallizing, tentatively and unevenly. Yet the assumption remains that a system (singular) of global governance will eventually come into being. It is next to impossible, on this understanding, to account for the disjuncture in the structural power and 'agential' capabilities of the World Bank.

The tensions between these competing modes of governance are crucial to explanations of the disjuncture.

Within this idea, the various well-known arguments can be accommodated about the ways in which the good governance agenda, for example, has floundered as a result of its incompatibility with the politics and institutional structures of the target countries. The effectiveness of World Bank programmes depends not only on the political will of neoliberal elites in national contexts, but also on the nature of states, economies and political systems, particularly with regard to institutional characteristics and levels of political, institutional and social – aside from policy-related – capacities. This point has been recognized frequently by those concerned to identify the reasons for the failures of the governance agenda in various parts of the world (Philip 1999; Beeson 2001; Clapham 2002; Harrison 2005). They draw particular attention to an intrinsic tension between the tenets of the agenda and the institutional, political and social conditions in which the Bank seeks to embed it. The precise arguments are different for Latin America, East Asia or sub-Saharan Africa, naturally, but the general thrust is to emphasize the absence of existing levels and types of institutional development for the effective implementation and implantation of the governance agenda, along with the nature of political systems, dominant patterns of political interactions and practices, and prevailing socioeconomic conditions and structures.

The issue of domestic and regional political obstacles to the effective realization of World Bank objectives could also be included in this category. Arguments abound which identify lack of political capacity and the inability of reforming elites to overcome opposition to their policy initiatives as central to the reasons for the incomplete implementation or rejection of the Bank's prescriptions. Charnock's (2005) analysis of Mexico, for example, emphasizes the manner in which the government lacked the 'ideological and material capacity' to persuade trade unions of the merits of labour reform; analyses of labour, fiscal and tax reforms in other parts of Latin America similarly have drawn attention, as at least part of an explanation, to patterns of government–business–labour relations which have posed political obstacles to government reform efforts (Phillips 2004). The issue of domestic politics manifestly intersects with the earlier points about the lack of consensus on the neoliberal project and the sorts of ideas about development that it embodies. In this particular context, it is notable that popular antipathy towards the IFIs and resentment of the consequences of neoliberal reform domestically have been pronounced across those parts of the world most affected by the associated processes of change since the 1980s, and in many ways have grown rather than diminished as the World Bank's thinking has involved into its 'second-generation' phases.

Yet, to present these domestic political obstacles as being erected by societal and economic interests to the reforming efforts of national governments is excessively simplistic. It is also the case that, in many countries, the effective implantation of the Bank's agenda has been hampered by existing divergences in the models of development associated with distinct political economies. Moreover, governments across the world have been increasingly confident in rejecting the Bank's orthodoxy in their development strategies. While it is most certainly the case that the Bank exercises enormous sway over governments that are constrained by dependence on its lending, the recent evolution of political debates in many regions has revealed a much greater questioning and contestation of the neoliberal orthodoxy as an appropriate development model. This has been particularly clear in Latin America, where a rash of left-leaning governments has been elected across the region since the late 1990s, which has sought to chart a rather different path even while adhering broadly to the tenets of market economics. This challenge, both regionally and globally, has also received particular stimulus from the Argentine government's handling of its negotiations with the IMF and international financial community since the economic collapse of late 2001. It can be argued convincingly that its successful pursuit of a hard-line in its negotiations, which led to creditors accepting debt restructuring terms that fell significantly short of their original demands, has set a new precedent in the relationship between debtor countries and the international financial community. Perhaps more significantly still, the Bush administration's response to the Argentine crisis was striking for its degree of support for the Argentine government *over* the interests of private creditors and the IFIs, particularly the IMF (Helleiner 2005).

Whether this represents a long-term rupture of the historically intimate link between the US and the IFIs remains to be seen. But it does serve to now substantiate the arguments made earlier that the challenge to the ideological orthodoxy and 'consensus' underpinning global governance emanates not only from outside but also from inside the transnational community associated with that ideological hegemony. It also adds further sustenance to the present arguments that the influence and dominance of the IFIs is much less monolithic and much more tenuous than many analyses would suggest, and will sharpen the disjuncture between their structural power and 'agential' capabilities as key institutions of global governance.

Institutional issues

The third and final set of issues that would form part of an explanation relate to the institution itself, recalling the fourth dimension of the framework set out earlier. There is a solid general literature devoted to the World Bank as an organization and the problems associated with its operations (among others, Payer 1982; Shihata 1991; Nelson 1995; Miller-Adams 1999; Harrison 2004). For present purposes, four particular issues deserve brief comment. The first and second are perhaps most immediately obvious in explaining the Bank's patchy record, and relate to the organizational characteristics of the Bank itself. On the one hand, the Bank itself lacks robust enforcement mechanisms and the capacity to impose sanctions for non-compliance with the conditions attaching to its loans. On the other, the Bank is an enormously unwieldy institution characterized by myriad operational inefficiencies. Indeed, a large part of the debate within and outside the Bank concerns the best means of resolving these organizational problems, which are seen to have hampered the effective pursuit of the Bank's strategies.

The third and fourth issues cluster around the Bank's legitimacy. One of these relates to the problems of governance *within* the Bank itself, and specifically the challenges of implanting in the organization the same characteristics of accountability, transparency and representation that is pursued globally in the form of the good governance agenda (Woods 2000, 2001), have been seen to undermine the credibility of the Bank's activities. The other brings together a range of the issues that have already been raised in this chapter, and relates to the actual and perceived dominance of the World Bank by the US. As in other multi-lateral institutions, the US claims the largest share in the Bank's voting structures (16.4 per cent) and as a consequence wields unique veto power given that major decisions require an 85 per cent majority. Under the terms of the Bretton Woods agreement, the US also claims responsibility for choosing the Bank's President. While this dominance is even more pronounced in the case of the IMF, and has been afforded significant attention in the context of the aptly dubbed 'Wall Street-Treasury-IMF complex' (Wade and Veneroso 1998), the Bank is also both shaped by these patterns of US dominance, perceived to be directly representative of those interests, and, consequently, highly politicized in its decision-making procedures. The implications for the legitimacy of the institution, then, are clear, especially at a time when contestation of the neoliberal ideological project and resistance to the aggressive assertion of US hegemony are so prevalent in global politics.

In this context, the Bush administration's successful nomination of Paul Wolfowitz as James Wolfensohn's replacement in 2005 is likely substantially to have sharpened the crisis of legitimacy that has unfolded from the time of the financial crises. Wolfowitz's appointment was greeted with widespread consternation, some of the primary concerns centring on his relative inexperience, his (hitherto) lack of concern with questions of development and his views on environmental issues. Perhaps greater concerns related to the manner in which his appointment augured an increased harnessing of the World Bank to the foreign policy objectives of the Bush administration – that is, of reinforcing the extent to which the Bank functioned primarily as an expression of US interests. Given the aforementioned challenge to the Bank's development agenda that has emanated from the Bush administration, these new organizational developments look likely to add up to a severe crisis of legitimacy for the Bank and its activities. In this sense, it seems entirely probable that the reasons outlined here for the disjuncture between the Bank's structural power and its capabilities as an agent of global governance are likely to be exacerbated, such that the disjuncture itself is sharpened rather than diminished in the next phase of the Bank's evolution. If that is the case, existing perspectives on global governance are likely to become even more problematic for its effective analysis.

Conclusion

A consideration of the puzzle posed at the beginning of this chapter offers a useful way of grasping the complexity of the World Bank's position in the architecture and politics of global governance. On the one hand, its immense structural power is primarily of an ideological and ideational variety, and the 'rethink' of the Bank's role that has occurred over the 1990s has aimed directly to position the

Bank as the prime institution generating and disseminating development ideas and knowledge. The governance agenda and other programmes captured within the Comprehensive Development Framework have consolidated an unprecedented reach into and control over the social, political and institutional systems of the countries in which the Bank is active. Yet we have also seen that this power is substantially contested, from both inside the transnational community associated with the neoliberal project and outside it. Equally, and on the other hand, we have seen that this reach and scope has not translated into significant efficacy or success in exercising what we have called 'agential' power. That is, the Bank's record in achieving its objectives has been at best patchy. This disjuncture between the Bank's structural power and its ability effectively to exercise that power have been explained with reference to a range of factors relating to the global environment in which the Bank operates and the organizational characteristics of the Bank itself.

It has also been explained with reference to difficulties in the conceptualizations and theorizations of global governance that inform and shape analyses of institutions such as the World Bank. The bifurcation between structuralist and agency-centred approaches to the study of global governance has meant that, on the whole, these analyses have offered only partial and unsatisfactory accounts of the nature, influence and significance of the major institutions of global governance, including the World Bank. Rather, it has been argued here that what is needed is due attention to both the structural dimensions of the Bank's place and role in global governance, and to the Bank as an 'agent' or actor operating within that structure.

Each of these elements invites a closer analysis of the various countries that exercise considerable power both within the architecture of global governance and in the structures of the World Bank itself. Although the Bank remains unquestionably dominated by the US, a simplistic assertion of this dominance risks overlooking important questions about the politics that surround the production of knowledge within the Bank and the elaboration of its strategies. It has been shown that some of the main challenges to the Bank and its development strategies have emanated recently from the orientation and practices of the Bush administration in the US, and indeed that the relationship between the IFIs and the US is much more ambiguous and, in some ways, tenuous than at any time since the Bretton Woods agreement. Equally, it has been shown that global governance has to be understood as involving different and competing modes of governance, and that patterns of contestation are fundamental to understanding the evolution of the Bank's position within the architecture of global governance. In this sense, the time would appear to be particularly ripe for more considered analyses of *politics* within the Bank as an institution, as well as the international politics of global governance more broadly, and a greater focus on the manner in which major countries such as Japan participate in and shape those arenas.

References

Beeson, Mark (2001) 'Globalisation, governance, and the political-economy of public policy reform in East Asia', *Governance: An International Journal of Policy, Administration and Institutions* 14, 4: 481–502.

Cammack, Paul (2004) 'What the World Bank means by poverty reduction, and why it matters', *New Political Economy* 9, 2: 189–211.

Charnock, Greig (2006) 'Improving the mechanisms of global governance? The ideational impact of the World Bank on national reform agendas', *New Political Economy* 10, 3: 73–98.

Clapham, Christopher (2002) 'The challenge to the state in a globalized world', *Development and Change* 33, 5: 775–95.

Cox, Robert (1996) 'Global *perestroika*', in Robert W. Cox with Timothy J. Sinclair, *Approaches to World Order*, Cambridge: Cambridge University Press, pp. 296–313.

ECLAC (United Nations Economic Commission for Latin America and the Caribbean) (2002) *Preliminary Overview of the Economies of Latin America and the Caribbean, 2002*, Santiago: United Nations.

Finkelstein, Lawrence S. (1995) 'What is global governance?', *Global Governance* 1, 4: 367–72.

Gamble, Andrew (2000) 'Economic Governance', in Jon Pierre (ed.) *Debating Governance: Authority, Steering, and Democracy*, Oxford: Oxford University Press, pp. 110–37.

Gill, Stephen (1995) 'Globalisation, market civilisation, and disciplinary neo-liberalism', *Millennium: Journal of International Studies* 24, 3: 399–423.

Global Development Network (2005), available online at http://www.gdnet.org, accessed on 14 May 2005.

Harrison, Graham (2004) *The World Bank and Africa: The Construction of Governance States*, London: Routledge.

—— (2005) 'The World Bank, governance and theories of political action in Africa', *British Journal of Politics and International Relations* 7, 2: 240–60.

Helleiner, Eric (2005) 'The strange story of Bush and the Argentine debt crisis', *Third World Quarterly* 26, 6: 951–69.

Kahler, Miles and Lake, David A. (eds) (2003) *Governance in a Global Economy: Political Authority in Transition*, Princeton, NJ: Princeton University Press.

Kaul, Inge, Grunberg, Isabelle and Stern, Marc A. (eds) (1999) *Global Public Goods: International Cooperation in the 21st century*, New York: Oxford University Press for the United Nations Development Programme.

Lake, David A. (1999) 'Global governance: a relational contracting approach', in Aseem Prakash and Jeffrey A. Hart (eds) *Globalization and Governance*, London: Routledge, pp. 31–53.

McGinnis, Michael D. (1999) 'Rent-seeking, redistribution, and reform in the governance of global markets', in Aseem Prakash and Jeffrey A. Hart (eds) *Globalization and Governance*, London: Routledge, pp. 54–76.

Miller-Adams, Michelle (1999) *The World Bank: New Agendas in a Changing World*, London: Routledge.

Murphy, Craig N. (2000) 'Global governance: poorly done and poorly understood', *International Affairs* 76, 4: 789–803.

Nelson, Paul (1995) *The World Bank and Non-governmental Organizations: The Limits of Apolitical Development*, Basingstoke: Macmillan.

Payer, Cheryl (1982) *The World Bank: A Critical Analysis*, New York: Monthly Review.

Payne, Anthony (2005a) 'The study of governance in a global political economy', in Nicola Phillips (ed.) *Globalizing International Political Economy*, Basingstoke: Palgrave, pp. 55–81.

—— (2005b) *The Global Politics of Unequal Development*, Basingstoke: Palgrave.

Philip, George (1999) 'The dilemmas of good governance: a Latin American perspective', *Government and Opposition* 34, 2: 226–42.

Phillips, Nicola (2004) *The Southern Cone Model: The Political Economy of Regional Capitalist Development in Latin America*, London: Routledge.

—— (2005a) 'Latin America in the global political economy', in Richard Stubbs and Geoffrey R. D. Underhill (eds) *Political Economy and the Changing Global Order*, Don Mills, ON: Oxford University Press, pp. 332–43.

—— (ed.) (2005b) *Globalizing International Political Economy*, Basingstoke: Palgrave.

Prakash, Aseem and Hart, Jeffrey A. (eds) (1999) *Globalization and Governance*, London: Routledge.

Rosenau, James N. (1997) *Along the Domestic–Foreign Frontier: Exploring Governance in a Turbulent World*, Cambridge: Cambridge University Press.

—— (2002) 'Change, complexity and governance in a globalizing space', in Jon Pierre (ed.) *Debating Governance: Authority, Steering, and Democracy*, Oxford: Oxford University Press, pp. 167–200.

Shihata, Ibrahim F. I. (1991) *The World Bank in a Changing World: Selected Essays*, Dordrecht and Boston, MA: Martinus Nijhoff.

Soederberg, Susanne (2004) 'The Emperor's new suit: the new international financial architecture as a reinvention of the Washington Consensus', *Global Governance* 7, 4: 453–67.

Standing, Guy (2000) 'Brave new worlds? a critique of Stiglitz's World Bank rethink', *Development and Change* 31, 1: 737–63.

Stiglitz, Joseph A. (2002) *Globalization and Its Discontents*, London: Penguin.

Swedberg, Richard (1986) 'The doctrine of economic neutrality of the IMF and the World Bank', *Journal of Peace Research* 23, 4: 377–90.

Tussie, Diana and Botzman, Mirta (1992) 'Sweet entanglement: Argentina and the World Bank 1985–9', in Ennio Rodríguez and Stephany Griffith-Jones (eds) *Cross-conditionality, Banking Regulation and Third World Debt*, London: Macmillan, pp. 156–90.

Wade, Robert and Veneroso, Frank (1998) 'The Asian crisis: the high debt model vs. the Wall Street-Treasury-IMF model', *New Left Review* 228: 3–27.

Wilkinson, Rorden (2002) 'Global governance: a preliminary interrogation', in Rorden Wilkinson and Steve Hughes (eds) *Global Governance: Critical Perspectives*, London: Routledge, pp. 1–13.

Wilkinson, Rorden and Hughes, Steve (eds) (2002) *Global Governance: Critical Perspectives*, London: Routledge.

Williams, David and Young, Tom (1994) 'Governance, the World Bank and liberal theory', *Political Studies* 42, 1: 84–100.

Woods, Ngaire (2000) 'The challenge of good governance for the IMF and the World Bank themselves', *World Development* 28, 5: 823–41.

—— (2001) 'Making the IMF and the World Bank more accountable', *International Affairs* 77, 1: 83–100.

World Bank (1989) *Sub-Saharan Africa: From Crisis to Sustainable Growth: A Long-term Perspective Study*, New York: Oxford University Press.

—— (1992) *Governance and Development*, Washington, DC: IBRD.

—— (1997) *World Development Report 1997: The State in a Changing World*, New York: Oxford University Press.

6 Global governance, Japan and the World Bank

Sasuga Katsuhiro

Introduction

This chapter discusses Japan's increasingly significant role in global multilateral economic institutions (MEIs) with particular reference to the changing relations between Japan and the World Bank from the perspective of global governance. Japan's foreign policy has typically been seen as *passive* and *reactive* (under domestic political pressure and the external pressure of the US) and as *constrained* (by the international circumstances in which Japan has found itself). However, relations between Japan and the World Bank in the 1990s and the early 2000s suggest a more proactive effort by Japan to mobilize its official development assistance (ODA) policy, with increasing emphasis being placed on multilateral aid. This proactive role in the provision of multilateral aid is in stark contrast to most of the existing literature on Japanese ODA, which still focuses on bilateral ODA relations. What is now needed is an extension of ODA analysis to take into account multilateral aid. Undoubtedly, Japanese ODA has been an integral, and perhaps the only visible, political and economic component of Japan's national interest as expressed through the foreign policy pursued. Certainly, in the post-cold war period, Japanese ODA has become a strong measure of foreign policy activity. This chapter argues that, despite the existence of many constraining factors, Japan's foreign economic policy has recently begun to emphasize the country's international responsibilities, with a new focus on MEIs. In terms of the implications of these trends for the emergent system of global governance, it is clear that Japan's stronger role in the World Bank has given it an opportunity to contribute more positively and more assertively to the functioning of governance on a global scale. Japan's role is especially significant because it derives from a primarily economic basis rather than from any overt politico-military role (although, as seen later, in the 1990s it became much more difficult to draw a clear dividing line between economics and politics); and it builds upon Japan's strong past record as a provider of bilateral ODA. This raises the key issue of how Japan actually exercises its influence within the World Bank and how *political* that role is, for example, in the development of World Bank policy through interactions with World Bank officials and the representatives of other governments, especially the US and the countries of the European Union (EU). The links between Japan's national policy-making institutions and networks, including its powerful Ministry of Finance (MOF, which is in charge of Japanese operations at the World Bank and other MEIs but delegates much decision-making power to the Ministry's International Finance Bureau, IFB), the Ministry of Foreign Affairs (MOFA), major ODA agencies in Japan, and the international policy-making level at the World Bank, are especially important in this respect. This involves the roles of both elected politicians and appointed officials. In the case of MOF, it is noteworthy that its aid decisions and actions are relatively unconstrained by political bodies, including the Japanese parliament.

Japan has also become a strong regional player in the system of global governance through its specifically East Asian focus on economic and financial issues, including developmental issues. In particular, Japan has come to play a major role in the Asian Development Bank (ADB, established in 1966). This highlights the view of global governance as a multi-level system, including both the global and regional levels of operation and a variety of multilateral programmes. In reality, global governance embraces regional and even sub-regional governance as well as the strictly global (international) level. Two of the most interesting questions as far as Japan is concerned are: how does it seek to combine its global and regional (East Asian) roles? And can the East Asian region justifiably be seen as an increasingly significant 'integrated' global player in the MEIs?

In sum, Japan's position illustrates well the complexity of global governance, since it draws attention to the relative roles of international institutions, regional and sub-regional institutions, the state level of decision making, and also bilateral relations between states. Increasingly, also, it is essential to pay attention to the significance of private-sector institutions, including banks and firms involved in the governance of global and regional production networks, and civil society (non-governmental) organizations in the emergent system of global governance. There is also a very important dimension of global governance that focuses on informal networking arrangements, for example, meetings of experts and scholars from different countries outside the 'official' institutional boundaries. This is especially important in terms of the developing intellectual and cognitive basis for global governance. One of the main arguments of this chapter is that global governance is, in both functional and spatial terms, immensely complex; it is not just a single system of authority or power. It is to be stressed that concepts such as 'globalization' and 'global governance' are at present highly contested, and the way in which these concepts are analysed depends on the view taken regarding the contemporary, post-cold war international political economy both horizontally and vertically, and in terms of political-power dynamics. From a policy-making point of view, what is also important in this respect is how Japanese policy makers and officials conceptualize these processes.

The chapter is divided into four sections. The first section discusses the changing relationship between Japan and the World Bank, stressing Japan's transformation from a borrower to a lender. The second section examines the impact of Japan as an increasingly influential state actor vis-à-vis the Bank's activity. The third section analyses the increasing role of Japan in terms of finance, human resources and funding projects. The fourth and final section considers the specific implications of Japan's changing World Bank role for the future of global governance, stressing that global governance is in transition and is an immensely complex, multi-tiered and fragmented phenomenon (so that the future is in fact very difficult to predict).

Japan: from a borrower to a lender

Japan's aid policy and behaviour in foreign policy can be traced back to the country's post-war transformation. For post-war Japan, 'reconstruction' and 'peace' were realized as ultimate values in contrast to the country's wartime ambition to challenge the international status quo. After achieving reconstruction, there was a new emphasis placed on 'prosperity', and this has continued to be a powerful norm for the Japanese people up to the present day. In 1945, after Japan's defeat, the Allied forces (dominated by the US) occupied Japan with the aim of achieving Japan's demilitarization and democratization. Japanese economic policy was set under the control of the US. This indirect rule by the US had a decisive effect on the shaping of Japan's post-war foreign policy. In these circumstances, Japan learned the importance of maintaining sincere cooperation and a low profile with the US in order to achieve its national objectives (Iokibe 2001: 7). Japan's security framework was established under the 1951 US–Japan Security Treaty, concluded on the same day as the San Francisco Peace Treaty (8 September). This allowed Japan to stick to a minimalist defence policy while constraining Japan's independent activity in the security field. Japan's position in the international community, as a member of the Western capitalist bloc, was thus settled. This enabled Japan to shift its priority to gaining independence in economic diplomacy and pursuing its own economic development.

In August 1952, with US support, Japan succeeded in obtaining entry to the World Bank. At this time, Japan was a relatively poor country, with an average income of just US$200 per year (Yasutomo 1995: 65), and was having difficulty with the management of its balance of payments. It needed a large amount of financial aid in order to re-establish basic industries. Japan hoped to join all the key international organizations at the earliest possible moment, not only for the purpose of reconstruction but also as an accepted legitimte member of the international community. In the reconstruction of the Japanese economy, Japan utilized first bilateral US aid and thereafter World Bank loans for establishing infrastructure and for investment in basic industries. Between 1953 and 1966, Japan borrowed more than US$863 million from the World Bank, and it finally completed repayment in July 1990. In 1953, the first loans from the World Bank were taken in order to support a power plant project. Then, later in the 1950s, the projects funded by the World Bank were extended to steel plants, the automobile industry (e.g. Toyota's truck and bus factory), ship-engine plant and agricultural development; and in the early 1960s to freeway and *shinkansen* (bullet train) development. These projects were seen as essential in order to compensate Japan for its shortages in the electricity, steel, coal and transportation sectors. The Bank assessed Japan's capability to absorb aid and promote the development of compatible institutions. In particular, MITI (the Ministry of International Trade and Industry, now the Ministry of Economy, Trade and Industry, METI) implemented various industrial and export promotion measures leading to structural change in the Japanese economy. By the end of the 1950s, the first reconstruction stage was almost complete, and Japan finished borrowing from the Bank in 1966 as it entered the decade of the so-called 'economic miracle'. From the late 1950s, with astute government economic policies, the private sector developed strong incentives to improve productivity and international competitiveness. Japan's reconstruction process was not the same as that of developing countries receiving development assistance, but its experience of utilizing loans did enhance the development role of the World Bank.

Japan's overseas aid started in the 1950s in the form of bilateral reparation payments to countries occupied by Japan during the Second World War. Japan was thus in a dual position: as a developing country (a borrower) and a developed country (a lender). The first war compensation agreement was concluded with Burma in 1955, followed in 1956 by an agreement with the Philippines, and then agreements with Indonesia in 1958 and Vietnam in 1959. Japan's first involvement in multilateral aid was through technical assistance as part of the British Colombo Plan in 1954 and 1958. Then Japan started to increase ODA through yen loans. The key characteristic of Japanese ODA was that it was implemented in response to requests from the recipient countries (the request-basis principle) and self-help efforts. Thus, ODA was carried out according to these criteria without any careful consideration of systematic planning policies. Such aid implementation, to some extent, indicated a lack of any autonomous Japanese decision-making strategy for aid. There was a focus on dealing with the past (the war and its impact) and on the vague possibility of reintegrating East Asia. Thus a large part of Japanese ODA was focused on Southeast Asian countries that had experienced war damage, and this was regarded by Japan as an atonement 'gift'. At the same time, businesses were able to take advantage of this situation, and MITI officials saw clearly the potential for Japan to again play a leading role in East Asia, as was also the case with the American planners, who were concerned about the Chinese economy being closed to Japan after Mao's takeover in 1949. Some institutions were established to put these policies into practice, such as the Overseas Economic Cooperation Fund (OECF) and the Overseas Technical Cooperation Agency (later known as the Japan International Cooperation Agency, JICA). Also, the US began putting pressure on Japan to increase aid to the Southeast Asian region; it saw that region as a major source of raw materials and as a potentially vital export market for Japan. In general, US Asian policy aimed to ensure the political stability of the non-communist Asian countries as part of the overall containment policy against communism. It was clear to US leaders that military assistance alone could not achieve the necessary regional stability. For Japan, it was essential to offer economic assistance to Southeast Asia in the form of trade promotion and resource acquisition. Although such economic cooperation benefited the Japanese private sector, more importantly it helped to increase Japan's international status and role in Southeast Asia.

By the early 1970s, the Japanese economy had reached a high level of performance, and the world started to pay attention to Japanese aid. In 1984,

Japan became the second largest contributor (behind the US) to the World Bank. Japanese ODA reached the world number one position between 1991 and 2000 (MOFA 2004a: 4). In the 1990s, Japanese ODA expenditure was consistently between US$10 billion and US$15 billion per annum. Though it dropped to US$8.88 billion in 2003, as financial recession took hold in Japan and fiscal deficit problems had to be dealt with (see Chapter 8 for details), it is still today the second largest national source of overseas aid. As part of Japanese ODA, the level of multilateral aid through international organizations and multilateral development banks (MDBs, including the World Bank, the Asian Development Bank, the Inter-American Development Bank, the African Development Bank, and the European Bank for Reconstruction and Development) varied between 13.3 per cent in 1996 and 30.0 per cent in 1997. In 2004, Japan's total subscription reached US$15.3 billion, amounting to an 8.1 per cent share of the IBRD's total fund of US$189.7 billion. In the IDA, Japan's subscription share has been maintained at about 22 per cent of the total fund in the last decade (see Table 6.1). In 2004, Japan's attendant voting shares reached 7.86 per cent in the IBRD and 10.89 per cent in the IDA. Thus, Japan has been the major contributor to the World Bank since the mid-1980s, thereby reflecting the Japanese government's commitment to multilateral aid as an integral part of its foreign policy and diplomatic activity; but Japanese policy did not begin to be reflected in the policy-making processes of the Bank until the early 1990s.

Despite the country's importance as a donor of ODA, the specific characteristics of Japanese ODA are not well known. The Asian region is the top priority for Japan's ODA. In 2003, 53.6 per cent of all Japan's bilateral ODA was provided to this region. In Japanese ODA there has been a strong focus on social infrastructure, transportation and energy projects. Among Japanese ministries, MOFA and MOF are key players in the implementation procedures of ODA. In the fiscal year 2004, the total ODA budget in the general account was 816.9 billion yen, representing a 4.8 per cent decrease from the previous year. MOFA's share of the ODA budget was 61.2 per cent and MOF's share was 26.9 per cent (MOFA 2004b). In the 2004 project budget (1,482.7 billion yen), MOF's share accounted for 59 per cent and MOFA's share was 34 per cent. The rest of the ODA budget is also shared by all other ministries, including Education, Culture, Sports,

Table 6.1 Japan's subscription shares and voting power in the IBRD and IDA (in percentage)

	1999	2000	2001	2002	2003	2004
Japan's subscription share in the IBRD	8.1	8.1	8.1	8.1	8.1	8.1
Voting power in the IBRD	7.93	7.91	7.87	7.87	7.87	7.86
Japan's subscription share in the IDA	21.5	22.5	22.1	22.1	22.8	22.3
Voting power in the IDA	10.73	10.61	10.90	11.03	10.92	10.89

Source: World Bank (2003 and 2004).

Science and Technology; Land, Infrastructure and Transport; Agriculture, Forestry and Fisheries; the Cabinet Office; the Financial Service Agency; Internal Affairs and Telecommunication; Justice; Health, Labour and Welfare, and so on.

National interests and development assistance

The World Bank is officially 'governed' by representatives of all its member countries and is thus inherently political, but in reality the representatives of the developed countries are by far the most important. There is considerable scope for conflicts of interest among members attempting to use their influence at the Bank. In the 1980s, the Reagan administration in the US emphasized the neo-liberal ideology promoting privatization and deregulation. The US, the major funder of the Bank, contributes the largest share of the Bank's funds, appoints the Bank's President, and controls the largest bloc of votes on the Bank's Executive Board. The US Congress has the power of decision over ODA; thus US security and national interest have been the primary concern in the use of ODA. For example, Egypt, an important recipient of US ODA, has supported the US interest in the Middle East. During the mid-1980s, the US Congress threatened to withhold future funds from the Bank unless it changed its practices. The Congress became increasingly doubtful about the MEIs' efficiency in relation to the US's interest. With its huge fiscal debt in the 1980s, the US was no longer generous towards the management of the Bank, and closely monitored the Bank's activities. Furthermore, the Bank's dependence on America's growing financial market increased the US influence on the Bank. In terms of Reagan's neo-liberal policies, an open market and the free flow of capital were seen as essential for economic growth, and these ideas were strongly supported by the IMF (the International Monetary Fund) and the World Bank (based in Washington, hence the term 'Washington Consensus'; see Williamson 2000). The end of the cold war gave more credibility to this dominant philosophy. The US Congress has used the opportunities to impose conditions on the overall governance and direction of the World Bank. In 1994, it followed through with its previous threat, withholding US$1 billion from the Bank. In 1998, the Congress threatened to cut funding for the IDA if the Bank made a controversial loan to China. The Bank was under pressure from the US and other Western donors to broaden its agenda to include issues of human rights and democracy. In 2000, the Meltzer report on the need to reform MEIs, expressing the voice of the US Congress, called for the World Bank to revise its functions and scale down its activities. The report proposed a change in name from the 'World Bank' to the 'World Development Agency', the latter suggesting more of a technical assistance centre focusing on Human Immunodeficiency Virus (HIV), natural disasters, environmental issues, and so forth. The 9/11 terror attacks on the US in 2001 also had a huge impact on America's ODA policies. Poverty was seen to be the hotbed of terrorism, and hence the poverty reduction promoted by the Bank was seen as an urgent, primary objective of US ODA. The Bush administration succeeded in persuading the Congress in this respect. It regarded good governance in the recipient countries as a core condition for the promotion of development.

Though there are few countervailing pressures from other shareholders, the Japanese government once challenged US dominance in the Bank. Japan increased its financial contribution substantially during the 1980s and 1990s, but it was uncomfortable with the Bank's dominant neo-liberal approach. In the late 1980s, the Japanese government began to voice its reservations. It criticized the neo-liberal approach, which paid little attention to the role of government, and adopted a more activist stance, advocating an alternative perspective based on Japanese and East Asian experience. Japan's developmental state model, which originally offered an explanation of Japan's own economic success, was subsequently applied to explain the pattern of development of East Asia under the name of the 'flying geese' model. The close cooperative relations between government and the private sector in Japan were called the 'developmental state' (Johnson 1982). Shiratori Masaaki, a former Vice Chairman of the OECF, made it his mission to impress on the Bank Japan's impatience with the prevailing neo-liberal philosophy. Sakakibara Eisuke (former Vice Minister of Finance for International Affairs, called 'Mr Yen') opposed structural adjustment by the IMF and the Bank, arguing the need for alternative paths following the Japanese model, such as a main bank system prior to launching full-scale privatization and deregulation (Terry 2000: 5–7). MOF proposed that the Bank should research East Asian economic development, and this resulted in the publication of *The East Asian Miracle: Economic Growth and Public Policy* in 1993. This report emphasized a 'market friendly approach' but also recognized the importance of the institutional environment, the role of government intervention in the private sector and the necessity of long-term planning. However, the emergence of the East Asian financial crisis in July 1997 called for a reassessment of the East Asian experience with political and economic governance and institutions. Japan attempted to launch an Asian Monetary Fund (AMF) with US$100 billion standby funds assembled from Asian donors. Sakakibara, the principal mover of this project, argued that an AMF would assist greatly with the bailout of Thailand, which was the first economy hit by the crisis in 1997. This proposal was harshly attacked by the US Treasury Department, with its strong interest in opening up financial and capital markets; it insisted that an AMF would undermine IMF discipline in the region. The US succeeded in replacing the AMF proposal by a policy of regional surveillance. Consequently, MOF's clumsy policy implementation, including inadequate personnel management towards the Bank, reinforced the continued dominance of the US. Nevertheless, in terms of development norms, the market-friendly intervention and policy coordination initiated by the Japanese government has helped to shift the Bank's emphasis on development strategies from a neo-liberal approach to a more institutionally focused concept of poverty reduction.

Japan's foreign aid policy and the Bank

In the 1980s, Japan's steady increase in financial contributions and voting strength did not automatically translate into policy influence at the World Bank. There were several reasons for this from an organizational viewpoint: the World

Bank operated a weighted voting system, so that winning coalitions of countries were necessary; Japan lacked expert knowledge and secretariat and management posts; and Japan also had little political experience of gaining a power basis sufficient to push its proposals through. Moreover, the Bank was located in the US (Washington, DC), was dominated by American staff, used the English language in its main deliberations and employed a US decision-making style. For Japan, this was a very complex and difficult institutional environment (Wan 2001: 145). These are all key factors in any international organization, and they have an enormous impact upon the nature, scope and style of governance. In the 1990s, Japan made strenuous efforts to overcome these barriers, and gradually mastered the art of intellectual and policy influence, not least by focusing on administrative and personnel issues, and by gaining the courage to give 'voice' to distinctly Japanese experience and approaches, especially Japan's own developmental model. Surprisingly, despite a sharp decrease in the total ODA budget since 2001, Japan has increased its subscription to the IDA and has gained strengthened voting power (see Table 6.1). Capital increases for the IBRD, International Finance Corporation (IFC) and Multilateral Investment Guarantee Agency (MIGA) were rare – just one each in the 1980s; only at the IDA do donor countries have a chance to increase their capital and hence their influence. Though the budget for the World Bank and other MDBs declined after 2000, Japanese ODA, as a share of the total expenditures for these institutions, has been maintained at a consistent level (see Table 6.2). This is due to the somewhat special characteristics of the Japanese ODA budgetary structure. The financial resources of Japanese ODA consist of the general account budget and other parts including Fiscal Investment and Loans (*Zaiseitōyūshi*), the special account, and government bonds. *Zaiseitōyūshi* is funded largely by postal savings, postal life insurance (*Kampo*), national pension funds, and such like. In the 2004 project budget, the *Zaiseitōyūshi* surprisingly accounted for 35 per cent of total Japanese ODA. The fact that these government bonds are charged by MOF itself makes it possible for MOF to allocate the budget without any interference from other ministries and politicians. Thus, despite the currently severe fiscal condition faced by the government, MOF retains its budgetary allocation power in relation to MEIs.

Despite Japan's enormous financial contribution to the World Bank, the number of Japanese staff at the Bank remains quite small. Among 3,381 professional staff, the number of Japanese staff was 81 in June 2002. In 2004, Japan had two Vice Presidents and one Executive Director at the Bank. Vice President Katsu Shigeo is in charge of Europe and Central Asia, and Yoshimura Yukio is the special representative for Japan. In the World Bank group, Ōmura Yukiko was appointed as Executive Vice President of MIGA in 2004. However, most of the Bank's staff is American, amounting in total to almost one quarter of the total of 10,000. Interestingly, other nationals, such as those of India and the Philippines, even though their countries' financial contributions to the Bank are much lower than the contribution of Japan, account for more than two or three times the number of Japanese employees (Ōno 2000: 224). It is noteworthy that those Japanese staff at the Bank who are employed as specialists on development issues do not in any sense work for the Japanese government, and hence their views

Table 6.2 Japan's ODA and the multilateral institutions (expenditure, US$ million and per cent share of total)

International Organizations	1993	1994	1995	1996	1997	1998	1999	2000	2001	2002	2003
Total expenditure of Japanese ODA	11,259	13,239	14,489	9,439	9,358	10,640	12,162	13,508	9,847	9,283	8,880
Japanese ODA as a share of total expenditure to international organizations	28.6	27.8	28.1	13.3	30.0	19.8	13.9	27.7	24.3	27.9	29.8
Japanese ODA as a share of total contributions and donations to UN agencies and other multilateral institutions	5.8	6.7	5.7	8.3	7.4	6.6	6.7	11.8	10.2	11.3	13.0
Japanese ODA as a share of total funding to the World Bank group	14.2	13.3	16.0	0.1	16.5	7.6	2.2	8.5	8.8	12.1	10.9
Japanese ODA as a share of total funding to other MDBs	9.3	9.6	7.0	4.9	6.3	5.8	5.3	7.6	5.6	5.0	6.2

Source: The author's calculations, based on figures from MOFA (2004a,b).

Notes

'MDBs' includes funding to the EBRD (European Bank for Reconstruction and Development). Total Japanese ODA does not include aid towards Eastern Europe and 'graduation' countries (those that have achieved successful economic development and are no longer recipients of aid).

are not necessarily in accordance with the Japanese national interest. Thus, the approaches towards the Bank from the Japanese side are crucial, and it is important to realize that the Development Institution of the International Bureau at MOF must cope with the decisions of the Board of Executive Directors of the World Bank. MOF continuously sends its staff to the Bank; in 2002, five persons from MOF were employed by the Bank (Motoda 2004: 128). In general, under these limitations, it is not possible to identify any clear, constructive and strategic approaches by Japan in its dealings with the World Bank. Japan's direct engagement can be seen in its co-financing lending activities and trust funds programmes. Co-financing involves coordinated finance projects between the Bank and its partners (such as export credit agencies and private investors), targeting specific projects of the Bank. Japan engaged in co-financing with the World Bank on structural adjustment lending from the mid-1980s through OECF and the Export–Import Bank of Japan (these two subsequently merged and became the Japan Bank for International Cooperation, JBIC). The average co-financing with OECF between 1988 and 1997 reached US$88 million per project, and for the Export–Import Bank of Japan US$123 million per project during the same period. In the 1990s, the relations between Japan and the Bank deepened through a widening of policy-level cooperation. This trend was initiated by the East Asian Miracle project, and the Japan Bank for International Cooperation (JBIC) has extended its cooperative relations with the Bank and now participates in the preparation of Poverty Reduction Strategic Papers (PRSP) in Vietnam, Laos and Bangladesh. In 2004, JBIC and the World Bank signed a co-financing agreement for the metro line 4 project in Sao Paulo, Brazil. JBIC will provide US$209 million for the project and the Bank will supervise the implementation of JBIC's loan. This will complement US$516 million financing from the Sao Paulo government and US$183 million from private investment. The Japanese private banks have also participated in co-financing projects and have played an important role in the implementation of projects.

Trust funds are financial and administrative arrangements between external donors and the Bank that provide grant funding to address diverse development needs. There are two particular trust funds in which Japan has been deeply engaged. The Japan Policy and Human Resources Development Fund (PHRD) was created in 1990 as a partnership between the Japanese government and the Bank. PHRD, one of the largest sources of grant funds, has provided nearly 3,500 grants in support of technical assistance activities to more than 140 countries. This seeks to promote poverty reduction in developing countries through technical assistance and institutional strengthening. It also provides funds for the analysis of Asia in the *World Development Report*. Another trust fund is the Japan Social Development Fund (JSDF), established in 2000, which is an untied grant facility. The Japanese government has donated funds of US$95 million with the aim of helping the World Bank to tackle poverty and the social consequences resulting from economic and financial crisis. The performance of the JSDF has been evaluated by annual joint meetings of the World Bank, the Japanese government and the ADB. Japan and the ADB established the Japan Fund for

Poverty Reduction (JFPR, a similar fund to the JSDF) in 2000. Both focus on the Asian region and actively try to utilize partnerships with non-governmental organizations (NGOs). In 2003, 68 per cent of the total grant to the JSDF was delivered to Asia. The JFPR embraces a unique opportunity for the ADB and Japan to test innovative poverty-reduction approaches incorporated with ADB loans. Japan makes the largest funding contribution to the ADB (equal to that of the US) and has always held the top position of the ADB presidency. Furthermore, Japanese expert staff account for 13.1 per cent of the total (Zaimushō 2003). It is noteworthy that reconstruction support for Afghanistan was seen as a co-formulation between Japanese bilateral and multilateral aid, in which the ADB played a vital role in bridging Japanese ODA with the JSDF projects under the World Bank (Zaimushō 2003). Another important project is that for the WBI (World Bank Institute), which aims to support human resource development in developing countries. Japan has been the largest donor to this programme, and has also sought to use the programme to apply the experience of its own economic development. In 2002, for example, some 94 per cent of approved projects utilized Japanese human resources or organizations. In general, this evidence underlines the increasingly proactive stance adopted by Japan in recent years.

For Japan, foreign aid is very significant not only for the fields of security and international trade but also for increasing Japan's international status and for supporting Japanese participation in the shaping of the international order. In Japan's development policies, the Bank is seen as a useful source of leverage to increase the capability for instrumentalizing Japanese foreign policy. Through multilateral aid, Japan is able to participate in aid projects for countries where its bilateral ODA is dislocated for reasons such as political sensitivity. In addition, the Bank has so far developed its comparative advantage in many development fields; thus Japan can efficiently use the Bank's resources. Capital increases and cooperation through trust funds in the Bank greatly help to underline Japan's policy and position in the international community. As seen earlier, Japan is able to express its own development philosophy based on its experience by supporting the Bank's projects. Japan's interest in Asia is carried out through the Bank, and this helps to actively involve Japan in the formation of the international order. Thus, in order to achieve its purposes, Japan needs to train development specialists who understand both Japan's national interest and the international public interest expressed by the World Bank.

In this respect, it is important to understand the political-strategic dimensions of Japan's revised ODA policy as they emerged in the 1990s. The Miyazawa Kiichi cabinet (1991–3) formally announced, in the 'ODA Charter' of 1992, that Japan's aid would henceforth give priority to diplomatic and political objectives, especially programmes related to democratization, human and civil rights, arms control, targeted military spending, economic liberalization, women's issues and the preservation of the human environment (Yasutomo 1995: 10–16). This new trend suggests that the traditional view that Japan's foreign and diplomatic policy is 'separate' from its economic policy is in need of revision. As Yasutomo puts it, 'For Japan, ODA is high politics in a post-cold war world where economic competition increasingly defines international relations' (1995: 3). Japanese ODA continued to be based on self-help efforts and direct requests by recipients until the late 1990s. Thus the yen loan was seen to support such self-help efforts in developing countries, and the 1992 ODA Charter clearly differed from the Bank's conditionality principles. Following the movement to revise the MEIs' aid policies in the late 1990s, Japan began to revise its own ODA policies. Though the new norms, such as 'poverty reduction' in the IMF and the World Bank, are also important for Japan, the Japanese emphasis is on promoting economic development as a means to reduce poverty in low-income countries. In this respect, for Japan, poverty reduction and economic growth are inseparable. In August 2003, the ODA Charter was again revised. The new version states that Japan will contribute to the peace and development of the international community, thereby helping to ensure Japan's own security and prosperity. The new ODA Charter reflects recent changes in the international political and economic environment, stressing current problems such as the gap between the poor and the rich, ethnic and religious conflicts, armed conflicts, terrorism, the suppression of freedom, human rights, democracy, environmental problems, infectious diseases, and gender issues. It also reflects the impact of public opinion in Japan and the increasingly voiced criticisms of the traditional approach to ODA (see Chapter 8 for details).

Japanese ODA is now undertaken not only by the national government and ministries but also by NGOs and local governments. While Japanese ODA led by the national government is seen to be inseparable from the country's economic national interests, the idea of ODA as an international contribution has gradually gained acceptance among Japanese citizens. The number of Japanese NGOs undertaking foreign assistance projects reached 351 in 1995 (Saotome 1997) and more than 400 in 2001 (Menju 2003: 99). The activities of NGOs target grassroots social and development projects such as the improvement of the medical environment, job training and environmental protection. NGOs are seen to play a vital role in the fight against poverty and the provision of humanitarian assistance. Now MOFA emphasizes this partnership with NGOs. Moreover, the foreign policy of Japanese local governments is often developed through 'sister city' relations. By 2002, the number of such schemes was 1,430 (Menju 2003: 50). With the rise of Japan's conception of aid as an international contribution, the activities of Japanese local governments in development assistance projects have also increased.

As the major domestic political controversies diminished in the early 1990s, Japanese politicians accepted the need to revise their relations with society, and they assumed important new roles in the process of compiling general budgets and fiscal plans. They also sought to change the structure of their interactions with the bureaucracy. This process culminated in a complete ministerial reorganization in 2001, combined with an effort to expand the politicians' role in administration and policy making. In these circumstances, the Liberal Democratic Party (LDP), which has remained the ruling party in Japan for most of the post-war period, has started to participate in the ODA budgetary process.

Moreover, many more NGOs and local governments now participate in the process of ODA formulation; and the key role of private-sector organizations has also been acknowledged. Thus, the implementation of Japanese ODA has become much more diversified in terms of forms and processes, thereby promoting strong new linkages between the domestic and international spheres.

In Chapter 8 Shirai stresses the marked change from ODA policy incoherence to a more integrated approach to ODA, partly in response to public opinion, and shows that there has been a move from the extreme fragmentation of policy making to greater coordination as exemplified by the establishment of the Inter-ministerial Meeting on ODA in March 2000, and the establishment of the Board on Comprehensive ODA Strategy in June 2002. In many areas, progress has been made but there are still major barriers in terms of a shortage of human resources and lack of institutional capacity. The stronger coordination of policy making, coupled with a more strategic approach to the targeting of ODA, has facilitated a clearer link between Japanese national interests and the implementation of ODA.

Global, regional and domestic governance

In the 1990s, there was a conspicuous increase in the scope of Japan's participation at the global and regional levels of international organizations, including the World Bank, the ADB, and a number of Asian/East Asian associations and forums. This trend reflected the spreading recognition in Japan and other Asian countries that globalization was an undeniable trend to which an appropriate policy response had to be made. No longer was an exclusive emphasis on national economic development through traditional means possible or desirable. The prosperity of any country was increasingly linked to global (including regional) economic, financial and trade relations. This change of circumstances was coupled with the shifting power politics of the world after the end of the cold war, and in particular the changing role of the US in relation to Japan and East Asia. More recently, the impact of the 1997–8 East Asian financial crisis, and especially its lessons concerning the extent of financial interdependence in the region, did much to stimulate Japan's determination to promote effective regional cooperation.

Without seeking any hegemonic role in the aforementioned organizations, Japan has steadfastly taken opportunities to challenge existing policies, and has used its strengthened 'voice', backed by its massive financial surpluses, to put forward its own ideas. This is most clear in the case of its questioning of World Bank opposition to government intervention in national economies. Japanese staff at the World Bank, many of them from MOF, 'felt that well-planned government intervention, which they considered essential to Japan's own success, should be applicable to other developing countries and play a bigger role in World Bank lending' (Langdon 1997: 4). The increasing intellectual exchange between the World Bank and the Japanese government in the 1990s facilitated the questioning of World Bank orthodoxy on developmental matters. While the Bank did not embrace the Japanese philosophy completely, it subsequently paid much more attention to the institutional context of domestic governance in countries receiving World Bank financial assistance, and acknowledged that each country is in this sense unique and requires an individualized response. One of the clearest lessons to be learned in this respect is that good global governance requires effective, domestic and non-corrupt domestic governance if it is to be successful. This in turn requires an effort to eradicate poverty, ignorance, social exclusion and ill-health as barriers to democratization. Since January 1999, the World Bank has formally instituted a programme to establish a 'Global Architecture of Governance' as part of a 'Comprehensive Development Framework' by linking its loans policies to social and structural policies, and to institutional and behavioural changes in recipient countries. This is now the official basis of the Bank's PRSP (see Cammack 2002). To achieve these ends, there is no doubt that the Bank has become increasingly dependent on Japanese financial inputs, and this economic power, coupled with an increasingly strong Japanese intellectual and cognitive contribution, has inevitably given Japan more of a political influence in the Bank.

At the same time, in the ADB and in East Asian regional organizations more generally, Japan has come to play the leading role, stressing its desire to focus on the economic growth and prosperity of the countries of the East Asian region. The ADB is especially important in stimulating sub-regional projects, for example, the Greater Mekong Subregion programme, the South Asia Subregional Economic Cooperation programme and the Central Asian Regional Economic Cooperation programme. Now nearly every sub-region in Asia has a cooperative programme initiated or supported by the ADB. In this way, the global, regional and sub-regional levels of development and governance are closely connected. This spatial interconnectedness highlights the need to understand global economic governance as existing simultaneously at different geographical levels. Japan is a global, regional and sub-regional actor, and any system of global governance, whether in the economic, financial or security fields, must allow scope for such vertical decentralization of decision making, and effective links between the three levels. What is most interesting about Japan's position is that it has sought to act independently of the US in developing a new framework for East Asian regionalism (Hayashi 2002: 3). In so doing, Japan has harnessed both government policy and foreign direct investment through the private sector to strengthen regional ties (2002: 9). The success of this approach cannot be doubted: the Japanese-dominated East Asian region has witnessed the emergence of a more effective environment for development than has the US-dominated Western hemisphere (Stallings 1995: 350). As a result, the Japanese approach has gained in credibility, even allowing for the 'shock' of the 1997–8 financial crisis. In the World Bank and other international institutions, Japan usually sees itself as a representative of East Asian, and often broader Asian, interests; one of the specific tasks to which Japan has committed itself is to achieve 'a fusion of the two viewpoints of globalism and regionalism' and the increasing global recognition of 'Asian values' (Ito 2001: 139).

Conclusion

In summary, Japan has achieved a position in which it plays a much more important role in global and regional governance than it did just 15–20 years ago.

This role is based on the mobilization and dispensation of the country's massive financial surpluses, especially through foreign aid of various kinds, in particular multilateral aid. This role is also supported by the fundamental changes in the international system that have occurred in the post-cold war period, the huge impact of economic globalization, the lessons learned from the 1997–8 East Asian financial crisis and the rise of East Asian regionalism. Japan's roles in the World Bank and Asian Development Bank illustrate these trends very well, but a full picture of Japan's involvement in global governance must take into account its contribution to other international and regional organizations, and also the Japanese state's relations with the major firms involved in global and regional production networks.

Global governance is a multi-tiered, spatially dispersed, and multi-institutional phenomenon that cannot be reduced to a single monolithic system of power. Here Rosenau's conclusion is apropos: 'Global governance is not so much a label for a high degree of integration and order as it is a summary term for highly complex and widely disparate activities that may culminate in a modicum of worldwide coherence or that may collapse into pervasive disarray' (Rosenau 1999). Global governance is the *sum* of an enormous number of levels and spheres of economic and political action. These have been described by Held and McGrew as 'a thickening web of multilateral agreements, global and regional institutions and regimes, transgovernmental policy networks and summits' (Held and McGrew 2002: xi). In this sense, this chapter has looked at only one piece of a very large jigsaw puzzle. As O'Brien and colleagues state, 'The nature of governance and authority in the field of multi-lateral economic institutions is going through a transitional stage. While it is clear what the transition is from, it is not as obvious where it is going' (O'Brien *et al*. 2002: 207). While the 'old multilateralism' was based primarily on the activity of states, a 'new multilateralism' is emerging in which numerous non-state actors are playing an increasingly important role (2002: 207–8). This process of transformation can clearly be seen in the World Bank's recent efforts to re-define its international role, to link its activities to the 'Global Architecture of Governance' strategy, and to establish positive relations with NGOs and civil society groups.

The short-term reality may be that the Japanese state is presently becoming a more assertive actor in the World Bank and other MEIs, but in the long-term the role of the Japanese state may become less important than the role of Japanese NGOs and civil society actors; or, put another way, it will be the dynamics of Japanese state, NGO and civil society relations that will ultimately be the key factor in shaping the patterns of Japanese participation in global governance arrangements.

References

Cammack, Paul (2002) 'The mother of all governments: the World Bank's matrix for global governance', in R. Wilkinson and S. Hughes (eds) *Global Governance: Critical Perspectives*, London: Routledge, pp. 36–53.

Hayashi, Shigeko (2002) *Japan and East Asian Monetary Regionalism: Towards a Proactive Leadership Role?* PhD thesis, University of Warwick (UK).

Held, David and McGrew, G. Anthony (eds) (2002) *Governing Globalization: Power, Authority and Global Governance*, Cambridge: Polity Press.

Iokibe, Makoto (2001) 'Nihon Gaikō 50-nen', *Kokusai Mondai* 500: 4–36.

Ito, Kunihiko (2001) 'Japan, the Asian Economy, the International Financial System, and the G8: a critical perspective', in John J. Kirton and G. M. von Furstenberg (eds), *New Directions in Global Economic Governance: Managing Globalization in the Twenty-first Century*, Aldershot: Ashgate, pp. 127–42.

Johnson, Chalmers (1982) *MITI and the Japanese Miracle: The Growth of Industrial Policy, 1925–1975*, Stanford, CA: Stanford University Press.

Langdon, Frank (1997) 'Japan's regional and global coalition participation: political and economic aspects', Institute of International Relations, University of British Columbia, Working Paper No. 14.

Menju, Toshihiro (ed.) (2003) *Kusanone no Kokusai Kōryū to Kokusai Kyōryoku*, Tokyo: Akashi Shoten.

MOFA (ed.) (2004a) *ODA Seifu Kaihatsu Enjo 2003 nendoban: Shin ODA Taikō no Mezasumono*, Tokyo: Kokuritsu Insatsukyoku.

MOFA (ed.) (2004b) *ODA Seifu Kaihatsu Enjo 2004 nendoban: Nihon no ODA 50-nen no Seika to Ayumi*, Tokyo: Kokuritsu Insatsukyoku.

Motoda, Yuka (2004) 'Sekai Ginkō', in Tadokoro Masayuki and Shiroyama Hideaki (eds) *Kokusai Kikan to Nihon*, Tokyo: Nihon Keizai Hyōronsha, pp. 89–141.

O'Brien, Robert, Goetz, Anne Marie, Scholte, Jan Aart and Williams, Marc (2002) *Contesting Global Governance*, Cambridge: Cambridge University Press.

Ōno, Izumi (2000) *Sekai Ginkō: Kaihatsu Enjo Senryaku no Henkaku*, Tokyo: NTT Shuppan.

Rosenau, James N. (1999) 'Toward an ontology for global governance', in Martin Hewson and Timothy J. Sinclair (eds) *Approaches to Global Governance Theory*, New York: State University of New York.

Saotome, Mitsuhiro (1997) 'Kokumin sankagata no kaihatsu kyōryoku: NGO to chihō jichitai no yakuwari o chūshin ni', *Kokusai Mondai* 451: 34–48.

Stallings, Barbara (ed.) (1995), *Global Change, Regional Response: The New International Context of Development*, Cambridge: Cambridge University Press.

Terry, Edith (2000) 'The World Bank and Japan: how Godzilla of Ginza and King Kong of H Street got hitched', Japan Policy Research Institute, Working Paper No. 70.

Wan, Ming (2001) *Japan between Asia and the West: Economic Power and Strategic Balance*, New York: M.E. Sharpe.

Williamson, John (2000) 'What should the World Bank think about the Washington Consensus?', *The World Bank Research Observer* 15, 2: 251–64.

World Bank (1993) *The East Asian Miracle: Economic Growth and Public Policy*, New York: Oxford University Press.

Yasutomo, Denis (1995) *The New Multilateralism in Japan's Foreign Policy*, New York: St Martin's Press.

Zaimushō (2003) 'MDBs'. Available on-line at: http://www.mof.go.jp/jouhou/kokkin/frame.html, accessed on 2 April 2005.

7 Global governance and the International Monetary Fund

Simon Lee

Introduction

The International Monetary Fund (IMF) has defined governance as a concept which 'encompasses all aspects of the way a country is governed, including its economic policies and regulatory framework'. On this basis, governance should be distinguished from the narrower concept of corruption, namely, 'the abuse of public authority or trust for private benefit' (IMF 2003a: 1). While the 'Purposes' of the IMF specified in Article 1 of its Articles of Agreement do not actually mention 'governance', let alone good governance, the IMF has maintained that it has always sought to promote good governance from its very inception. Its role has been to promote international monetary cooperation, facilitate the expansion and balanced growth of international trade, and promote exchange stability through shortening the duration and lessening 'the degree of disequilibrium in the international balances of payments of members' (IMF 2004a: 1).

This has led the IMF to intervene to encourage countries to both correct macro-economic imbalances and undertake market reforms, a process which in turn has caused the IMF to engage with a 'much broader range of institutional factors' in order 'to establish and maintain private sector confidence and thereby lay the basis for sustained growth' (IMF 1997: v). Largely as a consequence of the series of major financial crises during the past decade, the IMF has found itself drawn ever deeper into governance issues far beyond its original purposes. Indeed, the IMF has attempted to manage the aftermath of a series of capital account crises in liberalized financial markets, where volatility, panic and contagion have threatened the very stability of the global economy. At the same time, the IMF has sought to play a central role in the alleviation of global poverty and the achievement of the millennium development goals (MDGs). In fulfiling this broader and much more demanding role, like its sister international financial institutions (IFIs), the World Bank and World Trade Organization (WTO), the IMF has defined governance in orthodox neoclassical political economy terms, with an ultimately futile attempt made to separate the political from the economic aspects of governance, and to confine the role of the IMF to the latter. In this attempted de-politicization of governance, the role of politics has been defined as the building of institutions for the market, in accordance with certain general principles for governance, namely, that 'successful market-based economies need institutions that protect property rights, uphold the rule of law, provide appropriate regulation of markets, support macroeconomic stability, and promote social cohesion and stability' (IMF 2003b: 11).

Given the IMF's failure to anticipate major financial crises in developed, developing and emerging market economies for the past decade, the ineffectiveness of its responses to those crises, and the detrimental impact of the timing and conditionality of its structural adjustment loans upon the debt crisis and alleviation of poverty, criticism of the organization is often withering. A critique of its performance has suggested that 'the IMF is part of the problem, and not part of the solution' (Soros 1998: 148). The IMF's actions in response to the 1997 Asian financial crisis have been portrayed as anti-democratic, hypocritical, lacking transparency and based upon 'what seemed a curious blend of ideology and bad economics, dogma that sometimes seemed to be thinly veiled special interests' (Stiglitz 2002: xiii). The IMF's approach to poorer countries has been described as the 'Four Steps to Damnation', namely, privatization, capital market liberalization, market-based pricing leading to IMF-inspired rioting and the premature opening of markets to free trade (Palast 2001). In relation to governance issues, the IMF stands accused of intruding into and undermining legitimate domestic democratic governmental processes by imposing major structural and institutional reforms as conditions of its lending. Furthermore, the IMF's interventions are held to have been based on a flawed neoclassical political economy whose conception of governance has failed to deliver economic growth or provide a route out of poverty. Instead, these interventions are held to have delivered moral hazard, undermined market discipline and privileged the interests of private creditors over those of sovereign governments and the millions of citizens who democratically elected them. Moreover, in terms of its own internal governance, the IMF, like its sister IFIs, has been accused of possessing parallel deficits in the transparency, accountability and legitimacy of its decision-making processes, which have left it far short of the very standards of good governance which the IMF's conditionality has imposed upon others.

As a consequence of this avalanche of criticism of its decision-making and performance, one major recent study has suggested that 'the IMF is an institution in need of overhaul' (Bird 2003: 207). Another influential study has proclaimed that 'the most fundamental change that is required to make globalization work in the way that it should is a change in governance' (Stiglitz 2002: 226). In the light of these observations, this chapter explores aspects of the IMF's role in global governance and the actual governance of the IMF itself. The chapter begins by highlighting how both the IMF itself and students of its performance have wrongly and unsuccessfully attempted to de-politicize governance. Second, the chapter explores the democratic deficit in the internal governance of the IMF, highlighted by the controversies surrounding the selection of its new Managing Director. Third, the chapter analyses the deficiencies in the IMF's approach to the governance of financial markets. Fourth, the chapter identifies 'Four Steps to Redemption' for the IMF to reform the manner in which it provides important public goods towards the effective governance of the world economy. Finally, the chapter concludes that the prospects for wholesale reform are poor, at least until something akin to the economic conditions that inspired the IMF's creation recur in the US, and thereby persuade the incumbent administration that progressive multilateralism is more in accordance with the US's vital self-interest than neo-conservative aggressive unilateralism as a basis for ordering global governance.

The de-politicization of governance

When the IMF first sought to define its perspective on governance, it claimed that its role would be limited to economic aspects of governance alone. This reflected the orthodox neoclassical political economy underpinning the IMF's policies that sought to maintain a separation between the realms of politics and economics. Subsequently, the IMF has asserted that 'because of their economic nature, issues related to governance and corruption often fall directly within the mandate and expertise of the IMF' (IMF 2003a: 1). By also conceding that many, but not all, causes of corruption are economic in nature, the IMF has effectively admitted that other causes of the poor governance that is detrimental to economic performance are often political. Therefore, although it has maintained that it has a legitimate interest, mandate and expertise in the economic dimensions of governance, by its own admission the IMF cannot address the multifaceted nature of governance, unless it is prepared to engage with the political dimension of it.

The IMF has traced its explicit mandate to engage with questions of governance to 26 September 1996, when its Interim Committee, the precursor to today's International Monetary and Finance Committee (IMFC), declared the importance of 'promoting good governance in all its aspects, including by ensuring the rule of law, improving the efficiency and accountability of the public sector, and tackling corruption, as essential elements of a framework within which economies can prosper' (IMF 1996: 1). On 25 July 1997, following a series of meetings in which the IMF's Executive Board had developed a guidance framework, the IMF published a Guidance Note to formally define its role in governance. Insisting that its role in governance issues had evolved pragmatically (as opposed to in accordance with the tenets of its neoclassical political economy), the IMF stated that greater attention would now be paid by the IMF to its involvement in governance issues, through 'an evenhanded treatment of governance issues in all member countries' (IMF 1997: 2).

In promising an 'evenhanded treatment', the IMF maintained that, while the responsibility for governance issues would reside 'first and foremost with the national authorities', many such issues were 'integral to the IMF's normal activities' concerning macroeconomic stability, external viability and orderly economic growth.

The IMF was equally adamant that its involvement in governance 'should be limited to economic aspects of governance' (IMF 1997: 3). This broader and more intrusive role in governance issues raised two key questions. First, whether the sovereignty, self-determination and democratic autonomy of its member countries could be maintained in the face of the IMF's interventions. Second, whether a distinction would be sustainable between the economic, political and social aspects of governance that would enable the IMF to de-politicize its role in governance issues.

In relation to questions of national sovereignty, the IMF declared that, while it 'should not act on behalf of a member country in influencing another country's political orientation or behaviour', it would nevertheless need 'to take a view on whether the member is able to formulate and implement appropriate policies'. The conditionality attached to IMF lending had made it legitimate, in the eyes of the IMF, for it 'to seek information about the political situation in member countries as an essential element in judging the prospects for policy implementation' (IMF 1997: 4–5). Consequently, because poor governance might adversely affect macro-economic performance by undermining private market confidence and, in turn, reducing private capital inflows and investment, IMF staff should recommend a pattern of conditionality which would accord primacy to corrective measures to address weaknesses in governance (IMF 1997: 6–8).

The questionable viability of a distinction between the economic and other aspects of governance was immediately highlighted by the IMF's assertion that the contribution it could make to good governance, through its policy advice and technical assistance, would be in the two spheres of '*improving the management of public resources*', through reforms covering public sector institutions, and '*supporting the development and maintenance of a transparent and stable economic and regulatory environment conducive to efficient private sector activities* [original emphasis]' (IMF 1997: 3). The idea that reforms of the public sector could be regarded as de-politicized 'economic' aspects of governance would only be sustainable if the notion of politics was defined in narrow technocratic and ahistorical terms as the quest for administrative efficiency. This conception of politics ignored the central and, in most IMF member states, unresolved ideological debate over the appropriate roles of the public and private sectors, which would inevitably entail politics. It also offered no place for the role of vested interests in the political process, which would inevitably contest any reform of the public sector and question whether the efficiency of private sector activities should occupy such a privileged position on the political agenda to the potential detriment of rival political priorities.

Following the publication of the IMF's Guidance Note on Governance (GN), the financial crises in East Asia and Russia led to a significant expansion in the role of the IMF in governance issues. Indeed, from 1996 until the conduct of the February 2001 review of governance issues, the IMF's surveillance role and provision of technical assistance had extended its role in governance in no fewer than nine key areas (IMF 2001: 7). As a consequence of its greatly expanded role in governance issues, the IMF's Executive Board decided to review that experience, a process which included the publication of a study by the IMF's Policy Development and Review Department. This study concluded that the IMF's role, particularly in relation to the development of standards and codes of best practice and other related policies to promote transparency and accountability, had 'moved substantially beyond expectations at the time of the GN'. Moreover, there had been difficulty in many instances in precisely defining the macroeconomic significance of poor governance, for these effects could remain hidden for lengthy periods, 'like termites in the woodwork'. At the same time, the IMF needed to exercise 'careful judgments' when addressing governance issues requiring action beyond the IMF's expertise, especially when the appropriate agencies possessing the requisite expertise were not in a position to provide it (IMF 2001: 3). The clear implication was that the IMF had acted, on occasions, without due care and attention. The review also conceded that the instruction to eschew the political dimension of governance in favour of the economic dimension had proven 'difficult to do with precision', especially given the 'relatively general' boundaries specified in the GN (IMF 2001: 8). In effect, the IMF had conceded that the attempt to de-politicize governance issues was bound to fail.

'Do as I say, not as I do': the governance of the IMF

The principal decision-making organs of the IMF are its Board of Governors, its Executive Board, the International Monetary and Financial Committee (IMFC) and the Development Committee. The Board of Governors is the highest authority at the IMF. Although it usually meets only once a year, the Board has certain reserved powers under the IMF's Articles of Agreement. All other powers are exercised on a day-to-day basis by an Executive Board of twenty-four Directors, chaired by the Managing Director. The Board, whose members are elected or appointed by member countries or groups of member countries, tends to meet several times each week. The IMFC is an advisory body composed of twenty-four members, typically ministers or officials of high rank, from the same constituencies as the Executive Board. It tends to meet twice a year, fulfiling an advisory role to provide ministerial guidance to the Executive Board as well as reporting to the Board of Governors on matters relating to the management of the international monetary and financial system, including potential threats and possible amendments to the IMF's Articles of Agreement. The Development Committee, which tends to meet the day after IMFC meetings, is a joint IMF–World Bank committee, composed of twenty-four finance ministers or officials of equivalent rank (IMF 2003b: xi).

Ironically, the clearest critique of the limitations of the existing framework for the governance of the IMF has been published by the IMF itself. Van Houtven has identified what amount to parallel and intertwined democratic, accountability, participatory and transparency deficits in the IMF's governance. First, in terms of democracy, the IMF is deemed undemocratic because of the paradox that while the large majority of its 184 member states are borrowers drawn from the ranks of developing and transition economies, they remain simultaneously minority shareholders and stakeholders because of the dominance of the principal creditors from the industrialized economies. Second, there is a further democratic deficit arising from the selection process for the Managing Director of the IMF. In terms of transparency, selection remains a closed process of horse-trading between the US and the members of the European Union (EU), lacking procedural guidelines. Indeed, members of the Group of Seven (G7) industrialized economies had engaged in the kind of secretive 'Green Room' negotiations for decades before such practices became an issue for the WTO at the Seattle Ministerial Conference. Third, in terms of account-ability, the industrialized economies dominate the oversight of the IMF through their control of the Executive Board and other key IMF bodies, which lack representation and participation from the majority of developing economies. Fourth, in terms of participation, although the IMF is supposed to take decisions through consensus among its member states, in practice the rights of minority shareholders have been overridden by the interests of the G7 industrialized economies. This deficiency in the IMF's governance has been particularly marked in the operation of the IMFC, and its predecessor the Interim Committee. Non-governmental organizations (NGOs) and other actors from civil society remain marginalized or totally excluded from the IMF's principal decision-making structures and processes (Van Houtven 2002: 2–3).

The iniquities in the IMF's governance are vividly illustrated in the distribution of voting power. No less than 60 per cent of the voting power is controlled by twenty-four industrial economies, while the remaining 160 economies, 85 per cent of the membership, are left with only 40 per cent of the votes. While this distri-bution is a reflection of the financial quotas contributed by the members to the IMF's resources, this imbalance is also demonstrative of 'the lop-sidedness of governance of the international monetary system' (Van Houtven 2002: 66). Furthermore, for the Board of Governors, no fewer than thirteen categories of voting, relating to the most important issues such as the allocation of Special Drawing Rights (SDRs) or the adjustment of quotas, require 85 per cent of the total votes. For the Executive Board, 16 out of 14 categories of decisions require a similar 85 per cent of the vote. Because the US possesses more than 17 per cent of the voting power, it has a de facto veto over the IMF's key decisions, rendering it a 'Group of One' (Van Houtven 2002: 41, 73–4). For example, in 1997 a Fourth Amendment to the IMF's Articles of Agreement was adopted, which would provide a special one-off allocation of SDRs. This amendment eventually attracted the support of more than 100 member states and more than 70 per cent of the total voting power, but because the US would not give its support, the 85 per cent majority required could not be delivered (IMF 2002: 34). The principle of IMF governance by consent had been undermined by the unilateral veto of one member state. Since the other categories of special majority votes require endorsement by 70 per cent of the votes, the fact that the EU controls just under 30 per cent of the voting power has ensured that the US and the EU effectively control the IMF.

Inevitably, because the IMF needs to preserve the confidence of its creditors, those richer economies which have financed the majority of quotas will demand a majority of voting power. Nevertheless, the legitimacy of the IMF will always remain heavily constrained in the eyes of its overwhelming majority of developing economies, as long as their voice remains marginalized in the IMF's governance.

As Van Houtven has concluded, '[e]ffective governance of the IMF demands that the institutional benefits and burdens are equitably shared among the membership and that checks and balances operate efficiently in decision making' (Van Houtven 2002: 67). One possible reform of voting power has been suggested by the Quota Formula Reform Group, which has proposed that the principal factor in future quota allocation among the industrial economies should be gross domestic product (GDP). If this proposal was to be adopted, for example, the EU would see its quota allocation significantly reduced since its 30 per cent share of voting power has been achieved with a GDP smaller than of the US, which possesses just over 17 per cent of votes. Under this scenario, there would be a significant redistribution of voting power towards the Asian economies, notably Japan, whose paltry 6.2 per cent of votes is not proportionate to its status as the world's second largest economy, with a GDP around half that of the US.

It is not simply the formal inequalities in IMF voting power which are objectionable from the perspective of democratic governance. In its critique of the IMF's governance, the United Nations Development Programme (UNDP) has accorded equal importance to the informal influences and traditions which shape the IMF and other international institutions (UNDP 2002: 113). Most prominent among these has been the convention according to which the head of the World Bank and First Deputy Managing Director of the IMF have been nominated by the US while the Managing Director of the IMF has been nominated by the Europeans. This deficit in democratic governance has been highlighted by the recent dissent surrounding the appointment of Rodrigo de Rato y Figaredo (hereafter, Rodrigo Rato) as Horst Köhler's successor and the ninth consecutive European or Scandinavian to serve as Managing Director.

Following Köhler's announcement that he was to leave the IMF to mount what proved to be a successful campaign for the German Presidency, there was unprecedented pressure from both within and outwith the IMF for a more open leadership selection process. From within the IMF, on 19 March 2004, a self-appointed 'G11' group of eleven Executive Directors representing developing and emerging economies in Asia, Africa, Latin America and the Middle East, but also including the Executive Directors from Australia, Switzerland and the Russian Federation, took the unprecedented step of issuing a statement on the new Managing Director. They demanded that 'the process of identifying and selecting the candidate must be open and transparent, with the goal of attracting the best person for the job, regardless of nationality.' Moreover, 'a plurality of candidates representing the diversity of members across regions would be in the best interest of the Fund.' Furthermore, the process of selection should involve the consultation of all members of the Executive Board, who should be 'informed in a timely manner regarding candidates, including their credentials and knowledge of the institution' (IMF 2004b: 1). On 31 March, the G11 followed up its initial demands with a further statement that, conceding that while it would not be possible to apply the letter of the April 2001 Joint IMF/World Bank Report on Selection Procedures, nevertheless, it would be 'essential to abide by the *principles* underlying those recommendations' (IMF 2004c: 1).

In practice, the IMF has chosen to ignore those underlying principles. However, further unease from within the IMF about the degree of departure of the selection process for the new Managing Director from the principles of democratic governance was also expressed in an email sent by Jack Boorman, the former Director of Policy Development and Research at the IMF, to IMF staff. In his message, Boorman stated that he had thought that the principles underlying the April 2001 Report would guide the selection procedure to replace Köhler. Unfortunately, the process had turned out to be 'anything but open and transparent'. Therefore, since Fund staff had been excluded from the selection process now underway, Boorman invited staff to reply to his email, if they shared his concerns about the selection process. He would then convey those concerns to the Dean of the IMF's Executive Board. It was vital that staff should respond, and in the event, no fewer than 300 were reported to have done so, because, in Boorman's eyes, the IMF could not 'preach transparency, good governance, and other virtues to the membership and to the international community more broadly unless it is willing to apply those virtues in its own decision making' (Boorman 2004: 1).

The demands for a more transparent, open and inclusive selection process were echoed from outwith the IMF both by developing governmental and NGO representatives. For example, the Intergovernmental Group of Twenty-Four on International Monetary Affairs and Development (G24) expressed its concern that the selection process continued 'to fall far short of the standards of good governance' and backed the G11's call for a more open and transparent process (G24 2004: 3). This demand was repeated from the NGO sector by a letter sent by the Bretton Woods Project (BWP) and eleven other England-based NGOs on 12 March 2001 to UK Chancellor of the Exchequer Gordon Brown and ten other ministers and senior civil servants. The NGOs also reminded Brown of the principles underpinning the April 2001 Joint Working Group report. As an alternative, the NGOs recommended that the selection process should be 'merit-based, open to all nationalities, and subject to a clear and transparent set of selection criteria'. Using these criteria, a list of candidates should be drawn up for member governments by a search committee of 'independent stakeholder representatives' (BWP *et al.* 2004: 1).

A similar letter was sent by European NGOs to EU Finance ministers, prior to their meeting on 2 April demanding that European governments 'forgo their customary right to appoint the Managing Director of the International Monetary Fund' and urge President George W. Bush's administration to give up its right to appoint the IMF Deputy Director and World Bank President (Forum Syd and Diakonia 2004: 1). The official response to such NGO lobbying was predictable, but nonetheless disappointing, given the fact that, for example, the British government had previously spoken in favour of 'open and competitive processes for the selection of top management' at all the IFIs, including 'a clear process for taking the final decision, in which competence would be put above consideration of nationality' (DfID 2000: 100). However, while it had asserted in 2000 that 'developing countries are entitled to a stronger and more effective voice in all of these international institutions', when the actual question of the leadership of the

IMF arose, Britain chose not to support a more transparent and democratic approach to the IMF's governance. On the contrary, as Chair of the IMFC, the Chancellor of the Exchequer chose to ignore the respective demands of developing countries and NGOs for a more open process of selection.

The IMF and the governance of global markets

The shortcomings in both the IMF's flawed attempt to de-politicize governance and its own decision-making and internal governance have been compounded by the manifest deficiencies of its governance of global markets. In its 2003 Annual Report, the IMF conceded not only that global output growth from 1 May 2002 to 30 April 2003 was once more 'below trend' but also global trade 'was weaker than in any other year since the global recession of the 1980s' (IMF 2003b: ii). From a longer-term perspective, the IMF's own statistical analysis has demonstrated that, far from yielding increased stability, the 'Washington Consensus' has delivered greater volatility in global markets, an increased incidence of recessions and slower economic growth (IMF 2002). Thus, by its own admission, the IMF's governance of world markets has been ineffective. It has stood impotent in the face of large budget deficits in the world's two most important national economies while, in an ironic twist of fate, the US and UK, the countries of the architects of Bretton Woods, Harry Dexter White and John Maynard Keynes, are running unsustainable balance of payments' deficits.

IMF surveillance and conditionality have equally failed the poor. Köhler promised to work for a better form of globalization, but the greatest indictment of the existing pattern of global governance is its failure to deliver the millennium development goals (MDGs) (World Economic Forum 2005). At the current rate of progress, the goal of halving income poverty between 1990 and 2015 will not be met in Sub-Saharan Africa until 2147 and the goal of reducing child poverty by two-thirds in the same period will not be achieved until 2165. On a broader scale, the existing pattern of governance has delivered an underlying economic crisis for developing countries. During the 1990s, this was manifested in an average per capita income growth of less than 3 per cent in 125 developing and transition economies, while in 54 of those countries average per capita income actually fell. No fewer than 1.2 billion people try to survive on less than US$1 a day (UNDP 2003: 2–3, 5). It is not simply the failure of policy to be effective that has brought the governance of the IMF into disrepute. It is also the manner in which that policy has been conceived. For example, during the 1980s those countries which wished to borrow from the IMF and World Bank were required to meet between 6 and 10 performance criteria. However, during the 1990s that number mushroomed to no fewer than twenty-six (UNDP 2002: 112).

The IMF has sought to redress the shortcomings in its governance of global financial markets, for example, by strengthening its surveillance role, namely, 'oversight, including monitoring and analysis over its member states' exchange rate policies' (IMF 2003b: 3). This role is conducted at three levels – country or bilateral surveillance, global or multilateral surveillance and regional surveillance.

Between 1 May 2002 and 30 April 2003, the IMF held bilateral discussions with 136 of its 184 member countries. Köhler has also claimed that financial year 2002–3 had seen 'a consolidation of the reforms of the IMF itself, a key element of which has been to strengthen our ability to listen and learn' (IMF 2003b: vii). In terms of its own governance, Köhler pointed to a continuing increase in the transparency of the IMF's operations and finances, and the publication of the first reports from the IMF's own Independent Evaluation Office (IEO). Because the IEO is an internal part of the IMF, rather than a separate external monitoring mechanism, it has fallen far short of the demands for a truly autonomous evaluation unit. Possessing the form but not the substance of independence, the director of the IEO has been selected by a private firm, rather than through an open and transparent selection process. The IEO consequently lacks the prestige or political authority to counterbalance the agenda and interests of the IMF's existing internal evaluation units, notably, the Office of Inspection and the Policy Development Review Department.

Despite these weaknesses, the IEO's initial reports have proven highly embarrassing to the IMF, since they have further exposed the flaws both in its role in global governance and its own internal decision-making processes. In its first report, the IEO's evaluation of the prolonged use of IMF resources found that their general use tended to 'be associated with a negative impact on growth' and 'an overoptimistic bias as regards projections of real GDP growth and (for users of concessional facilities) export growth'. In terms of governance, the IMF's approach to structural reforms had until recently been 'often characterized by insufficient emphasis on fostering the deep institutional changes needed in critical areas'. Insufficient priority had been given in programme design 'to a proper assessment of the implementation capacity constraints that a program might face, be they related to political feasibility or to administrative capacity' (IEO 2002: 11–12). As a consequence, the IEO recommended that 'the IMF should strengthen the ability of its staff to analyse political economy issues in order to achieve a better understanding of the forces that are likely to block or enhance reforms and to take these into account in program design' (IEO 2002: 15). There could not have been a more prescient critique of the IMF's flawed efforts to de-politicize governance issues.

Further critical IEO evaluations have followed on fiscal adjustment in IMF-supported programmes, and the Poverty Reduction Strategy Papers and the Poverty Reduction Growth Facility (IEO 2003, 2004a). However, the most damning indictment of the IMF's surveillance, conditionality and crisis prevention measures has come in the IEO's evaluation of the IMF's role in Argentina. Here, the IEO has delivered a critique as devastating as any of the many furnished by the IMF's critics among the academic and NGO communities. It has criticized the IMF for supporting Argentina 'despite repeated policy inadequacies'; lambasted IMF staff for not bringing vital exchange rate issues to the attention of the Executive Board; claimed that 'the IMF's surveillance and program conditionality were handi-capped by analytical weaknesses and data limitations', but 'the more critical error of the IMF, however, was its weak enforcement of fiscal conditionality'; and concluded that 'the remarkable feature of the successive IMF-supported programs with Argentina was the paucity of formal structural conditionality' (IEO 2004b: 6–8). Moreover, in terms of the IMF's own internal governance, the IEO has asserted that 'the IMF's management of the Argentine crisis reveals several weaknesses in its decision-making process', including a failure in the oversight responsibility of the Executive Board. Consequently, the tenth lesson the IEO has drawn from the crisis is that 'the IMF's decision-making process must be improved in terms of risk analysis, accountability, and predictability' (IEO 2004b: 9–10).

Four steps to redemption: reforming the IMF

In order to remedy the aforementioned 'Four Steps to Damnation' which the IMF is held to have inflicted upon its borrowers, the IMF needs to take at least four steps along the road to redemption which will reform both its own internal governance and its role in the governance of global markets. First, in terms of ideology, the IMF needs to further reconsider its adherence to the orthodoxy of neoclassical political economy enshrined in the 'Washington Consensus'. Second, in terms of interests, the US, as the IMF's largest single financial stakeholder, has to be persuaded that its own self-interest is best pursued through an approach to global governance of progressive multilateralism rather than aggressive neo-conservative unilateralism. Third, in terms of institutional reform, the IMF must redress the democratic deficits in its own internal governance to move closer to the openness, transparency and accountability which it constantly demands of other public and private actors. Fourth, in terms of policy, the IMF needs to take the lead from its recent questioning of the benefits of the liberalization of capital markets for growth and development, to evaluate some of its other principal policies, and indeed the very model of political economy upon which they are based.

The first step, of an ideological departure from neoclassical political economy, is the hardest and least likely. As Will Hutton has observed, 'the so-called "Washington consensus", enshrining balanced budgets and the urgency of implementing pro-market solutions, is not just an economic doctrine to be applied universally; it has profound social and political repercussions' (Hutton 2002: 11–12). Those who remain in the vanguard of the ideological assault upon market fundamentalism have sought to apply social democratic principles to the institutions of global governance. The ambition to create a global social democracy has started from the belief that certain fundamental cosmopolitan values and ethical principles must be deployed to form the basis of a 'new internationalism' (Held 2004: 171).

These cosmopolitan principles have a clear meaning for governance, namely, a commitment to the idea that 'legitimate political authority, at all levels, must uphold, and be delimited by, a commitment to the values and principles which underpin political equality, democratic politics, human rights, political and social justice, and the sound stewardship of the environment' (Held 2004: 162). Thus, global social democracy seeks a new global covenant, embracing greater transparency, accountability and democracy in global governance. In the longer term, the reform of governance will mean democratization of national and suprastate governance to create multilevel citizenship, a global constitutional convention to explore the rules and mandates of new democratic global bodies, and the enhanced provision of global public goods (Held 2004: 164–5). However, the principal flaw in this agenda, which its advocates have yet to adequately address, concerns its political viability. Having been routed by the dogma of Thatcherism and Reaganomics, disappointed by the New Democrat and New Labour 'Third Ways' of US President Bill Clinton and UK Prime Minister Blair, and finally further dislocated by the neo-conservatism of George W. Bush standing 'shoulder-to-shoulder' with Blair, the proponents of a return to social democracy have yet to explain why a project which has been so widely rejected at the national level should offer convincing solutions on the global stage. This is perhaps their greatest challenge.

The second step, of a realignment of American self-interest to wholeheartedly embrace the principles of progressive multilateralism, appears as unlikely as the first. The creation of the Bretton Woods' institutions was the clearest recognition that the effective governance of the world economy would require multilateral institutions capable of furnishing public goods and services. Global integration has deepened the need for such public goods (Van Houtven 2002: 1), but these will not be achievable if they are provided 'as any one country dictates, or as a by-product of what it considers its interests' (Hutton 2002: 11). The Bush administration's scepticism towards the benefits of multilateralism has been reflected in its stance towards the IMF, whose interventions it has claimed have led to moral hazard, namely, 'an increase in risky behaviour (in this case on the part of the borrowing countries and their lenders) when insurance or a guarantee is provided' (in this case by the IMF) (CEA 2002: 285). Indeed, the IMF has been accused of having 'essentially lost its original role' in the early 1970s, following the abandonment of the Bretton Woods' fixed exchange rate system.

The Bush administration has sought to narrow the role of the IMF, and thereby to substantially reduce its level of lending, through a more focused approach to conditionality in IMF programmes. This approach was affirmed in the April 2002 Action Plan agreed by G7 Finance Ministers and Central Bank Governors. The Plan committed the G7 to work with the IMF towards a 'market-oriented' approach to sovereign debt restructuring. This effectively undermined IMF First Deputy Managing Director Anne Krueger's alternative proposals for an 'international workout mechanism', modelled on a domestic bankruptcy court, which would have provided debtor economies with legal protection from those creditors who might obstruct a necessary debt restructuring. The Plan also committed the G7 to working with the IMF 'to improve the quality, transparency, and predictability of official decision-making as a key means of crisis prevention' (G7 2002: 2).

Since the publication of the G7 Action Plan, the Bush administration has maintained the pressure for rapid IMF reform and a narrower form of multilateralism, and has succeeded in implementing collective action clauses in external sovereign bonds and creating clearer limits and criteria for exceptional borrowing from the

IMF. To this end, US Treasury Secretary John Snow has used his chairmanship of the G7 Finance Ministers and Central Bank Governors to advance a 'strategic review and new directions' initiative for the IFIs by the G7, whose aims include 'improving assessments of economic policies and potential risks and refocusing the IMF and World Bank on their core mandates' (G7 2004: 2). The US Treasury wishes the IMF to concentrate on its core responsibilities of 'monetary policy, fiscal policy, financial markets, and exchange rates' (US Treasury 2004: 7), and thereby to reduce the risk of the IMF's interventions leading to moral hazard. However, despite its attempts to reign in the role of the multilateral institutions, and the US's financial contribution towards them, the past precedent of exposure of US investors and financial institutions to major financial crises, such as those in Mexico and Asia, is likely to lead to strong domestic pressure from powerful constituencies for future US and IMF intervention. Furthermore, despite its preference for market-based approaches to sovereign debt rescheduling, the Bush administration might be advised to note the IEO's eighth lesson from the Argentinian crisis, namely, that 'voluntary, market-based debt restructuring is costly and unlikely to improve debt sustainability if it is undertaken under crisis conditions and without a credible, comprehensive economic strategy' (IEO 2004b: 11).

The third step, of major institutional reform to render the IMF more open, transparent and accountable, is one which Rodrigo Rato and Horst Köhler have claimed that the IMF has already undertaken. Both have claimed that IMF 'transparency has taken a quantum leap in the last decade' (IMF 2004d: 2). However, the demands for even greater transparency have been echoed from within the IMF by its own IEO's *Annual Report 2004*. Following on from its damning critique of IMF decision-making during the recent financial crisis in Argentina, the IEO has identified three messages for IMF decision-making. First, 'the candour of assessments tends to become muted as they are transmitted through the institution', and despite recent efforts to strengthen IMF surveillance, it 'remains to be seen' whether greater candour will result. Second, 'there is a reluctance by the institution to address explicitly the question of what should be the alternative strategy if the preferred approach fails', with an absence of alternative contingency plans. Third, 'any political considerations, which are inevitably present in decisions on financing, should be taken into account in a transparent manner, with decisions and accountability clearly at the level of the Executive Board and on the basis of candid technical assessments by the staff' (IEO 2004c: 42). The IEO has suggested that such issues raise 'complex issues of accountability when highly sensitive information is involved' (IEO 2004c: 42). On the contrary, such issues raise simple issues of accountability, namely, the need for the Executive Board to conform to the same standards of openness and transparency it demands of others.

The fourth step, a major re-assessment of the IMF's policies, is largely contingent upon the other three steps having first been taken. One IMF research paper has concluded that, while international financial integration should in principle help countries to reduce macroeconomic volatility, in practice, 'the available evidence suggests that developing countries have not fully attained this potential benefit. Indeed, the process of capital account liberalization appears to have been accompanied in some cases by increased vulnerability to crises' (IMF 2003c: 5). Although this has yet to be acknowledged in official IMF policy, this marks a considerable departure from the IMF's September 1997 Annual Meeting, when the IMF was seeking an amendment to its Articles of Agreement to permit it to promote freedom of capital movements (Lee 2002: 286). Indeed, in its 2003 Annual Report, the IMF has conceded that 'while derivatives could play a positive role in contributing to a more efficient allocation of risks in financial markets, these instruments could also be used to avoid prudential safeguards and take on excessive leverage' (IMF 2003b: 14). This is a frank admission of the limits to the IMF's capacity to govern liberalized financial markets. The principal constraint on the IMF's foresight remains the inherent uncertainty and volatility which characterizes liberalized financial markets and their constant capacity of unfettered entrepreneurship to produce new, innovative financial products. Since it also can only exhort the world's largest debtor economy, the US, to reform its fiscal policies, the IMF has the power neither to stabilize private markets nor to reform the conduct of macroeconomic policy in major economies, notably the US and Japan.

There remain similarly huge flaws in the IMF's use of conditionality in its lending policies. IMF conditionality is supposed to act as a signalling device, which both reduces uncertainty and provides additional information about future economic policy and performance. This signalling of better economic fortunes ahead is supposed to provide borrower governments with greater credibility among markets and investors about the efficacy of their reform programmes and thereby to attract additional private capital to their economies. However, there is little evidence of a significant and positive catalysis between multilateral lending by the IMF and World Bank and private capital flows (Bird 2003: 84). Indeed, Bird has suggested that 'neither theoretical analysis nor empirical evidence is consistent with the signalling role of IMF conditionality.' This is not surprising since the mechanism upon which signalling is based, namely, conditionality and credibility, is itself 'defective' (Bird 2003: 131, 137). Because of this, Bird has concluded that 'one of the key stated purposes of Fund programmes is not being fulfilled' (Bird 2003: 156). Consequently, what is required is nothing less than a 'fundamental reassessment of conditionality' (Bird 2003: 207).

Conclusion

As an archetypal technocrat, Rodrigo Rato has claimed that the IMF can promote financial stability, and respond to the risks of contagion which financial globalization has brought, through improved surveillance, and better crisis management and resolution (IMF 2004d: 2). However, irrespective of how complex and nuanced the IMF's surveillance role becomes, the fact remains that a fundamental characteristic of liberalized markets is their proclivity for volatility and uncertainty which may induce in turn panic, manias and crises, precisely because of the freedom and trust which has been accorded to entrepreneurs, arbitrageurs and corporations to innovate in the pursuit of profit. Any debate about the redefinition of the IMF's role which limits that discourse to a refocusing of policy within the existing parameters of the neo-liberal orthodoxy, and leaves unchallenged the principles underpinning the IMF's perspective towards the governance of states and markets, will inevitably be limited in its effectiveness. Unless and until those principles are challenged and opposed by an alternative political economy, which recognizes the constraints which neo-liberal political economy has placed upon trade and development, the world economy will continue to experience damaging contagion, instability and volatility. The original creation of the IMF was inspired by a desire in 1944 not to revisit the depression and political trauma of the inter-war period. It would be unfortunate, to put it mildly, if the global economy has to await a similar depression in the US and beyond before the debate on governance and the IMF can agree upon the need to move on beyond the constraints of the current orthodoxy.

The need to re-evaluate the IMF's overall approach to global governance, and in particular its relationship to the World Bank, has been given renewed momentum by the failure of the international community to deliver the MDGs. In relation to the achievement of the millennium goals for peace and security, hunger and poverty, education, health and the environment, global progress during 2004 has scored no higher than between 2 and 4 out of 10 (where 10 constitutes only a mere passing grade or satisfactory progress) (World Economic Forum 2005: v). The importance of investing in the quality of governance to redress these parallel developmental deficits has been emphasized in a major report from the UN. The report, *Investing in Development* (UNDP 2005), has been welcomed by the IMF as 'an important contribution to the international community's efforts to halve global poverty by 2015' (IMF 2005: 1). For their part, the IMF and World Bank have asserted that the three key areas where they must take action to promote progress towards the MDGs are refining and strengthening their institutional roles in low-income countries; furthering progress on the MDGs' results agenda; and improving the selectivity and coordination of their respective programmes (World Bank/IMF 2004: xx). However, the capacity of the IMF to deliver will in turn largely depend upon the role played by its most powerful member states, and their willingness to support the drive towards poverty reduction. It is these themes which are addressed in Chapter 8.

References

Bird, Graham (2003) *The IMF and the Future: Issues and Options Facing the Fund*, London: Routledge.

Boorman, Jack (2004) *Selection of a New Managing Director*. Available on-line at: www.financialpolicy.org/IMFDemocracy/boorman.htm, accessed on 6 August 2004.

Bretton Woods Project *et al.* (2004) Letter to the Rt Hon Gordon Brown MP, London: Bretton Woods Project. Available on-line at: www.financialpolicy.org/IMFDemocracy/bwproject.htm, accessed on 6 August 2004.

CEA (2002) *Economic Report of the President Together with the Annual Report of the Council of Economic Advisers*, Washington, DC: United States Government Printing Office.

DfID (2000) *Eliminating World Poverty: Making Globalisation Work for the Poor*, London: Department for International Development.

Forum Syd and Diakonia (2004) *Joint Letter from European NGOs to the EU Ministers Prior to the ECOFIN Meeting,* April 2, 2004, Stockholm: Forum Syd and Diakonia.

G7 (2002) *Action Plan: Statement of G7 Finance Ministers and Central Bank Governors,* Washington, DC, 20 April, Ottawa: Group of Seven.

—— (2004) *Statement by US Treasury Secretary John Snow following the G7 Finance Ministers' Meeting,* Washington, DC, 24 April, Ottawa: Group of Seven.

G24 (2004) *Intergovernmental Group of Twenty-four on International Monetary Affairs and Development Communiqué,* 23 April, Geneva: Group of Twenty-Four.

Held, David (2004) *Global Covenant: The Social Democratic Alternative to the Washington Consensus,* Oxford: Polity.

Hutton, Will (2002) *The World We're In,* London: Little, Brown.

IEO (2002) *Evaluation of Prolonged Use of IMF Resources,* Washington, DC: Independent Evaluation Office, International Monetary Fund.

—— (2003) *Fiscal Adjustment in IMF-supported Programs,* Washington, DC: Independent Evaluation Office, International Monetary Fund.

—— (2004a) *Report on the Evaluation of Poverty Reduction Strategy Papers (PRSPs) and the Poverty Reduction and Growth Facility (PRGF),* Washington, DC: Independent Evaluation Office, International Monetary Fund.

—— (2004b) *Report on the Evaluation of the Role of the IMF in Argentina, 1991–2001,* Washington, DC: Independent Evaluation Office, International Monetary Fund.

—— (2004c) *Annual Report 2004,* Washington, DC: Independent Evaluation Office, International Monetary Fund.

IMF (1996) *Partnership for Sustainable Global Growth: Interim Committee Declaration,* Washington, DC: International Monetary Fund.

—— (1997) *Good Governance: The IMF's Role,* Washington, DC: International Monetary Fund.

—— (2001) *Review of the Fund's Experience in Governance Issues,* Washington, DC: International Monetary Fund.

—— (2002) *World Economic Outlook, Recessions and Recoveries: April,* Washington, DC: International Monetary Fund.

—— (2003a) *The IMF and Good Governance: A Factsheet,* Washington, DC: International Monetary Fund. Available on-line at: www.imf.org/external/np/exr/facts.gov.htm, accessed on 18 August 2004.

—— (2003b) *Annual Report 2003: Making the Global Economy Work for All,* Washington, DC: International Monetary Fund.

—— (2003c) *Effects of Financial Globalization on Developing Countries: Some Empirical Evidence,* Washington, DC: International Monetary Fund.

—— (2004a) *Articles of Agreement of the International Monetary Fund,* Washington, DC: International Monetary Fund. Available on-line at: www.imf.org/external/pubs/ft/aa/aa01.htm, accessed on 19 August 2004.

—— (2004b) *Statement by a Group of IMF Executive Directors on the Selection Process for a New Managing Director, Press Release No. 04/55,* Washington, DC: International Monetary Fund.

—— (2004c) *Statement by the G11 Executive Directors of the IMF on the Selection Procedures for Appointing the IMF Managing Director, Press Release No.04/64,* Washington, DC: International Monetary Fund.

—— (2004d) *The IMF at 60 – Evolving Challenges, Evolving Role,* Washington, DC: International Monetary Fund. Available on-line at: www.imf.org/external/np/speeches/2004/061404.htm, accessed on 2 July 2004.

IMF (2005) *IMF Managing Director Rodrigo de Rato Welcomes UN Millennium Project's Report on Achieving Millennium Development Goals*, Press Release No. 05/6, Washington, DC: International Monetary Fund. Available on-line at:www.imf.org/external/np/sec/pr/2005/pr0506.htm, accessed on 18 March 2005.

Lee, Simon (2002) 'The International Monetary Fund', *New Political Economy* 7, 2: 283–97.

Palast, Gregory (2001) 'IMF's four steps to damnation', *The Observer*, 29 April.

Soros, George (1998) *The Crisis of Global Capitalism: Open Society Endangered*, London: Little, Brown.

Stiglitz, Joseph (2002), *Globalization and its Discontents*, London: Allen Lane.

UNDP (2002) *Deepening Democracy in a Fragmented World: Human Development Report 2002*, New York: United Nations Development Programme.

—— (2003), *Millennium Development Goals: A Compact among Nations to End Human Poverty. Human Development Report 2003*, New York: United Nations Development Programme.

—— (2005) *Investing in Development: A Practical Plan to Achieve the Millennium Development Goals*, New York: United Nations Development Programme.

US Treasury (2004) *The Bush Administration's Reform Agenda at the Bretton Woods Institutions: A Progress Report and the Next Steps*, Washington, DC: United States Department of the Treasury, Office of Public Affairs.

Van Houtven, Leo (2002) *Governance of the IMF: Decision Making, Institutional Oversight, Transparency, and Accountability*, Washington, DC: International Monetary Fund.

World Bank/IMF (2004) *Global Monitoring Report 2004*, Washington, DC: World Bank.

World Economic Forum (2005) *Global Governance Initiative Annual Report 2005*, Geneva: Switzerland.

8 Global governance, Japan and the International Monetary Fund

Shirai Sayuri

Introduction

Over the last two decades, one of the most important challenges for improving global governance has been poverty reduction in low-income countries. This reflects how the prevalence of extreme poverty, especially in Sub-Saharan Africa, is closely associated with internal, regional and global conflicts; with marginalized groups of people and resultant social tensions; and with an imbalance in global prosperity. Despite the rising global living standards over the period examined here, nearly half of the world's six billion people still live on less than US$2 a day; while one-fifth live on less than US$1 a day and are without basic human needs.

The growing global concern about problems associated with poverty has also led to the United Nations Millennium Development Declaration of 189 nations, and to joint commitments by the United Nations, International Monetary Fund (IMF), World Bank and the Organization for Economic Cooperation and Development (OECD) in 2000, with respect to achieving specific targets for poverty reduction known as the Millennium Development Goals (MDGs). The achievement of the MDGs depends on effective economic policies and the improvement of governance (both at country and global levels) with the closer collaboration of all stakeholders, including international organizations, developing countries, donor countries and non-governmental organizations (NGOs). To assist developing countries to meet the MDGs, twenty-two Development Assistance Committee (DAC) donor countries are expected to raise the amount of their official development assistance (ODA) from the current level of 0.2 per cent of gross national product (GNP) to the 0.7 per cent target established in the 1970 Pearson Commission Report and re-confirmed by the donor countries under the 2002 Monterrey Consensus.

In January 2005, the UN Millennium Project, commissioned by the UN Secretary-General, released the report entitled 'Investing in Development: A Practical Plan to Achieve the Millennium Development Goals'. By stressing the positive impact of aid volumes on raising economic growth rates, the report indicated that donor countries should provide at least US$69 billion in 2006 (0.44 per cent of GNP), rising to US$195 billion (0.54 per cent) by 2015. Given that Japan's ODA accounts for only 0.2 per cent of GNP and the amount of ODA has been in decline, its greater contribution and initiatives for promoting global governance has been increasingly expected by the international community; especially as Japan is the world's second largest economic power. However, the increasing pressure for reducing the large fiscal deficit at home, a growing sense of 'aid fatigue', and weak economic and historical relationships with Sub-Saharan Africa make it difficult for the Japanese government to gain public support for an increase in ODA. In addition, Japan is reluctant to accept full-cancellation of the yen loans provided in the past to low-income countries any more than those provided to the Highly Indebted Poor Countries (HIPCs). Moreover, Japan's greater proportion of yen loans over grants in the total volume of ODA has been criticized by the donor community, as demonstrated in the G7 meeting held in early February 2005, as being at odds with the global trend toward grants. In these circumstances, Japan needs to provide a more convincing rationale for its present ODA policy, while searching for an alternative and more effective aid approach to assist developing countries.

As one of the major international financial organizations, moreover, the IMF has since the 1980s begun to tackle the economic development of low-income developing countries by providing highly concessional lending to these countries. It introduced the low-interest medium-term structural adjustment facility (SAF) in 1986, followed by the enhanced structural adjustment facility (ESAF) in 1987. The IMF, together with the World Bank, introduced the HIPCs Initiative in 1996 in order to reduce the external debt burdens of developing countries to sustainable levels. The IMF also launched the Poverty Reduction Growth Facility (PRGF) in 1999, replacing the ESAF, with the aim of making the objectives of poverty reduction and growth more central to lending operations in low-income developing countries. The IMF (and the World Bank) has also begun to stress country ownership in designing a country's development strategy, as evidenced by the introduction of the Poverty Reduction Strategic Paper (PRSP). It is expected that both international financial organizations and bilateral donor countries, such as Japan, would increase collaboration and concentrate their financial assistance on achieving development strategies in developing countries that are envisaged in PRSPs. While Japan has been making efforts to coordinate its ODA policy in line with the MDGs, its reluctance to promote debt relief and raise ODA makes it difficult to take a leadership role within the IMF and influence IMF policies.

Japan provides the second largest quota (US$17.4 billion) to the IMF and its vote accounts for 6.1 per cent of the total votes of all member countries, while the United States provides US$48.7 billion and its vote accounts for the largest 17.1 per cent. Despite its significant financial contribution, Japan has so far failed to convince the IMF Executive Board to raise the quotas and votes of other East Asian countries to the level at least comparable to their economic sizes. As a result, the presence of the disproportionately large voices of West European countries, together with the dominance of the United States, makes it difficult for Japan and East Asia to collectively and effectively reflect their concerns and express a commensurate voice over the IMF decision-making process.

This chapter first focuses on Japan as one of the major donor countries of the IMF and undertakes a critical overview of its recent efforts in promoting a better system of global governance. It next examines the role of the IMF as one of the major international financial institutions providing concessionary loans to low-income countries. It then goes on to discuss a number of recent initiatives and Japan's role in improving global governance before concluding with some policy recommendations.

Economic growth, poverty reduction and Japan

Japan's ODA policy and contributions

Since the 1980s, Japan has placed high national priority on ODA and enlarged the size and variety of its aid programmes. As a result, Japan became one of the world's top ODA donors in value terms, and maintained its status as the largest ODA provider until 2001. Since then, Japan has been the second largest ODA provider after the United States. As of 2002, Japan's ODA amounted to US$9.28 billion, accounting for 15.9 per cent of total net ODA of DAC countries: second largest after the United States (US$13.3 billion and 23 per cent). Japan's bilateral ODA (excluding contributions to international organizations) amounts to US$6.7 billion, accounting for 16 per cent of total net ODA of DAC countries. Moreover, Japan's untied ratio for total ODA is more than 80 per cent and higher than Canada (25 per cent), Italy (38 per cent), Spain (47 per cent) and France (68 per cent). In particular, Japan's untied ratio for ODA loans has been substantially higher than other major industrialized donor countries.

Furthermore, the share of net ODA loans in total ODA accounted for 40 per cent in Japan in 2002 and was the highest among the donor countries. Figure 8.1 indicates the ratio of net ODA loans to total bilateral net ODA for the four largest donor countries. The greater ratio of ODA loans in Japan reflects two factors: one is that about one-third of Japan's ODA is financed by the Fiscal Investment and Loan (*zaiseitōyūshi*) whose funds are largely from postal savings deposits and public insurance (*kanpo*). Another 10 per cent is financed by the issuance of government bonds and mainly allocated as contributions to the increase in the capital of international financial organizations. Given that a substantial amount of ODA is sourced from borrowed funds, it is inevitable for Japan to provide a greater amount of loans over grants, relative to other countries, and compensate for back spread (the gap between lending and borrowing interest rates) in the ordinary budget.

The other factor is related to Japan's principle that ODA should be used to promote self-reliance incentives among recipient countries, rather than promoting dependence on foreign grants with no repayment obligation. This reflects the successful experience of the East Asian region, where the expansion of economic infrastructure assisted by Japan's ODA has contributed to high economic growth. Loans not only enable long-term, large-scale financing (which is necessary for promoting fixed capital formation), but also requires recipient countries to produce

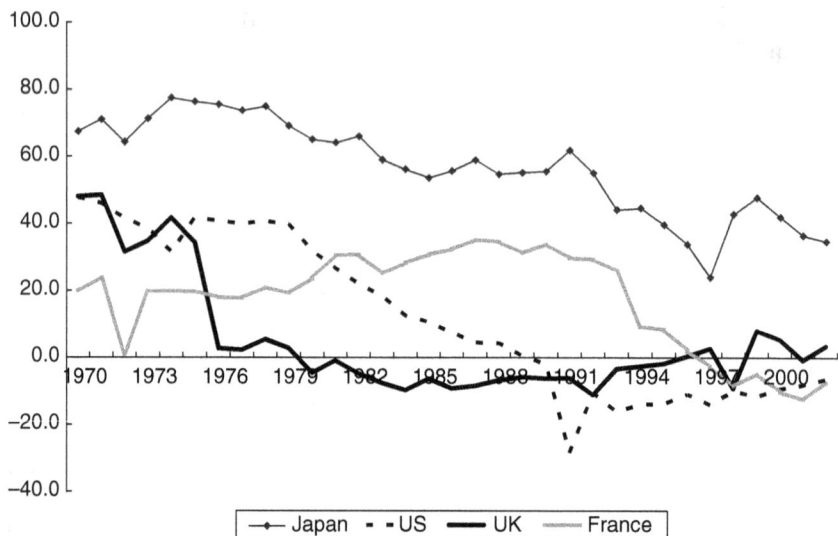

Figure 8.1 Trends in bilateral net ODA loans (per cent of total bilateral net ODA).
Source: OECD/DAC geographic distribution of financial flows to developing countries.

high returns and, at the same time, conduct prudent fiscal policy. Therefore, Japan is of the view that loans could contribute positively to the economic development of other regions as well as in favour of the East Asian development model. It is also of the view that yen loans would not adversely affect low-income countries given that they are largely untied and their grant element (GE) is higher (72 per cent) than the United States (69.2 per cent), the United Kingdom (43.4 per cent), France (55 per cent) and Germany (66 per cent).

In terms of geographic contribution, Japan's ODA policy has played a crucial role in helping achieve high, sustainable economic growth in many East Asian countries, as noted earlier. This has also been aided by massive private credit flows from Japan to Asian countries. Japan's active outward foreign direct investment (FDI) since the 1980s has helped to improve the productive base, increase employment, boost foreign reserves and raise corporate income tax revenues in these recipient countries. Further, Japan's ODA has been instrumental in helping lay down essential economic infrastructure and set the stage for an economic take-off for many Asian countries that have registered impressive recent economic gains. For example, Japan allocated ODA loans to establish industrial sea ports and industrial estates in Map Ta Phut (¥12 billion on a contractual basis) and Laem Chabang (¥19 billion) in Thailand in the mid-1980s. These loans have contributed to attracting FDI from Japan as well as other countries, and thus helped Thailand to achieve higher export-driven economic growth. In addition, Japanese firms operating abroad have employed more than three million people (nearly two million in Asia) each year during 1999–2000. The Japan Bank for

International Cooperation (JBIC), an administrator of ODA loans, has provided an assessment that Japan's ODA loans from 1980 to 1999 raised 1999 GDP by 3.2 per cent (on year-average, 0.17 per cent each year) in Thailand and 1.4 per cent (0.08 per cent) in the Philippines (JBIC 2002). While the contribution of Japan's ODA to the East Asian region could be substantial, it should be emphasized that other factors have been equally important contributors. Those include high educational levels, high savings, well-planned development strategies together with relatively good governance at the government level, and promotion of private sector development together with better legal and institutional infrastructure and rapid globalization in the region.

Moreover, Japan's food aid, which is included in the Ministry of Foreign Affairs (MOFA) ODA budget, has been LDC-untied, so that recipient countries are able to purchase rice from other developing countries using Japan's grant, thus helping rice-exporting developing countries to accumulate foreign reserves and generate income. Further, Japan's aid for food speeded-up production, although the volume has been declining in recent years, helped a number of developing countries to achieve food self-reliance by enabling them to purchase fertilizer, agricultural equipment, and learn advanced farming skills. Consequently, some countries, such as Thailand, Cambodia, Vietnam and Myanmar, have increased rice production and been transformed from net rice importers to net rice exporters. According to the DAC, 37 per cent of all agriculture-related ODA comes from Japan.

Japanese public views

The amount of Japan's ODA began to decline from 2002, since Japan's fiscal deficit problems led the government to make fiscal reform a top priority, illustrated by the passing of the Fiscal Restructuring Law in December 1997. Moreover, the prolonged recession (1.2 per cent growth in 1992–2003 compared to 3 per cent growth in 1980–91) and a high unemployment rate (4.4 per cent in 2004 compared to around 2 per cent in 1974–94) in Japan, together with a growing fiscal deficit, induced the Japanese public to question whether Japan should continue to provide assistance to other countries when it faces so many domestic problems of its own. Public feeling increasingly has stressed that national interest should be given a higher priority, and that this should be reflected in ODA programmes toward developing countries. A public opinion survey conducted by the Cabinet Office in 2003 with respect to the level of ODA, for example, revealed that 73 per cent of respondents supported 'maintain status quo', 'should do less', or 'should terminate', increasing from 59.5 per cent in 1993 (Figure 8.2). The public has also criticized Japan's ODA policy for its lack of transparency and effectiveness and that it should contribute to helping overcome Japan's recession (Figure 8.3).

The growing criticism of Japan's ODA policy has left the government no choice but to lower the ratio of untied loans since 1999, while increasingly allocating ODA toward environmental areas (currently more than 30 per cent), human rights, peace restoration and so on. Many now have the view that Japan's ODA loans should not be used to hire companies operating in other OECD countries to build highways or other infrastructure under their corporate names in developing

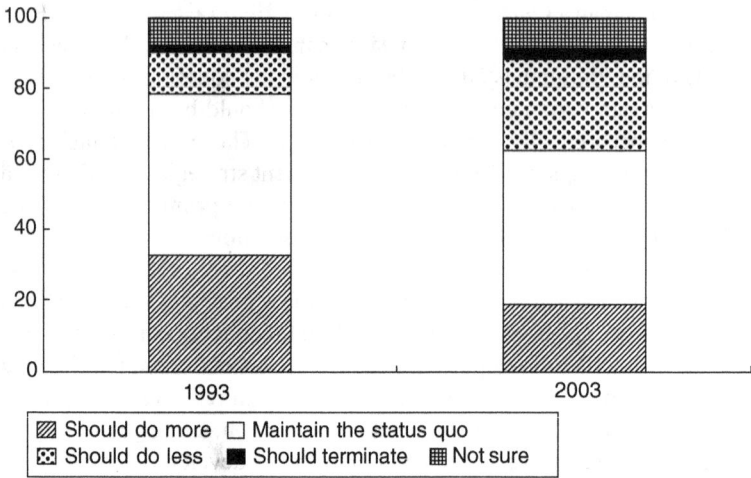

Figure 8.2 Public opinion surveys concerning the amount of ODA (per cent).

Source: Cabinet Office, Keizai Kyōryoku ni kansuru Yoronchōsa, 2003.

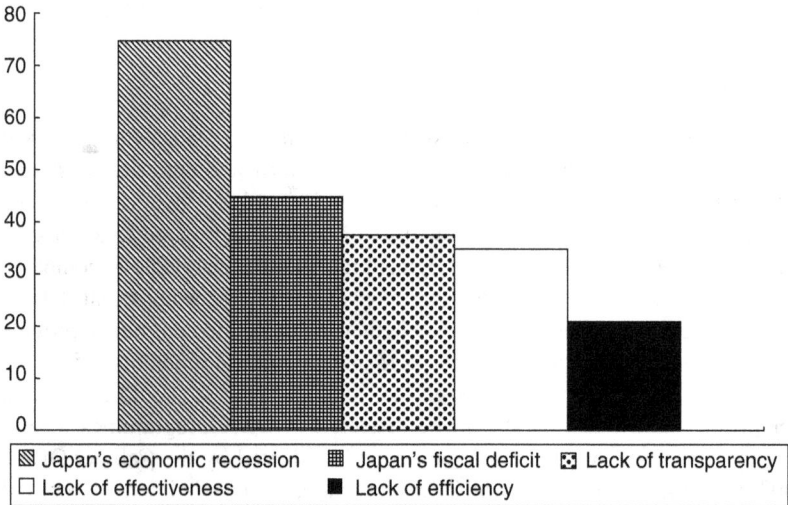

Figure 8.3 Public opinion surveys concerning reasons for choosing 'should do less or terminate' (per cent).

Source: Cabinet Office, Keizai Kyōryoku ni kansuru Yoronchōsa, 2003.

countries, since residents in recipient countries are unlikely to realize this reflects Japan's contribution. Since ODA constitutes the main part of Japan's foreign policy, the public view is that money should be used as policy 'to explicitly reveal Japan's face'. In other words, there is a growing consensus that Japan's national interests should be given greater salience in ODA policy, as reflected in the revised ODA Charter (revised in 2003), while allocating ODA more selectively to restore peace in Afghanistan, Sri Lanka, Iraq and other war-torn countries, and to solve environmental problems.

Given the close economic linkages and geographical proximity, Japan's ODA has been historically concentrated in East Asia, even though ODA has been extended to 150 nations in total. While the ratio of Japan's bilateral ODA toward Asia to total bilateral ODA has declined from 98 per cent in 1970 to 71 per cent in 1980, and further to 57 per cent in 2002, the ratio remains high. One reason for Japan's bias toward Asia is explained by the fact that ODA was initiated in the process of paying post-war compensation and quasi-compensation to Asian countries on the basis of the 1951 San Francisco Peace Treaty. Another reason is that ODA was used to promote Japan's economic recovery from economic devastation through promoting its exports to neighbouring countries including India (for example, by actively using trade credit). While these two reasons explain Japan's bias toward Asia in the early stage, it may be no longer justified since many of these assisted Asian countries have achieved high economic growth and have been enjoying inflows of private sector capital from the rest of the world. Indeed, some countries, such as South Korea, Thailand and Malaysia, have been shifting from the status of ODA recipient countries to that of ODA donor countries. The persistent Asian bias until today reflects Japanese public views that ODA should be used in a manner that is mutually beneficial. According to the aforementioned Cabinet Office survey, 49 per cent of respondents pointed to Asia as the region to enhance further economic cooperation, while Africa accounted for only 9 per cent. As a result, the revised ODA Charter stresses the achievement of mutual economic growth in East Asia where economic linkages with Japan have been strong.

As for ODA toward China, on the other hand, the provision of substantial amounts of ODA to the country (the second largest recipient, accounting for about 10 per cent of Japan's total ODA) has generated strong criticism in Japan (for example, by the Economic Cooperation Evaluation Subcommittee of the Liberal Democratic Party's Special Committee on External Economic Cooperation and the Advisory Group on Japan's Economic Assistance to China in the 21st Century). Criticism has mainly focused on China's massive military expenditure; concerns about its violation of basic human rights; the lack of public recognition or appreciation by Chinese citizens for Japan's aid; China's assistance to other countries (it is rumoured that part of Japan's ODA has been reallocated to countries of strategic importance to China); and its high economic growth and position as a net exporter. At the end of January 2005, the government announced a plan to gradually reduce yen loans to China and terminate them by 2008; its assistance to China will thenceforth be concentrated on technical assistance and some grants.

Challenges over Japan's ODA policy

Japan's ODA policy faces various challenges. First, Japan had to provide a greater amount of debt relief to the HIPCs than other donor countries, given that the ratio of

ODA loans to total ODA has been largest among DAC countries. In accordance with the HIPCs initiative, moreover, the government decided to carry out full-cancellation of the claims for HIPCs in 2003. In the past, Japan avoided debt cancellation but performed debt relief by providing grant aid for debt relief. In this process, recipient countries needed to repay their yen loans first and subsequently received grants from the Japanese government to offset the payment. This was burdensome for the recipient countries due to administrative and foreign currency procurement costs. The amount of Japan's debt relief under this mechanism reached US$9 billion (of which, ODA loans reached US$8 billion), accounting for 26 per cent of total debt relief undertaken by the G7 nations. Debt cancellation helps recipient countries to reduce these costs and thus should be evaluated highly. Nonetheless, the presence of a large amount of outstanding ODA claims to developing countries makes it difficult for Japan to expand the HIPCs initiative to other low-income countries that are not eligible for the HIPCs initiative. This makes it difficult for Japan to take the lead over the debt relief initiatives in the donor community. Additionally, the growing global expectation regarding Japan's leadership role on the issue of debt relief suggests that a greater portion of grants, not loans, should be provided to low-income developing countries in future ODA allocations.

Second, despite the large amount, Japan's ODA has been small in terms of its GNP, accounting for only 0.23 per cent (eighteenth ranking) and being far below the 0.7 per cent target committed under the Monterrey Consensus (Table 8.1). Also, Japan's per capita ODA reaches only US$77.4 (ninth ranking). The severe fiscal deficit (more than 7 per cent of GDP) and growing public debt (about 140 per cent of GDP) make it extremely difficult for Japan to increase ODA from the current level. This indicates that Japan needs to play a more active role in reducing poverty in developing countries, mainly through improving the effectiveness of its ODA policy. In particular, a greater amount of ODA needs to be allocated to Sub-Saharan African countries with a more carefully designed ODA policy targeting the poor and, at the same time, promote private sector trade and investment flows. It may be necessary to earmark a certain portion of ODA for Sub-Saharan Africa. This regional reallocation of the ODA budget is necessary for Japan in order to assist developing countries to fulfil MDGs. In doing so, the amount of ODA could be reduced for some Asian countries that are able to receive private sector capital flows, and this reduction could be offset partially by an increase in other offical flows (OOF, official loans other than ODA loans) toward them.

Third, Japan's ODA concentrates on economic infrastructure covering transportation and energy infrastructure relative to social infrastructure (such as education, health and access to safe water). The ratio of economic infrastructure accounted for 35 per cent of total bilateral ODA in 2001, greater than the United States (3.6 per cent), United Kingdom (8 per cent), France (7.7 per cent) and the DAC average (14.9 per cent). Japan's greater bias toward economic infrastructure reflects in part its own development experience. To reconstruct Japan from the post-war economic devastation, for example, it borrowed funds from the World Bank in 1952 and allocated them to promoting fixed capital formation in the steel, automobile, ship-building industries as well as to constructing dams in the 1950s.

Table 8.1 Net ODA of DAC countries

	GNP ranking	2002 (%)	Per capita ranking	2001 (US$)
Denmark	1	0.96	2	304.9
Norway	2	0.89	3	298.4
Sweden	3	0.83	5	187.2
Netherlands	4	0.81	4	198.4
Luxembourg	5	0.77	1	320.5
Belgium	6	0.43	7	84.3
Ireland	7	0.40	11	74.7
France	8	0.38	12	70.9
Finland	9	0.35	10	74.8
Switzerland	10	0.32	6	125.6
UK	11	0.31	8	77.9
Canada	12	0.28	15	49.3
Germany	13	0.27	14	60.6
Portugal	14	0.27	21	25.9
Australia	15	0.26	13	65.6
Spain	16	0.26	17	43.1
Austria	17	0.26	16	44.8
Japan	18	0.23	9	77.4
New Zealand	19	0.22	19	29.1
Greece	20	0.21	22	18.4
Italy	21	0.20	20	28.4
US	22	0.13	18	40.1
Average		0.23		104.6

Source: ODA White Paper 2003, Ministry of Foreign Affairs.

In the 1960s, the borrowed funds were allocated extensively to building highways and railroads for express trains (Watanabe and Miura 2003). Moreover, Japan's ODA is essentially request-driven and many East Asian countries have been willing to utilize yen loans to expand their economic infrastructure, following Japan's successful development model. In recent years, however, many donor countries allocate more funds for social infrastructure, shifting away from economic infrastructure (Figure 8.4 in the case of Japan and the United States). The development community now understands that developing better governance and institutions and promoting human capital and basic human needs are essential for raising the contribution to economic infrastructure for economic growth. Thus, Japan may need to shift its emphasis from economic infrastructure to social infrastructure to some extent.

Policy coherence: *toward an integrated ODA policy*

In recent years, policy coherence has become an important issue related to ODA policy. Policy incoherence occurs when contradictory policies are implemented by donor countries. For example, countries may spend large amounts of ODA to strengthen trade capacities in developing countries, while at the same time

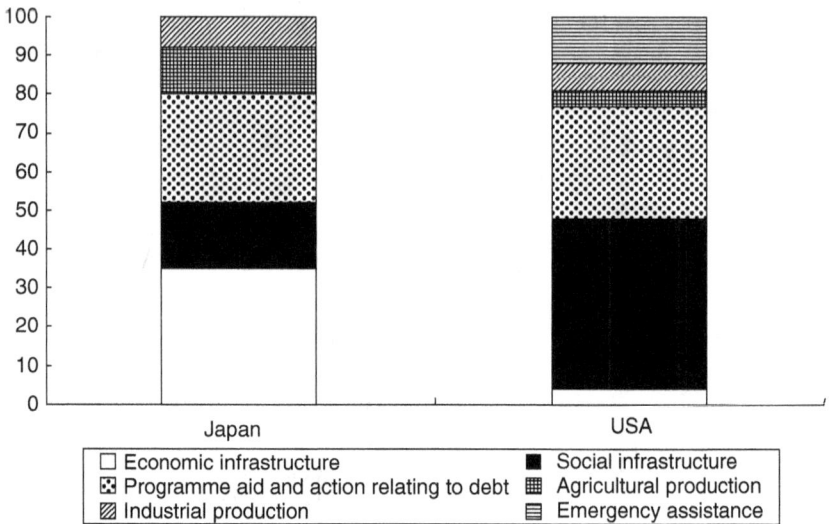

Figure 8.4 Sector allocation of Japan's and US's bilateral ODA in 2001(commitment base, per cent of total).

Source: ODA White Paper 2003, Ministry of Foreign Affairs.

restricting access to their markets (OECD 2002). Formally, policy coherence can be thought of as being attainable through three stages: (1) between the different instruments of development cooperation (e.g. grant, loans, humanitarian aid and technical cooperation), (2) between development and domestic policies (e.g. agricultural and fishery policies) and (3) between development policies and other areas of international policy (e.g. international investment, trade, security and environmental policies). It has been increasingly recognized in the international development community that donor countries should expand their economic cooperation for development in low-income countries not just by increasing ODA and improving its effectiveness (as envisaged in Stage 1), but to promote broader economic cooperation through achieving better policy coherence (as envisaged in Stages 2 and 3). With respect to the first stage of policy coherence aimed at achieving an integrated ODA policy, Japan has been making efforts to achieve greater ODA policy coherence between the different instruments of development cooperation (although less effort has been made for the second and third stages). One factor making Japan's ODA policy complicated and opaque arises from the complex ODA budgetary allocation process. Japan's ODA budget has been allocated among twelve ministries and the Cabinet Office. The lack of an integrated budget makes it complicated for the government to implement a mutually consistent ODA policy. In particular, close collaboration between the MOFA and the Ministry of Finance (MOF) is the key to achieving an integrated ODA policy, given that most of the budget is allocated to MOFA (31.5 per cent of the total budget) and MOF (60 per cent). The MOFA's budget is allocated subsequently to technical cooperation executed by the Japan International Cooperation Agency ([JICA] accounting for 35 per cent of the MOFA's total budget), contributions to international organizations (20 per cent), and grants including food aid (50 per cent). The MOF's budget is distributed to the JBIC (accounting for 80 per cent of the total MOF budget) and contributions to other international organizations, such as the World Bank and the Asian Development Bank. The rest of the budget (8.5 per cent) is allocated to sector-based assistance programmes (largely, technical cooperation) executed by the remaining ministries and the Cabinet Office. In the past, yen-denominated loan projects were determined through coordination among MOFA, MOF, the Ministry of Economy, Trade and Industry (METI), and the Cabinet Office, while grants and technical cooperation programmes used to be determined by the MOFA.

In recent years, the government has adopted several measures to improve coordination of ODA policy: first, the Council of Overseas Economic Cooperation-related Ministers was re-opened in December 2000, after its abolishment in 1993, with growing awareness of the need to promote exchanges of views and improve collaboration among relevant ministries. However, the Council, presided over by the Chief Cabinet Secretary and participated in by the ministers of the relevant ministries, does not meet regularly. This is a high-level council convened to discuss Japan's main foreign policy, positioned above the Inter-ministerial Meeting on ODA described later. The Secretariat is located in the Cabinet Office. Agenda items discussed are generally coordinated in advance by the MOFA through communications with relevant ministries. In this sense, the Council has been passive since issues have been selected from the bottom up, not at the initiative of the Ministerial Council, which would be top-down and more active on the part of the Council. So far, the Council has discussed and made decisions to revise the ODA Charter; to formulate medium-term ODA policy; and to invite public comments on the ODA Charter.

Second, the Inter-ministerial Meeting on ODA was established in March 2000 to serve as a forum for discussion on major ODA-related issues among the twelve ministries and the Cabinet Office. For example, a meeting in October 2001 discussed measures to be taken by Japan in reaction to the September 11 terrorist attacks on the United States. In March 2002, the topic addressed was support for the reconstruction of Afghanistan. The meeting discussed the total ODA budget and inter-ministerial collaboration in September 2002 and the basic principle of the ODA Charter revision in March 2003.

Third, the Bureau Meeting for Inter-ministerial Groups on ODA now functions as a forum to conduct discussions and collaboration at desk level to support the Inter-ministerial Meeting on ODA among the twelve ministries and the Cabinet Office. All important negotiations take place at this level. Thus, the meeting of this forum takes place more frequently than the Inter-ministerial Meetings. For example, in October 2002, the Bureau Meeting discussed a proposal for ODA Reform made by the Liberal Democratic Party's Special Committee on External Economic Cooperation, the transformation of the JICA to an Independent

Administrative Institution, the ODA White Paper, and assistance to Afghanistan. In January 2003, the Bureau Meeting discussed the final report on ODA Reform submitted by the Liberal Democratic Party's Special Committee on External Economic Cooperation, the schedule and direction of ODA Charter revision, and the present conditions and future plans in relation to country assistance programmes. In addition, the Bureau Meeting has been given a position superior to the three subordinate Experts Meetings described later.

Fourth, given that all ODA-budgeted ministries provide technical cooperation, the Experts Meeting of Technical Cooperation was established in April 1997 as a forum to exchange information and views and collaborate on related projects in order to implement projects effectively and efficiently, and to reduce the overlapping of projects among the twelve ministries and the Cabinet Office. The Directors of these ministries serve as members. In addition, the Experts Meeting of ODA Evaluation was established in July 2001 with members being the division directors from relevant ministries, along with scholars, experts and representatives of NGOs and international organizations as observers. This meeting provides a forum to formulate guidelines on project evaluation and to review evaluation outcomes related to ODA in order to strengthen Japan's ODA evaluation system. In March 2002, the meeting adopted the Reference Method of Technical Program Evaluation in ODA-related ministries to use as a reference in evaluating ODA activities involving the dispatch of experts and the acceptance of trainees overseen by various ministries. In November 2002, February 2003 and April 2003, meetings discussed the Reference Method and reviewed evaluations performed by relevant ministries and agencies.

Moreover, the Experts Meeting of Financial Cooperation was established in November 2002. These meetings provide a forum to discuss and coordinate programmes and projects in developing countries in relation to grants, ODA loans, OOF and trade credits among the MOFA, MOF, METI, JICA, JBIC and the Nippon Export and Investment Insurance. For example, in November 2002 the meeting discussed the present conditions of financial cooperation with Indonesia and Vietnam. It focused mainly on financial cooperation with India in January 2003; with Sri Lanka and Vietnam in February 2003; with Bangladesh, and collaboration between the JICA and JBIC, and bilateral and multilateral financial assistance in March 2003; with China, and the strengthening of field-level collaboration in April 2003, and with Cambodia and Thailand in June 2003.

Fifth, in addition to the role of coordinating ODA projects among relevant ministries, the MOFA has been given a stronger mandate to formulate country assistance programmes with close collaboration with governments in recipient countries, the Board on Comprehensive ODA Strategy, the ODA Task Force (both discussed later), embassies, international organizations, other donors, NGOs and the general public. The MOFA has been making efforts to better align the country assistance programmes formulated by Japan with recipient country-owned development plans including the PRSPs. Also, efforts have been made to better align Japan's aid projects and programmes with those of recipient country-owned sector strategies. Japan's ODA policy has now shifted toward formulating and strengthening existing country assistance programmes in line with the revised ODA Charter. To support this move, the MOFA is currently being reorganized to back up its strengthened authority with respect to its overall responsibility for ODA policy and to coordinating roles with other ODA-budgeted ministries. Additionally, in April 2003 the MOFA strengthened collaboration with related ministries in relation to ODA policy by newly appointing a Senior Vice-Minister in charge of ODA. To further enhance inter-ministerial coordination, the Director General of the Economic Cooperation Bureau (ECB) of the MOFA was appointed from METI, and the Deputy Director General and the Senior Coordinator (to the Loan Division of ECB) both from the Cabinet Office.

Sixth, the Board on Comprehensive ODA Strategy was established in June 2002 and is chaired by the Minister of Foreign Affairs. The members consist of the Senior Vice-Minister, a journalist, a development journal editor, NGO repre-sentatives, experts, academics, think tank representatives, firm representatives and so on. In addition to reviewing the ODA Charter, its mandate is to review and formulate country assistance programmes, and discuss major ODA agenda items. The meeting is generally held once a month. Relevant ministries, JICA and JBIC send staff as observers. The Board plays an important role in determining future target countries where assistance programmes are to be applied and reviewing as well as revising the existing fifteen country assistance programmes (those already formulated before the establishment of the Board). However, the fact that Board members are public representatives and that the Board is essentially an advisory council to the MOFA makes it difficult to expect it to emerge as a place to negotiate policy coherence issues, although discussions on policy coherence can be held. Even though other relevant ministries send their officials as observers to the Board, their roles are mostly to simply report discussions to their respective ministries and the Cabinet Office.

Seventh, in line with its mandate to improve the transparency and effectiveness of ODA policy, the MOFA has strengthened field-level participation in the process of policy formulation. At the end of 2002 the MOFA instructed embassies, JICA and JBIC representative offices to organize ODA Task Forces for fifty-one countries (covering Asia, Latin America, Middle East, Eastern Europe and Africa) and to form field-level networks with JICA experts, NGOs, the Japan Foundation and others. The ODA Task Force collects information in relation to macroeconomic performance and development plans of recipient countries, exchanges views and negotiates with recipient governments, and closely collaborates with other donors and international organizations to reduce administrative overlap or burden on governments in recipient countries. The Task Force organizes frequent meetings in the recipient country and reports regularly to MOFA headquarters, which in turn utilizes the information and suggestions in formulating country assistance programmes and in selection of country strategies.

While these changes are welcome and on the right track, Japan still faces difficulty in developing a comprehensive, integrated, attractive aid policy for developing countries and coordinating a national role in global governance. As Japan's ODA volume is declining, the better coordination among relevant ministries and agencies is becoming an even more urgent task. Japan's current budgetary allocation practices on ODA budget is not suitable to deal with the broader global agenda. For example, issues such as how to improve governance needs to be addressed at a recipient country level (e.g. bureaucratic efficiency, government expenditure management, legal and judiciary systems, sound financial systems) as well as at a global level (e.g. promoting trade and financial liberalization, reducing global income disparity and tensions, improving collective security and reducing terrorism, limiting the emergence of economic and external debt crises, ameliorating environmental problems). Country-level governance also needs to be dealt with regionally and globally, since developing countries tend to face the same problems; for example, lack of governance often deters the effective use of ODA funds for development purposes. Also, ODA policy needs to be closely coordinated with other issues including free trade area (FTA) arrangements, inward and outward foreign direct investment policies, environmental policy and the WTO Agreement on Trade-Related Aspects of Intellectual Property Rights (TRIPS Agreement). Accordingly, Japan needs to seriously investigate its present governmental organizational and budgetary structures so that new policies related to these issues can be formulated in a timely and effective manner.

Successful examples of policy coherence regarding integrated ODA policy

Vietnam (Japan is its top aid donor) is the first country whose existing country assistance programme (formulated in 2000) has been revised based on a consensus achieved at the Board on Comprehensive ODA Policy. This move significantly differs from past practices of formulating country assistance programmes, since the Embassy of Japan in Vietnam and representative offices of the JICA and JBIC have been closely collaborating with members of the Board on Comprehensive ODA Policy in the process of revising Vietnam's country assistance programme. The ODA Task Force in Vietnam was established in March 2003. The Task Force concentrates on issues such as developing a new Country Assistance Programme. Special meetings are also held with Japanese NGOs. This field-based approach is different from that followed in the past, when such field-level collaboration and collaboration between field-level agents and the MOFA was limited. Close collaboration with other donors and partners such as the World Bank, the IMF and the United Nations Development Program (UNDP) has also been successfully realized. While this approach is welcome, the application of the same level of assistance to other countries, especially in Sub-Saharan Africa, may be difficult to achieve owing to the lack of sufficient manpower in Japan. As a result, closer collaboration with other donors is likely to become important in the near future.

Another example is that Japan has been promoting the Tokyo International Conference on African Development (TICAD) process since the 1990s with a view to realizing ownership and partnerships in development and economic adjustment programmes in countries in Africa. This process represents Japan's continuing commitment to resolving Africa's problems and its determination to work in cooperation with Africa in the international community. As part of its initiative in the area of investment, the MOFA held the Tokyo International Conference on Investment to Africa in February 2003. The conference featured lively discussions in which participants drew on their experiences, and many constructive proposals were made regarding issues that should be addressed to promote investment in Africa. TICAD III was held in Tokyo in September 2003, followed by the TICAD Asia–Africa Trade-Investment Conference held in Tokyo in November 2004.

Poverty reduction, the IMF and Japan

Limited impact of IMF policies

Article 1(2) of the Articles of Agreement stipulates that the purpose of the IMF is 'to facilitate the expansion and balanced growth of international trade, and to contribute thereby to the promotion and maintenance of high levels of employment and real income and to the development of the productive resources of all members as primary objectives of economic policy'. While this purpose could be considered as its long-term and ultimate goal, the immediate goals of the IMF concern prudent macroeconomic policies and related structural reforms (e.g. exchange rate policy, tax policy, fiscal management, privatization, domestic price reform).

Notwithstanding these goals, the results of the impact of IMF economic policies on macroeconomic performance have been mixed. For example, Reichmann and Stillson (1978) found that IMF programmes had no effect on the balance of payments. On the other hand, Pastor (1987) reported an improvement in the balance of payments in IMF-programme countries. Moreover, many studies found that IMF programmes had no effect on inflation (Pastor 1987; Edwards and Santaella 1993), while Killick (1995) reported that IMF programmes were effective in reducing inflation. In addition, Killick (1995) and Pastor (1987) found no effect of IMF programmes on the international current account, while Khan (1990) and Edwards and Santaella (1993) discovered their positive contribution. Furthermore, Reichmann and Stillson (1978) and Pastor (1987) reported no effect of IMF programmes on economic growth, while Killick (1995) found ambiguous effects. Meanwhile, Conway (1994) found that while growth declined in the first year of the programmes, the negative effects diminished thereafter.

As for the impact of IMF economic policies on poverty reduction, the results have been largely negative. For example, Pastor (1987), focusing on IMF-supported programmes in eighteen Latin American countries for 1985–91, compared macroeconomic indicators in the year preceding the programme to those in the final year of the programme. Using non-parametric techniques, Pastor found that the programme reduced labour's share of income relative to both the pre-programme levels and a control group of Latin American countries that did not undertake IMF-supported programmes. Assuming that the average changes in total income were positive, the finding suggests that returns on capital increased amid a declining share of income for labour; hence poverty and inequality worsened.

In the recent literature, Easterly (2000) examined the effect of IMF (and World Bank) adjustment lending on poverty reduction, based on household survey data of sixty-five countries for 1980–98. Using the number of adjustment loans per year during the poverty spell, no direct effect was traced for lending on poverty reduction. However, he found that such lending had a strong positive interaction effect with economic growth. Namely, such lending lowers the growth elasticity of poverty reduction by smoothening consumption for the poor and lowering the rise in poverty for a given contraction, but lowers the fall in poverty for a given expansion. This result is not favourable for the IMF, because it gives the poor less of a stake in overall good economic performance, and thus, suggests that growth under adjustment lending is less pro-poor than in economies without it.

In addition, Garuda (2000) estimated the effects of IMF-supported programmes on income measures of both poverty and inequality based on a database of fifty-eight programmes in thirty-nine countries for 1975–91. Garuda introduced counterfactual thinking by using a propensity score estimation method in order to reduce the selection bias inherent in comparing programme and non-programme countries. Propensity scores represent the probability that either programme or non-programme countries would have agreed to an IMF-supported programme at some point before the decision is made, regardless of what they ultimately decided to do. Once the scores are generated, observations are divided into groups by the extent of the scores, within which countries are further subdivided into programme and non-programme countries to control for systematic differences between them prior to the decision. Garuda found that countries with a low propensity and IMF involvement showed an improvement of 10–15 percentage points in their Gini Coefficient, average level of income and income level of the lowest quintile, relative to the control groups. As propensity scores increase, countries with IMF-supported programmes showed less significant improvements than those that did not have IMF support, suggesting that the IMF role in lowering poverty and inequality has been less effective.

Furthermore, Shirai (2004a) examined factors affecting the level of poverty and the impact of the IMF-supported programmes on poverty reduction by focusing on seventy-seven countries (those eligible for ESAF or PRGF assistance) rather than extending to broader ranges of developing countries as done in many previous studies. In the absence of income measures of poverty for many low-income countries, Shirai (2004a) used non-income poverty measures, typically education and health indicators, and found a weak or negative impact of the IMF on poverty reduction, based on panel data for 1981–2000. The results suggested that the IMF needs to redesign its programmes targeting low-income developing countries toward more education- and health-oriented objectives.

IMF initiatives for poverty reduction

The weak effect of IMF economic policies on poverty reduction is consistent with growing criticism over IMF programmes. In the past, the IMF has placed priority on improving macroeconomic performance over poverty reduction. This reflected the view that achieving an overall improvement in macroeconomic performance would help lower poverty in developing countries. However, prolonged sluggish economic growth and the worldwide prevalence of poverty in developing countries have given rise to doubts about IMF adjustment programmes. In particular, it has been pointed out that ESAF-supported programmes have failed to achieve economic growth and external debt sustainability in developing countries. Moreover, the programmes have been criticized for prioritizing short-run stabilization (i.e. fiscal and monetary tightening) over poverty reduction, by squeezing education and health care spending (IMF 1999). These growing criticisms finally persuaded the IMF to undertake an internal staff review of the ESAF in 1997, followed by an external evaluation in 1998 (IMF 1997 and 1998). These reviews concluded that more should be done to ensure that macroeconomic, structural and social policies complement each other and that ESAF-supported programmes aim to accelerate growth and shift the composition of fiscal expenditure in favour of health care, education, and other basic social and economic infrastructure.

In response to these recommendations, the IMF replaced ESAF with the PRGF in 1999 to integrate the objectives of poverty reduction and growth more fully into its operations for low-income countries, and to base these operations on national poverty-reduction strategies prepared by the country (IMF 2000). While PRGF-supported programmes still focus on prudent macroeconomic policies and structural reforms, they now include poverty and social impact analysis (PSIA) of the policies adopted, which has enabled countries to weigh the trade-offs arising from the implementation of the policies and thus take countervailing measures to mitigate adverse impacts. These programmes also more flexibly accommodate rising budget deficits, and place more emphasis on an increase in budgetary resources for poverty-reduction purposes.

While it is still too early to make a comprehensive assessment, an internal staff review has concluded that the PRGF-adopted countries do now allocate more resources to education, health care and capital expenditure as measured in terms of gross domestic product (GDP) and total government spending (IMF 2002). However, the review concluded that PSIAs should be carried out more systematically, and that the quality and efficiency of government spending should be improved. In addition, Inchauste (2002), an IMF staff member, concluded that there is room for improving programme designs and implementation of countervailing measures used to offset potentially negative impacts. In 1999, the IMF, in close collaboration with the World Bank, introduced PRSP, a comprehensive country-based strategy for poverty reduction. It is formulated around a participatory process involving the governments of low-income countries, the IMF, the World Bank, donor countries, NGOs and other relevant stakeholders with the goal of meeting MDGs. The PRSP also provides the operational basis for IMF and World Bank concessional lending and for debt relief under the HIPCs Initiative, described earlier. It is updated every three years with annual progress reports, describing a country's macroeconomic, structural and social policies and programmes over a three year or longer horizon to promote broad-based growth and reduce poverty, as well as associated external financing needs and major sources of financing.

Shirai (2004b) reviewed the PRSPs of thirteen selected countries and found that they lacked proper sequence and adequate coordination between policies (e.g. between rural development and education policies). Also, too much emphasis was being placed on describing poverty analysis and governance issues, thus providing little in the way of detailed, step-by-step strategies. Moreover, the PRSPs were seen to pay little attention to trade policies, notwithstanding that the domestic markets in these countries are small, indicating that they need to develop export-oriented economic growth strategies. Thus, the content of PRSPs needs to be greatly improved to make them more realistic country-strategic papers. As the second largest financier of the IMF, Japan should play a more active role within the IMF in view to developing better PRSPs by stressing the role of the state in improving governance at country and regional levels and performing outward-oriented and private sector development strategies following its own experience. It should also support this approach by linking its bilateral ODA policy more closely with projects and programmes that are conducive to the strategies envisaged in the PRSPs.

HIPCs initiative

The HIPCs initiative was introduced by the IMF and the World Bank in September 1996 to provide a comprehensive, generous debt relief mechanism involving all creditors (bilateral, multilateral and commercial creditors) with new inflows of aid. It was followed by the 'Enhanced HIPCs' Initiative in October 1999, which eased the eligibility criteria by lowering the ratio of total external debt to annual exports from 200–250 per cent to 150 per cent and thus expanded membership.

To be considered as eligible for HIPCs Initiative assistance, a developing country must (1) face an unsustainable debt burden (i.e. external debt of more than 150 per cent of annual exports) and (2) have established a track record of reform and sound policies through the IMF- and World Bank-supported programmes for more than three years. Once an eligible country has prepared a PRSP, it is able to reach the 'decision point', when the needed debt relief is assessed or committed and interim debt relief is provided and front-loaded. As soon as successfully having implemented a set of predefined reforms envisaged in the PRSP for at least one year, the country is able to reach the 'compression point', when the full stock-of-debt reduction is performed. As of April 2004, the HIPCs debt reduction packages have been approved for twenty-seven countries (twenty-three of them in Africa), providing US$31 billion (net present value terms) in debt service relief over time. The HIPCs initiative differs from the previous Paris Club restructurings, since multinational creditors (i.e. the IMF, the World Bank and the regional development banks), which have historically held the preferred creditor status and thus have not rescheduled their loans, now have to provide debt relief. While full-cancellation of bilateral loans has been making progress, however, that of multilateral loans has been slow so far. The main factor behind this tardiness is that donor countries have not been able to agree on the sources of doing so. At the G7 meeting held in early February 2005, it was agreed on a case-by-case analysis of HIPCs, based on the willingness to provide as much as 100 per cent multilateral debt relief (about US$80 billion). The phrase 'as much as' was inserted in the common communiqué, reflecting Japan's opposition to full-cancellation of debt and Germany's concerns about the dangers of blanket debt relief for all debtors. Moreover, while it was agreed that debt cancellation on IMF claims could be financed by its gold sales (US$33 billion at present prices), the issue of how to implement this policy has been unresolved owing to concerns by some gold producing countries over the negative impact on world gold prices. Also, Japan's lack of willingness to actively participate in further debt relief initiatives has been weakening its presence not only at the G7 meeting but also within the IMF. If Japan continues to maintain its present stance, the growing criticism of Japan's policy makes it inevitable for the government to come up with good rationales for doing so. It is likely that Japan will be increasingly asked to come up with alternative development strategies for Sub-Saharan Africa if providing further debt relief remains difficult. Without taking any new initiatives along these lines, Japan is not only unable to contribute substantially to improving global governance, but also this stance weakens its leadership role despite its greater financial contributions and its status as the second largest economic power.

Conclusion and policy recommendations

In recent years, it has been widely acknowledged that development strategies should give greater attention to preparing appropriate conditions for the poor to benefit from growth, and further for growth rates to rise and be sustainable. These conditions include improving governance, easing constraints on domestic credit markets, reducing labour market distortions, building human capital and increasing access to trade markets.

This process is closely associated with the HIPCs initiative, since debt relief frees up financial resources from debt servicing for the task of poverty reduction and dealing with the earlier issues. In particular, the improvement of global governance is important for the effectiveness of ODA policy, since improving human capital, for example, depends on how efficiently available funds are spent and how well they are targeted on the poor; this requires well-designed and well-sequenced pro-poor economic development strategies with good governance and institutions. In this sense, the PRSPs should be more carefully designed with greater focus on producing mutually consistent, well-sequenced realistic policies and the issue of how to improve governance. So far, in preparing the PRSPs, stakeholders spend less time on prioritizing the allocation of available resources in line with poverty-reduction targets than on analysis of poverty, governance and institution. Also, little work has been done on the direct relationship between external debt and poverty and between debt relief and governance. Japan, as the second largest financier of the IMF, should make greater efforts to improve IMF policies targeting poverty reduction and produce more realistic and pro-growth poverty-reduction strategies.

As for Japan's bilateral ODA policy, while the government has implemented new measures to improve an integrated ODA policy, a more systematic approach is necessary to increase the effectiveness of its ODA. While Japan's ODA policy development is on the right track, it appears that it will take some time to develop more integrated field-level approaches equivalent to that taken in Vietnam, given the lack of human resources and institutional capacity in the field. To facilitate this process, the MOFA needs to allocate a bigger budget allowance to provide for training experts and JBIC/JICA/Embassy staff together with some kind of reallocation of the ODA budget towards achieving this end, while increasing collaboration with other donor countries and the IMF.

An ideal way to produce a mutually consistent ODA policy and improve global governance would be to establish one aid agency that managed all ODA budgets and formulated integrated and consistent ODA policies by setting priorities for various projects in accordance with the needs expressed by recipient countries, and in close collaboration with other donor countries and international organizations. While this would facilitate policy coherence with other relevant ministries, the realities of the current political and vertical bureaucratic structures make it unrealistic to envisage such reorganization in the near future. Another way could be to strengthen the role of the Council of Overseas Economic Cooperation-Related Ministers, at least to a level equivalent to the *Council on Economic and Fiscal Policy*, as a place to regularly discuss the issues of policy coherence and formulate ODA and external strategies among the ministers of relevant ministries, the prime minister, high-level government officials, private sector representatives, academics and so on. To do so, the Secretariat of the Council of Overseas Economic Cooperation-Related Ministers needs to develop an analytical and information-gathering capacity.

It should be noted, however, that the earlier proposals aim solely at improving policy coherence among ODA policies carried out by individual ministries and agencies. Japan faces greater challenges in terms of improving policy coherence between ODA policy and agricultural and fishery policy, on the one hand, and between ODA policy and trade and investment policies, on the other. Until Japan starts to address these issues comprehensively and radically, its contribution to improving global governance is likely to remain limited. It is crucial for Japan to recognize that paying attention to the improvement of global governance is as important as dealing with domestic problems, as this would ultimately produce benefits not only for the global community but also bring prosperity and security to Japanese citizen.

References

Conway, Patrick (1994) 'IMF lending programmes: participation and impact', *Journal of Development Economics* 45, 2: 365–91.

Easterly, William (2000) 'The effect of International Monetary Fund and World Bank Programmes on Poverty', World Bank, mimeo.

Edwards, Sebastian and Santaella, Julio A. (1993) 'Devaluation controversies in the developing countries: lessons from the Bretton Woods era', in Michael D. Bordo and

Barry Eichengreen B. (eds) *A Retrospective on the Bretton Woods System*, Chicago, IL: University of Chicago, pp. 405–55.

Garuda, Gopal (2000) 'The distributional effects of IMF programmes: a cross-country analysis', *World Development* 28, 6: 1031–51.

Inchauste, Gabriela (2002) 'Poverty and social impact analysis in PRGF-supported programmes,' IMF Policy Discussion Paper PDP/02/11, Washington DC: IMF.

International Monetary Fund (1997) 'The ESAF at ten years: economic adjustment and reform in low-income countries', Occasional Paper 156, Washington, DC: IMF.

—— (1998) 'External evaluation of the ESAF: report by a group of independent experts', Washington, DC: IMF.

—— (1999) 'The IMF's enhanced structural adjustment facility (ESAF): is it working?', Washington, DC: IMF.

—— (2000) 'Key features of IMF Poverty Reduction and Growth Facility (PRFG) supported programmes', prepared by the Policy Department and Review Department, 16 August 2000, Washington, DC: IMF.

—— (2002), 'Review of the Poverty Reduction and Growth Facility: issues and options', Washington, DC: IMF.

Japanese Bank for International Cooperation (2002) 'ODA: En Shakkan Katsudō Report 2002', Tokyo: JBIC.

Khan, Mohsin S. (1990) 'The macroeconomic effects of fund-supported adjustment programmes', *IMF Staff Papers* 37, 2: 1–23.

Killick, Tony (1995) *IMF Programmes in Developing Countries: Design and Impact*, London: Routledge.

Organization for Economic Cooperation and Development (2002) 'Policy coherence for development', 2001 Development Cooperation Report, pp. 33–52.

Pastor, Manuel (1987) 'The effects of IMF programmes in the Third World: debate and evidence from Latin America', *World Development* 15, 2: 249–62.

Reichmann, Thomas M. and Stillson, Richard T. (1978) 'Experience with programmes of balance of payments adjustment: stand-by arrangements in the highest tranches, 1963–72', *IMF Staff Papers* 25, 2: 292–310.

Shirai, Sayuri (2004a) 'The impact of IMF economic policies on poverty reduction in low-income countries', *Kokusai Keizai* 55: 119–61.

—— (2004b) Hinkonkoku no Minkan Sector Kaihatsu ni okeru Bōeki Tōshi ga Keizai Seichō ni oyobosu Kōka, Japan International Cooperation Agency: Tokyo, Visiting Scholar Report JR 03-58. Available on-line at: http://www.jica.go.jp/activities/report/kyakuin/200403_03.html, accessed on 4 April 2005.

Watanabe, Toshio and Miura, Yūji (2003) *ODA: Nihon ni nani ga dekiru ka*, Tokyo: Chūkō Shinsho.

9 Global governance and the World Trade Organization

Rorden Wilkinson

Introduction

For those seeking a detailed and considered account of the World Trade Organization's (WTO) role in global governance, the popular, practitioner and scholarly literature can be rather frustrating. A quick glance through the existing commentary uncovers a dearth of work in this area. In probing further, it becomes apparent that even in those few works purporting to be both centrally and peripherally concerned with the WTO's role in the governance of global life, almost none define or engage with the term global governance or explore the Organization's role therein. What becomes apparent is that existing commentary has been confined to accounts of the Organization's shortcomings variously perceived and the myriad ways in which it could be reformed, refashioned and, occasionally, disbanded. Indeed, it is only in the most fleeting of moments that the WTO's role in global governance is discussed; even then this is done without clarity or precision.

Three brief forays into the literature serve to illustrate this point. Popular accounts of both the WTO and its role in global governance tend to perceive the Organization as an instrument designed to prise open 'emerging' markets and bolster the economic advantages of leading industrial states and their economic agents to the detriment of, variously, developing states, the global environment, organized and unorganized labour, consumers and democratic freedoms (see, for instance, Monbiot 2003; Wallach and Woodall 2004). The problem here is not so much the way in which the WTO is conceptualized, but the way in which these accounts treat the Organization, its system of rules and the concept of global governance as interchangeable terms. Lori Wallach's work is indicative of this tradition. For her, the WTO is an organization which acts at the behest of corporate interests, and its body of rules constitutes a system of global governance (Wallach 2004: 1–5, 7–17; also Sukthankar and Nova 2004). Yet, Wallach's discussion of the constitutive elements of global governance extends only as far as an assertion that the WTO's legal framework comprises trade-related as well as trade-specific disciplines. Moreover, she does not fully explain how the WTO governs commercial activity or acts as an agent of transnational capital.

Practitioner accounts of the WTO and its role in global governance offer little more. These tend to treat global governance as a synonym for international organization; debate the various ways in which the Organization could be improved to deliver the fruits of trade liberalization; and explore the need for greater coherence among the principal global (largely, though not exclusively) economic institutions in response to the challenges thrown up by increasing interdependence and the extension of economic liberalization. While these accounts eschew the corporate conspiracy evident in Wallach's work, they take the role of the WTO, the economic system of which it is part, and the idea of global governance at face value and as inalienable public goods. In doing so, they offer little more than a limited understanding of global governance and the WTO's role therein. The writing of former WTO Director-General Mike Moore typifies this perspective. Moore treats global governance as a synonym for the coordination of interstate relations and emphatically rejects charges that equate the WTO with a proto-world government (WTO 1999; Moore 2003: 11, 235). He sees the WTO's role in global governance as facilitating the ability of its members to share in the 'benefits of globalisation' (for him a blend of technological innovation, global change and free trade) (Moore 2003: 11, 18–42); and the task ahead is to improve the Organization's existing procedures, the most pressing of which is to enhance the representation of member governments (Moore 2003: 217, 223–5). Similarly, Gary Sampson, in the introductory chapter to a book specifically entitled *The Role of the WTO in Global Governance*, rejects the need to define global governance preferring instead to refer the reader, via a footnote, to the 1995 definition of governance (note the lack of 'global' as a prefix) put forward by the Commission on Global Governance (Sampson 2001: 1, 17). Like Moore, Sampson treats multilateral coordination synonymously with global governance; argues that the international economic architecture is in need of reform (see also Sutherland *et al.* 2001); suggests that WTO obligations have locked developing countries into 'outward-orientated' domestic policy reforms (which he deems positive); reasons that the Organization's remit should be limited to trade-specific issues; celebrates the WTO's one-member-one veto decision-making processes as an exemplar of democratic international practice; and argues for the exclusion of public interest groups in the Organization's decision-making procedures (Sampson 2001: 3–17).

Academic accounts tend to take a slightly different tack, though they too are frustratingly limited. With very few exceptions (see, for instance, McMichael 2000; Jackson 2001; Rodrik 2001), scholars working on the WTO tend to concentrate on the Organization's rules-based, member-driven, consensus-orientated nature and confine debate to the perceived merits of modifying, refining and extending the Organization's legal framework. Herein the Organization's role is treated uncritically with the general assumption being that the outcome of WTO negotiations, dispute-settlement procedures and administrative activities are, to a large degree, equitable and welfare enhancing for all (see Krueger 1998) and where they are not, modifications at the margins will suffice. Within this literature few deal specifically with the role of the WTO in global governance, and those that do, concern themselves with thinking about what the Organization's function could be rather than establishing the precise nature of that role.

Andrew Guzman's work exploring the WTO's utility as a basis for the creation of a World Economic Organization (WEO) – an idea also developed by Marco Bronkers (Bronkers 2001) – is a case in point. His claim is that, rather than pruning back the sphere of activity regulated by the WTO's legal framework as a growing number of liberal economists (see Bhagwati 2001) and popular commentators (see Monbiot 2003; Wallach and Woodall 2004) have suggested, the Organization's remit can and ought to be developed in such a way that it deals with the regulation of international trade as well as a host of non-trade issues (including worker rights, environmental standards, human rights and competition policy among others) (Guzman 2002). What is striking about Guzman's account, and others like it, is the absence of (1) any engagement with, or definition of the concept of global governance (again, it is assumed to be a self-explanatory term) and (2) a discussion of the WTO's current role therein. At best, Guzman treats global governance as a synonym for the regulation of state activity and the WTO's role as a means of coordinating commercial behaviour. At worst, John McGinnis and Mark Movsesian charge him with equating global governance with world government (McGinnis and Movsesian 2004: 2).

What the literature presents, then, is a paradox. At a time when interest in global governance is on the rise, and when anxiety about the kind of global governance currently in place finds expression not only in mass public demonstrations during the meetings of world and regional organizations but also in the less visible debt relief, human rights and environmental campaigns, among others, the role of one of the institutions deemed to be at the core of contemporary global governance is insufficiently understood. The consequence of this paradox is significant, not least because it fails to accurately describe and understand the way in which global life generally, and international trade more specifically, is governed. This chapter attempts to overcome some of the problems inherent in the literature and advance a more detailed, contextualized and critical account of the WTO's role in global governance. In contrast to much of the popular, practitioner and academic literature, it argues that the WTO is more than just an instance of interstate cooperation that coordinates commercial policy among its member states, a blunt instrument designed to promote corporate interests, or the potential platform for a world economic organization. The chapter takes as a starting point an understanding of global governance that sees the system of regulation administered by the WTO as one among a burgeoning number of transnational, regional and global actors, processes and mechanisms that contribute to what James Rosenau calls the 'overarching pattern of governance' within and across the globe (Rosenau 1995: 18). Rather than treating these actors, processes and mechanisms as neutral or passive entities or crude agents of transnational capital as the literature variously does, the core assumption here is that they are in varying degrees both the product of and forces involved in shaping global configurations of power. In this way, they contribute to the production and shaping of particular modes of behaviour consistent with the overarching logic of that power configuration.

The argument presented here is that the WTO's role in global governance can be critically and more fully uncovered through an examination of (1) the unique historical circumstances in which the institution of international trade regulation was created and the specific purposes it was intended to serve; and (2) the manner in which that institution has evolved through time. The chapter argues that the General Agreement on Tariffs and Trade (GATT), as the precursor to the WTO and one-third of a post-war economic triumvirate (see Wilkinson 2002), was fashioned for the specific purpose of facilitating the exploitation of the economic opportunities presented to the US and, to a lesser extent, its Western allies in the post-Second World War era. To enable these opportunities to be fully realized, the GATT's architects put in place a system of international trade regulation that facilitated an increase in the volume and value of trade in manufactured, semi-manufactured and industrial goods but which, both from the outset and through time, excluded goods of political and economic significance (largely agriculture and textiles and clothing) from the institution's remit. The chapter argues that the regulation of trade in this fashion contributed to the consolidation of US hegemony in the post-war era and to the structural disadvantagement of its potential competitors, particularly those in the global South. The chapter further argues that, despite high profile contestations among member states over the proposed extension of the liberalization agenda most notably resulting in the collapse of the Seattle and Cancún ministerial meetings (1999 and 2003 respectively) and the breakdown of the Doha round (the so-called Doha Development Agenda – DDA) in July 2006, this asymmetry of opportunity was and continues to be extended under the auspices of the WTO. This, in turn, has contributed (and continues to contribute) to the preservation of the post-war and post-cold war global configuration of power. In this way, the WTO's role in global governance is better conceived of as one means by which a US-centred neoliberal world order has emerged and been perpetuated.

In presenting its argument, the chapter unfolds as follows. It begins by exploring the unique circumstances in which the modern system of international trade regulation was fashioned. It then examines the development of international trade regulation through time. In doing so, the chapter illustrates how the circumstances in which it was created, and the manner in which it has evolved, has imbued the system of international trade regulation with asymmetries of opportunity that advantage the economic interests of advanced industrial states over their developing counterparts. The chapter then explores how these asymmetries of opportunity have been carried over into the WTO as well as how the contribution of international trade regulation to the maintenance of the current global configuration of power has been consolidated. It also examines how, under a cloud of political contestation, this system is likely to be further extended. The final section summarizes the chapter's argument and offers its concluding remarks.

Global governance and the WTO

Seldom sufficiently acknowledged is the WTO's evolution from and intrinsic connection to a post-Second World War institutional apparatus designed to implement a quite specific international economic policy and cement an emergent world order. The Organization's general purpose, core principles, legal framework and operating procedures are all continuations, adaptations, variations or developments of aspects of a trade institution – what began as the International Trade Organization (ITO) but which, as we see later, became the GATT – fashioned for the purposes of reconstructing a war-ravaged world economy and resurrecting a system of international commerce around the broad notion (though, as it turned out, not a realization) of non-discrimination in international commerce (see Patterson 1966; Wilkinson 2000). Yet, the construction of a post-war economic institutional apparatus (comprising at its core the IMF, World Bank and, originally, the ITO) was not an 'allied' project as is often suggested by the literature. While the final shape of the post-war economic architecture was the result of a process of negotiation among the allies, it was US power, its special interests, its ideas and its material capabilities that provided the structural context in which this post-war institutional apparatus was forged (Knorr 1948; Crick 1951; Diebold 1952; Ikenberry 1992). The other allies were merely Greeks at the Roman court.

The active crafting of a post-war institutional architecture by the US was guided by a self-interest that emerged from its changed political and economic circumstances. Politically, the end of the war posed new strategic challenges. While the war had settled one ideological conflict, its conclusion garnered another. The emergence of the Soviet Union as an economic, military and, most importantly, an ideological competitor threatened American interests. But the creation of a series of economic institutions presented the US with an opportunity for economic aggrandizement and strategic consolidation. Although in principle open to Soviet membership, the antitheticism of the core principles of the post-war economic architecture to the USSR precluded its accession (see Feis 1948: 41; Knorr 1948: 35–6). The result was to put the US in the unique position of not only wielding influence in the institutions' creation but also their subsequent development.

Economically, the two world wars proved to be uniquely beneficial to the US. The First World War decimated the productive base of the dominant European powers and transformed the US into a major exporter of mass-produced goods. American industrial expansion was further enhanced by the demand for US products stimulated by Europe's post-First World War reconstruction process. The net result was to accelerate the rate at which the US overtook its principal rivals. The onset of the Second World War and its impact on the European industrial base further stimulated demand for US produce, and the post-war reconstruction process promised additional returns. It was thus in the US's interest to pursue a post-war international economic policy that would enable American industry to fully exploit these opportunities. As Klaus Knorr put it, '[m]ultilateral commerce is eminently suited to the American system of government and economic organization. Prewar trade practices were not, and their continuation would either harm American trade or compel further extensions of governmental controls over private business' (Knorr 1948: 19).

US plans for an integrated international economic policy designed to enable American goods to flow more freely did, however, have a significant caveat.

The depression of the 1930s hit the US agricultural sector particularly hard. The inefficiencies resulting therefrom ushered in the implementation of a system of production controls and price-support schemes, import quotas and export subsidies. Moreover, the relative political strength of the agricultural lobby made any attempt to pursue a blanket liberalization policy unlikely and at variance with US national interests (Gardner 1956: 3, 20–1). The result was that while the US was willing to liberalize trade in those sectors in which it could accrue economic gain (and wherein, it should be noted, the US faced little competition) it was not willing to do the same in areas of political and economic sensitivity.

US efforts to create a post-war economic architecture were thus guided by the desire to secure increasing market opportunities for its burgeoning industrial sector while at the same time protecting domestic agricultural production. But the process of establishing an institutional apparatus to satisfy those interests proved more difficult than was at first imagined. The negotiation of the ITO's legal framework – what eventually became the Havana Charter – was torturous. The core principles were subject to a plethora of exception clauses that threatened to nullify any economic benefit that might be accrued therefrom; consternation over the content of the Charter emerged not only among the sixty delegations but, more crucially, within the US; and the intensification of the cold war shifted focus away from the creation of a formal trade institution. The result was the still-birth of the ITO and the collapse of efforts to create a trade institution (see Diebold 1952).

The outcome of this crisis was not, however, the collapse of efforts to reconstruct world trade; on the contrary, a *de facto* trade institution emerged that proved to be more congruous with US interests than the ITO would have been. Frustrated by the sloth of the ITO negotiations, and under US leadership, twenty-three states engaged in a 'round' of negotiations during a special session of the ITO's Preparatory Committee in Geneva between April and October 1947. In an effort to give contractual force to the outcome of these discussions, the contracting parties negoti-ated the GATT. In contrast to the slow, fraught and stuttering ITO negotiations, the GATT appeared lithe and streamlined. The first round saw negotiations on some 45,000 items, the duties on all of which were bound against future increases until 1951 with a significant number being reduced (Gorter 1954: 11). By early autumn 1948, a date of April 1949 had been agreed for the start of a second round of trade negotiations; and a third round of negotiations was followed in September 1950.

This early progress, however, belied a more troublesome development. Reflecting its initial purpose, the GATT was deployed in a manner that sought merely to liberalize trade flows in goods. Even then it was deployed in such a way that it only liberalized trade in *some* goods. The exigencies of European reconstruction and the US's ability to act as a willing supplier led to a natural concentration on liberalization of industrial and related goods. This was com-pounded by an absence of developing country representation during the initial negotiations. The result was to imbue the *General Agreement* with a distinct institutional bias towards the economic needs of its industrial contracting parties. The GATT was, in short, an industrial nations' club.

Three developments are notable in this regard. First, slower-than-expected European reconstruction in the immediate post-war years reinforced an almost exclusive concentration on the liberalization of industrial, manufactured and some semi-manufactured goods. This concentration did not, however, desist once European recovery had firmly taken hold despite widespread recognition of the negative impact of such a course of action. The 1952 GATT report provided impetus for liberalization of trade in this targeted fashion. It observed that the pre-war decline in manufactured output and trade arising therefrom had continued since the cessation of hostilities (GATT 1953; ITO Report 1953: 587–8). But by 1954 the GATT report noted that this trend had been reversed and that a relative increase in trade within and among industrial countries had taken place. However, it also noted that a relative decline in trade between non-industrial and industrial countries had emerged (GATT 1955; ITO Report 1955: 597). As the 1954 Report noted, '[i]t is obvious that the problem arising from these divergent trends ... is one which is likely to loom large in the future course of economic development everywhere' (GATT 1955: 16). Yet, the narrow fashion in which liberalization was pursued continued. The result was to compound the growing gap between the economic opportunities and benefits available to the GATT's industrial contracting parties and their developing counterparts.

The second development that reinforced the GATT's emerging industrial character was the incremental exclusion of agriculture from the *General Agreement's* remit. As early as the fourth meeting of the contracting parties (23 February to 4 April 1950) the US was actively excluding its agricultural sectors from the GATT's purview (ITO Report 1950: 496). This was consolidated by a number of measures that steadily increased the degree to which US agricultural markets were protected and the extent to which American domestic overproduction and 'surplus dumping' disrupted normal patterns of trade. The US was of course not the only country seeking to protect its agricultural markets. Quantitative restrictions on agricultural imports were also imposed and maintained by most of the European powers, and many subsidized both the production and export of agricultural produce. Attempts were made to reverse this growth in agricultural protection both by warning against its deleterious effects (as in the 1954 GATT report among others) and through efforts during periodic trade negotiations (most notably during the Kennedy (1964–7) and Tokyo (1973–9) rounds). Nevertheless, remedial action was not forthcoming.

A third development came in the form of a withdrawal of textiles and clothing from the GATT's remit. In response to competition from overseas textile and clothing producers in the newly independent world, the industrial countries, most notably the US and the UK, sought to introduce measures to protect domestic producers. This involved, in the first instance, extracting a series of voluntary quotas limiting imports from Japan, Hong Kong, Pakistan and India. Thereafter, these restrictions were codified first during the Dillon Round (1960–1) with the negotiation of the Short-term Agreement on Cotton Textiles. This, in turn, morphed into the 1962 Long-term Agreement Regarding Trade in Cotton Textiles, and subsequently the 1974 Multi-fibre Agreement (MFA). Needless to say, efforts to reverse these developments were not forthcoming.

Taken together these three developments resulted in the evolution of a commercially restrictive trade institution: one that targeted the economic needs of its industrial contracting parties and presided over the steady increase in protectionism in those areas of commercial interest to their developing counterparts. Agricultural and textile and clothing producers in the industrial states were protected from the growing competitiveness of developing and newly independent producers by the manner in which the GATT was deployed. Producers in industrial states were, nevertheless, able to benefit from negotiated reductions in barriers to trade in manufactured, semi-manufactured, low and high technology goods. But for developing states, the combination of the constraints of their own lack of development, the absence of substantive opportunity arising from the GATT, and their diminishing share of world trade served to amplify the value of the institutional advantages afforded the industrial states. Clearly, the purpose of the post-war institutional architecture was not to construct an equitable and mutually beneficial trade regime, but rather to serve US economic interests. This remained, and the manner in which the GATT evolved throughout the years that followed consolidated rather than enervated its character.

Attempts were made to redress these imbalances; they were, however, few and far between, and lacking in substance. In 1965 the contracting parties negotiated a protocol amending the GATT (effective in 1966 and known as 'Part IV') in an effort to address some of the concerns of developing countries. It was, however, acutely inadequate. Part of the problem lay in its reliance upon the good will of industrial states to consider adopting measures to assist developing countries in their commercial activities, rather than compelling them to put into place remedial measures. Thereafter, few attempts were forthcoming, though discussions during subsequent trade rounds on the problems facing developing countries did grow in intensity. Indeed, it was not until the Uruguay Round (1986–94) that a concerted effort to broaden the GATT's commercial remit to include those areas of economic interest to developing countries took place. Yet, rather than attending to the asymmetry of opportunity arising from the manner in which the GATT was deployed, the Uruguay Round actually presided over a consolidation and extension of a system of international trade regulation that structured commercial behaviour in such a way as to contribute to the perpetuation of a US-centred, but generally industrially-focused, global configuration of power. This outcome was the result of a bargain struck between industrial and developing states at the conclusion of the Uruguay Round that, at one level, appeared broadly positive, but which, at another level, remained acutely asymmetrical.

The conclusion of the Uruguay Round saw the inclusion of agreements on agriculture, and textiles and clothing within a wider suite of trade agreements administered by the soon-to-be-created WTO and the adoption of a range of provisions throughout the Organization's legal framework to ease some of the pressure for reform generated by the new rules. It also resulted in the adoption of agreements on services (the General Agreement on Trade in Services – GATS), intellectual property (the Agreement on Trade Related Intellectual Property Rights – TRIPs) and investment measures (the Agreement on Trade Related Investment Measures – TRIMs). Yet, while the inclusion of agriculture and textiles and clothing rectified an existing imbalance in the way in which the GATT had previously been deployed and the sprinkling of development sensitive provisions represented a step forward from the GATT era, the introduction of new rules in services, intellectual property and investment measures simply generated additional asymmetry. Whereas under Uruguay rules developing states could finally hope to benefit from the liberalization of agricultural and textiles and clothing markets, their lack of capacity and resources ensured that this was not to be the case in the new areas. The potential fruits of Uruguay were, however, much larger for the industrial states. Not only were they existing beneficiaries of trade liberalization in areas covered by GATT rules, their economic make-up ensured they would be the principal beneficiaries of the market opportunities presented by the liberalization of services and investment measures, and the codification of trade-related intellectual property rights. What Uruguay clearly did, then, was to further divide up the arenas of economic activity in which member states could specialize and, in so doing, accentuated the problems facing developing countries seeking to diversify their export portfolios. Moreover, not only were the industrial states better suited to taking advantage of these new rules, their ability to utilize the market opportunities presented therein enabled them to develop a competitive advantage over future market entrants. The result was to carry across the transition in institutions from GATT to WTO the contribution of international trade regulation to the reinforcement and perpetuation of a global configuration of power that privileged the core to the detriment of the periphery.

Other aspects of the Uruguay Round agreements are notable in this regard. First, the Organization's legal agreements firmly tied the WTO to, and consolidated the character of, a cluster of economic institutions (principally, the IMF and World Bank) in a move to increase the coherence of global economic policymaking (see Wilkinson 2002). Central to this development was the removal of cross-conditionality: that is, the erosion of policy prescriptions and requirements by each of the institutions that are at variance with one another. Second, in deepening and widening the commercial arena covered by WTO rules, the Uruguay agreements brought into the newly consolidated institutional core a supporting cast of institutions comprising, among others, the World Intellectual Property Organization (WIPO), the International Telecommunications Union (ITU), the Office International des Epizooties (The World Organization for Animal Health) and the International Organization for Standardization (ISO). Third, in carrying forward GATT rules on customs unions and free trade areas WTO rules ensured that the commercial behaviour of a host of member and non-member states was reinforced at the regional level. Fourth, the increasing encroachment of WTO rules on national policymaking (so-called behind the border measures) served to lock member states more tightly into a liberal world order. Fifth, the collapse of the Soviet Union and the movement towards market liberalism in its successor states and their brethren in East and Central Europe, the Caribbean and East and Southeast Asia and their combined rush to accede to the WTO extended the geographic reach of WTO rules locking a growing proportion of the world's population into a liberal order. Finally, the commitments made during the Uruguay Round were reinforced by the negotiation of a much revamped and, more importantly, legally binding dispute-settlement process. In combination these developments served to further cement the post-cold war economic order.

Although the WTO enjoyed something of a honeymoon period in its first three years of operation, by the time the Organization's members met to convene the third ministerial meeting in Seattle in 1999 significant tensions had begun to emerge among its members – tensions which threatened to roll back the commitments made during the Uruguay Round. The tensions arose from the lack of substantive movement forward in liberalizing the complex and extensive agricultural support systems of the industrial states and the opening up of markets in this area. Significant problems also emerged over the implementation of Uruguay Round commitments. Not only was there much sloth in implementing agreed provisions, many developing countries were struggling with the legal burden with which they had been presented. These tensions were exacerbated by growing pressure from the US and EU to extend yet again the remit of WTO rules to include the four 'Singapore issues' (competition policy, government procurement, investment and trade facilitation – so called because the 1996 Singapore ministerial declaration established a mandate for working groups to be set-up exploring the relationship between trade and each of these issues) as well as to launch a new trade round. Moreover, talk of increasing the involvement of civil society organizations and exploring linkages between WTO rules and worker rights by industrial members was felt by many developing states to be diverting attention from the problems of development. Ill advisedly scheduled during the run-up to a US presidential election, and amid mass demonstrations, these tensions came to a head at Seattle. The result was the collapse of the meeting and the injection of temporary inertia into the process of trade liberalization (Wilkinson 2001; Wilkinson 2006a).

The most obvious response to the collapse of the Seattle meeting was the engagement in a public confidence-building exercise, and an accompanying effort to improve and increase the Organization's general profile. This comprised not only an increase in the usage of the WTO's website as the Organization's principal medium as a response to accusations of poor transparency, but also a public relations strategy to intensify the WTO's courtship of non-governmental organizations (NGOs). Behind the scenes, however, the Director-General, Secretariat, notable international public officials (including United Nations Secretary-General Kofi Annan) and key member states put considerable effort into rebuilding the image, of the WTO among developing countries. This confidence-building exercise was not merely intended to rehabilitate the Organization's image, it was also intended to generate support for the launch of a new trade round. The chosen strategy for nurturing a new consensus was to place 'development' at the heart of any new negotiations, thereby pacifying what were seen to be the most hostile elements of the membership, but nevertheless maintaining a commitment to extend WTO rules into new areas. What followed was a twenty-month period of intense confidence building and behind-the-scenes negotiation with a view to re-launching the millennium round (albeit renamed the Doha Development Agenda) at the Organization's fourth ministerial meeting in Doha in November 2001.

Despite the post-Seattle rehabilitation process, significant differences remained among the membership and the launch of a new round was by no means a forgone conclusion. Divisions still persisted over the precise balance between addressing long-standing concerns about the implementation of the Uruguay Round accords and redressing imbalances therein, and the pursuit of further industrial tariff cuts and extending WTO rules into new areas. Although the post-Seattle process had in large measure nurtured a broad consensus, and the absence of civil disruption in Doha contributed to a more conciliatory climate, the meeting's successful conclusion and with it the launch of the DDA owed as much to a change in the political climate and the hesitancy of members to be obstructive following the 11 September 2001 terrorist attacks on targets in the US as it did to the efforts of the round's supporters.

For all the talk of putting development issues at the heart of the new round the DDA did not promise to attenuate the asymmetry of opportunity-embedded WTO rules. Instead, the DDA firmly married a commitment to revisit the Uruguay Round agreements (coupled with promises to explore the relationship among trade, debt and finance, the plight of small economies, the transfer of technology, technical cooperation and capacity building, and a commitment to review and strengthen special and differential provisions) to the commencement of negotiations in investment, government procurement, trade facilitation and competition policy (and, potentially, e-commerce) should an 'explicit consensus' have been forthcoming at the WTO's Cancun meeting date. The intention was that a new bargain would result that would mollify developing world concerns with a commitment to revisit a previous agreement but which at the same time would drive the trade agenda forward in a manner that would provide additional economic opportunities for the Organization's industrial members. Had the DDA been quickly concluded, the WTO's contribution to cementing and perpetuating the current global configuration of power would have been enhanced.

The Cancun meeting did not, however, go to plan. The meeting collapsed after a spectacular bout of coalition and counter-coalition formation generated by tensions over the content of a draft framework for taking the DDA negotiations forward (see Bhagwati 2004; Narlikar and Wilkinson 2004; Wilkinson 2004). But the collapse of the meeting did not, however, derail the negotiations or alter to any significant degree the asymmetry of opportunity evident in the negotiating agenda, as many have argued and is popularly conceived. What emerged instead was an agreement to modify aspects of negotiations but which nevertheless kept the asymmetry of any bargain that would be struck firmly intact. In July 2004 members agreed to a framework for negotiating modalities in agriculture and non-agricultural market access (NAMA); movement forward in service negotiations; a commitment to continue the consultation process on the extension of the TRIPs agreement; the commencement of negotiations on only one of the Singapore issues (trade facilitation) and the ejection of the remaining three (government procurement, investment and competition policy); and an extension in the time frame of the overall negotiations with a view to their conclusion at the WTO's December 2005 Hong Kong ministerial meeting.

Progress in the wake of the July meeting was, however, slow. Deadlines were consistently missed and member states arrived at the Hong Kong ministerial meeting having scaled back expectations. As a result, the meeting was only partially successful. Although full modalities (the means by which commitments to liberalize are translated into actual cuts) for the negotiations were not forthcoming, members did agree to modest movements forward in NAMA, agriculture and services, as well as a package of measures designed to help the Least Developed Countries (see Wilkinson 2006b). Hong Kong also set out a timescale for the rest of the negotiations. April 2006 was identified as the point at which members should agree to full negotiating modalities and December 2006 the point at which the round should be concluded.

However, the modest progress made in Hong Kong proved unable to bridge remaining differences among member states and to keep the round on track. The April 2006 deadline for the agreement of negotiating modalities was missed; little progress was made in the negotiations generally; and the round came to an abrupt halt in July 2006. Inevitably, this has led to a resurgence of speculation that the DDA was increasingly moribund. The looming expiry of US Trade Promotion Authority (more commonly known as 'Fast Track') in mid-2007 added to this speculation and few beyond the WTO Secretariat publicly stated their belief that the round would be completed much before the end of the decade, if at all.

Yet, while the breakdown of the talks and the prospect of an expiry of fast track authority is significant, the general pattern of rounds to date (which since at least the Kennedy Round has been as tortuous as the current negotiations) suggests that the DDA will be concluded. The renewal of fast track authority has so far not been a problem when it has run out during a round (though, of course, this is not to claim that it will be unproblematic in this case); and nearly all of the previous 8 rounds have overrun with the DDA's immediate predecessors – the Tokyo and Uruguay Rounds – doing so by some 4 years. Moreover, despite the ejection of the contentious Singapore issues in the summer of 2004, it should be concluded the DDA remains set to disproportionately favour economic interests in the industrial states over their counterparts in the global South. The negotiation of a substantial Aid for Trade package beyond that agreed in Hong Kong, or some other sweetener aimed at developing countries, will do little to correct this imbalance. As a result, the asymmetry of opportunity arising from the way in which liberalization is pursued under WTO auspices will be at least perpetuated by the conclusion of the DDA if not further amplified.

Conclusion

What is clear from the preceding analysis is that the WTO's role in global governance is more complex than the literature suggests. Rather than serving as a means of coordinating interstate relations in the pursuit of ever freer trade, a crude agent of transnational capital or a platform for a world economic organization, international trade regulation has a more organic purpose. It is both the product of, and has been an agent involved in, the creation and perpetuation of a particular global configuration of power that has as a central component the economic interests of core industrial states but which evolved from the economic (and political) opportunities presented to the US in the post-war era. Understanding the WTO in this fashion has important consequences for the way in which Japan's role in global governance is conceived – the wider concern of this book. If, as much of the populist literature suggests, the WTO were merely an agent of transnational capital, then Japan's role would simply be to secure the best deal for its corporate sector. If, as the practitioner literature encourages, the WTO's role in global governance was merely accepted as providing a forum for governing the conduct of trade and a means of liberalizing trade flows through periodic negotiation, understanding Japan's role therein would be confined to an examination of the performance of its delegations in securing favourable deals during trade rounds, an account of the losses and gains during dispute-settlement activities, or the extent to which key Japanese officials are able to exercise agency within the institution during day-to-day operations as well as over its future evolution. And if speculation were allowed on the possibilities of utilizing the WTO's legal framework as a basis for a larger World Economic Organization, as Guzman and Bronkers suggest (Bronkers 2001; Guzman 2002), exploring Japan's role therein would be limited to an assessment of its potential to shape aspects of that institution's evolving architecture. However, if, as this chapter argues, international trade regulation is conceived as the product of, as well as a key element in the emergence and consolidation of a US-centred but nevertheless industrially focused global configuration of power, then Japan's role therein needs to be understood quite differently. In this first instance, the WTO, and the GATT before it, need to be understood as a mechanism through which Japan's commercial behaviour has been shaped and constrained in such a fashion that it is conducive to the overall logic of the global configuration of power.[1] Moreover, it requires an understanding that Japanese post-war reconstruction and economic development thereafter has been structured in part through its involvement in this system of regulation. And it suggests that the GATT and WTO have structured Japan's commercial behaviour such that it is consistent with the maintenance and perpetuation of the current global order. It is in this context that the next chapter unfolds.

Note

1 It is clear that Japanese economic development was subject to limitations imposed through its involvement in international trade regulation from the outset. The withholding of most-favoured-nation status by 40 per cent of the GATT's contracting parties at Japan's point of accession in 1955 inhibited Japan from enjoying fully the benefits accorded by the *General Agreement*, particularly given that the fourteen states involved (Australia, Austria, Belgium, Brazil, Cuba, France, Haiti, India, Luxembourg, the Netherlands, New Zealand, the Federation of Rhodesia and Nyasaland, South Africa and the UK) represented markets of chief economic importance (Patterson 1966:

274–300); and the exclusion of textiles and clothing from the GATT's remit had an impact on Japan's economic development.

References

Bhagwati, Jagdish (2001) 'After Seattle: free trade and the WTO', *International Affairs* 77, 1: 15–29.
—— (2004) 'Don't cry for Cancún', *Foreign Affairs* 83, 1: 52–64.
Bronkers, Marco C. E. J. (2001) 'More power to the WTO?', *Journal of International Economic Law* 4, 1: 41–65.
Crick, W. F. (1951) 'International financial relations: some concealed problems', *International Affairs* 27, 3: 297–305.
Diebold Jr, William (1952) 'The end of the ITO', *Essays in International Finance* No. 16, International Finance Section, Department of Economics, Princeton University.
Feis, Herbert (1948) 'The Geneva proposal for an International Trade Charter', *International Organization* 2, 1: 39–52.
Gardner, Richard N. (1956) *Sterling–Dollar Diplomacy: Anglo-American Collaboration in the Reconstruction of Multilateral Trade*, Oxford: Clarendon Press.
GATT (1953) *International Trade, 1952*, Geneva: GATT.
—— (1955) *International Trade, 1954*, Geneva: GATT.
Gorter, Wytze (1954) 'GATT after six years: an appraisal', *International Organization* 8, 1: 1–18.
Guzman, Andrew T. (2002) 'Global governance and the WTO', *UC Berkeley Public Law and Legal Theory Research Paper series* No. 89.
Ikenberry, G. John (1992) 'A world economy restored: expert consensus and the Anglo-American postwar settlement', *International Organization* 46, 1: 289–321.
ITO Report (1950) *International Organization* 4, 3: 494–7.
—— (1953) *International Organization* 7, 4: 584–8.
—— (1955) *International Organization* 9, 2: 278–9.
Jackson, John H. (2001) 'The WTO "constitution" and proposed reforms: seven "mantras" revisited', *Journal of International Economic Law* 4, 1: 67–78.
Knorr, Klaus (1948) 'The Bretton Woods institutions in transition', *International Organization* 2, 1: 19–38.
Krueger, Anne O. (ed.) (1998) *The WTO as an International Organization*, Chicago, IL: Chicago University Press.
McGinnis, John O. and Movsesian, Mark L. (2004) 'Against global governance in the WTO', *Northwestern Public Law Research Paper* No. 04-03.
McMichael, Philip (2000) 'Sleepless since Seattle: what is the WTO about?', *Review of International Political Economy* 7, 3: 466–74.
Monbiot, George (2003) *The Age of Consent: A Manifesto for a New World Order*, London: Flamingo.
Moore, Mike (2003) *A World without Walls: Freedom, Development, Free Trade and Global Governance*, Cambridge: Cambridge University Press.
Narlikar, Amrita and Wilkinson, Rorden (2004) 'Collapse at the WTO: a Cancun post-mortem', *Third World Quarterly* 25, 3: 447–60.
Patterson, Gardner (1966) *Discrimination in International Trade: The Policy Issues 1945–1965*, Princeton, NJ: Princeton University Press.
Rodrik, Dani (2001) 'The global governance of trade: as if development really mattered', *Background Paper*, New York: United Nations Development Programme.

Rosenau, James N. (1995) 'Governance in the twenty-first century', *Global Governance* 1, 1: 13–43.

Sampson, Gary P. (2001) 'Overview', in Gary P. Sampson (ed.) *The Role of the World Trade Organization in Global Governance*, Tokyo: United Nations University Press, pp. 1–18.

Sukthankar, Ashwini and Nova, Scott (2004) 'Human and labor rights under the WTO', in Lori Wallach and Patrick Woodall (eds) *Whose Trade Organization? A Comprehensive Guide to the WTO*, New York: The New Press, pp. 219–38.

Sutherland, Peter, Sewell, John and Weiner, David (2001) 'Challenges facing the WTO and policies to address global governance', in Gary P. Sampson (ed.) *The Role of the World Trade Organization in Global Governance*, Tokyo: United Nations University Press, pp. 81–111.

Wallach, Lori (2004) 'Introduction: it's not about trade', in Lori Wallach and Patrick Woodall (eds) *Whose Trade Organization? A Comprehensive Guide to the WTO*, New York: The New Press, pp. 1–17.

Wallach, Lori and Woodall, Patrick (2004) *Whose Trade Organization? A Comprehensive Guide to the WTO*, New York: The New Press.

Wilkinson, Rorden (2000) *Multilateralism and the World Trade Organisation: The Architecture and Extension of International Trade Regulation*, London: Routledge, 2000.

—— (2001) 'The WTO in Crisis: exploring the dimensions of institutional inertia', *Journal of World Trade* 35, 3: 397–419.

—— (2002) 'Peripheralising labour: the ILO, WTO and the completion of the Bretton Woods project', in Jeffery Harrod and Robert O'Brien (eds) *Globalized Unions? Theory and Strategies of Organized Labour in the Global Political Economy*, London: Routledge, pp. 204–20.

—— (2004) 'Crisis in Cancun', *Global Governance* 10, 2: 149–55.

—— (2006a) *The WTO: Crisis and the Governance of Global Trade*, London: Routledge.

—— (2006b) 'The WTO in Hong Kong: what it really means for the Doha development agenda', *New Political Economy* 11, 2: 291–303.

WTO (1999) 'The WTO is not a world government and no one has any intention of making it one Moore tells NGOs', *WTO Press Release* No. 155 (29 November).

10 Global governance, Japan and the World Trade Organization

Araki Ichirō

Introduction

The Japanese people often regard themselves as a nation dependent on foreign trade (*bōeki rikkoku*). Scarce in natural resources and arable land, but rich in a well-educated labour force and technology, Japan has had to utilize this comparative advantage and export its industrial products to overseas market in order to maintain the current level of economic growth and prosperity, so the thinking goes.[1] Although such an idea smacks of mercantilism, rather than the full embrace of liberal trade policies based on the notion of comparative advantage, this awareness of dependence on trade is so deeply ingrained in the Japanese psyche that popular support for the liberal world trade order is strong in Japan. Unlike other developed countries, civil society movements critical of the General Agreement on Tariffs and Trade (GATT) and the World Trade Organization (WTO) are not very active, and labour complaints about the 'giant sucking sound' from developing country competitors are seldom heard.[2]

Against this background, the government often claims that Japan has been the prime beneficiary of the liberal international economic order embodied in the GATT/WTO and that it is committed to the maintenance and strengthening of the multilateral trading system (see, for example, MOFA 2002).[3] However, historically, Japan has not been a major political force in the global quest for freer trade. In other words, Japan has not played the role of protagonist in global governance of the world trading system. According to one observer, 'Japan conformed to the practices and procedures embodied in the international system when it was compelled to do so, and deviated when it had the opportunity' (Noland 2000). However, there are signs of positive change. At least in the area of dispute settlement, Japan is using the WTO's dispute settlement mechanism actively both as a complainant and a respondent. This is a marked departure from the bilateralism of the past. While Japan's presence in other areas of negotiations is not conspicuous, there are other areas where Japan is becoming more active in the global governance of trade at the WTO.

This chapter first traces the historical development of Japan's trade policy, which will be followed by a brief sketch of Japan's so-called aggressive legalism in dealing with trade disputes. Then, other aspects of Japan's contribution to the

WTO's governance will be examined, with some concluding observations regarding Japan's performance in the current negotiating round called the Doha Development Agenda (DDA).

Historical development of Japan's trade policy

The modern origin of Japan's trade policy can be traced back to the mid-nineteenth century, when Japan signed the Treaty of Friendship and Commerce with the US in 1858, following the forced 'opening' of the country by Commodore Matthew Perry several years earlier. Similar treaties were concluded with the Netherlands, Russia, Britain and France as well. The shock of these 'unequal treaties' was one of the major reasons for the Meiji Restoration in 1868. For half a century thereafter, Japan embarked upon a remarkable process of modernization, adapting Western social and technological innovations to its own ends (Morishima 1982: 70–7). Under the 'unequal treaties', the Japanese government's ability to impose import tariffs was severely limited. The maximum rate of duty allowed was 5 per cent *ad valorem*. This low level of tariff binding (to use modern terminology) may have actually fostered Japan's development by forcing the country to specialize along the lines of its comparative advantage. The limitation on tariffs also encouraged the use of other policy tools such as low-interest loans and government procurement preferences for 'strategic' industries, establishing a precedent of what came to be known at a later stage as industrial policy (Noland 2000: n2).

As the volume of Japanese exports grew, they were met by discriminatory trade restrictions imposed by Japan's trade partners fearing 'import surges'.[4] On its part, Japan began raising its tariffs significantly during the slump which followed the conclusion of the First World War and the Great Kantō Earthquake of 1923. This was possible because full tariff autonomy had been restored in 1911 as the 'unequal' treaties had been amended in Japan's favour. The policy adopted was a set of selective tariffs with heavy duties on luxury imports, on a wide range of manufactures, especially finished and consumer goods and, at the insistence of the farm lobby, controls and duties on foodstuffs (Macpherson 1987: 39). During the Great Depression, Japan's friction with its trading partners became more intense. Japan started to export its products aggressively, partially helped by the 1931 devaluation of yen. However, Japanese products were subjected to severe trade restrictions in such markets as India, Canada and Australia, where Japan had to conclude a series of voluntary export restraint (VER) agreements due to pressure from the UK (Ikeda 1996). The US market was no exception. It is well-known that the US reversed its course on protectionism (which started with the Smoot-Hawley Act of 1930) after the enactment of the Reciprocal Trade Agreements Act (RTAA) of 1934. However, unlike some European and many Latin American countries, Japan was not a beneficiary of the RTAA. US Secretary of State Cordell Hull, the visionary free trader and the chief architect of the RTAA, demanded that Japan place VERs on a range of exports from pencils to cans of tuna and textile products. Japan had little choice but to comply. Yoshida Shigeru, Japan's post-war Prime Minister (who was then Japanese Ambassador to Britain), and other Japanese diplomats of the time were reluctant to accept the US demands. A query to Hull was made as to whether he was not contradicting himself by, on the one hand, seeking trade liberalization through the RTAA, while on the other asking Japan to impose VERs. Hull made no direct reply, but instead criticized Japan's 'heavy, competitive exports' as posing 'serious outside interference' to the US (Butler 1998: 159–62). Thereafter, the world plunged into the downward spiral of shrinking trade, with beggar-thy-neighbour policies practiced everywhere. As the international economic system literally disintegrated, Japan desperately launched the Pacific War in late 1941 with the aim of creating an autarkic Greater East Asian Co-prosperity Sphere. The war ended in ruin, defeat and occupation by US military forces.

After the occupation ended in 1952, Japan applied to join the GATT. Japan's GATT application was initially opposed by a number of countries, but the US strongly supported the application, and Japan was granted provisional membership in 1953 and full membership in 1955. However, Japan's accession came with a price. While the Japanese negotiators tried their best to avoid the invocation of GATT Article XXV ('opting out' clause)[5] by its trading partners during the accession negotiations, in the end, a number of countries (fourteen in total) including the UK, France and Italy invoked the provision against Japan for fear of the re-emergence of the pre-war aggressive export behaviour (Cortell and Davis 2005: 11; also see Note 1 in Chapter 9 in this book). Thus, although it was a contracting party to the GATT, it still faced discrimination by many trading partners. Thus, the most pressing negotiating agenda for Japan was securing disinvocation of GATT Article XXXV. To achieve this goal, Japan had to offer additional GATT 'concessions' and voluntary export restraints of certain products such as automobiles and motorcycles (Pekkanen 2001: 709).

While Japan participated in successive rounds of multilateral trade negotiations held under the auspices of the GATT, it did not play a central role in the agenda setting or in the conduct of multilateral negotiations. True, Japan was part of the so-called Bridge Club (consisting of the US, European Economic Community, Japan and the UK – not unlike the 'Quad' group in the Uruguay Round thirty years later) in the Kennedy Round (1964–7), but its role as the driving force of the negotiations was limited (Endo 2005: 172). In the Tokyo Round (1973–9), Japan tried to play a more active role, starting with the hosting of the inaugural GATT ministerial meeting in Tokyo. However, toward the end of the negotiations, Japan's role was rather limited. It had to accept the outcome of the negotiations on safeguards and government procurement despite its initial positions on these issues (Endo 2005: 173).

In contrast to its passive attitude in the multilateral trade negotiations, during the 1960s, 1970s and 1980s, Japan favoured a bilateral approach in settling trade disputes with its trading partners, including the use of VERs, despite the criticism in the GATT about the non-transparent and discriminatory nature of those bilateral arrangements. A press release on the result of the first trade policy review report under the WTO is suggestive of the old image of Japan in the GATT. It reads in part as follows (WTO 1995):

> Japan's elimination of a number of voluntary export restraints with the United States and the European Community (EC), its increased use of international standards and its growing trade and investment in Asia should help Japan shift from 'its past emphasis on bilateralism in trade relations' to one which confirms its greater integration in the multilateral trading system. A new report by the WTO Secretariat on Japan's trade policies and practices also notes that firm progress in domestic deregulation, combined with the implementation of the Uruguay Round Agreements, should ensure improved access to Japan's market.... The report states that Japan has reduced the number and scope of restrictions on exports. Also, a number of 'voluntary' export restraints on machine tools, automobiles and steel to the United States and on machine tools to the EC were eliminated in 1993 or early 1994. Other long-standing restraints on pottery, chinaware and cutlery exports to the United States were to expire at the end of 1994 while the monitoring arrangement on car exports to the European Union is to be eliminated in 1999. Furthermore, since 1992, 17 of 28 export cartels have been abolished while many others have been reduced in scope. Export cartels related to VERs, to the protection of quality or intellectual property or to import monopolies in partner countries are to be reviewed with the objective of their elimination by 1999.

The very fact that these new policy orientations by Japan are hailed by the newly created WTO Secretariat strongly suggests that, up to this point, Japan had been seen as a country that favoured bilateral approaches over multilateral solutions in dealing with trade frictions and disputes, heavily dependent upon the use of VERs, a tradition dating back to the 1930s, as we have seen earlier. So, while being keenly aware of the sense of *bōeki rikkoku*, the Japanese trade negotiators did not place full confidence in the multilateral trading system as a guarantor of non-discrimination and the liberal trade order. Rather, they were pursuing a more pragmatic solution to the trade frictions they were facing.

However, as the press release mentioned earlier indicates, at around the time of the establishment of the WTO in 1995, this attitude of Japan had already changed. In fact, Japan's full embrace of the multilateral trading system preceded the establishment of the WTO. While it is difficult to pinpoint the exact watershed, observers agree that the change of attitude occurred sometime in the late 1980s. Saadia Pekkanen suggests that the critical incident was Japan's victory in the Spruce, Pine and Fir (SPF) Dimension Lumber panel of 1988, where Canada had filed a complaint against Japan's tariff classification of certain wood products (Pekkanen 2001: 709). Iwasawa Yūji and this author argue that the victory in the Parts and Components panel of 1989, where Japan had complained against the EC's anti-dumping measures, had a more profound impact on the thinking of Japan's trade policymakers (Iwasawa 2000: 477; Araki 2004: 153).

This new attitude of Japan toward the multilateral trading system coincided with the intensification of negotiations in the Uruguay Round. Japan's most important negotiating objective in the round was to strengthen the rules-based multilateral trading system. The need for this was keenly felt because of the unilateral trade policy pursued by the US under the 1988 Omnibus Trade and Competitiveness Act, with its Super 301 provisions. The restraint of US unilateralism was one major common goal pursued by all participants of the Uruguay Round (except the US, of course), but Japan played a significant role in the negotiations of the WTO Dispute Settlement Understanding, which has successfully constrained recourse to unilateral trade actions by the US (Endo 2005: 174). Another area of priority for Japan in the Uruguay Round was the anti-dumping rules. Japan sought to tighten disciplines on the use of anti-dumping measures through the negotiations. Although it partially succeeded in achieving this objective, on balance, the negotiated results were not satisfactory to Japan because the Anti-dumping Agreement left room for arbitrary calculation of dumping margins (Endo 2005: 175). Nevertheless, the energy and efforts devoted by the Japanese trade negotiators on the reform of anti-dumping rules were unprecedented. This was particularly noteworthy because toward the end of the round, anti-dumping became one of the most contentious issues owing to strong political pressure from the US. As a veteran US trade negotiator vividly explains:

> The draft [anti-dumping code of December 1993] attempted to place restraints on the unilateral application of anti-dumping duties, which was subject to protectionist abuse, particularly in the United States. US negotiators had presented eleven key changes to the draft code that would effectively maintain existing US freedom of action in this area. Jeffrey Garten, Department of Commerce Undersecretary and senior US negotiator, arrived in Geneva insisting that all eleven changes be accepted. He was credibly supported by an avalanche of congressional and private-sector leaders with anti-dumping as their top priority. Senate Finance Committee Chairman Patrick Moynihan and senior committee member Jay Rockefeller held a series of meetings with an ultimatum warning about committee support for the Uruguay Round agreement. Senate Minority Leader Robert Dole and House Majority Leader Richard Gephardt led a group of eleven corporate leaders, representing steel, semiconductor, automobile and other sectors who delivered a similar message. Various other members of the Congress, including Chairman Dan Rostenkowski of the House Ways and Means Committee and countless industry representatives, added to the anti-dumping blitz. The peremptory manner of the US lobbying irritated others, but they also accepted political reality and were prepared to make limited further concessions.
>
> (Preeg 1995: 169–70)

Japan was among the 'others' who caved in to the US pressure but was widely recognized as a key player in that group along with countries like Hong Kong, South Korea and Singapore. In the end, it reluctantly agreed to the revision of the draft code accommodating some of the US demands (but not all of the eleven points), but Japan's aggressive negotiating stance on anti-dumping issues during the Uruguay Round is well remembered among the Geneva trade diplomats. A recent text book on WTO law written by a former WTO Secretariat staff member highlights this (and nothing else) as Japan's significant contribution to rulemaking in the Uruguay Round (Van den Bossche 2005: 515). This treatment appears to be representative of the trade community's view today.

Japan also played an important role in the Uruguay Round as a member of the Quad group, consisting of the US, EC, Canada and Japan. The group met at both ministerial and official levels. The group's role was prominent during the preparatory period leading up to the Punta Del Este Declaration of September 1986. Their activities intensified again after the collapse of the Brussels ministerial meeting in December 1990 (Preeg 1995: 111). In particular, the Quad ministerial meeting in Tokyo in July 1993 was significant in breaking the deadlock in the market access negotiations:

> As leaders arrived in Tokyo, however, agreement had still not been achieved, and considerable pessimism prevailed. US press briefings attempted to 'downplay expectations'. In particular, the United States did not intend to offer further cuts in high tariffs on textiles and apparel of interest to European exporters, and the EC continued to resist deep cuts in semiconductors and other electronics products. The Sutherland warning that an unclear outcome would be a negative one was nevertheless understood. Trade representatives continued a six-hour negotiating session until 3 a.m. on July 7 and finally came up with a package agreement that extended significantly market-access commitments. The critical move came from Japan, who surprisingly agreed to zero duties for 'coloured' distilled spirits, including scotch and bourbon. This triggered response by Canada to eliminate duties on beer and furniture, and by the EC, who had been pressing Canada on furniture, to eliminate duties on farm equipment. The overall agreement involved duty elimination in eight sectors, harmonization of tariffs at low levels for the chemicals sector, minimum average cuts of one-third for four other sectors, and tariff cuts of up to 50 per cent for high tariffs in the ceramics, glass, textiles, and apparel sectors.

> (Preeg 1995: 160)

However, the Japanese agenda during the Uruguay Round was not wholly positive. As is well-known, Japan took an extremely defensive posture in the agricultural negotiations. The Japanese delegation was preoccupied with the idea of food security. They would point to the fact that Japan's food self-sufficiency ratio was only 40 per cent (an unusually low figure for a developed country, it was claimed) and that Japan was the world's largest net importer of agricultural products already. In particular, since rice was the staple food of the Japanese and the only main food product with respect to which Japan remained self-sufficient, the opening of the rice market became the most contested issue for Japan in the agricultural negotiations of the Uruguay Round. Enormous attention was focused on the rice issue by politicians and media coverage was intensive 'as if it had been the only subject of the Uruguay Round' (Endo 2005: 174). At the final moment of the negotiations, Japan decided to accept the minimum access commitments in rice, abandoning the previously announced policy of 'not a single grain of rice shall be imported'. Again, an interesting observation was made by the US negotiator:

> The political repercussions to the final outcome for rice were very different in Tokyo and Seoul. Japanese Prime Minister Morihiro Hosokawa announced on December 7 [1993] that his country would open its market to rice imports because it benefited from the world's free-trade system and thus needed to bear a proportional burden for successful conclusion of the Uruguay Round. The news of this pending commitment had been rumoured for a couple of weeks, and the Japanese public reacted relatively mildly despite the political sensitivity accorded to rice farmers. In contrast, on December 9, South Korean President Kim Young-Sam announced the undertaking to liberalize rice imports and apologized publicly for breaking his presidential campaign pledge not to do so. He posed the question: 'Are we to live as an orphan by rejecting the GATT system, or lead our country toward globalization and internationalization by accepting the GATT framework?' The Korean people, taken more by surprise, were not prepared for such a display of international leadership, and rioting broke out in the streets, much of it anti-American.
>
> (Preeg 1995: 168–9)

The Japanese reaction described here is consistent with the key thesis of this chapter: the mantra of *bōeki rikkoku*. It will return to the contrast with the Korean reaction when the activities of civil society groups in Japan are discussed later.

In any event, there is no denying that since its establishment in 1995 Japan has been an active member of the WTO. Some observers even claim that Japan has embraced the strategy of aggressive legalism – active use of the legal rules in the treaties and agreements overseen by the WTO to stake out positions, to advance and rebut claims, and to embroil all concerned in an intricate legal game in dealing with trade issues (Pekkanen 2001: 732). The next section attempts to sketch briefly the state-of-play of Japan vis-à-vis the WTO's dispute settlement mechanism to see how aggressive Japan really is. The analysis begins with dispute settlement because the dispute settlement mechanism is supposedly the most successful component of the WTO system, functioning as the 'central element in providing security and predictability to the multilateral trading system' according to Article 3.2 of the WTO's Dispute Settlement Understanding (DSU).

Japan and the WTO dispute settlement mechanism

Among the members of the WTO, Japan has had fairly frequent recourse to the dispute settlement mechanism under the DSU. In terms of the number of cases involved, Japan ranks seventh as a complaining party and fifth as a responding party among the total membership of the WTO (currently 149) although only about one-third of the membership has ever had recourse to the DSU. While not reaching the level of the two giants in the WTO system, the US and the EC, Japan's involvement in the dispute settlement system appears to be moderately active, commensurate with its economic and political power in the world (Araki 2006: 783). However, trade officials at the Ministry of Economy, Trade and Industry (METI) do not seem to be content with the status quo. Based on essentially the same statistical analysis as earlier, a recent trade policy report by METI laments the existence of a 'significant gap' between the performance of the US and the EC on the one hand and that of Japan on the other hand 'regarding the active use of international economic rules toward securing compliance with WTO obligations' (METI 2004b: 347–58). The report emphasizes the importance of improving Japan's initiatives toward securing its trading partners' compliance with the existing international trade rules, based on the recognition that such initiatives are inadequate at present (interestingly, this part of the report is not translated into its official English edition). This is not a statement that is expected from officials of a country that has embraced the strategy of aggressive legalism in the WTO.

Still, the drastic change in Japan's trade policy position in the late 1980s, namely, the departure from the traditional non-legalistic and bilateral tendencies and the embrace of aggressive legalism, was a dramatic event both for the Japanese and Japan's trading partners. In hindsight, the US–Japan automobile dispute in the summer of 1995 (WT/DS6) was probably the climax, symbolizing the new directions of Japan's trade policy, where Japan simply refused to accept the US demand for further market opening and instead filed a WTO complaint regarding the US unilateral threat (Pekkanen 2001: 722–4). Thereafter, with the prolonged recession in Japan, and the rise of economic powers in other parts of the world, bilateral disputes between Japan and the US started to fade away from the major trade agenda. Thus, while METI has consistently emphasized the importance of rules-based trade policy, Japan's activity in the WTO dispute settlement system remained relatively moderate. However, Japan is far more aggressive than in the past in utilizing the rules of the GATT/WTO to advance its national interests. It will never revert to the infamous practice of bilateralism and VERs.

It is true that Japan came close to demanding openly VERs from China in the mushroom–onion–tatami dispute of 2001 (Nakagawa 2003), but the circumstances were special since the dispute was with a country that was not yet a member of the WTO. If a similar dispute arises between Japan and China in the future, both countries as responsible WTO members will have to act more legalistically. In a more recent dispute with South Korea involving import quotas on seaweed, while the two parties announced a bilateral settlement in early 2006, this only occurred after South Korea successfully argued before the panel as regards the illegality of Japan's import quota (WT/DS323). Immediately before the scheduled issuance of the interim report, Japan offered a bilateral deal, which was acceptable to South Korea. The terms of the settlement were a simple and straightforward expansion of the quota amount. While the WTO-consistency of this settlement is dubious, no trace of VERs is in evidence here.

As these events show, aggressive legalism is a double-edged sword (Pekkanen 2001: 734). If Japan asks its trading partners to play by the rules, then it must accept the principle of fair play. Thus, Japan will continue to uphold the integrity of the WTO dispute settlement mechanism and will contribute to the strengthening of the governance of the world trading system. Furthermore, Japan is trying to contribute to the improvement of the dispute settlement mechanism by promoting discussion on this subject. As mandated by the ministerial decision taken at Marrakesh in 1994, the DSU is subject to review by the WTO membership. As part of this exercise, in the lead-up to the failed Seattle ministerial meeting in December 1999, there was an attempt to amend the DSU to deal with the question of 'sequencing' between the determination of compliance with the panel/Appellate Body recommendations (Article 21.5) and the authorization of retaliation (Article 22.6). If the doomed Seattle ministerial meeting had not ended in failure, an agreement on this amendment might have been possible. In 2000 and 2001, informal efforts to reach agreement on the amendment continued under Japanese leadership. These efforts resulted in October 2001 in a revised proposal for amending the DSU tabled by a group of fourteen WTO members chaired by Japan (but not including the US and the EC). However, the WTO membership again failed to reach agreement on this proposal, but Japan's role in this process was significant (Van den Bossche 2005: 290). Today, the Japanese government still continues to engage actively in the negotiations of the DSU in the context of the DDA.

Other aspects of Japan's contribution to the WTO

In the previous two sections, this chapter reviewed how Japan has utilized the WTO system to advance its national interests. While active participation in the dispute settlement process has the effect of enhancing the global governance of world trade, the motive to participate for each WTO member is that of enlightened self-interest. This section will examine how Japan is contributing positively to the governance of the WTO, first financially and then with respect to human resources.

In the WTO, contributions to the Secretariat budget are determined according to each member's share of international trade, based on trade in goods, services and intellectual property rights for the last three years for which data is available. For the 2005 budget, Japan contributed 10.2 million Swiss francs, which represented 6.125 per cent of the total budget of 167.4 million Swiss francs. The largest contributor was the US (15.798 per cent), followed by Germany (8.872 per cent). Japan ranked third in terms of contribution, followed by the UK (5.704 per cent) France (5.152 per cent), Italy (4.087 per cent), Canada (3.921 per cent), China (3.599 per cent), the Netherlands (3.388 per cent), Hong Kong (3.122 per cent), and so on (WTO 2005a: 112–4). Due to the automatic nature of the contributions assessment, it would be difficult for Japan (or any other country) to deviate largely from the prescribed share, except for the possibility of establishing special trust funds for specific purposes (e.g. capacity building). To the extent that the multilateral trading system is a global public good characterized by non-excludability and non-rivalry, this method of contributions assessment would seem appropriate.

Regarding the contributions to trust funds, it was recently announced that the Japanese government donated 50 million yen in 2006 to finance technical assistance and training activities organized by the WTO. According to the WTO Secretariat, after this latest donation, Japan's total contribution to the DDA's Global Trust Fund reached 5.3 million Swiss francs. As of July 2006, Japan was the fifth largest voluntary contributor to the WTO (WTO 2006).

In contrast to financial contributions, human resources are the one area Japan could contribute more to the governance of the system. Since all the staff members of the Secretariat are selected on the basis of merit, so long as there are individuals who are capable and willing to work at the Secretariat, Japan should be able to contribute positively to the daily operation of the multilateral trading system. However, the reality is disappointing. As of 2005, there were only 4 Japanese officers (1 female and 3 males) in the organization with 630 regular staff members (WTO 2005a). All of them were middle-level professionals (posted respectively at the trade policy review division, legal affairs division, rules division and development division). Three of them were previously trade officials with METI. None of the senior management team of the Secretariat (Director-General, Deputy Director-Generals and divisional directors) was Japanese. While accepting the fact that Europeans have a natural advantage in their linguistic abilities (as of 2005, there were 165 French, 82 British, 47 Spanish and 35 Swiss nationals working at the Secretariat, WTO 2005a) and that East Asians are generally under-represented in the WTO Secretariat, there is much more room for improvement. Particularly, in view of the fact that there are already seven Chinese staff members (5 females and 2 males), it must be said that Japan's contribution through human resources to the Secretariat is less than what is expected of a country that has been the member of the system since 1955 (China has been a member since 2001).

Of course, the Secretariat alone does not represent the human aspects of the multilateral trading system. The WTO is often regarded as a member-driven organization. So, inputs by member governments play an important role. It is difficult to measure the level of Japan's contribution in this regard, but Japan's influence in agenda setting in the WTO seems to be diminishing. As noted, Japan was a member of the Quad group during the Uruguay Round. However, this way of handling the negotiations came to be seen with increasing levels of scepticism. Particularly, after the failure of the Seattle ministerial meeting, the Quad ceased to function (Sutherland, Sewell and Weiner 2001: 88). This was because many developing countries felt that they had been short-changed in the Uruguay Round, and they were determined not to let that happen again. This came as something of a surprise to the Quad, but it was inevitable (*The Economist* 2000). As the negotiations of the DDA started to pick up, a new coalition emerged among the influential members of the WTO. However, since the main focus of the negotiations was agriculture, the membership of this new group was different from the Quad – initially the US, EC, Australia, Brazil and India. Then, as the agenda moved to other issues such as services, the group of the US, EC, Brazil and India came to be known as the 'new Quad'. Japan appears to play a very limited role in the agenda setting of the current round.

This is not to say that few Japanese officials are involved in the WTO negotiations. On the contrary, many are working hard day and night, but their work results in little output (apart from the dispute settlement activities noted earlier). Regarding Japanese participation in the Cancun ministerial meeting of September 2003, one observer noted:

> Japan had a huge delegation of officials – 235 – by far the biggest, as far as I could tell. This compares with 53 officials from China, 59 from India and 132 from the United States. As most of the time nothing was happening in Cancun – since the agenda could not be moved forward – taxpayers in Japan may want to ask themselves what all of these 235 officials were doing. The breakdown of the official delegation is quite revealing. It included 44 officials from the Foreign Ministry, 11 from the Finance Ministry, 39 from the Ministry of Economy, Trade and Industry, and 72 from the Ministry of Agriculture, Forestry and Fisheries! The delegation included a handful of officials from other ministries such as posts and telecommunications, health and welfare, land and transport, etc. From the Japanese Permanent Mission to the WTO in Geneva there were 10 people..., while from the Japanese Embassy in Mexico there were 45 people. ... Almost as massively present as the Japanese official delegation were Japanese non-government organizations, or NGOs, representing farming and fishery interests. So far as I could judge, that was it!
>
> (Lehmann 2003)

This apparent inefficiency of the Japanese trade bureaucracy is (as is implied by Jean-Francois Lehmann) largely due to inter-ministerial rivalries. What is more, while it is often said that NGOs are playing more and more important roles in the negotiations of the WTO (Wilkinson 2002), the 'NGOs' mentioned in Lehmann's report are not civil society representatives. As mentioned at the outset of this chapter, civil society groups based in Japan are not very active on trade issues. It is as if the leaders of those groups have accepted the premise of *bōeki rikkoku*. Accordingly, the Japanese government does not feel compelled to undertake elaborate consultations with civil society groups before they form their trade policy, unlike the situation in Canada (Hocking 2004). The government occasionally holds town meetings and public symposia on the WTO inviting a wide range of NGOs and social activists, but it is not clear how the results of those dialogues are reflected in actual policy formation.

Conclusion

It is not clear to what extent current Japanese behaviour in WTO negotiations is dependent upon its historical path. A critic of this historical approach would highlight the difference between Japan and South Korea. In view of the active civil society engagements in the trade agenda in South Korea, which shares a similar path of economic growth with Japan, it may be wrong to conclude that the way in which Japan is engaged in trade negotiations is historically determined. However, as argued in the previous chapter, if the WTO is be understood as a mechanism through which Japan's commercial behaviour has been shaped and constrained in such a fashion that it is conducive to the overall logic of the global configuration of power, then the historical analysis becomes relevant. Throughout its history since the 'opening' of the country in the nineteenth century, Japan's engagement with the world trade system has been rather passive. When it opened its trade with the outside world, its rules of conduct were determined by the prevalent rules of the day. When it tried the beggar-thy-neighbour policies of the 1930s, it had to accept voluntary export restraints as a consequence. When it rejoined the world trading system in 1955, it had to accept, again, the prevalent rules of the game, and to deal with the imminent trade frictions with the US and Europe, it had to turn to bilateral, pragmatic, not-so-legal approaches. This began to change in the late 1980s, and at least on the dispute settlement front, Japan has now embraced what is called aggressive legalism, although, as we have seen, how aggressive Japan is remains an open question. Its contribution to the governance of the multilateral trading system is still limited in terms of budgetary contributions and intellectual inputs through human resources.

Will this change? One might become pessimistic when observing Japan's slippage from the old Quad leadership to the current obscurity and the apparent apathy of civil society groups on trade agenda. However, there are encouraging signs both at the government level and the civil society level.

First, the Japanese trade negotiators may finally be becoming proactive in agenda setting in the DDA, not for defensive purposes like a series of protectionist agricultural proposals and not simply following up its Uruguay Round agenda in anti-dumping and dispute settlement. On the eve of the Hong Kong Ministerial in December 2005, Prime Minister Koizumi Junichirō stated:

> Japan has decided to announce a comprehensive 'development initiative' on the occasion of the Hong Kong Ministerial Conference with a view to promoting the empowerment of developing countries through the DDA and help them reap the benefits of the multilateral trading system. In this initiative, Japan expresses its commitment to provide duty-free and quota-free market access for essentially all products originating from all least-developed countries. This initiative also includes a package of extensive development assistance, which is composed of four methods of support, 'Knowledge and Technology', 'Financial Assistance', 'People' and 'System' to be employed at three different phases of trading by developing countries; 'Produce' 'Sell' and 'Buy'. As part of the Japanese ODA Initiative announced at the G8 Gleneagles Summit, 10 billion US dollars in financial assistance in trade, production, and distribution infrastructure will be provided over the next three years. There will be an exchange of a total of ten thousand trainees and experts in these fields during the same period.
>
> (Koizumi 2005)

It is easy to dismiss this as an empty gesture to buy off the opposition from developing countries (*The Economist* 2005). However, at least this initiative came from innovative thinkers within the Japanese bureaucracy. The proposal has been well received by civil society groups and developing countries alike. Of course, if Japan fails to deliver on its promises, it will be subjected to severe criticism, but this may be a first step in the right direction. Japan may finally be moving from (mildly) aggressive legalism to (mildly) aggressive agenda setting. If that is the case, Japanese trade officials will have to resist the current fad for regional/bilateral trade initiatives. Furthermore, while the prospect of the DDA is still very murky, as negotiators get serious about market access negotiations, Japan appears to be making a slow comeback to the centre stage. The old Quad is dead, but apart from the new Quad, the group of six comprising of the US, EC, Australia, Brazil, India and Japan are meeting to discuss the modalities of market access negotiations. It is too early to tell at this stage whether this group will play the role of the old Quad (as they met in Tokyo in July 1993) in the market access negotiations, but it is a welcome sign that Japan is back to the negotiating table despite the collapse of the group's Geneva ministerial meeting in July 2006.

Second, the record of NGO/civil society participation in trade issues is clearly improving. Unlike at Cancun, genuine civil society groups were accredited from Japan at the Hong Kong ministerial meeting. A total of forty-four organizations were accredited as based in Japan, out of 811 such organizations. While this figure is comparable to other developed countries (US: 180; Canada: 76; Belgium: 50; France: 49; Germany: 26 and Australia: 26), as it was the case with Cancun, most of them were industry representatives such as agricultural cooperatives and industry associations, but judging from the names, at least ten of them represented civil society interests, such as those who were concerned about sustainable development.[6] While some of them were Japan branches of a global civil society organization (such as Oxfam Japan), most appeared to be indigenous organizations based in Japan (WTO 2005b). Interestingly, as for South Korea, out of the eleven accredited organizations, only one ('Korean NGOs Coalition for the WTO Round concerning Agriculture, Environment and Livelihood') appeared to be the representative of civil society. All others were representatives of agricultural, fishery or industrial interests. Yet, as was widely reported, South Korean protesters were the most militant in the streets of Hong Kong during the ministerial meeting (Harney 2005). Certainly, accredited farmers and fishermen also joined the demonstrations, but there are likely to have been diehard South Korean protesters who dared not register in the NGO list. Japanese farmers and civil society groups were relatively well-behaved (none was detained by the Hong Kong police), but the South Korean protesters made headlines, reminiscent of the stark contrast in the two countries' reactions to the rice market opening in 1993 as noted earlier. Where does this difference come from? It is an intriguing question, but it is the subject of another study.

Notes

1 For example, Nakagawa Shōichi, who took office as trade minister on 22 September 2004 stated at a press conference as follows: 'Japan is a country dependent on trade (*bōeki rikkoku*) both in imports and exports' (METI 2004a). Even the executive director of the Central Union of Agricultural Cooperatives (ZENCHU) concedes that Japan is a country dependent on trade (Yamada 2006).

2 The Japanese Trade Union Confederation (RENGO) does not list import competition or job exports as its major challenges in its latest action agenda, although it does seem wary of the spread of regional trade agreements in Asia (RENGO 2006). Compare this with the view of the American Federation of Labor and Congress of Industrial Organizations on the global economy (AFL-CIO 2006).

3 It is interesting to note, though, that the notion of *bōeki rikkoku* is not statistically supported. The ratio of trade to total output in Japan has been constantly declining since 1913, unlike the US or Europe. The ratio of merchandise trade to GDP was about 30 per cent in 1913, while it is less than 20 per cent today (*The Economist* 1997).

4 For an overview of the history of Western criticisms of Japanese exports since the nineteenth century, see Saxonhouse 1996.

5 The operative part of Article XXXV reads as follows: 'This Agreement... shall not apply as between any contracting party and any other contracting party if (a) the two contracting parties have not entered into tariff negotiations with each other, and (b) either of the contracting parties, at the time either becomes a contracting party, does not consent to such application.'

6 Action for Solidarity, Equality, Environment and Development Japan; Advocacy and Monitoring Network on Sustainable Development; Consumers Union of Japan; Forum for Peace Rights and Environment; Global Guardian Trust; Japan Centre for a Sustainable Environment and Society; Oxfam Japan; Pacific Asia Resource Centre; People's Plan Study Group; and the 21st Century Public Policy Institute.

References

AFL-CIO (2006) *Global Economy*. Available online at http://www.aflcio.org/issues/jobseconomy/globaleconomy, accessed on 27 July 2006.

Araki, Ichiro (2004) 'Beyond aggressive legalism: Japan and the GATT/WTO dispute', in Matsushita, Mitsuo and Ahn, Dukgeun (eds) *WTO and East Asia: New Perspectives*, London: Cameron, May, pp. 149–76.

——— (2006) 'The evolution of Japan's aggressive legalism', *The World Economy* 30: 783–803.

Butler, Michael A. (1998) *Cautious Visionary: Cordell Hull and Trade Reform, 1933–1937*, Kent: Kent State University Press.

Cortell, Andrew P. and Davis, James W. (2005) 'When norms clash: international norms, domestic practices, and Japan's internalisation of the GATT/WTO', *Review of International Studies* 31, 1: 3–25.

The Economist (1997) 'One world?', 16 October.

——— (2000) 'A different, new world order', 9 November.

——— (2005) 'The Doha trade round is still alive, but hardly healthy', 20 December.

Endo, Minoru (2005) 'Japan', in Patrick F. J. Macrory, Arthur E. Appleton and Michael G. Plummer (eds) *The World Trade Organization: Legal, Economic and Political Analysis, Vol. III*, New York: Springer, pp. 171–81.

Harney, Alexandra (2005) 'Journal from the WTO protests in Hong Kong', *The Financial Times*, 14 December.

Hocking, Brian (2004) 'Changing the terms of trade policymaking: from the "club" to the "multistakeholder" model', *World Trade Review* 3, 1: 3–26.

Ikeda, Michiko (1996) *Protectionism and Discrimination against Japan's Foreign Trade, 1926–1937*, Tokyo: International Library Foundation.

Iwasawa, Yuji (2000) 'WTO dispute settlement and Japan', in Marco Bronckers and Reinhard Quick (eds) *New Directions in International Economic Law*, The Hague: Kluwer Law International, pp. 473–90.

Koizumi, Junichiro (2005) 'Creating an upward spiral of trade and development (Japan's development initiative for the WTO Hong Kong ministerial conference)', 9 December. Available online at: http://www.infojapan.org/policy/economy/wto/min05/initiative.html, accessed on 27 July 2006.

Lehmann, Jean-Francois (2003) 'Japan at Cancun – so little done with so many', *The Japan Times*, 25 September.

Macpherson, W. J. (1987) *The Economic Development of Japan 1868–1941*, Basingstoke: Macmillan.

METI (2004a) 'Shokakugigo no daijin kaisha kaiken no gaiyō', 22 September. Available online at: http://www.meti.go.jp/speeches/data_ed/ed030922-2j.html, accessed on 27 July 2006.

—— (2004b) *Fukōsei Bōeki Hōkokusho*, Tokyo: Keizai Sangyō Chōsakai.

MOFA (2002) 'Japan's basic strategy for the WTO new round negotiations', 4 October. Available online at: http://www.mofa.go.jp/policy/economy/wto/round0210.html, accessed on 27 July 2006.

Morishima, Michio (1982) *Why Has Japan 'Succeeded'?: Western Technology and the Japanese Ethos*, Cambridge: Cambridge University Press.

Nakagawa, Junji (2003) 'Lessons from the Japan–China "Welsh Onion" War', *Journal of World Trade* 36, 6: 1019–36.

Noland, Marcus (2000) 'Japan and the international economic institutions'. Available online at: http://www.iie.com/publications/papers/paper.cfm?ResearchID=380, accessed on 27 July 2006.

Pekkanen, Saadia (2001) 'Aggressive legalism: the rules of the WTO and Japan's emerging trade strategy', *The World Economy*, 24: 707–37.

Preeg, Ernst (1995) *Traders in a Brave New World: The Uruguay Round and the Future of the International Trading System*, Chicago, IL: The University of Chicago Press.

RENGO (Japanese Trade Union Confederation) (2006) *Action Policy 2006–2007*. Available online at: http://www.jtuc-rengo.org/about/actionpolicy/a_policy.html, accessed on 27 July 2006.

Saxonhouse, Gary (1996) 'A short summary of the long history of unfair trade allegations against Japan', in Jagdish N. Bhagwati and Robert E. Hudec (eds) *Fair Trade and Harmonization*, Vol. 1, Cambridge: MIT Press, pp. 471–513.

Sutherland, Peter, Sewell, John and Weiner, David (2001) 'Challenges facing the WTO and policies to address global governance', in Gary P. Sampson (ed.) *The Role of the World Trade Organization in Global Governance*, Tokyo: The United Nations University, pp. 81–111.

Van den Bossche, Peter (2005) *The Law and Policy of the World Trade Organization*, Cambridge: Cambridge University Press.

Wilkinson, Rorden (2002) 'The contours of courtship: the WTO and civil society', in Rorden Wilkinson and Steve Hughes (eds) *Global Governance: Critical Perspectives*, London: Routledge, pp. 193–211.

WTO (1995) 'Trade Policy Review of Japan', PRESS/TPRB/5, 29 March.

—— (2005a) *Annual Report 2005*. Available online at: http://www.wto.org/English/res_e/booksp_e/anrep_e/anrep05_e.pdf, accessed on 27 July 2006.

—— (2005b) *NGOs Attendance to the WTO Sixth Ministerial Conference*. Available online at: http://www.wto.org/english/thewto_e/minist_e/min05_e/list_ngo_hk05_e.pdf, accessed on 27 July 2006.

—— (2006) 'Japan donates Yen 50 million to finance technical assistance', PRESS/445, 12 July.

Yamada, Toshio (2006) 'Ikkoku niseido o dō kokufuku suru ka', *FAE Forum*, 20 March. Available online at: http://www.fae-forum.org/2kaisou/forum_meseiji/forum_meseiji.html, accessed on 27 July 2006.

11 Global governance and the United Nations

Shaun Breslin

Introduction

The UN's record as a key institution in the promotion of global governance is somewhat mixed. From one perspective, the UN has probably done more than any other international organization. The UN has published and endorsed some of the most explicit calls for the establishment of new norms of global governance based on liberal conceptions of the best way of constructing a peaceful and prosperous global order. But this vision of the UN as a definer and promoter of global governance sits in stark contrast to visions of the UN as an ineffective and/or unwilling actor in war-ravaged societies. When millions die in civil wars in Africa, and major powers ignore the UN if it gets in the way of their agendas, where is the evidence that the UN does anything at all in practical terms to establish new forms of global governance?

These conflicting perspectives largely reflect the distinction between the UN as a generator of ideas relating to global governance, and the way in which the member states of the UN have differential power to establish and impose norms through UN-sanctioned actions. It also reflects a distinction between different norms. Many member states fiercely defend the principle of sovereignty, and the practice of non-interference in the domestic affairs of sovereign states which they believe should be the bottom line in all UN activity. But this traditional norm is increasingly being challenged by emerging norms of global governance promoted by UN commissions, agencies, programmes and some member states. At the heart of this challenge to sovereignty is the argument in *Our Global Neighborhood* that 'although states are sovereign, they are not free individually to do whatever they want' (UN 1995). For proponents of this view, the UN not only has a right to intervene to prevent bloodshed, but in fact has a duty to protect all of the citizens of the world from tyranny. Although this contradiction has been at the heart of much of the thinking and debates within the UN since its inception, in the post-cold war era there has been a key shift in understandings of not only the relationship between sovereignty and intervention, but also what is the best (perhaps only) path to development, and appropriate forms of national (as well as global) governance.

This chapter focuses on the impact of this dual contradiction – between agents of power in the UN and between different conceptions of the limits of state sovereignty – on the UN's position as an instrument of global governance. It suggests that the national interest of member states – particularly those with veto power in the UN Security Council (UNSC) – normally prevent emerging norms of intervention and new conceptions of the limits of state sovereignty from being transferred into UN-sanctioned policy. Put another way, the existing power structure of the UN gives key sovereign states the power to define what privileges are provided to sovereign states in the international system. Furthermore, this structure of power and the actions (and inactions) of UNSC members threatens to undermine the legitimacy of the UN as a whole, and as a guarantor of security for all the peoples of the world in particular. Nevertheless, this chapter also starts from the assumption that ideas are important. The ideational changes promoted by proponents of global governance in the UN system reinforce the dominance of the hegemonic liberal ideas and ideals. And crucially, in terms of developmental ideas at least, the UN has been transformed from a site of ideational conflict and competition to one where the neoliberal orthodoxy is increasingly unchallenged and unchecked.

Power and interest in the UN system

In writing about the UN system, the question of 'who' is involved can become rather complex. Although the UN is a state-based system over 1,500 NGOs are formally affiliated to the UN represented by the Conference on Non-governmental Organizations in Consultative Status with the Economic and Social Council. Otto (1996: 109) argues that:

> There is no doubt that the extent of NGO involvement in UN activities has vastly exceeded the expectations of those who drafted the Charter and dramatically outstripped the scope of these legal provisions [in the original charter].

In terms of establishing norms, organizations such as Amnesty International do have influence in setting agendas and as 'standard bearers' – not least because of the specialist technical knowledge that they possess (Martens 2004). Nevertheless, the primacy of states in the UN means that such influence is only on an 'ad hoc basis' and proposals to formalize NGO participation in decision-making processes remain yet to be realized (Barnett 1997: 538–9).[1]

Even putting NGOs to one side, who or what leads in the UN in relation to establishing norms and modes of global governance remains a complicated issue. International organizations are much more than just a community of member states and an arena in which competing national interests are played out. As a wide number of observers from often competing perspectives have observed, international organizations can become 'independent actors with their own agendas, but they may embody multiple agendas and contain multiple sources of agency' (Barnett and Finnemore 1999: 705). As will be argued later, there is an internal conflict (or at least potential for conflict) between the promoters of ideas, and the authorizers of action within the UN system. There is also conflict between different parts of the UN structure – some of it linked to this division between promoters and actors, and some of it based on the differential power of member states in the UN's organizational structure. Most clearly, those who hold veto power in the UNSC have the ultimate power to decide when to act and on what grounds – and some even have the power to ignore the UN altogether if it gets in the way of the promotion of national interests.

There are six peak organizations at the apex of the UN organizational structure: the Secretariat, the General Assembly, the UNSC, the Economic and Social Council, the Trusteeship Council and the International Court of Justice (ICJ). This chapter focuses on the first four with the focus in the Secretariat on the Office of the General Secretary, and in the Economic and Social Council and its programmes and funds such as the UN Conference on Trade and Development (UNCTAD), and its functional agencies such as the Human Rights Commission (UNHCR).

The Trusteeship Council (which controlled territories liberated from enemy states at the end of the Second World War to oversee their transition to liberation) is ignored as it was suspended in 1994 with full independence of the last trusteeship territory, Palau, and Kofi Annan has proposed that it now be removed from the UN Charter. The International Court of Justice in the Hague is responsible for providing advisory opinions on legal questions that are referred to it by member states, selected UN organs and agencies. The Court does play an important role in not only providing opinion on whether international laws have been breached, but also in defining what international law actually is.

The ICJ partly defines[2] international law in terms of the binding treaties and conventions that states have formally accepted by signing and ratifying. Even here there is room for ambiguity as the court has the right to interpret what the treaty really meant, and also to decide whether 'at the time of the interpretation', the original meaning of the treaty needs to be reconsidered. The ICJ also has the power to put aside international law, and 'settle a dispute without strict regard for the existing rules of international law, but in the light of the justice and merits of the case' if both parties agree – something that has yet to happen since 1946.

More important for this chapter, the ICJ also defines international law as 'international custom, as evidence of a general practice accepted as law' and/or 'the general principles of law recognized by civilized nations'. In these cases, 'a State which relies on an alleged international custom practised by States must, generally speaking, demonstrate to the ICJ's satisfaction that this custom has become so established as to be legally binding on the other party.' Perhaps not surprisingly, the ICJ has been reluctant to impose its judgement on when custom becomes legally binding, and has tended to respect state sovereignty in such cases. But there have been cases when, notwithstanding the lack of legality defined by treaties, the ICJ has attempted to define what customary law actually is. In 1986, the US was condemned for training, arming, equipping and financing Contra activity in Nicaragua and for attacks on Nicaraguan territory. It found that the US had 'acted, against the Republic of Nicaragua, in breach of its obligation under customary international law not to use force against another State'.[3] Even here, the decision was only taken on a majority (12 to 3) with one Judge arguing that the court did not have jurisdiction to decide on matters 'in lieu of the relevant multilateral treaties'. And as the decisions of the ICJ are not binding in any way, findings based on customary law in one case do not force the defendant (nor anybody else) to modify current or future behaviour accordingly.

The Security Council, the General Assembly and changing conceptions of sovereignty

In many of the cases brought before it, the key question is whether one state has abrogated the sovereignty of another. And for many of the UN's member states, the norm of state sovereignty is, or at least should be, at the heart of the UN system. To be sure, individual states might find it impossible to have total autonomy over domestic affairs.[4] But for states that take a hard line on sovereignty like China, neither the UN nor individual states have any right whatsoever to interfere in the domestic politics of sovereign states no matter what is happening within that state's borders.[5] A less absolutist position considers the infringement of sovereignty as tolerable only when international security is threatened by events in a sovereign state under the principle of 'collective security' (Cuellar 2004). For adherents of both positions, state sovereignty overrides any proposal to intervene when the domestic affairs of a sovereign state are abhorrent and/or uncivilized.

It is oft stated that the conception of sovereignty was embedded in international relations with the Treaty of Westphalia in 1648. In reality, Westphalia was more important as a symbol of change. Quite apart from the fact that many of the modern nation states of Europe were still some time away from being created, the creation of mechanisms to manage diplomatic relations between sovereign states did not really occur until the end of the Napoleonic Wars with the 1815 Congress of Vienna.[6]

Furthermore, sovereignty was a principle that was largely reserved for European states. The Berlin conference of 1884–5 that divided the conference into different spheres of influence saw participation only from the major Western powers,[7] and the resulting cartography of Africa owed everything to the interests of the great powers, and nothing to concerns for sovereignty. China was forced to accept Western norms of statehood and sovereignty in the nineteenth century through the superior military force of first the British and later other Western powers. And notwithstanding the importance of Woodrow Wilson's fourteen points for establishing the principle of self-determination, negotiations at the Paris Peace Conference still managed to ignore Chinese sovereignty in delivering former German territories in China to the Japanese. It is slightly ironic that China, which was in many ways forced to accept externally defined universal norms of statehood and sovereignty, is now one of the strongest defenders of those norms in opposition to attempts to establish new externally defined universal norms.

Perhaps not surprisingly, attempts to establish a new forum for ensuring international peace have typically followed war. This is partly out of the need to redraw boundaries at the end of war – for example, the redrawing of Europe at Westphalia at the end of the Eighty and Thirty years wars. But it also is partly a 'never again' phenomenon – for example, the congresses of the nineteenth century to stop the likes of the Napoleonic war ever happening again. And there is also an extent to which new treaties and organizations are inspired by a desire to ensure that the failings of previous treaties and organizations are not repeated. The League of Nations sought to overcome the failing of the 1899 International Peace Conference[8] to prevent the First World War, and the UN sought to overcome the League of Nation's failure to prevent the Second World War.

It is not just history that is written by the winners – so too are treaties and the constitutions of international institutions. In 1814, all representatives of all European countries were called to attend a congress in Vienna to negotiate a new peace for Europe in the wake of the defeat of the Napoleonic armies. According to de Ligne '*Le congres ne marche pas, il danse*' – hence, 'the dancing congress' – the majority of participants found ways to fill their time while representatives of the five major powers[9] engaged in the real business of negotiation. Although negotiations at the congress of Vienna were strictly limited to the major powers, they explicitly and deliberately drew the defeated French back into diplomatic activity. By contrast, while the negotiations to establish the League of Nations were primarily dominated by the victorious powers[10] they explicitly and deliberately not only kept the defeated powers out of the negotiations, but also constructed a punitive peace.

So the creation of the UN has many historical precedents. Indeed, the term 'United Nations' was first used by Roosevelt as shorthand for the Allied Powers in the 'Declaration of United Nations' in January 1942. As with the League of Nations, the UN was negotiated by the victors with the Charter of the 'United Nations' signed by victorious powers of the Second World War on 26 June 1945 in San Francisco.

Despite much talk about fundamental principles and state sovereignty, even in its inception, the construction of the UN entailed elements of political fudge based on great power rivalries. For example, Stalin's concerns that the UN would be weighted towards the interests of the US and the UK had much to do with the establishment of the type of veto powers that are still enjoyed by the permanent members of the Security Council.[11] Even fundamental conceptions of statehood were subject to political fudge. Stalin's argument that there should be a seat for each of the separate Soviet Republics (if each state of the British Empire was to have one each) eventually resulted in one seat for the USSR and one each for the Ukraine and Byelorussia, but not for the other Soviet Republics. As a result, it is not just the states that have a veto that is largely a consequence of the great power rivalries and the emerging cold war politics at the end of the Second World War, but the extent to which veto power can be used.

It is also worth noting that the current permanent membership of the Security Council is in some ways accidental. The Chinese seat was created for the nationalist Guomindang on the understanding that they would be returned to power in China after the defeat of the Japanese. While the Guomindang did indeed occupy the seat supposedly representing all of China even after defeat in the Chinese civil war, the switch from Republic of China to the People's Republic of China in 1971 gave a permanent seat and veto power to another communist party state – something that had not been envisaged when the UN was being drawn up at the end of the Second World War. In addition, the seat currently occupied by the Russian federation was created for the Soviet Union. Bourantonis and Panagiotou (2004) argue that the ease at which Russia simply assumed the SU seat was because the UK and France in particular were opposed to a wide ranging and open debate in the General Assembly as it would bring back to the fore attention on the legitimacy of the constitution of the UNSC and their privileged role within it.

And it is this question of the legitimacy of the UNSC that occupies much attention in considerations of leadership in the UN. The current makeup of the UNSC is widely considered to be unrepresentative no matter which calculation of representation is used. Simply in terms of size, five permanent members in 1945 represented 10 per cent of the original 1945 membership of 51 states as opposed to 191 members today. In terms of global powers, while all five members are nuclear powers, they do not have sole control over global nuclear weapons, and the conception of France and Britain as global powers above non-members looks increasingly anomalous. Taking economics as an indicator, then the absence of Japan and Germany and perhaps increasingly India looks unfair. After the US, Japan is the leading provider of funds for the UN, but has no final say in the Security Council. Geographically, three European states out of five with no representative from Africa or Latin America is widely considered to be iniquitous. And with Chinese economic growth, the lack of representation for developing countries is increasingly marked. Suggested criteria to be used for considering new UNSC members include a wide range including 'peacekeeping contributions; contribution to the UN budget; population; size; political and economic power and potential; stability of economic system; military force; reduction of military expenditures; eradication of poverty; promotion of education; and influence of civilization' (UN 2004a: 25).

As Featherston (2004: 202) argues:

> The Security Council is a relic of the geopolitics of 1945. To be legitimate today it must reflect contemporary realities. It needs to accommodate today's powers that are currently excluded – Japan and Germany, and contemplate the accommodation of tomorrow's big states – India and Brazil. It must also address the extraordinary powers inherent in the veto. Legitimacy is not to be found in the uneven distribution of such clout. As the many failed attempts at reform instruct us, positive change is not easy.

Schlichtmann (1999: 5–8) goes further than most arguing that the composition of the UNSC actually breaches the UN's own charter in respect to principle of equal rights for all member states, the principle of equal sovereignty and the principle of equal representation of all geographic regions. This view was echoed by a General Assembly report on the UNSC, which noted that:

> Numerous delegations expressed the view that the veto was anachronistic, discriminatory and undemocratic. They maintained that the actual use and threat of using the veto represented a complete erosion of the principles of transparency and accountability in the working methods and procedures of the Security Council. It was considered by many speakers that the use of the veto created two categories of membership in the Security Council, despite the principle of sovereign equality contained in Article 2.1 of the Charter. The view was expressed that in no other United Nations body was the principle of sovereign equality violated.
>
> (UN 2004a: 30)

At the very least, the use of the veto in support of national interests, rather than in support of 'collective interests', undermines the legitimacy of not just the UNSC itself, but the entire UN system and the UN's Millennium Declaration in 2000 noted the need to intensify activity 'to achieve a comprehensive reform of the Security Council in all its aspects'.[12]

Ironically, the legitimacy of the UNSC is also undermined when the veto is not allowed to be used in those cases where major powers choose to go outside the UN system to pursue policy – as was the case with the use of force by NATO in Yugoslavia without UNSC endorsement, and the decision not to hold a second UNSC vote before the invasion of Iraq. But as Wheeler argues, while ignoring the UNSC might be considered an emasculation of the UN by the great powers, an alternative argument is that the UNSC (or permanent members of the UNSC) has emasculated the UN. There is no agreed framework in the UNSC for defining when intervention is justified, and the national interest, rather than principle, often results in action being vetoed:

> Security Council inaction in cases where atrocities shock the conscience of humankind equally undermines the authority of the UN . . . having willed the ends of policy, the Security Council was failing in its duty by not willing the military means to implement its demands in the face of persistent non-compliance.
>
> (Wheeler 2001: 119)

Without reform of the SC, and perhaps even with it, there is significant differential ability for member states to decide on norms – and most importantly, to decide when intervention should be sanctioned notwithstanding the principle of state sovereignty. Schabas (2004: 719) argues that in designing the UN, Roosevelt deliberately constructed the UNSC as the real site of authority, leaving the General Assembly as 'a place for the majority of small states to "let off steam"'. Even if this is apocrophal, the lack of binding authority for General Assembly resolutions is juxtaposed against the authority of the UNSC in general, the ability of the permanent members to exercise the veto and the ability of the hegemon to go beyond the UN system when the national interest dictates.

Changing conceptions of sovereignty

From the outset, the UN has played an important role in establishing global norms with claims to universal applicability. The adoption of the Universal Declaration of Human Rights in December 1948 being perhaps the highest profile case of the General Assembly attempting to establish a norm of basic freedoms 'as a common standard of achievement for all peoples and all nations'.[13] But since the end of the cold war the agenda has changed. Not only has previous reticence about impinging on sovereignty been overcome, but there is also a move towards establishing liberal ideals as the basis for UN policy (Barnett 1997: 536).

Doyle (2001) argues that Agenda for Peace in 1992 and reformulation of the UN Charter fundamentally changed traditional conceptions of sovereignty. It is now up to the UNSC to decide what a 'threat to peace' actually means, and when such a threat to peace justifies the abrogation of sovereignty and intervention. Events that take place entirely within a sovereign state – be they civil war or violations of rights – can lead to them losing the 'protection afforded them by the rules of sovereignty and non-intervention'(Wheeler 2001: 127), with the only obstacle to the UNSC endorsing intervention being the veto power of the five permanent members.

Following Reisman, David and Held, Paris (2003: 450–1) suggests that it is not so much that the legitimate sovereignty of states has been relegated below other concerns/issues, but that the fundamental understanding of what actually constitutes legitimate statehood has been redefined. Increasingly, for states to be granted freedom from external interference in their sovereign domestic affairs, they have to be liberal democracies. Clearly, many of the UN's members would not meet these criteria, and the mere lack of democratic institutions is not enough on its own to justify intervention. But rather than simply talk about respect for human freedom, UN statements on what these standards should be are now much more explicit in asserting that 'governance should be underpinned by democracy at all levels'. For Paul Taylor (1999: 540), this 'proactive cosmopolitanism' entails 'a deliberate attempt to create a consensus about values and behaviour' based on 'the civil and political values of Western liberal states'. As Barnett (1997: 529) argues, the UN has become, through its official reports at least, 'an agent of normative integration that can increase the number of actors who identify with and uphold the values of a liberal international order'. Furthermore, he suggests that the UN commissions are aware that many states – particularly developing states – do not buy into these principles and pose serious challenges to the universal adoption of these values and norms. As such, while the UN might have been characterized by East–West conflict during the cold war, it has increasingly become an arena in which North–South issues are now played out (Barnett 1997: 545–6).

It is not just that democracy is the best form of government for ensuring the protection of basic human rights. But alongside the economic prescriptions outlined earlier, democracy is also portrayed as the basis for development (Forsythe 1997). Where the right to development may stay firmly embedded in the UN (Pace 1998), increasingly developmental/socio-economic rights are not seen as being separate from human/political rights, but establishing human/political rights and democratic institutions is seen as the prerequisite for assuring developmental/ socio-economic rights. Such an understanding has been at the heart of the agenda of both Boutros Boutros-Ghali[14] and Kofi Annan (2005). Indeed, for Forsythe (1997), a key sea change in UN thinking on global governance occurred with the election of Boutros Boutros-Ghali to Secretary General of the UN. In Boutros-Ghali, the UN also had a secretary general who identified himself (and thus the UN) with new thinking on how best to establish global governance and indeed what the guiding principles of global governance should be – not least by explicitly linking democracy with development – in 'Agenda for Peace'[15] and the 1995 publication of the Commission on Global Governance's *Our Global Neighbourhood*. Although the commission on global governance is not an official UN organization,[16] it carried the endorsement of Boutros-Ghali and secured part funding from UNDP trust funds. If anything Kofi Annan's 2005 report, *In Larger Freedom* (Annan 2005), goes even further in establishing a normative position that undermines the principle of state sovereignty, and explicitly promotes democracy and free market capitalism as the correct form of governance, the best guarantors of international peace, and the basis of economic development.

While recognizing that Sovereign states are the 'basic and indispensable building blocks of the international system', Annan argued that states alone can no longer provide the stability and economic development that they should promote for their people without the active participation of both civil society and the private sector which now occupy 'the space formerly reserved for States alone' (Annan 2005: 6). Furthermore, neither norms nor legal principles of sovereignty should ever prevent the UN from intervening to stop severe abuses of human rights and suffering in sovereign states. Crucially, such a need to intervene is no longer simply couched in terms of intervention to ensure international peace and collective security, but instead is based on an 'emerging norm that there is a collective responsibility to protect',[17] which should not be subject to arbitrary and selective application in the UNSC.

Although Annan (like Boutros-Ghali before him) talks in terms of a growing 'consensus', the consensus is far from total. China, Mexico, Pakistan, Peru, Russia, South Africa and Tunisia have all consistently rejected the establishment of peace-keeping operations built on notions of humanitarian intervention (Pugh 2004: 45). The former Russian PM and Foreign Minister, Yevgeny Primakov (2004: 49), is explicit in rejecting any move towards a duty of care to global citizens as being anything to do with the UN: 'The UN charter limits the use of force to protect or restore international peace; it does not condone the interference in the internal affairs of a state.' Indeed, for representatives of many (primarily developing) states, the promotion of a norm of humanitarian intervention even when international peace and stability is not threatened smacks of an attempt to use the UN as an agent of Western cultural imperialism (Wheeler 2001: 127–8). Attempts to construct new mechanisms of global governance – not just through the UN – are often perceived as a means of imposing Western preferences to ensure the continued privileged position of Western states in the global order (Held *et al.* 1999: 6).

As such, the formal position of the Secretary General of the UN conflicts with the position of a number of the UN's member states. And no matter what the Secretary General or any of his endorsed reports say, it is the member states that ultimately decide on whether action should be taken and under what conditions. As Russia and China are both resistant to emerging new norms, and both have veto power as permanent UNSC members, then there are sizeable obstacles to translating ideas into policies. As such, the apparent contradiction between principles of sovereignty and intervention are in many respects replicated by the division between the UN as a generator of ideas and ideals on one hand, and the practical actions of the UN in UNSC-mandated actions on the other.

Developmental norms and neoliberalism

Most of the focus on the UN as a promoter of norms focuses on political issues. And quite clearly, the UN is far less important in terms of global economic governance than the World Bank, the IMF and the WTO. Nevertheless, the UN does play a role – albeit a minimal one, in reinforcing if not establishing global economic norms. On one level, the UN has taken a number of steps to embody principles of human rights within international economic activity. In 2003, the Commission on Human Rights published a draft, 'Norms on the Responsibilities of Transnational Corporations and Other Business Enterprises with Regard to Human Rights' (UN 2003). Vagts (2003) argues that the 'norms' simply call for corporations to adhere to existing treaties covering labour standards, the environment and broadly defined human rights in their overseas operations, and therefore makes little concrete difference. Perhaps at best, the norms have symbolic importance in establishing the right of the UNHCR to concern itself with the economic activity of private economic actors, and in recognizing that notwithstanding the principle that states remain ultimately responsible for ensuring that TNCs do not abrogate basic rights, it is not always that easy for states to exercise this responsibility in a globalized economy.[18]

On another level, the UN reinforces at least the hegemony of neoliberal economics as not so much the best as the only economic strategy that will deliver countries from underdevelopment. As Annan (2005: 7) put it, there is 'an unprecedented consensus on how to promote global economic and social development'. This consensus – the 2002 Monterrey Consensus – recognizes that the international economic order contains important structural constraints on developing countries; not least among them lack of access to the most lucrative potential markets as a result of protectionist trade policies. But at its heart is a commitment to the promotion of:

> sound macroeconomic policies aimed at sustaining high rates of economic growth, full employment, poverty eradication, price stability and sustainable

fiscal and external balances to ensure that the benefits of growth reach all people, especially the poor. Governments should attach priority to avoiding inflationary distortions and abrupt economic fluctuations that negatively affect income distribution and resource allocation. Along with prudent fiscal and monetary policies, an appropriate exchange rate regime is required.

(UN 2002: 4)

The Monterrey Consensus also emphasizes the importance of private capital flows through Foreign direct investment (FDI) as a means of generating development:

Foreign direct investment contributes toward financing sustained economic growth over the long term. It is especially important for its potential to transfer knowledge and technology, create jobs, boost overall productivity, enhance competitiveness and entrepreneurship, and ultimately eradicate poverty through economic growth and development. A central challenge, therefore, is to create the necessary domestic and international conditions to facilitate direct investment flows, conducive to achieving national development.... To attract and enhance inflows of productive capital, countries need to continue their efforts to achieve a transparent, stable and predictable investment climate, with proper contract enforcement and respect for property rights, embedded in sound macroeconomic policies and institutions that allow businesses, both domestic and international, to operate efficiently and profitably and with maximum development impact. Special efforts are required in such priority areas as economic policy and regulatory frameworks for promoting and protecting investments.

(UN 2002: 5)

The importance of policy adjustments to allow the private sector to flourish was also at the heart of The Commission on the Private Sector and Development's 2004 report, 'Unleashing Entrepreneurship: Making Business Work for the Poor' (and echoed in Kofi Annan's 2005 report). It is important to note that while these various reports all argue that developed countries need to make changes to domestic and multilateral policy to ensure equity, the bottom line is that free market capitalism is the only road to development: and 'the primary responsibility for achieving growth and equitable development lies with developing countries' (UN 2004b: 1), and is not the fault of the international economic order.

How important is all this? Given the recommendations of these various reports, there is very little that the UN can do to effect change. The responsibility for change is primarily in the hands of governments in developing states. And where the international order might need attention to ensure equity, the onus falls primarily on the WTO and to lesser extents the World Bank and the IMF. But the very fact that these reports emanate from the UN and not the WTO, IMF or World Bank in many ways increases their significance. As they are not tied to the organs of economic governance which are largely expected to promote neoliberalism, their policy prescriptions carry an air of neutrality. It is particularly notable that the Commission on the Private Sector and Development was jointly chaired by Canadian PM Paul Martin, and the former Mexican President, Ernesto Zedillo, and notwithstanding three US-based commissioners, was dominated by representatives from the South. It might not be the authentic voice of the South, but neither does it appear to be the voice of the developed North alone. As such, the UN can be seen as promoting what Gosovic (2000) calls the 'Global Intellectual Hegemony' designed to influence and homogenize world public opinion. Ideational promotion by the UN increasingly reflects the interests and agendas of developed states with the UN development agenda no longer reflecting either the ideas or the interests of the South. Selected words and terminologies from the old development agenda have been co-opted and given new meanings to support the neoliberal hegemony (Gosovic 2000: 450), while other terms and concepts have 'virtually disappeared from public usage' (Gosovic 2000: 451).

In many respects, it is what is not said in UN developmental discourse that is as important as what is said. For example, although Lavelle (2001) acknowledges the many differences of opinion given the diversity in the G77, and the lack of Southern unity within UNCTAD, she argues that at the very least both provided an essential alternative (or alternatives) to neoliberal development discourses. The G77 used UNCTAD as a means of promoting an alternative ideology emphasizing the structural failings of the global trading system and the capitalist global economy which perpetuated the exploitation of poorer countries by the rich. While current UN thinking on development places the onus for change on the developing countries themselves, the call for a New International Economic Order required a root and branch reform of the system itself. But for this study, perhaps more important than specific policy prescriptions were simply that alternative models and ideas were on the UN agenda:

> The key ideological feature which cemented a strikingly heterogeneous institutional alliance was not a point of theory upon which all agreed, but rather one upon which all agreed not to agree. The third world institutional alliance was grounded in developing countries' refusal from the start to accept a universal model of development.
>
> (Lavelle 2001: 31)

Although there may not have been a clear, distinct and coherent G77 approach before, the disbanding of the coalition marked the end of the 'African input into the discourse on development' (Lavelle 2001: 27).

While Ian Taylor (2003: 410) shares this view of the decline of UNCTAD as a source of alternative developmental discourses, he follows Augelli and Murphy (1988) by placing a much stronger emphasis on its deliberate emasculation by governments in the North, and by the US and the UK in particular under Reagan and Thatcher. The resulting re-invention of UNCTAD as a proponent of neoliberal economic reform in developing states (as epitomized by the 2004 São Paulo Consensus (UNCTAD 2004)) represents a retreat from demands for structural change, the near abandonment of alternative developmental discourses and an: '[a]cceptance of the hegemonic discourse while (at best) attempting to ameliorate the worst aspects of the established order.... This was a remarkable sea-change in UNCTAD's normative posture' (Taylor 2003: 412). In short, the development discourse in the UN has moved from one of ideational competition (if not conflict) to one of unanimity and consensus. While the UN may not be *that* important as a promoter of economic and developmental norms when compared to the other agencies of global economic governance, crucially, it is no longer the arena for alternative ideas and norms that it once was, and which Gosovic (2000) argues were part and parcel of the original developmental objectives of the UN Charter. For Otto (1996), this leaves the task of promoting 'postliberal' approaches within the UN to NGOs.

Between theory and practice

So much for ideas. As noted later, the extent to which these ideas are put into practice within the UN system is, however, a different matter. There are some areas in which the ideas promoted by or through the UN are supported by specific action. On one level, Kofi Annan (2005: 39) has committed himself to providing more concrete support through the UN system to promote democratization:

> The United Nations should not restrict its role to norm-setting but should expand its help to its members to further broaden and deepen democratic trends throughout the world. *To that end, I support the creation of a democracy fund at the United Nations to provide assistance to countries seeking to establish or strengthen their democracy. Furthermore, I intend to ensure that our activities in this area are more closely coordinated by establishing a more explicit link between the democratic governance work of the United Nations Development Programme and the Electoral Assistance Division of the Department of Political Affairs* (original emphasis).

On another level, there is evidence that in its peace-keeping activities, the UN is implementing policies designed to construct new post-conflict orders as liberal democracies. For Richmond (2004: 92):

> the creation of the liberal peace requires an agreement on method, which can be found in a peacebuilding consensus framed by the notion of peace-as-governance. This occurs in the context of peace operations in which peacebuilding recreates the state-centric order, territorial integrity and basic human rights, while also attempting to institutionalize political, social and economic reform according to the precepts of the democratic peace, which have been widely accepted in the post-cold war environment.

Pugh (2004) similarly argues that in promotion of Peacebuilding and Peace Support Operations, UN actions promote the preferred policy preferences of hegemonic powers built on liberal ideas of both state construction and economic paradigms. Indeed, holding successful elections has become a measure of the success of UN peace-keeping operations (Barnett and Finnemore 1999: 720). Moreover, in establishing new orders, ideational principles can override local interests and practicalities. There is a strong literature that warns against the 'dangers of hasty democratization in deeply divided countries',[19] and if the new order is built by and largely dependent on external forces with weak local support (Richmond 2004: 93), then there is a danger that it can create instability and violence rather than build peace. For example, Barnett and Finnemore (1999: 720) argue that the result of pushing for quick elections in Bosnia and parts of Africa was the very ethnic cleansing and exacerbated ethnic tensions that the operations were designed to prevent in the first place.

Given that 'the UN's peacekeepers derive part of their authority from the claim that they are independent, objective, neutral actors who simply implement Security Council resolutions' (Barnett and Finnemore 1999: 709), at the very least, there is concern about whether the UN's dual role as a promoter of norms and a hands-on actor can be reconciled (Kent 2004), and the legitimacy of UN peace-keeping actions maintained. At worst, for Mégret and Hoffmann (2003), if the local populations are forced to accept democratic structures against their wishes, then the UN itself might violate, rather than protect, the rights of those that it is trying to build a democratic peace for.[20]

Notwithstanding the apparent increasing imposition of democratic norms in peace-keeping and peace-building operations, while many of the pronouncements associated with the UN are built on liberal principles, in action, realist principles of national interest and hard-nosed power balancing often trump utopian ideals. For example, Forsythe argues that notwithstanding the rhetorical commitment to linking development aid to democratization, there is no evidence that this has actually occurred in any of the 150 countries where the UNDP is involved in development programmes. Furthermore, when the UNDP did attempt to implement a democracy criterion in 1990, it had to backtrack in the face of opposition from developing country members of the UN (Forsythe 1997: 343). When principle and pragmatism collided, pragmatism and the power of sovereign member states within the UN won out.

Perhaps a better example is the actual promotion of a universal conception of human rights that should be protected and promoted by the international community through the UN. On one level, the UN's ability to enforce change on recalcitrant states is limited. On another, and perhaps more significant, the UN system has, to say the least, been partial in exposing and criticizing abuses of human rights in member states. Although a 1995 censure of China's human rights record failed by only one vote, Chinese diplomatic efforts have subsequently resulted in other critical resolutions not even being discussed on the floor of the United Nations Human Rights Commission (UNHRC). In 2004 the commission adopted resolutions critical of North Korea, Cuba, Belarus and Turkmenistan – but rejected resolutions against China and Russian action in Chechnya as well as Zimbabwe.

At the time, Zimbabwe was one of the fifty-three member states that formed the membership of the UNHRC in its annual meeting. Each year, a country is elected to Chair this meeting – in practice, this means that each of the five regional groupings[21] nominate a country to act on their behalf for that session, and no vote was needed from the founding of the commission in 1997 until 2003. In 2003, it was the turn of the African grouping to elect a chair and they nominated Libya, a country that was still under some international sanctions after the Lockerbie bombing, and which was accused of breaching a wide range of human rights by international NGOs at the time.

Not surprisingly, Libya's nomination generated considerable opposition from human rights NGOs, with Human Rights Watch arguing that it not only undermined the legitimacy of the UNHRC, but also of (New Partnership for Africa's Development) NEPAD's commitments to promoting and monitoring human rights in Africa.[22] It also generated opposition from developed countries, most notably the US that for the first time in the UNHCR's history forced a vote (which Libya won 33-3 with 17 abstentions). Notably, the decision to force a vote in itself generated condemnation of the US for violating the norm that allowed regional groupings to nominate their own representative. The established modus operandi within the UN was, for some, much more important than the legitimacy of the UNHRC.

And the fact that it was the US that had forced a vote, and that the US consistently vetoes resolutions that are critical of Israel, was crucially important here. Indeed, in the same 2003 session, the US was the only member of the UNHRC to vote against a resolution condemning the treatment of Lebanese detainees in Israel. So on one side there is the accusation that human rights abusers, not least through their participation on the UNHRC itself, can avoid criticism and emasculate the objectives of the UNHRC in particular and the UN in general, as a promoter of universal human rights norms. On the other side, there is the feeling that the permanent members of the Security Council, and the US in particular, use their privileged position to protect allies and decide who should be subject to these norms, when, and with what consequences.

Criticism of US actions in the UN abound. The US has withheld funding for the UN when policy has been unpopular at home, and though both Afghanistan and the US have failed to make their required payments to the UN in the past, Afghanistan suffered a loss of voting rights as a result but not the US. The US also vetoed the reappointment of Boutros Boutros-Ghali as Secretary General in a 14–0–1 vote in 1996 (Chollet and Orr 2001). Cannon (2004) even argues that the US is trying to undermine the World Health Organization (WHO) strategy on diet and health because of the relationship between the Bush Presidency and US sugar producers.

Perhaps most important of all for the legitimacy of the UN as a promoter of global norms is the US refusal to adhere to the International Criminal Court (ICC) which, according to Lavalle (2003: 195), 'set off, in June and July 2002, a crisis so severe that it threatened the survival of all United Nations peace operations'. Although Clinton was supportive of the ICC, and in the process of negotiating the terms of the treaty a number of concessions were made to the US that some argue diluted its original intentions (Weller 2002: 696), it was not ratified in the US Senate and the Bush administration informed the UN that it was not a party to the treaty in May 2002. The US administration argued that it was not prepared to allow its citizens to be subject to extra-national law in the ICC – partly as a matter of absolute principle, partly because of fears that other nations would use the ICC as a way of 'getting back' at the US, and partly because as the US carries most weight in military activities either within or without the UN and is therefore more likely to be subject to potential charges than other countries.

For Schabas (2004), these arguments are largely unconvincing as the same questions arise when considering myriad other treaties and conventions that the US has signed and ratified, and the US was for a long time the main champion of international criminal justice. The key is that the original draft for the ICC conceived as the Security Council having the final authority, while the final agreement gave the court considerable independence. While the US is prepared to subject itself to the jurisdication of international organizations such as the UN, this is conditional on its ability to influence if not control those international organizations – and in the case of the UN, to ultimately be able to veto unfavourable outcomes. The sole superpower is only prepared to accept new norms of global governance when it does not infringe on its own sovereignty – a privilege that it is not prepared to extend to all other states.

The US is not alone in refusing to ratify the ICC – neither have Russia, China, Israel and Turkey. And the US is far from the only power that defends its sovereignty and national interest in the UN system. But Cronin (2001) argues that the US is different, and that US actions are much more likely to undermine the legitimacy of the UN system than similar actions by other states. The UN, along with other international organizations, was largely constructed by the hegemon to promote a hegemonic world order. Indeed, the hegemon relies on these international organizations as a means of legitimating its interests through the creation of legally binding treaties. Having done more than most to establish a norm – in this case built around conceptions of rights and the need to hold states to account if they abrogate rights – not submitting themselves to the norm not only undermines the institution itself, but the liberal principles that underpin the hegemonic world order *per se*:

> When a hegemon fails to act within the boundaries established by its role, the credibility of the institutions and rules it helped to establish weakens. IOs act as the chief legitimizing agents of global politics. When these organizations are undermined, the legitimacy of the international order itself is threatened.
> (Cronin 2001: 113)

Conclusions

The US does not ratify the convention of the ICC because it considers it an illegitimate infringement of its sovereignty. Other states consider the US's and other states' decisions to abandon the UNSC to use force against other sovereign states as undermining the legitimacy of the UN. When permanent members veto action, this is taken as also undermining UN legitimacy through the selective application of principles based solely on national interest – indeed, for many the use of veto in the UNSC in itself is illegitimate and in contravention of the UN's own charter. For some, it is the failure to apply principles of humanitarianism that reduces legitimacy – for others it is simply illegitimate for the UN to abrogate sovereignty and concern itself with the domestic affairs of sovereign member states. No wonder that there is a general consensus that the UN needs to be reformed – and no wonder that there is little consensus on how it should be reformed.

The latest in a relatively long list of calls to reform the UNSC came in Kofi Annan's 2005 report proposing an expanded UNSC (one model proposing extra permanent seats and another proposing four-year renewable seats). But the immediate responses to the proposals indicate that while there might be wide agreement that the UNSC needs to be reformed, how, and who should join, remains an area of contention. For example, during the debates over reform proposals in 1993 and 1995, Non-aligned Movement states expressed concern over another advanced industrialized country joining the UNSC. If Japan and/or Germany were to join, then three other developing nations should also join to provide balance – one each for Africa, Latin America and Asia. But even then there were severe divisions over whether new permanent members should have the same veto powers as the existing powers, and which country should get the extra seats from each region (Bourantonis and Panagiotou 2004).

Even prior to the publication of Annan's report in 2005 calling for UNSC reform, Brazil, Germany, Japan and India indicated their claims to UNSC membership, and mutual support for each other's bids.[23] Pakistan was reported to be hostile to the idea of an Indian seat, Italy about a German seat, Argentina and Mexico about Brazil, and China and both Koreas expressed immediate opposition to Japan. Popular opinion in both countries remains highly hostile towards Japan, and Annan's report resulted in a number of Japanese-owned shops and companies in China coming under attack from rioters in April 2005. As existing UNSC members have the ultimate right to veto any proposals for change, and given China's reticence and at times downright hostility to Japan's UNSC pretensions, it remains unlikely (at the very least) that China would allow a permanent veto power seat for Japan. It is perhaps not surprising, then, that the Security Council reforms quietly slipped off the agenda, and were not even discussed in the General Assembly.

Given all this, it is tempting to argue that by promoting norms of global governance through official reports and commissions that it cannot deliver upon or are even blocked by its member states, the UN not only fails to promote, but actually undermines attempts to establish global governance. Manifestations of hostility to the promotion of liberal norms by some states, and the failure of others to always act according to either their own avowed principles, or the principles established by the Secretary General, simply point to the futility of trying to build global orders that will not simply be ignored when they conflict with perceived national interests.

But the importance of ideational promotion should not be wholly dismissed. Despite opposition from some states, and the uneven (at best) transformation of principle into practice, the post-cold war era has seen the UN change. Whether the UN was ever conceived as being an organization solely designed to promote international peace is debateable. But in the recent era, it has become much more clearly an organization concerned with promoting ideas on how best to achieve development, and how best to organize national governance and governmental structures. It has also become an arena in which liberal political and developmental ideas are promoted.

Gosovic's (2000) conception of the homogenization of global public opinion noted in the discussion of developmental paradigms earlier is an idea that echoes Gramsci's conception of the 'common sense'.[24] By common sense, Gramsci meant 'the folklore of the future, a relatively rigidified phase of popular knowledge in a given time and place' (Gramsci 1985: 421) – the promotion of a single idea that becomes accepted as obvious as not to be contested (or if it is, for that contestation to be considered as irrelevant, absurd or counter-intuitive). It is going too far to suggest that liberal ideals inform action in the UN system; but the UN system has become a vehicle through which a distinctive set of liberal norms are promoted, even though they are not yet universally accepted, nor universally applied.

Notes

1 As Barnett also points out, formalizing a role for NGOs in the decision-making process was one of the proposals of the Commission on Global Governance.
2 In Article 38, paragraph 1, of the Statute of the Court.
3 Case Concerning the Military and Paramilitary Activities in and Against Nicaragua (Nicaragua v. United States of America) Judgment of 27 June 1986. Available on-line at: http://www.icj-cij.org/icjwww/icases/inus/inus_isummaries/inus_isummary_19860627.html, accessed on 4 December 2006.
4 Strange (1999) argued that the sovereign state system had failed – failed to provide global financial stability and failed to manage transnational environmental governance.
5 Though note that this position is not always maintained by the Chinese who supported intervention in Afghanistan after 9/11. But the principle that China's own state sovereignty should never be impinged remains firm.
6 And the subsequent Congresses that codified the post-Napoleonic peace – Aix-la-Chapelle (1818), Troppau (1820), Laibach (1821) and Verona (1822).
7 Great Britain, Austria-Hungary, France, Germany, Russia, the US, Portugal, Denmark, Spain, Italy, the Netherlands, Sweden, Belgium and Turkey.
8 This established The Hague Convention for the Pacific Settlement of International Disputes and the Permanent Court of Arbitration (1902).
9 England, Austria, Prussia, Russia and France.
10 Italy, the US, France and the UK.
11 For details on how different conceptions of how the veto should work were argued through in the creation of the UN, see Gowan (2003).
12 General Assembly resolution 55/2, para. 30. Available on-line at: http://www.ohchr.org/english/law/millennium.html, accessed on 4 December 2006.
13 Though of course not all states have ratified the declaration.
14 Perhaps most clearly enunciated in Boutros-Ghali (1995). See also Forsythe (1997).
15 The 1995 publication of Agenda for Peace was officially the supplement to his original report adopted by the Security Council in January 1992.
16 It is funded by national governments, educational foundations, and nine individual national governments and was established with a membership of twenty-eight selected (i.e. non-elected) individuals.

17 Annan was quoting here the High-level Panel on Threats, Challenges and Change's report on 'A more secure world: our shared responsibility' (UN 2004c).
18 This argument was made by Felice (1999) in his discussion of the Maastricht guidelines on violations of economic social and cultural rights, but also holds true here.
19 This literature is summarized in Paris (2003).
20 Furthermore, the UN is not subject even to its own treaties – these only bind the UN's member states and not the UN itself.
21 Africa, Asia, Latin American and Caribbean states, Central and Eastern Europe, and Western European and other states which includes Australasia, Canada and the US.
22 Available at on-line at: http://hrw.org/press/2002/08/libya080902.html, accessed on 4 December 2006.
23 After a meeting in New York on 21 September 2004.
24 Many thanks to Ian Taylor for pointing this out to me.

References

Annan, Kofi (2005) *In Larger Freedom: Towards Development, Security and Human Rights for All*, New York: United Nations.

Augelli, Enrico and Murphy, Craig (1988) *America's Quest for Supremacy and the Third World: A Gramscian Analysis*, London: Pinter.

Barnett, Michael (1997) 'Bringing in the new world order: liberalism, legitimacy, and the United Nations', *World Politics* 49, 4: 526–51.

Barnett, Michael and Finnemore, Martha (1999) 'The politics, power, and pathologies of international organizations', *International Organization* 53, 4: 699–732.

Bourantonis, Dimitris and Panagiotou, Ritsa (2004) 'Russia's attitude towards the reform of the United Nations Security Council, 1990–2000', *The Journal of Communist Studies and Transition Politics* 20, 4: 79–102.

Boutros-Ghali, Boutros (1995) *Agenda for Peace* (2nd edn), New York: United Nations.

Cannon, Geoffrey (2004) 'Why the Bush administration and the global sugar industry are determined to demolish the 2004 WHO Global Strategy on Diet, Physical Activity and Health', *Public Health Nutrition* 7, 3: 369–80.

Chollet, Derek and Orr, Robert (2001) 'Carpe diem: reclaiming success at the United Nations', *The Washington Quarterly* 24, 4: 7–18.

Cronin, Bruce (2001) 'The paradox of hegemony: America's ambiguous relationship with the United Nations', *European Journal of International Relations* 7, 1: 103–29.

Cuellar, Mariano-Florentino (2004) 'Reflections on sovereignty and collective security', *Stanford Journal of International Law* 40, 211: 211–57.

Doyle, Michael (2001) 'The new interventionism', *Metaphilosophy* 32, 1–2: 212–35.

Featherston, Scott (2004) 'Review of Stephen C. Schlesinger act of creation: the founding of the United Nations', *SAIS Review* 24, 1: 201–03.

Felice, William (1999) 'The viability of the United Nations approach to economic and social human rights in a globalized economy', *International Affairs* 75, 3: 563–98.

Forsythe, David (1997) 'The United Nations, human rights, and development', *Human Rights Quarterly* 19, 2: 334–49.

Gosovic, Branislav (2000) 'Global intellectual hegemony and the international development agenda', *International Social Science Journal* 52, 166: 447–56.

Gowan, Peter (2003) 'US: UN', *New Left Review* 24: 5–28.

Gramsci, Antonio (1985) *Selections from Cultural Writings*, London: Lawrence and Wishart.

Held, David, McGrew, Anthony, Goldblatt, G. David and Perraton, Jonathan (1999) *Global Transformations: Politics, Economics and Culture*, Cambridge: Polity.

Kent, Randolph (2004) 'The United Nations' humanitarian pillar: refocusing the UN's disaster and emergency roles and responsibilities', *Disasters* 28, 2: 216–33.

Lavelle, Kathryn (2001) 'Ideas within a context of power: the African Group in an evolving UNCTAD', *The Journal of Modern African Studies* 39, 1: 25–50.

Lavalle, Roberto (2003) 'A vicious storm in a teacup: the action by the United Nations Security Council to narrow the jurisdiction of the International Criminal Court', *Criminal Law Forum* 14, 4: 487–8.

Martens, Kerstin (2004) 'An appraisal of Amnesty International's work at the United Nations: established areas of activities and shifting priorities since the 1990s', *Human Rights Quarterly* 26: 1050–70.

Mégret, Frédéric and Hoffmann, Florian (2003) 'The UN as a human rights violator? Some reflections on the United Nations changing human rights responsibilities', *Human Rights Quarterly* 25, 2: 314–42.

Otto, Dianne (1996) 'Nongovernmental Organizations in the United Nations system: the emerging role of international civil society', *Human Rights Quarterly* 18, 1: 107–41.

Pace, John (1998) 'The development of Human Rights Law in the United Nations, its control and monitoring machinery', *International Social Science Journal* 50, 158: 499–511.

Paris, Roland (2003) 'Peacekeeping and the constraints of global culture', *European Journal of International Relations* 9, 3: 441–73.

Primakov, Yevgeny (2004) 'Rather the United Nations than US unilateralism', *New Perspectives Quarterly* 21, 2: 49–59.

Pugh, Michael (2004) 'Peacekeeping and critical theory', *International Peacekeeping*, 11, 1: 39–58.

Richmond, Oliver (2004) 'UN Peace Operations and the dilemmas of the peacebuilding Consensus', *International Peacekeeping* 11, 1: 83–101.

Schabas, William (2004) 'United States hostility to the International Criminal Court: it's all about the Security Council', *European Journal of International Law* 15, 4: 701–20.

Schlichtmann, Klaus (1999) 'A draft on Security Council reform', *Peace and Change* 24, 4: 505–35.

Strange, Susan (1999) 'The westfailure system', *Review of International Studies* 25, 3: 345–54.

Taylor, Ian (2003) 'The United Nations Conference on Trade and Development', *New Political Economy* 8, 3: 409–18.

Taylor, Paul (1999) 'The United Nations in the 1990s: proactive cosmopolitanism and the issue of sovereignty', *Political Studies* 47, 3: 538–65.

UN (1995) *Our Global Neighborhood: Report of the Commission on Global Governance*, Oxford: Oxford University Press.

—— (2002) *Report of the International Conference on Financing for Development*, New York: United Nations.

—— (2003) *Norms on the Responsibilities of Transnational Corporations and Other Business Enterprises with Regard to Human Rights: Commission on Human Rights, Sub-commission on the Promotion and Protection of Human Rights*, New York: United Nations.

—— (2004a) *Report of the Open-ended Working Group on the Question of Equitable Representation on and Increase in the Membership of the Security Council and Other Matters related to the Security Council: General Assembly Official Records*, New York: United Nations.

UN (2004b) *Unleashing Entrepreneurship: Making Business Work for the Poor: Commission on the Private Sector and Development Report to The Secretary-General of the United Nations*, New York: United Nations.

—— (2004c) Report of the Secretary General's High Level Panel. A More Secure World: Our Shared Responsibility. Available on-line at: http://www.un.org/secureworld, accessed on 5 December 2006.

Vagts, Detlev (2003) 'The UN norms for transnational corporations', *Leiden Journal of International Law* 16: 795–802.

Weller, Marc (2002) 'Undoing the global constitution: UN Security Council action on the International Criminal Court', *International Affairs* 78, 4: 693–712.

Wheeler, Nicholas (2001) 'Review article: humanitarian intervention after Kosovo: emergent norm, moral duty or the coming anarchy?' *International Affairs* 77, 1: 113–28.

12 Global governance, Japan and the United Nations

Hoshino Toshiya

Introduction

The UN was created to 'save the succeeding generations from the scourge of war' (Preamble). It was the second attempt in the twentieth century to establish an international mechanism for peace and security by incorporating lessons learned from the first attempt, the ill-fated League of Nations. After debating extensively about its nature, structure and function, those delegates from fifty countries who gathered at the historic Opera House in San Francisco, California, unanimously adopted the Charter of this new international organization on 25 June 1945. On the following day, they held a signing ceremony at the Herbst Theatre auditorium of the Veterans' War Memorial Building next door (later, Poland was added to the group to make the official number of original members of the UN fifty-one). The 111-article Charter subsequently came into effect on 24 October, the day which is commemorated as 'UN Day'. Although the particular expression was not directly used in the languages of the Charter, the idea of *collective security* (and its fulfilment) was recognized as the essential goal of this world body. The UN Charter stresses that the main purpose of the organization is 'to maintain international peace and security', and 'to that end: to take effective collective measures for the prevention and removal of threats to the peace, and for the suppression of acts of aggression or other breaches of the peace, and acts of aggression' (Preamble, Chapter I, Article 1-1 and Chapter VII, among others). The creation of the UN, with the concept of collective security at its core, can be seen as a manifestation of an attempt at global governance.

Thousands of miles away, due west and southwest in the Pacific theatre, across the international date line, Japan was still at war with the Allied powers (also known as the 'United Nations') when the Charter of this global governance mechanism was signed. As the name represents, the United Nations Organization was founded on war-time alliance relations, which in itself was a realization of a 'collective security' mechanism against the aggressors. Obviously, Japan, as an Axis power, was one of those targets of the mechanism against which the new organization had had to be built. It was for this reason that the Charter maintained special provisions for the 'enemy states', against which the signatories of the Charter would be permitted to take necessary enforcement measures without explicit authorization from the Security Council (UNSC) 'for preventing further aggression by such a state' (Articles 53 and 107). As this episode clearly demonstrates, Japan's place in the UN at the very starting point of this organization was certainly not a positive one.

But a number of important events happened during the next sixty years, among which the transformation of Japan–UN relations can be seen as one of the most significant changes. Indeed, it was the story of an imperial power – a totalitarian 'Axis' power in East Asia – turned into a major democracy after the Second World War. The people of Japan believed that Japan's admission to the organization in December 1956 was the true international recognition of their country as a 'peace-loving state' (Article 4). Furthermore, by the year 2005, when the UN marked the 60th anniversary of its founding, Japan had long established itself has an indispensable power in the UN, the second largest financial contributor and a key candidate as a permanent member of the UNSC. Japan has transformed itself from the former aggressor state to a key member state of the organization and has aspired to find a place at its core decision-making body, the UNSC, which is the central organ of the UN's collective security apparatus.

In addition to these changes of Japan's relative and absolute status in the UN, although the Charter's 'former enemy' clause has not fully been revised, it is also important to recognize that the concept of collective security has significantly changed over time. In fact, the ideas of 'comprehensive collective security' – the key concept that the Report of the High-level Panel on Threats, Challenges and Change of December 2004 – and the pursuit of 'larger freedom' – the words that were highlighted in the title of the Secretary-General's Report for the UN Reform in March 2005 – underline the renewed as well as continuing relevance of the ideas of collective security in the UN, and its relevance in a global governance mechanism in today's context. Moreover, Japan's assertive candidacy for a permanent seat on the UNSC in 2005, though it did not materialize in that year for various reasons discussed later, can be interpreted as the demonstration of Tokyo's strong will to play its parts, both potential and actual, in the fulfilment of redefined collective security in the more contemporary global governance environment, in which the UN would prove to be an important forum.

Having laid out the overall changes in the understandings of collective security, and Japan's transformation within it, what is paradoxical from the contemporary global governance perspective is a sea change in the hitherto generally positive public perception in Japan of the UN. It has shown a serious downturn as the UN commemorates its 60th anniversary. The most direct cause was the Iraq War of 2003, when the US bypassed the process of UNSC authorization in engaging in its unilateral and even pre-emptive military actions against Iraq. The general public viewed the UN as helpless in avoiding the war. It was a serious disillusionment, which in itself was based on rather a naïve sense of idealism embedded in basic Japanese post-war perceptions of the UN. The Secretary-General's office quickly recognized the mood change. Kofi Annan's rather abrupt visit to Japan in February 2004 therefore had one specific purpose of preventing Japan, and the people of Japan for that matter, from further distancing themselves from the organization. The objective situation that surrounds the UN was unfavourable, too, when the debates for UNSC reform, as Annan himself admitted, had 'gone on for so long with so little progress' and the series of scandals within the UN, most notably the one that surrounded the 'Oil-for-Food' programme in Iraq, were unfolding (Annan 2004).

Against these backgrounds, this chapter analyses Japan's policies towards the UN and its related organizations, funds and programmes, during the last sixty-plus years and tries to identify the ideas and activities in which both the government and the people of Japan have made particular efforts to advance values that are relevant to global governance. For this purpose, the first section will revisit Japan's basic thinking behind its UN policies. The second section will assess Japan's policy innovations in the area related to the broadly defined area of collective security. The third section will discuss the role that Japan can play in global governance in the area of peace and security through the mechanisms of the UN.

Japan and the UN: their past and present

When the UN was established, both the government and the people of Japan viewed it as a major positive stride for peace in the war-torn international community. Here the discontinuity from the war period, and the image of a fresh start in the post-war era, was stressed both in the name and substance of the organization. As seen earlier, exactly the same name, 'United Nations' (*Rengōkoku*), which was originally coined by President Franklin D. Roosevelt to describe the war-time alliance against the Axis powers, was given to this world organization. But the Japanese name of the organization, which the Ministry of Foreign Affairs (MOFA) adopted after the defeat of the war and upon envisioning its re-entry into the post-war international community, was *Kokusai Rengō*, literally meaning the 'International Union' in English. By giving two different translations to the 'United Nations', it can be assumed that the post-war Japanese political leaders wanted to make an explicit disconnection with the past, and to explore joining the organization in a totally new context.

Japan's favourable view *vis-à-vis* the UN was moulded almost immediately after its defeat in the Second World War in 1945 when Japan found its future vision in the language of the UN Charter and particularly during its campaign to be a member of the organization. In those days, Japan equated its admission to the UN with its full return to the international community. Moreover, Japan made clear its commitment to subscribe to the spirit of the Charter in its Peace Constitution of 1947 even before its formal membership of the organization was granted in December 1956, and, upon its entry, designated *Kokuren chūshinshugi* (UN centrism) as one of the three principles of Japanese foreign policy in the spring of 1957, along with 'cooperation with the (Western) Liberal Camp' and 'membership in Asia'. With certain ups and downs, this was the basic orientation of Japan's policy during the cold war period.

After the end of the cold war, and particularly after the terrorist attacks against the US on 11 September 2001, many countries changed their priorities in foreign and national security policies. Japan was not an exception. Terrorism is by no means a new challenge to our society. But the incidents, with their magnitude of human deaths and material damage to the US, coupled with the overwhelming shock which was multiplied by the real-time television coverage of unfolding events, largely, if not completely, changed the international agenda. In fact, the opening of the general debate at the fifty-sixth session of the General Assembly of the UN was delayed exactly because of the dreadful crisis that took place in the city where the UN headquarters is located. The sessions were almost totally dominated by the question of anti-terrorism. Japan's head delegate, former Prime Minister Miyazawa Kiichi, also took up the subject and discussed Tokyo's strong determination to take a comprehensive approach to eliminate terrorism (Miyazawa 2001).

A year previously, when the world was not yet preoccupied with this daunting question, then-Prime Minister Mori Yoshirō stressed three points in his prepared remarks on the opening day of the UN's historic Millennium Summit in September 2000 (Mori 2000). First was the importance of 'human security', an approach in dealing with issues confronting the international community from a human-centred point of view. Second was the need for UN reform with particular reference to the need for the expansion of the UNSC's permanent and non-permanent members. During the address, Mori did not directly appeal for Japan's entry into a reformed UNSC as a permanent member although Japan's interest in this regard had long been expressed. Third was the government's plan to submit a new draft resolution on the elimination of nuclear weapons. Considering the time restraint of just five minutes allocated to each of the 190 delegations that gathered at the summit, there was no doubt that these were the three priority messages that Japan wanted to emphasize at the start of the new millennium. They were also indicative of the identity that Japan would be willing to pursue in international society at large and in the UN in particular.

Then, came the year 2005. Secretary-General Annan, in his report submitted to the General Assembly on 21 March, laid out the reform package in what he called 'a historic opportunity in 2005' (Annan 2005). The vision of Annan was eloquent:

> Five years into the new millennium, we have it in our power to pass on to our children a brighter inheritance than that bequeathed to any previous generation. We can halve global poverty and halt the spread of major known diseases in the next ten years. We can reduce the prevalence of violent conflict and terrorism. We can increase respect for human dignity in every land. And we can forge a set of updated international institutions to help humanity achieve these noble goals. If we act boldly – and if we act together – we can make people everywhere more secure, more prosperous and better able to enjoy their fundamental human rights.
>
> (Annan 2005)

Annan's initiative was ambitious in a sense that he wanted to make certain 'vital and achievable' advancements in the fields of development, security and human rights in a package, together with the institutional changes of the organization, most contentiously UNSC reform, all by the scheduled UN World Summit in New York in September 2005. In echoing the Secretary-General's reform efforts that culminated in the earlier report, and taking advantage of the momentum, Japan started its campaign for a permanent UNSC seat, the most direct and enthusiastic one ever. It began with Prime Minister Koizumi Junichirō's address at the fifty-ninth General Assembly in September 2004, in which he noted Japan's contributions in the fields of peace and security, economic and social issues, and he emphasized that '[we] believe that the role that Japan has played provides a solid basis for its assumption of permanent membership on the Security Council' (Koizumi 2004).

Japan has come a long way to secure its current position in international society. Certainly, Japan's bid for a permanent seat in the Security Council is not assured by any means. This is a fundamentally difficult task of changing the world's most powerful decision-making structure in peace-time by diplomacy. As history eloquently records, these drastic rule-changes in international power structures normally only take place after catastrophic world wars. Moreover, Japan's tactic, namely, the formation of a so-called Group of Four or G4, namely, collaboration with three other aspirant countries for permanent seats, Brazil, Germany and India, has been faced with challenges both from within and without.

With these developments aside, Japan's relationship with the UN has had many faces. In retrospect, the sixty years of its history can be divided into three periods. The first is from 1945 to 1956, the period during which Japan viewed the UN as a means for promoting its own individual (as opposed to collective) security interests. The second is from 1957 to 1989, during which the reality and integrity of Japan's pronounced 'UN centrism' were tested constantly under the rubric of the cold war. And the third is from 1990 until today, during which Japan began to actively become involved in the deliberation and implementation of the actions that support the 'maintenance of international peace and security'. All actions that Japan has taken were interpreted within the framework of its Peace Constitution. Nonetheless, just like the UN Charter is now under scrutiny in order to make it match reality, the Constitution of Japan is also undergoing the test of time.

The first period of Japan–UN relations dates back to the time of Japan's surrender to the Allied power (1945), followed by the nearly six-and-a half years of Occupation period and the eventual conclusion of the San Francisco Peace Treaty (1951), until its admission to the UN (1956). Japan submitted its application for entry to the UN as soon as the Peace Treaty took effect in April 1952. As noted earlier, Japan in those years equated its membership in the UN with its return to the international community from which it had been alienated since it unilaterally left the League of Nations in 1933. In the shadow of the cold war, however, the world was divided into the East and West blocs. Tokyo's main concern was, then, to explore the way to secure peace and security, not of the international community as a whole but of itself. Theoretically, there were at least five options that Japan considered for its own security, namely, autonomous defence, a Locarno Treaty-type international peace guarantee with neighbouring states, security through the UN, security through the US–Japan cooperation and permanent neutrality

(Hoshino 1995). It became a matter of real policy choice as the Allied Occupation period drew to a close.

Under the total demilitarization and disarmament mandated by the Occupation authority, the autonomous defence option was considered a non-starter. Neither was the conclusion of a peace treaty with all the Allied powers, including the Eastern bloc countries, while the stark cold war rivalry existed. Likewise, a permanent neutrality option was deemed unrealistic. The international peace guarantee option was considered inappropriate for an independent sovereign state. As a result, what was actually left for Japan were two options, namely, the security of Japan would be provided either through the UN or through the US–Japan cooperation. In the final analysis, maintaining Japan's security through the UN was also deemed impractical in the divided world of the cold war. It was for these reasons that Tokyo took a strategic decision to pursue US–Japan security arrangements. Prime Minister Yoshida Shigeru initiated this idea and sent his close associate, Finance Minister Ikeda Hayato, to Washington, under the official cover of an economic mission, to privately convey the message to Washington that Japan would be open to conclude a bilateral security agreement with the US which enabled the stationing of US forces on the soil of Japan even after the Occupation period expired. This is the genesis of the US–Japan Security Treaty. It was also a decision to place Japan firmly in the Western bloc. The war on the Korean Peninsula strongly motivated Tokyo and Washington to move closer to each other. Subsequently, Japan concluded the Peace Treaty in San Francisco on 8 September 1951, at the Opera House, incidentally the same location where the UN Charter was voted on six years earlier. No Eastern bloc countries joined the pact. Prime Minister Yoshida, the head delegate to the Peace Conference, left the Opera House later that day to a separate location in this city, the Presidio, to conclude the Security Treaty with the US. This time it was Yoshida alone who signed the document to show his determination to take full responsibility for his strategic choice of allying with the US.

It can be said that the first casualty of opting for the US–Japan alliance was Japan's bid for UN membership. By firmly tying itself to US strategy, Japan was repeatedly denied admission to the UN. The Soviet Union cast a veto three times to block the entry of Japan to the UN and it was only after the normalization of diplomatic relations between Tokyo and Moscow under the Hatoyama government (October 1956) that Moscow agreed to acquiesce in Japan's admission (December 1956).

As noted earlier, the Constitution of Japan (1947) clearly endorsed the overall spirit of the UN Charter (1945). Also recognized in the Constitution was the right of individual and collective self-defence, as stipulated in Article 51 of the Charter, on which the US–Japan Security Treaty (1951) was formed. And finally, the Security Treaty denoted in Article 10 that

> [t]his Treaty shall remain in force until in the opinion of the Governments of Japan and the United States of America there shall have come into force such United Nations arrangements as will satisfactorily provide for the maintenance of international peace and security in the Japan area.

In this way, three key documents that Japan adhered to in its post-Second World War formative years were interrelated both ideationally and institutionally. It is important to recognize their mutual complementarities. But at the same time, it is correct to believe that the main imperative on the part of Japan in this first period was its interest in protecting its own individual (as opposed to collective and international) peace and economic recovery.

The second period of Japan–UN relations covers the next thirty years, during which the reality and integrity of Japan's pronounced 'UN centrism' were constantly tested. The idea of 'UN centrism' first appeared in the Diet speech of Prime Minister Ishibashi Tanzan in February 1957, in which he said 'from now on, Japan should make it a basic principle of our diplomacy to contribute to world peace and prosperity, with the UN in its centre'. It did not take much time to formalize that this concept of 'UN centrism' was systematically incorporated into the three pillars of Japanese diplomacy, which was made public in the first-ever volume of the *Diplomatic Bluebook* of Japan published in March 1957 under Prime Minister Kishi Nobusuke, who succeeded Ishibashi.

'UN centrism' is an abstract idea. Moreover, it has never been officially defined. Naturally, much attention has been given to the actual weight of 'UN centrism' in the subsequent policy practices of Japan. One standard account looks at the weight given to the principle in comparison with the other two, namely, 'cooperation with the (Western) Liberal Camp' (*jiyūshugi jinei to no kyōchō*) and 'membership of Asia' (*Ajia no ichiin*) to find out what kind of gap exists between the rhetoric and reality of 'UN centrism'. Reinhard Drifte, for instance, conducted a survey of the official Japanese statements in the *Diplomatic Bluebooks* and foreign ministers' addresses spanning over thirty years and found, apart from the first two editions of the *Bluebook* in 1957 and 1958, that even the official position on 'UN centrism' became more critical and that it was not until 1989–90 that the term *Kokuren chūshinshugi* reappeared in foreign ministers' addresses, together with a variation of *Kokuren jūshi* (giving greater importance to the UN) concept (Drifte 2000). Drifte argues that the resurgence of the term around the 1989–90 timeframe particularly coincided with 'the endeavor of the government to smooth the discussion of the Peacekeeping Operations (PKO) bill' in the wake of the Gulf War, when Japan was trying to expand the scope of the hitherto financially oriented international contribution to a more physical one. It was also the time when Japan began to pursue explicitly an ambition to achieve a seat on the UNSC.

There was no doubt that Japan's first foreign and security policy priority would always be placed on the alliance with the US. Kishi himself was the proponent of strengthening this bilateral treaty, which was revised in 1960 to make it more effective. But on the UN front, Japan was far from inactive. In fact, Japan was first elected a non-permanent member of the UNSC as early as 1957, and then gained a seat on the Economic and Social Council in 1959. In addition to sending a judge to the International Court of Justice in 1960, Japan was successful in obtaining board membership of almost all specialized agencies by 1963. Certainly, Japan was not ready to respond positively to the request from Secretary-General Dag Hammarskjöld to dispatch its Self-Defence Forces (SDF) personnel to a peacekeeping mission in Lebanon in 1957. But Japan steadily broadened its contribution in the non-military sector. According to Akashi Yasushi, the first Japanese career UN official, who witnessed the development of Japan–UN relations over the years, Japan in the 1960s 'expanded its ground in the UN by learning multilateral diplomacy', in the 1970s 'faced difficulty in managing the relationship between Western developed countries and developing or non-aligned countries, as Japan was taking relatively accommodating approaches to developing world', and in the 1980s Japan promoted UN administrative and budgetary reform 'to restrain the institutional expansion from the position of positively recognizing the significance and roles of the UN system' (Akashi 2005: 24). It was a Japanese way of taking a middle ground role between the UN and the openly confrontational US which adamantly pressed for management reform of the organization.

It would be too much of an exaggeration to call Japan's UN policies during this period a realization of 'UN centrism' given the fact that the term itself was no longer widely articulated in its official discourse. Moreover, the international strategic environment of the cold war made it very difficult for Japan to take positions *other than* a US–Japan alliance-centred approach. Nonetheless, it would be correct to assume that Tokyo was fully cognizant of the significance of the UN and used it as an integral, if not a central, platform for Japan to play international roles, largely in non-military areas, well beyond the previous preoccupation of maintaining Japan's own security. The scope of Japan's internationalism began to widen as the cold war situation drew to a close in the late 1980s.

The third period in Japan–UN relations is the post-cold war and then post-9/11 periods. In these periods, Japan has gradually but substantially expanded its role in international peace and security. The first wave came in the wake of the Gulf Crisis/War of 1990–1. Because of the conspicuous absence of its physical participation in the coalition against Iraq, in spite of its huge amount of financial contributions (US$13 billion), Japan was exposed to severe international criticism. This traumatic experience led the political leaders to openly pursue the options to send Japanese personnel, preferably uniformed contingents, to troubled regions. Subsequently, the so-called International Peace Cooperation Law (or the PKO Law) was enacted in June 1992 and the SDF units were deployed to Cambodia and to Mozambique later that year. Japan, thereafter, became more proactive in dispatching the SDF overseas.

Over the years, the legal and administrative mechanisms that enabled the SDF to become generally more proactive were instituted. It was not so much a planned development as an event-driven one. Two lines of crises in the 1990s, national/regional ones, on the one hand, and international/global ones, on the other hand, triggered the trend. In post-cold war Northeast Asia, political developments on the Korean Peninsula and in China–Taiwan relations among others necessitated the upgrading of US–Japan defence cooperation. On the international/global security side, it was the crises caused by Iraq-related matters and the new challenges of international terrorism that stimulated Japan's legal response to the new situation. Two special measures laws were enacted for Japan to actively participate in international peace cooperation activities that were not covered by the International Peace Cooperation Law. The Anti-terrorism Special Measures Law authorized the Japanese Maritime SDF's dispatch to the Indian Ocean to supply fuel to the coalition vessels involved in the war against terrorism, and the Iraq Reconstruction Assistance Special Measures Law pertained to the activities of the Ground SDF in southern Iraqi city of Samawah for humanitarian and reconstruction missions.

The government of Japan stressed that all of these missions did not infringe upon the Constitutional restraints. No combat missions were involved, and no Japanese SDF were expected to operate in a combat zone. Having said this, however, the missions are conducted by Japanese troops for the purpose of enhancing international (and not national) peace and security. Though limited from the traditional viewpoint, they are the missions that can contribute to a 'collective security' interest broadly defined. In this connection, it should be pointed out that the government always made sure to obtain the authorization from the UN as a prerequisite of Japan's involvement in every overseas mission. Japan's participation in the humanitarian and reconstruction mission in Iraq may deserve special attention because Japanese troops acted as a part of the coalition force particularly after sovereignty was transferred to the local Iraqi transitional government. Since it was the first Japanese participation in the multinational force operating in an unstable foreign land, Tokyo took extra care to manoeuvre diplomatically at the UN Security Council, mainly through the US, in order to incorporate the specific mandate of humanitarian and reconstruction in the resolution so that the government of Japan can stress the legitimacy of SDF activities in the field.

In retrospect, the changing nature, mission and capabilities of Japan's UN policies can be characterized as the transformation from its own individual security to a collective but non-military security, further to a collective and military (but non-combat) security. In one respect, it can be viewed as the process of Japan's progressive approach to a traditionally defined collective military security. But as reflected in the 2004 report of the High-level Panel, it was the definition of the collective security concept itself that has been broadened to be more 'comprehensive' (UN 2004). By bringing these two directions together, it would be legitimate to expect that there will be sufficient ground where Japan's international policy and the UN's redefined concept of 'comprehensive collective security' can converge. And in view of their universality and fundamentality, the meeting points will most likely cover the important aspects of global governance in the contemporary world. So, in order to clarify these meeting points, the next section will review Japan's salient policy initiatives, both military and non-military, that may have close relevance to the global governance system.

Japan's policy innovation in the areas of international peace and security

For many years, the term 'collective security' has had an unpopular connotation for the people of Japan. The reason is its traditionally highly militaristic implications, which recognize military actions and the use of force even for the legitimate purpose of responding to aggressors. It is easy to find Japan's remorse towards, and its strong desire to distant itself from, the militarist and aggressive past. As a result, Japan's post-Second World War pacifist sentiment has created a unique atmosphere in Japan to take overly cautious, and even negative, views of the military establishment and its actions.

The Constitution of 1947, particularly Article 9, states that '[a]spiring sincerely to an international peace based on justice and order, the Japanese people forever renounce war as a sovereign right of the nation and the threat or use of force as means of settling international disputes.' The second paragraph of the same article says that '[i]n order to accomplish the aim of the preceding paragraph, land, sea, and air forces, as well as other war potential, will never be maintained.' This wording, originally drafted by the American Occupation force after the war but deeply accepted by the people of Japan, has made it very difficult to justify the status of its military, namely, the Ground, Maritime, and Air Self-defence Forces. The official government explanation stresses the exclusively defensive nature of the mission of these forces as opposed to full-fledged armed forces. But this sort of interpretation did not prevent the leftist parties from questioning the government's position, together with their criticism against the US–Japan security alliance that, they said, could entrap Japan in unwanted wars.

In recent years, however, those critical and ideological sentiments, which were rather loudly expressed during the cold war period by left wingers, were replaced by a more 'real' sense of security, mainly driven by the series of threats primarily originating from North Korea and China. The Pyongyang government's test launch of a long-range Taepodong missile, its involvement in the abduction of Japanese nationals and the repeated infiltration by its spy ships are the salient examples that exacerbated the Japanese sense of insecurity regarding this dictatorial state. Moreover, China's rise and its rapid pace of military modernization without much transparency concerns many Japanese, together with the series of disputes over many bilateral political issues ranging from history-related ones (such as Japanese history textbooks and Prime Minister Koizumi's controversial visit to Yasukuni shrine), to territorial and resource-related ones in the East China Sea.

The level of public acceptance of the US–Japan alliance has increased. In fact, today, the security alliance is generally considered a prerequisite to discussion of both the defence posture and policies of Japan. While the relocation and realignment of US forces and installations in Japan, particularly the question of relocating the US Marine Corps Futenma Air Station in Okinawa and other controversial plans in the wake of the US Global Posture Review process, have caused concern in the local municipalities, there is a basic understanding about the *raison d'être* of the alliance. Two recent exceptions to the rule are the increased sense of alarm in the cities that host US bases for fear of collateral damage due to terrorist attacks after 9/11, on the one hand, and the opposition to the Bush administration's decision to go to war in Iraq, on the other hand.

Against these and more real security policy backgrounds, how has Japan developed its policies towards international, as opposed to the more national, peace and security arena? There are four key policy areas: (1) the SDF's overseas activities; (2) disarmament, arms control and non-proliferation; (3) human security; and (4) official development assistance (ODA) with a focus on peace building. Many of the policies hitherto taken under these four areas may not have been coordinated, but they are indeed inter-connected, and have a potential to restore peace and stability in the country which experienced severe internal conflict. As will be discussed later, these are the steps that can open the avenue for Japan to make an effective contribution to 'collective security' in its broader sense.

First, on the SDF's overseas activities, as discussed in the previous section, Japan's proactive participation in what Japan calls 'international peace cooperation' opened the avenue for both civilian and SDF personnel to join UN authorized or UN requested activities. In the Japanese context, the term 'international peace cooperation' activities is defined in the International Peace Cooperation Law of 1992, and its subsequent revisions, to include peacekeeping operations international humanitarian relief operations and election support operations. Although they were revised later-on, the main assignments for the SDF's ground troops were 'frozen' at the time of enacting the law, even though those tasks were considered doable within the framework of the Peace Constitution of Japan.

These are certainly welcome developments. The fact of the matter is that, however, in this term 'international peace cooperation', Japan's participation, in the form of logistical support (fuel supply in the Indian Ocean), in support of Operation Enduring Freedom to fight against terrorism in Afghanistan, and its role in Iraq in the form of humanitarian and reconstruction assistance, were not included. Legally speaking, they were considered outside the purview of the International Peace Cooperation Law, because both of the SDF's activities were related to the coalition forces rather than UN-sanctioned ones, so that two new special measures laws, one on anti-terrorism (for Afghanistan operation) and the other on humanitarian and reconstruction assistance (for activities in Iraq), have had to be enacted while the latter two activities can legitimately occupy a place in the concept of international peace cooperation. (The latter activity was first conducted as a part of the US-led coalition forces, but after the return of Iraqi sovereignty to the local interim government, SDF troops became part of the multinational forces for the first time in Japanese history.) Moreover, the dispatch of the SDF overseas in the context of the US–Japan security alliance to respond to more regional contingencies, though there have been no instance of this sort, is legislated separately. In view of these separate and somewhat confusing legal structures, an effort has been made to systematize the procedure to approve the dispatch of the SDF for overseas missions.

Second, in the field of disarmament, arms control and non-proliferation, Japan's focus is twofold. One is its leadership on the issue of nuclear disarmament and non-proliferation. Japan, as the only country which has the direct experiences of suffering from nuclear devastations in Hiroshima and Nagasaki, has put on the agenda the eventual elimination of nuclear weapons. This position has the potential to contradict Japan's alliance with the US, particularly when Japan relies on the US nuclear umbrella. But by combining the efforts to promote the non-proliferation of weapons of mass destruction and the reduction of reliance on nuclear deterrence, Japan and the US have been exploring common and overlapping interests.

The other focus is on the control of conventional weapons. Here, Japan has taken a leadership role in two sub-areas: the system of UN registery of conventional arms, on the one hand, and small arms and light weapons, on the other hand. The former was launched in 1992 as a joint Japan-the then-European Community (EC) project, which is aimed at improving arms transparency and openness of arms transfer by encouraging UN members to disclose export/import figures in seven categories of equipment, namely, battle tanks, armoured combat vehicles, large-calibre artillery systems, combat aircraft, attack helicopters, warships and missiles/missile launchers. The latter is an initiative to control conventional weapons but much smaller in size, namely, assault rifles, pistols and submachine guns. These weapons, though they may be 'small' or 'light' in appearance, constitute a new concern for the world as a huge number of them are actually used in civil wars to take out the lives of millions of people. Japan has been taking a leading role in tackling the issue of small arms and light weapons by putting forward the UN General Assembly resolutions on this matter since 1995, by establishing two UN Governmental Groups of Experts on Small Arms, and by making financial contribution of over US$3.5 million in support of UN activities in this area.

Third, Japan has been actively promoting the idea of 'human security' mainly in terms of coping with human suffering that easily transcends national borders. While the term 'human security' has been around for a while, Japan promotes a unique perspective, as described by Prime Minister Obuchi Keizō who said in his Hanoi speech in December 1998, 'human security' is 'a concept that takes a comprehensive view of all threats to human survival, life and dignity and stresses the need to respond to such threats' (Obuchi 1998a; Hoshino 2002). In this speech, Obuchi announced Japan's decision to contribute 500 million yen (approximately US$4.2 million) for the establishment of the 'Human Security Fund' under the UN to provide support not just for recovery from the economic crisis that Asian countries had experienced in 1997–8 but also for more medium-to-longer-term problems. His successor, Prime Minister Mori, further added to the fund in September 2000, as announced in his address at the UN Millennium Summit.

The concept of human security has subsequently been refined and elaborated through the works of the Commission on Human Security, jointly headed by Ogata Sadako, former UN High Commissioner for Refugee, and Nobel Prize winning economist, Amartya Sen (Commission on Human Security 2003). The bottom line of the commission report was to focus on 'protection' and 'empowerment' of people under extremely harsh situations by ensuring their 'freedom from fear' and 'freedom from want'. The idea of focusing on human 'freedoms' has largely affected and guided the overall discourse of UN reform as evidenced in the title of the Secretary-General's report of March 2005, *In Larger Freedom*, in which the needs were identified to promote 'freedom from want' (development), 'freedom from fear' (peace and security) and 'freedom to live in dignity' (human rights) (Annan 2005). Here, although it is not directly mentioned, it is the basic idea of 'human security' that enabled the integrative approach of bringing together three policy areas (peace and security, development and human rights).

The language of 'human security', which takes people as the referent of security (as opposed to national governments), has not necessarily been well-received by many member states of the UN as it could undermine their basic adherence to sovereign rights. In this regard, it was an important step forward to note that world leaders agreed, with the active persuasion of Japan, to incorporate a paragraph on human security in the World Summit Outcome Document (UN 2005). This was the first time that the term was explicitly written into an official UN document. It recognized that 'all individuals, in particular vulnerable people, are entitled to freedom from fear and freedom from want, with an equal opportunity to enjoy all their rights and fully develop their potential', and the member states pledged to 'commit ourselves to discussion and defining the notion of human security in the General Assembly' (UN 2005). The introduction of the concept of 'human security' will have other implications that help expand the scope of the concept of collective security, which primarily dealt with national security challenges in a collective manner (namely, collective *national* security), to include actions to tackle human security challenges also by collective means (namely, collective *human* security). This sort of conceptual expansion will certainly give more room for Japan to utilize its resources.

Fourth, Japan's ODA policy has to be put into perspective in this context. As is widely known, Japan considers its ODA a prime tool of international contribution. A certain set of approaches has been identified as the Japanese way of extending ODA that stresses the self-help efforts and local initiatives of the recipient countries. This approach has then been adopted in the international arena as a 'new development strategy', an effort to combine the ownership of the developing world and partnership of the developed world to comprehensively pursue development assistance and market-oriented economy. It was Obuchi who introduced the concept of a 'new development strategy' in his statement at the Fifty-third Session of the General Assembly of the UN in 1998 entitled 'Toward achieving peace, development, and United Nations reform' (Obuchi 1998b).

Probably one of the key challenges for Japan to increase the effectiveness of its ODA was to utilize it not just for social and economic development but for broader stability and peace in the recipient countries. It was 1992 when Japan formulated the ODA Charter to take into account the post-cold war international situation and the government's new policy priorities. Then, as noted earlier, in 1998, Japan introduced the concept of 'human security' in ODA policy in its response to the Asian financial crisis. Next came an attempt to connect its development assistance with other policy objectives such as conflict prevention, emergency humanitarian assistance, and post-conflict recovery and reconstruction. The 'Action from Japan on Conflict and Development' document was released in July 2000, marking a new willingness on the part of the Japanese government to overcome the traditional policy divides between development and conflict management. It was an element of policy innovation that Japan put forward when it hosted the G8 Summit meetings in Kyūshū and Okinawa. This approach was subsequently incorporated into the concept of 'peace consolidation and nation-building', a policy idea that Koizumi stressed at his speech in Sydney in May 2002 (Koizumi 2002). This speech was instrumental in the process of revising the ODA Charter, and the new Charter, released in 2003, included 'peacebuilding' as one of the formal priorities together with poverty reduction, sustainable development and addressing global issues. (These new steps were further elaborated in the 'ODA Medium-term Policy' documents of February 2005.)

With regard to the past practice of Japan's ODA policies, it is useful to recognize its renewed focus in Africa as most vividly shown in the Tokyo International Conference on African Development (TICAD) project. Japan has hosted three conferences over the past decade and demonstrated its willingness to extend economic assistance well beyond the traditional geographic scope of Asia. Also, beyond the conventional focus on socio and economic development, Japan has expressed its interest in incorporating conflict prevention and peacebuilding factors as well as the aforementioned 'human security' focus.

Japan's ODA will continue to play a key role in its foreign policy but problems remain. The biggest among them are financial resources and public support, both of which have contracted over the years against the background of Japan's economic difficulties. The good news is that the slow but steady recovery of the Japanese economy, which may not immediately allow Tokyo to increase the amount of its ODA to the internationally stressed level of 0.7 per cent of GDP (the level of Japan's ODA in GDP ratio was 0.2 per cent in 2005), is providing an impetus to reverse the trend and encourage the more dynamic use of ODA.

Having seen the policy developments of Japan in the earlier four areas, namely, SDF's overseas activities; disarmament, arms control and non-proliferation; human security; and ODA with a renewed peacebuilding focus, it seems that the basic 'tools' exist. What is necessary next is to explore the way to combine these tools to form a strategy for Japan to effectively promote global governance in the area of international security. The next section will look at the possible steps to bring together these policy tools under the rubric of 'comprehensive collective security'.

Japan's position in a comprehensive collective security system

No term is more symbolic than 'collective security' in portraying the trans-formation of Japan from the aggressive 'enemy', that is, one of the target states of the Second World War collective security mechanism of the 'United Nations', to a peace-loving and even major peace-contributing member of the post-war universal international inter-governmental organization for collective security, the United Nations. Today, the policy tools that Japan has been accumulating are indeed relevant to what may be called a 'comprehensive collective security'.

The term 'comprehensive collective security' can be found in the High-level Panel Report, *A More Secure World: Our Shared Responsibility* (UN 2004). In it, Secretary-General Kofi Annan endorsed the report's 'core arguments for a broader, more comprehensive concept of collective security: one that tackles new and old threats and addresses the security concerns of all States – rich and poor, weak and strong' (para. 5). The reasons that the High-level Panel focused their attention on the utility of both the comprehensive and collective aspects of contemporary security means are obvious. One is certainly related to the inter-connectedness of threats that plague our society. The report identified six clusters of threats, namely, economic and social threats (including poverty, infectious diseases and environmental degradation), inter-state conflict, internal conflict (including civil war, genocide and other large-scale atrocities), nuclear, radioactive, chemical and biological weapons, terrorism and transnational organized crime. As they affect the security of state and human beings in a comprehensive manner, the means to respond to them have to be comprehensive and collective. The other is unilateralism led mainly by the US in its response to Iraq. The military action the US took in March 2003 was not authorized by the UNSC due to the division among the permanent members over the interests, evidence and rationality in justifying military solution. The UN, which was created to 'take effective collective measures' (Article 1-1) for the maintenance of international peace and security, not just lost its face but was physically attacked. The terrible bombing of the UN headquarters in Baghdad on 19 August 2003 was one of the most tragic examples.

The original and traditional idea of collective security was to respond to military aggression by one state against another state, which constitutes a violation of that victim state's national sovereignty, with the means, including military enforce-ment under UN authorization, which are conducted collectively as an expression of the disapproval of the rest of the world. The necessity of this approach remains today as most vividly practiced in the international response to Iraq's invasion of Kuwait in 1990, which brought about the multinational forces' military action against Baghdad in 1991. But given the multidimensional and inter-connected nature of the issues that threaten both national sovereignty and human life and dignity, collective and comprehensive responses, in which a military option is a necessary factor but not always a sufficient one, have to be employed. And the collective efforts, among which the most legitimate are those that are anchored to the UN, to secure peace in this globalized world can be considered a manifes-tation of global governance.

Where, then, can Japan find its place in this global governance of comprehensive collective security? In fact, there are many ways. Although direct military means are restricted by the Constitution, Japan has a set of tools to take an effective part in an entire collective effort to bring peace to the states in trouble or the people under severe suffering. The four areas of policies, the SDF's overseas missions, disarmament-related efforts and expertise, human security-focus and the dynamic use of ODA for peace consolidation, can be combined in a variety of creative ways. While its long aspiration of becoming a permanent member of the UNSC has met an unfortunate deadlock, Japan can make a difference. Playing a leading role in the UN Peacebuilding Commission, which was created as a result of intense reform debates on the UN's 60th anniversary year in 2005, is a good place to start, while it is still necessary to skill up its political mediation role and start involving itself at the early stage of peacemaking as the process of building peace, contrary to the general perception, does not start at the conclusion of a peace agreement. It is important to recognize that to make an effective contribution to global governance in the areas of peace and security, efforts begin at a very local level of conflict management, resolution and reconciliation in a solid and sustainable manner.

References

Akashi, Yasushi (2005) 'Kokuren kamei kara anpori jōnin rijikoku e', *Gaikō Fōramu,* August: 22–7.

Annan, Kofi (2004) 'The Secretary-General's address to the Japanese parliament', 24 February. Available on-line at: http://www.un.org/apps/sg/sgstats.asp?nid = 789, accessed on 26 June 2006.

—— (2005) *In Larger Freedom: Towards Development, Security and Human Rights for All: Report of the Secretary-General*, UN Document A/59/2005. Available on-line at: http://daccessdds.un.org/doc/UNDOC/GEN/N05/270/78/PDF/N0527078.pdf?OpenElement, accessed on 26 June 2006.

Commission on Human Security (2003) *Human Security Now.* Available on-line at: http://www.humansecurity-chs.org/finalreport/English/FinalReport.pdf, accessed on 26 June 2006.

Drifte, Reinhard (2000) *Japan's Quest for a Permanent Security Council Seat: A Matter of Pride or Justice?*, London: Macmillan.

Hoshino, Toshiya (1995) 'Nihon no anzenhoshō to kokuren: bai no sentaku, maruchi no sentaku', in Umemoto Tetsuya and Kusano Atsushi (eds) *Gendai Nihon Gaikō no Bunseki*, Tokyo: Tokyo Daigaku Shuppankai, pp. 2–30.

—— (2002) 'Ningen no anzenhoshō to Nihon no kokusai seisaku', *Kokusai Anzenhoshō*, 30, 3: 9–25.

Koizumi, Junichirō (2002) 'Japan and Australia toward a creative partnership: speech at the Asia Society Dinner, Sydney Australia', 1 May. Available on-line at: http://www.mofa.go.jp/region/asia-paci/pmv0204/speech.html, accessed on 26 June 2006.

—— (2004) 'Address at the fifty-ninth session of the general assembly of the United Nations: a new United Nations for the new era', 21 September. Available on-line at: http://www.mofa.go.jp/policy/un/adress0409.html, accessed on 26 June 2006.

Miyazawa, Kiichi (2001) 'Statement by H.E. Mr Kiichi Miyazawa: taking a comprehensive approach to the elimination of terrorism', 11 November. Available on-line at: http://www.mofa.go.jp/policy/un/assembly2001/state.html, accessed on 26 June 2006.

Mori, Yoshirō (2000) 'Statement by H.E. Mr Yoshiro Mori at the Millennium Summit of the United Nations', 7 September. Available on-line at: http://www.mofa.go.jp/policy/un/summit2000/pmstate.html, accessed on 26 June 2006.

Obuchi, Keizō (1998a) 'Toward the creation of a bright future for Asia: a policy speech at the lecture program hosted by the Institute of International Relations, Hanoi, Vietnam', 16 December. Available on-line at: http://www.infojapan.org/region/asia-paci/asean/pmv9812/policyspeech.html, accessed on 26 June 2006.

—— (1998b) 'Statement at the Fifty-third Session of the General Assembly of the United Nations: toward achieving peace, development and United Nations reform', 21 September. Available on-line at: http://www.mofa.go.jp/announce/announce/1998/9/921.html, accessed on 26 June 2006.

UN (2004) *A More Secure World: Our Shared Responsibility – Report of the High-level Panel on Threats, Challenges and Change*, 2 December. UN Document A/59/565. Available on-line at: http://www.un.org/secureworld/report.pdf, accessed on 26 June 2006.

—— (2005) *2005 World Summit Outcome*, 24 October, UN Document A/RES/60/1. Available on-line at: http://unpan1.un.org/intradoc/groups/public/documents/UN/UNPAN021752.pdf, accessed on 26 June 2006.

Conclusion
The meaning of global governance
Andrew Gamble

Introduction

Global governance has become a new organizing idea in political science and international politics all over the world. Many recent books and articles in Japan and Britain have been devoted to it. It is attractive to so many scholars because it brings together two voluminous literatures, on globalization and on governance, suggesting that the insights of the two can be combined in a new synthesis. But its meaning is hard to pin down, and the more that it is used the harder that becomes. There is a danger as with so many political concepts that global governance becomes such a contested term that it no longer refers to anything precise. At the same time it is continually invoked as a shorthand in political debate and political analysis which implies that it does have a clear meaning. But before we can start using the term 'global governance' we need to confront some of the issues which the use of this term raises. This chapter seeks to clear some of the ground in thinking about global governance by posing some basic questions.

Does global governance exist?

There is a good case for arguing that it does not. The term implies the existence of something that is truly 'global' rather than merely national or international, and which requires 'governing'. It has been criticized from two broad directions, one realist, one neo-liberal. Realists argue that there is no such thing as a global economy or global civil society. There is instead an international state system which divides the world into separate jurisdictions (Hirst and Thompson 1996; Zysman 1996). States negotiate and co-operate and conflict, but ultimately the character of politics is at best international rather than global; it is always mediated through states (Gilpin 1987; Tsuchiyama 2000). Economies are primarily national spaces, governed by local rules and institutions, rather than part of a supranational space. Governance does exist but it is predominantly national in character. Where supranational institutions appear to exist, on closer inspection these turn out to be the result of intergovernmental bargaining, and are only sustained by the will and resources of national governments.

A rather different objection is made by neo-liberals. They have no doubt that a global economy exists, but they reject the notion that it has to be governed by anybody. Their global economy is a global market, a spontaneous order, which works best when it is left alone, spreading prosperity, growth and development around the world. National jurisdictions frequently create obstacles to the global market, and more often than not hinder the creation of wealth. Keeping governance strictly limited to the core functions of internal and external security, enforcement of laws on property and contract and the provision of sound money are what is required. Anything beyond that threatens the basic foundations of a market order (Hayek 1960). These functions are necessary and are best provided locally. Any attempt to provide them at the global level risks creating regulatory authorities which will attempt to intervene too much and will damage the working of the global market. All the global market requires to succeed is the free movement of goods, capital and people. The last thing it needs is the creation of a political space which allows intervention in the way it operates.

Any analysis of global governance must first surmount these two objections. It has to assert that there is a global phenomenon, such as a global economy or global civil society or global ideology, in which the term global is not merely decorative, but denotes a substantive reality. This does not mean that the global phenomenon whatever it is has to be fully formed; it may be in the process of developing. But it has clearly to exist as a level or space which is distinct from other levels and spaces, whether regional, national or local. Second, any such analysis has to make the claim that this global level, however it is conceived, requires governance, not on normative grounds but as a matter of fact (Payne 2005a). This is a fundamental point, and one which is contested. Does an economy or a society have to be governed either through a state or other institutions? Should we conceive of economies and societies as self-governing, as spontaneous orders or catallaxies which do not require to be planned or steered by institutions external to them? Or are they always embedded in such external institutions, on which they depend for their survival?

The important insight of the literature on governance is that the process of governing can be separated from the particular institution of government (Pierre and Peters 2000). Governance refers therefore to the steering capacities of a political system, the ways in which governing is carried out, but leaves it open as to which agents and institutions are responsible for the steering. What is implied in the use of the term is that governance is integral to the functioning of any social system, not an optional extra, as some neo-liberal analyses apply. This is because the notion of governance has two key aspects; it comprises first a set of fundamental laws, rules and standards – the ordering principles which provide the constitutional framework for governing; and second, a set of techniques, tools and practices which define how governing is carried out. Neo-liberals can accept the need for these two aspects of governance but argue that both can be supplied internally through markets themselves. The more the global market can be self-governing and self-regulating the better it will perform. The more it is invaded by the practices and institutions of 'global governance' the more sluggish it will become. But for those who take the perspective of global governance this is a false opposition. Global governance is not optional, but is a necessary aspect of the capitalist world economy, reflecting the way in which that economy and society have been constituted. Its modes, institutions and procedures determine such things as the division of powers, the representation of interests, the locus of decision-making, the limits within which power is exercised, the boundary between public and private, and the objectives of policy.

One way of understanding the debate between the partisans of global governance and their critics is to relate it to different conceptions of world order which are associated with the three positions. The realists hold a territorial conception of world order, which treats sovereign states as the basic building block of the international state system. The world economy is not a global economy but an international economy, mediated through the separate and independent jurisdictions of nation-states. The order that becomes established depends on the calculations made by nation-states of the advantages to themselves to be derived from co-operation rather than conflict (Bull 1977). A balance of power may result which ensures reasonable stability, although it is a stability which is always fragile and capable of being undermined, because states can at any time review their interests and decide they are not being well served by current arrangements. So long as they see their interests being served, however, states will co-operate, and quite extensive forms of interdependence may arise. But their foundation remains the interest of the states in preserving their territorial security. From this perspective national control can always be reasserted and powers that have been pooled or shared can be restored. The state may choose to permit free movement of goods and capital and even people, but this is always conditional, and in extreme circumstances the powers can be revoked.

Neo-liberals offer a complete contrast, since they hold a cosmopolitan conception of world order, which emphasizes not state sovereignty but market sovereignty. Their basic claim, which is both empirical and normative, is that the state and politics are subordinate to the way in which the economy is organized. The market supplies the ordering principles for both economy and society. The rise of the global market is regarded as the key development in the construction of modernity, because it allowed the development of an interdependent system of global production and exchange which escaped the control of states and national jurisdictions and became an overarching reality to which states found they had to adjust. Their autonomy was undermined and circumscribed by the global market. States and the separate jurisdictions associated with them have not disappeared or been destroyed, but the global market has created powers, resources, networks and institutions which constantly reach beyond them and tower over them. States find they cannot reject the constraints which markets place upon them without destroying the conditions for the economic growth and prosperity of the territories they control, and with that the fiscal basis for their own existence. The ordering principle in this conception lies in the logic of markets rather than the instrumental calculus of state interest.

The global governance perspective incorporates aspects of both the territorial and the cosmopolitan conceptions, but transcends them. It is primarily concerned with the political conditions of world order (Archibugi and Held 1995). It accepts the reality of the global economy which the neo-liberals so eloquently describe, but at the same time notes the persistence of the international state system, and the necessity for the global market to be embedded in non-market institutions and practices. It asks the question how are the institutions and the functions which the global market requires provided? Who provides them? And in whose interests are they provided?

This conception of order may be termed hegemonic, because it examines the forms of governance which have emerged and which are emerging in the global economy and in global society, and which however imperfectly and unevenly provide a set of ordering principles to tackle the problems thrown up by the tensions between an increasingly interdependent global economy and global civil society, and the continuing fragmentation of political rule (Wallerstein 1974). Hegemony has in the past been associated with the existence of a hegemon, a sovereign state which by virtue of its economic, financial and military predominance exercises rule-making functions for the global economy and society. But such periods of dominance have tended to be short, because rivals arise to challenge the hegemon, and because the hegemon is caught in a perpetual tension between pursuit of its own interests and acting in the interests of the system as a whole. At particular times Wallerstein and others have argued that the existence of a hegemonic state has been a key factor in providing the conditions which enable expansion, prosperity and profitability in the global economy, the peaceful movement of peoples and transfer of technologies. But such times are unusual. In future it is unlikely that one state will be able or willing to assume the role of hegemon. What is emerging instead are collective forms of hegemony, centred on key transnational institutions such as the World Trade Organization (WTO), Internationl Monetary Fund (IMF) and World Bank (Wilkinson 2000).

The term hegemony has a number of meanings associated with it, and there are both strong and weak senses. In the weak sense the hegemon is simply the dominant power able to impose its leadership on others. In the strong sense the power of the hegemon becomes authority, and is exercised through consent. This latter kind of hegemony is always likely to be more durable because its roots lie both in ideological legitimation of what the hegemon does, and also in the accommodation of the interests of those over whom rule is exercised. Global governance to be successful has to aspire to hegemony in this sense. It has to find a means of ideological legitimation which make its purposes and its methods appear legitimate, and it has to be flexible enough to make concessions to accommodate the vital interests of the ruled (Cox 1987). One of the key issues in analysing global governance is to estimate the extent to which the institutions and agents of global governance are coming to be accepted as legitimate authorities for an embryonic global polity, or by contrast are seen as little more than the agents of dominant powers. This relates in particular to the third question discussed.

Is global governance new?

If global governance exists, it follows that it cannot be new. It must have existed at least as long as the modern world system has existed; it cannot have been invented in the last twenty years. The political conditions for order in a world system characterized by increasing global economic interdependence and fragmented political rule have common features that stretch back to the beginnings of the modern period, and certainly to the period of the last 200 years. There have of course been important developments and changes in that time, but the basic problematic of global governance is still recognizable. What is apparent however in recent decades is that the institutionalization of global governance has been gathering pace.

This argument also entails that globalization itself is not new. The capitalist world economy since the sixteenth century inaugurated trends towards cultural, political, ideological, economic and racial homogenization – the creation of one world. Progress towards this has been very uneven, and is unlikely ever to be complete. This reflects the fact that globalization is not an uncontrollable force of nature but a specific set of practices and discourses, of which global governance is one (Hay and Marsh 2000). From the beginning globalization has been constituted and propelled by politics, in particular by those nation-states which have been economically and politically by dominant in particular periods.

Territorial, cosmopolitan and hegemonic conceptions of world order are both alternative ways of thinking about the capitalist world economy, as well as necessary components of it, reflecting its different and interrelated aspects. In different periods one or other of these conceptions may be in the ascendancy, as territorial conceptions undoubtedly were in the 1930s, and have been increasing in importance again post 9/11. In a purely territorial vision of world order small states would fear absorption by large states, through conquest and territorial expansion. This was after all how all the large states were formed, even the two island empires, Britain and Japan, emerging as single states after centuries of internal warfare and territorial aggrandizement (Tsuzuki 2000; Gamble 2003); it was the basis of the rapacious European colonial empires, the consolidation of the jurisdiction of the United States over the greater part of the landmass of North America, the Napoleonic conquests in Europe and the German project of MittlelEuropa. Territorial ambitions of states have often known no limit, only checked by the countervailing power of rivals. The territorial principle of world order conceives an order that is inherently fragile, and always liable to break down, since no state can be certain that it is secure in the possession of its territory. Taken to its extreme the territorial principle therefore points to perpetual conflict unless and until it is superseded by the emergence of a single world empire, and the creation of a central world authority.

States do well to survive in a world ruled by the territorial principle, but they are also threatened by the cosmopolitan principle. A cosmopolitan order is one which breaks down boundaries and overwhelms separate jurisdictions, and therefore potentially destroys the capacities which all states, but particularly smaller states, require to preserve their separate and diverse institutions and policies, and so leads to convergence. A cosmopolitan order is central to the discourse of globalization, with its emphasis on the benefits of free exchange and free movement. It is not possible to imagine the contemporary world system without the cosmopolitan principle, but by itself it is not a sufficient principle of order any more than the territorial principle is. Only the hegemonic principle, when it is realized in institutions of global governance, can ensure a proper balance between the territorial and the cosmopolitan principles, and create the political space to give small states some autonomy.

The hegemonic principle, however, and global governance are not necessarily benign. They are easily perverted, and have often been associated with oppressive and asymmetrical relationships. If the hegemon is a single large state it will have territorial or other political ambitions of its own, and the nature of the hegemonic institutions that evolve is likely to be highly imperfect, and certainly unrepresentative of most of the states in the world system, and not accountable in any democratic sense (Held 2004). Global governance has been an important part of the world economy for 200 years, but it has been highly dependent first on Britain and then on the United States. There has been continuity between the two, so that it is possible to speak of 'Anglo-America' as the most powerful determinant of the way the system of global governance has evolved, because these two states have actively encouraged the development of a liberal, cosmopolitan order, and have done so partly by establishing rules and norms for such an order, and partly by holding in check territorial claims of other states. Britain's period of hegemony was marked by the simultaneous pursuit of an informal cosmopolitan empire alongside a formal territorial empire. British policy was always pulled in two directions, but the more important legacy of British hegemony was the cosmopolitan empire, the empire of trade. The opportunity for this to develop to the extent it did in the nineteenth century owed much to the successful breakaway of the American colonies from Britain's territorial empire.

US hegemony has been on a quite different scale to the British. After 1945 the United States rebuilt the institutions of the liberal world order which Britain had established, only this time the claims have been more universal, less compromised by the direct possession of a territorial empire, or the harbouring of specific territorial claims. What this liberal order has permitted is the creation of conditions for the flourishing of a large number of small and relatively autonomous states; respect for the territorial principle and national self-determination (where this did not conflict with US security or economic interests) conferred sovereignty and territorial jurisdiction upon a wide range of states, while the maintenance of a (relatively) open system of trade and finance offered opportunities for states to adjust their domestic policies to take full advantage of them (Katzenstein 1985). The spur which economic openness provided to these states was the result of the conditions which US hegemony established. But territorial sovereignty was also key.

This postwar constellation appeared threatened in the 1980s and 1990s by the new imperatives of globalization. But globalization has to be understood in its proper historical context. It is a particular discourse and a particular political project, the latest project indeed of Anglo-America for maintaining its 200-year-old hegemony and ensuring that the world economy continues to be governed by liberal rules and objectives. Globalization is only the latest doctrine that has been used to promote the virtues and advantages of a liberal world order. The international

Keynesianism of Bretton Woods, or the free trade doctrines of the nineteenth century are earlier examples (Gilpin 1987). The new policy doctrines in the discourse of globalization emerged in the 1970s, mainly in the United States and Britain, and quickly became established in the main agencies of global governance, the financial markets and the networks of transnational capital. By the 1980s aided by two like-minded ideological regimes in the United States and Britain, led by Reagan and Thatcher, they became crystallized in the Washington consensus.

The significance of this for other states is that the globalization discourse first emerged in a bid by the governing institutions of the postwar order to re-establish control of how states responded to the financial crises and economic recessions of the new era. In particular, the governing institutions wanted to discourage protectionism and any retreat to closed blocs or autarchy. At the same time the purpose of globalization was also to take the attack to those countries, particularly Japan, who were seen as free-riding on the liberal world order by not opening their domestic markets sufficiently to goods from the rest of the world. By proposing new trade rules the aim was to recast the basis of the liberal world order in a way which served the interests of the United States rather better than it had in the past, when the United States had been prepared to take more sacrifices in the interests of rebuilding the liberal world order and containing communism. Japan had indeed benefited greatly from the postwar liberal trading order, and had emerged as the second most important industrial power and a major financial power. But the Japanese were very reluctant to accede to the demands of the United States to open their markets, fearing that this could lead to the destruction of key features of the Japanese model which had served them so well in the postwar era (Weiss 1998; Dore 2000). Yet at the same time Japan, although a full member of the G8, appeared reluctant to take on wider responsibilities for managing the global system, or to reshape the institutional pattern of US hegemony, for fear of disrupting the international order which had served it so well (Lincoln 1993).

The emergence of modern forms of economy, state and society in the last 200 years provides the historical context for understanding contemporary forms of global governance: the creation of market economies and clearly defined property rights, the widening and deepening of the division of labour, the exploitation of new technologies, making possible a cumulative advance in living standards, the establishment of the state as an independent public power, the elaboration of the institutions and organizations of civil society, and the breakdown of local regional self-sufficiency through the emergence of a global economy.

It is the complex structure of modern societies which makes possible several different modes through which economies can be governed, as well as several different levels (local, sectoral, sub-regional, national, regional, global) at which governance can be located. There are pressures towards uniformity, but also at the same time significant pressures sustaining and creating diversity. The patterns of governance which emerge together make up an economic and social constitution, the distillation of dominant practices and doctrines which define the parameters within which the governing of the global economy takes place in a particular period (Gamble 1999). Such constitutions arise incrementally and reflect the political purposes of particular agents as well as the distribution of political power between groups. To that extent they are politically and socially constructed rather than the spontaneous creation of markets.

This point can be illustrated with reference to the first modern global economic constitution, the liberal economic constitution of the nineteenth century which reflected the practice and beliefs of a particular national economy, that of Britain, the leading economy of the time. This economic constitution not only became the model for other states throughout the global economy, but also became the constitution for that global economy itself, based on an attempt to universalize certain rules about property, finance and trade. The liberal economic constitution was therefore both a doctrine, centred on the ideals of liberal political economy – free trade, sound finance and laissez-faire – and a reflection of the institutional means by which the British economy and the global economy were co-ordinated and governed. The celebration of the power, productivity and efficiency of markets as the main instrument of economic governance was the backbone of the laissez-faire vision. The state had an important role, but it was a minimal one; it had to remove the obstacles to the working of the free market, and ensure that they were not re-established. The state had specific functions to discharge – enforcement of law, maintenance of social order, safeguarding of the currency – and was much more active than the normal caricature of laissez-faire suggests, since there were a great number of obstacles to the efficient working of markets. But under this liberal economic constitution there was no requirement for the state at the national level to be responsible for the level of employment or for economic prosperity. Its responsibilities for human capital and for infrastructure were also small. What the liberal economic constitution assumed was that once the basic laws and institutions had been established the economy was in principle self-governing. The market itself provided the steering and corrective mechanisms, in particular the price system, which were required for successful economic governance. Interventions by the state risked disturbing the delicate mechanism which co-ordinated economic activity across the globe and ensured such high and rising levels of prosperity.

The policy rules for national governments contained in this economic constitution were that governments should pursue sound finance, by maintaining balanced budgets and keeping expenditure and therefore taxation to a minimum; they should adhere to the gold standard, thus imposing on themselves a severe external financial discipline which would ensure that money would be stable in value; they should support open markets and free trade, and resist the lobbying of special interests whatever the implications for particular sectors of the economy, in order to maximize wealth for the whole community; and they should confine their internal interventions to make sure that markets were as competitive as possible, and that all restraints on trade, from whatever source they came, were outlawed. The division between the public and the private was relatively clear-cut. There was an important if limited public sphere and an important role for the public interest in defining and enforcing the conditions for a thriving market economy. But the dynamism emanated from the private sphere itself. Economic agency in the liberal constitution is located in private individuals. The role of the state is restricted to maintaining the conditions for the market to function.

As many of its critics pointed out, however, the very success of the liberal economic constitution obscured the foundations of its own success, by making it appear that the only mode of governance on which it relied was the market. Schumpeter argued that the liberal civilization of the nineteenth century, brilliant though it was, rested on non-market and often non-liberal institutions – such as religion and community which gave legitimacy to the social order, and in particular to existing property rights, while at the same time imposing certain limits within which wealth-seeking was conducted (Schumpeter 1943). The capitalist economy was governed through pre-capitalist institutions which originated outside the processes of market exchange. It relied upon a strong civic culture and the willingness of individuals to act in the public interest and pursue public purposes, as well as trusting one another in economic exchange. Without these non-market forms of governance market relations themselves could not have been sustained.

The crucial role played by the state was emphasized by Karl Polanyi, who argued that far from being a natural, spontaneous development, the liberal economic order in important respects was created and sustained by the state (Polanyi 2001). It was an artificial and vulnerable political creation which required continuous political support. It was successfully established in Britain and some other countries, but elsewhere key elements were resisted, and states emerged with very different economic aims, which eventually led to the creation of different national economic constitutions, which rejected some key elements of the liberal constitution, particularly in relation to the role of the state in the economy. Protection was used as a weapon to establish industries which could compete with Britain, and some countries like Germany began to develop novel policies towards human capital, welfare and investment. So long as Britain, however, remained the world's leading industrial and financial power the liberal constitution was the one which ruled the global economy.

In the twentieth century the liberal economic constitution came under sustained assault both at the global and at the national level, and was substantially modified, and in many countries was rejected altogether as a framework for governance. This occurred in the context of an enormous expansion in the scope and scale of government, measured by the size of the public sector, the growth of public spending and taxation as a proportion of gross domestic product, and by the extensive new responsibilities which national governments assumed. These changes were fuelled by the new pressures of democratic polities, major new technological advances, increasing military and economic competition between states, and the rise of collectivist ideologies of right and left.

The twentieth century was notable for the fierceness of its ideological disputes. The economy and how it should be governed has often been central; two key debates were the case for capitalism and socialism as alternative economic systems and the merits of different institutional models of capitalism (Coates 2000). Both debates moved public discourse on political economy away from many of the assumptions of the liberal economic constitution of the nineteenth century.

The economic constitutions which came to dominate the twentieth century at both global and national level were much more collectivist, nationalist and protectionist in their basic assumptions. One of the most successful alternative models was developed by Japan, the only country outside the leading industrial states in 1900 to subsequently join the leading group (Arrighi 1994).

The rise and fall of different national models, like the Japanese, has taken place within the context of the economic constitution established at the global level. There have been three such economic constitutions in the last 200 years, the liberal economic constitution of the nineteenth and early twentieth century, the national protectionist constitution of the short twentieth century (1917–91), and the neo-liberal constitution which has been emerging since 1971 and became fully dominant in the 1990s.

Whose interests does global governance serve?

The emergence of collective forms of global governance, to some extent separate from the dominant powers, has not stilled argument about the interests that they serve. The idea that there is an uncomplicated way in which the institutions of global governance can identify and pursue the public interest and the public good is no more true for the global polity than it is for national polities. One of the problems therefore in analysing the structures and institutions of global governance that are emerging is to pinpoint the interests that they are serving. To what extent are they merely ciphers for US interests or the interests of the G8 or of a transnational business class, and to what extent do they provide genuine autonomous spaces for other states and interests?

The position is complicated because of disagreements over the legitimacy and purpose of these institutions within the dominant states themselves. Many neo-liberals are suspicious of the very idea of global governance, and oppose the creation or further extension of bodies which claim the authority to intervene in the way in which the global market works. They would happily scrap the World Bank and the IMF, seeing them as relics of the Keynesian era. Critics from the left, however, often regard these same institutions as the embodiment of neo-liberalism, and the driving force for neo-liberal policies.

The truth has to lie somewhere in between. If the institutions of global governance received direct instructions from the US State Department, then their legitimacy and credibility would be extremely low, especially in an era in which the United States has found it increasingly difficult to assert its leadership. The unease of neo-liberals with many of these institutions demonstrates that they have achieved some autonomy, and have begun to consider themselves (although still very tentatively) as the instruments of a global polity rather than of any particular state. But their understanding of their role remains heavily conditioned by the assumptions of the neo-liberal world order, and in that sense reflects the deeper structural realities of the world economy. The extent to which other states, including major states within the G8 such as Japan, are or could play a role in reshaping the institutions of global governance is a critical question. The tolerance of different models of capitalism and paths of development is one of the issues at stake. Japan has the economic and financial weight to assert itself and propose alternative ways to govern the world economy. It is increasingly seeking to do within its own region. But it has not so far done so at the global level, content to follow the US lead.

One of the key issues for the future is whether a more collective and pluralist hegemony, in which Japan would play an important role (Inoguchi 2005), can gradually replace the hegemony of the United States. In the security field this looks unlikely, because of the huge dominance which the United States has established. But it is much more promising in the economic sphere and also in dealing with new problems that threaten the whole world such as climate change. The question is whether there are ways of opening existing institutions and processes of governing the world economy to reflect the interests not just of the leading economic states, but also of the rising economic states, and of the poor. The global campaign to 'Make Poverty History' was an example of the new power of global civil society, and it had some, if limited, success in making the G8 respond to its demands, and some changes did follow. But the most important change of all, reversing the discrimination against poor countries and giving them access to the markets of Europe, North America and Japan, has made little progress. Until the international institutions work in the interests of the world's poorest, they will continue to be seen as biased in favour of the small group of rich countries (Payne 2005b).

What is the future of global governance?

George Bush has declared that 9/11 changed everything, so now the United States is changing the world. As a succinct summary of neocon thinking it is hard to beat. What is undoubtedly true is that there has been a rethink about globalization since 9/11, and a notably darker, more sombre appreciation of the perils facing global governance has emerged. US policy has once again become dominated by security issues, and by a much narrower focus on its national interests. But try as it might it cannot entirely disengage from the structures of global governance which it was responsible for developing, and there is a vigorous internal debate in the United States about the degree to which an 'America Alone' strategy is in long-term US interests. The heady optimism at the end of the cold war has certainly been dissipated, but the premise of a united global civilization, One World under US leadership, initially formulated by Fukuyama (although he now disowns it) (Fukuyama 2006) has been taken up by the neocons, but given a new twist (Stelzer 2004), shaped by the declaration of the global war on terror, combating Bush's 'axis of evil' (Frum and Perle 2003).

Re-integrating the United States within the structures of global governance has become one of the most difficult contemporary problems. As Joseph Nye has pointed out (Nye 2002), its huge military superiority is not matched in other arenas, such as the world economy, where the United Statess is already counterbalanced by the EU and by Japan, and will be in the future by India and China as well. In other areas of interdependence, such as the environment, crime, migration, disease, drugs and poverty, the United States is dependent on collective transnational solutions which it cannot achieve by itself, and no longer appears capable of brokering. Yet despite the difficulties of dealing with the United States, the need for the global economy and global society to be governed remains pressing, so the institutions of global governance are unlikely to disappear, although they may become the sites for increasingly rancorous arguments and negotiations, as recently with the Doha Round in the WTO. The extent to which global governance can be detached from the United States, or can survive without the active involvement of the United States, is a key issue for the future.

Of all the many scenarios that have been put forward, three of particular interest are the scenario of Empire, the scenario of blocs and rival civilizations, and the scenario of new medievalism. The scenario of Empire (from both its supporters and its critics) brushes aside US weakness, believing that over time the United States has the resources and the political will to remake the world in its own image in the way that George Bush predicts. This involves making all states into client states of the United States, particularly those that are currently viewed as rogue states and part of the axis of evil. The process has already begun with Afghanistan and Iraq. After such an imperial reconstruction the world will be ready again for a more consensual US leadership.

The scenario of the blocs is Orwell's nightmare in *1984* of a world divided between three rival totalitarian powers – Eastasia, Oceania and Eurasia. This was a world of perpetual war and mobilization in which two of the powers were always fighting the third. The names of the powers reflected the geopolitical realities of the 1930s and 1940s, with Japan the leading power in Eastasia, Germany in Eurasia and the United States, in alliance with Britain, in Oceania. Fears that such rivalry between blocs might return in the 1990s have so far proved unfounded, but the idea has gained new life by mutating into the thesis of the clash of civilizations (Huntington 1996). Here once again the political unity of the world is fractured, and any hope for One World or for a universal global civilization is dashed. Instead, the world divides along lines of culture and identity, Christianity, Islam and Confucianism being the three organizing principles. Rooted in different ultimate values these three civilizations make claims which are exclusive and beyond negotiation, and therefore any conflict once begun becomes bitter and prolonged, a return to holy wars.

The third scenario is both more interesting and more plausible. It suggests that we may be moving into an era in which the two key features of the capitalist world economy will become still more marked. Political rule will become even more fragmented, while global interdependence will continue to increase. This will create huge tensions and problems, as well as more concerted attempts to manage them through the institutions of global governance. This may never amount to a world government, but neither will power return to nation-states. Political authority will be defined less through territoriality and sovereignty and more through a complex network of cross-cutting identities, jurisdictions and authorities. There will be no single-state hegemon, but increasing reliance on the collective hegemony embodied in the institutions of global governance. This would not amount however to a political capacity to deal with global problems at the global level of the kind that is familiar from the history of the modern nation-state. Instead, the steering functions are likely to be continued to be shared among a wide range of public and private agencies, including transnational corporate networks and transnational civil society groups. There will be a large role in such a world for regionalist projects and local solutions. It will be a world of considerable conflict and disorder, and little stability, and as a result the institutions of global governance will expand their range and their authority. They are unlikely to wither away.

References

Archibugi, Daniele and Held, David (eds) (1995) *Cosmopolitan Democracy: An Agenda for a New World Order*, Cambridge: Polity.

Arrighi, Giovanni (1994) *The Long Twentieth Century: Money Power, and the Origins of Our Times*, London: Verso.

Bull, Hedley (1977) *The Anarchical Society*, London: Macmillan.

Coates, David (2000) *Models of Capitalism*, Cambridge: Polity.

Cox, Robert (1987) *Production, Power, and World Order*, New York: Columbia University Press.

Dore, Ronald (2000) *Stock Market Capitalism, Welfare Capitalism: Japan, Germany and the Anglo-Saxons*, Oxford: Oxford University Press.

Frum, David and Perle, Richard (2003) *An End to Evil: How to Win the War on Terror*, New York: Random House.

Fukuyama, Francis (2006) *After the Neocons*, New York: Profile Books.

Gamble, Andrew (1999) 'Economic Governance', in Jon Pierred (ed.) *Debating Governance*, Oxford: Oxford University Press, pp. 110–37.

—— (2003) *Between Europe and America: The Future of British Politics*, London: Palgrave Macmillan.

Gilpin, Robert (1987) *The Political Economy of International Relations*, Princeton, NJ: Princeton University Press.

Hay, Colin and Marsh, David (eds) (2000) *Demystifying Globalization*, London: Palgrave Macmillan.

Hayek, F. A. (1960) *The Constitution of Liberty*, London: Routledge.

Held, David (2004) *Global Covenant: The Social Democratic Alternative to the Washington Consensus*, Cambridge: Polity.

Hirst, Paul and Thompson, Grahame (1996) *Globalisation in Question*, Cambridge: Polity.

Huntington, Samuel (1996) *The Clash of Civilizations and the Remaking of World Order*, New York: Simon and Schuster.

Inoguchi, Takashi (2005) *Kokusaiseiji no Mikata. 9.11 go no Nihon Gaikō*, Tokyo: Chikumashinsho.

Katzenstein, Peter (1985) *Small States in World Markets*, Cornell: Cornell University Press.

Lincoln, Edward (1993) *Japan's New Global Role*, Washington, DC: Brookings Institution.

Nye, Joseph (2002) *The Paradox of American Power: Why the World's only Superpower Can't go it Alone*, New York: Oxford University Press.

Payne, Anthony (2005a) 'The study of governance in a global political economy', in Nicolla J. Phillips (ed.) *Globalizing International Political Economy*, London: Palgrave Macmillan.

—— (2005b) *The Global Politics of Unequal Development*, London: Palgrave Macmillan.

Pierre, Jon and Peters, B. Guy (2000) *Governance, Politics and the State*, London: Palgrave Macmillan.

Polanyi, Karl (2001) *The Great Transformation: The Political and Economic Origins of Our Time*, Boston, MA: Beacon Press.

Schumpeter, Joseph (1943) *Capitalism, Socialism and Democracy*, London: Allen and Unwin.

Stelzer, Irwin (ed.) (2004) *Neo-conservatism*, London: Atlantic Books.

Tsuchiyama, Jitsuo (2000) 'Realism no saikōchiku wa kanō ka', *Kokusai Seiji* 124: 45–63.

Tsuzuki, Chushichi (2000) *The Pursuit of Power in Modern Japan, 1825–1995*, Oxford: Oxford University Press.

Wallerstein, Immanuel (1974) *The Modern World System*, New York, Academic Press.

Weiss, Linda (1998) *The Myth of the Powerless State*, Cambridge, Polity.

Wilkinson, Rorden (2000) *Multilateralism and the World Trade Organisation: The Architecture and Extension of International Trade Regulation*, London: Routledge.

Zysman, John (1996) 'The myth of the global economy: enduring national foundations and emerging regional realities', *New Political Economy* 1, 2: 157–84.

Glossary

Japanese

Ajia no ichiin	membership of Asia
bōeki rikkoku	dependence on foreign trade
chūshinkoku	middle-level developed country
Daitōa kyōeiken	Greater East Asian Co-prosperity Sphere
jiyūshugi jinei to no kyōchō	cooperation with the (Western) liberal camp
Kokuren chūshinshugi	UN centrism
Kokuren jūshi	giving greater importance to the UN
Ron-Yasu	The close personal relationship between Japanese Prime Minister Nakasone Yasuhiro and US President Ronald Reagan
seiji taikoku	a political great power

Non-Japanese

Nixon shock	US President Richard Nixon's shock visit to Beijing and diplomatic recognition of the People's Republic of China

Index

For Product Safety Concerns and Information please contact our EU
representative GPSR@taylorandfrancis.com
Taylor & Francis Verlag GmbH, Kaufingerstraße 24, 80331 München, Germany

www.ingramcontent.com/pod-product-compliance
Lightning Source LLC
Chambersburg PA
CBHW070609270326
41926CB00013B/2483

* 9 7 8 0 4 1 5 4 2 4 0 1 1 *